The Politics Today companion to American government

Politics Today

Series editor: Bill Jones

Ideology and politics in Britain today
 Ian Adams
Political ideology today, 2nd edition
 Ian Adams
Scandinavian politics today
 David Arter
US politics today
 Edward Ashbee and Nigel Ashford
Pressure groups today
 Rob Baggott
Local government today, 3rd edition
 J. A. Chandler
Political issues in Ireland today,
 2nd edition
 Neil Collins (editor)
Irish politics today, 4th edition
 Neil Collins and Terry Cradden
General Elections today, 2nd edition
 Frank Conley
East Central European politics today
 Keith Crawford
US elections today (Elections USA,
 2nd edition)
 Philip John Davies
Political issues in America today
 Philip John Davies and Fredric A.
 Waldstein (editors)
British political parties today, 2nd edition
 Robert Garner and Richard Kelly
Spanish politics today
 John Gibbons
Political issues in Britain today,
 5th edition
 Bill Jones (editor)

British politics today, 6th edition
 Bill Jones and Dennis Kavanagh
Trade unions in Britain today, 2nd edition
 John McIlroy
French politics today
 Peter Morris
Italian politics today
 Hilary Partridge
Britain in the European Union today,
 2nd edition
 Colin Pilkington
The Civil Service in Britain today
 Colin Pilkington
*The Politics Today companion to the British
 constitution*
 Colin Pilkington
Representative democracy in Britain today
 Colin Pilkington
German politics today
 Geoffrey Roberts
European politics today
 Geoffrey Roberts and Patricia
 Hogwood
Debates in British politics today
 Lynton Robins and Bill Jones (editors)
Government and the economy today
 Graham P. Thomas
Prime Minister and Cabinet today
 Graham P. Thomas
Political communication today
 Duncan Watts

The Politics Today companion to American government

Alan Grant and Edward Ashbee

Manchester University Press

Manchester and New York

distributed exclusively in the USA by Palgrave

Published by Manchester University Press
Oxford Road, Manchester M13 9NR, UK
and Room 400, 175 Fifth Avenue, New York, NY 10010, USA
www.manchesteruniversitypress.co.uk

Distributed exclusively in the USA by
Palgrave, 175 Fifth Avenue, New York,
NY 10010, USA

Distributed exclusively in Canada by
UBC Press, University of British Columbia, 2029 West Mall,
Vancouver, BC, Canada V6T 1Z2

British Library Cataloguing-in-Publication Data
A catalogue record for this book is available from the British Library

Library of Congress Cataloging-in-Publication Data applied for

ISBN 0 7190 5891 0 *hardback*
     0 7190 5892 9 *paperback*

First published 2002

10 09 08 07 06 05 04 03 02   10 9 8 7 6 5 4 3 2 1

Typeset in Photina
by Graphicraft Limited, Hong Kong
Printed in Great Britain
by Biddles Ltd, Guildford and King's Lynn

Contents

List of tables and boxes

Tables

Boxes

Introduction

There are a number of American government and politics textbooks and *The Politics Today Companion to American government* aims to complement rather than replace them. It offers further materials and resources for those studying the subject. These include:

- Simple and straightforward introductions to key debates and issues
- Glossaries of important terms and concepts
- Statistics and other forms of data
- Guides to further reading and websites

The coverage has been written to include the 2000 presidential election, its bitter aftermath and the first year of the new Bush administration, including the terrorist attacks of 11 September 2001.

We would like to thank Kaye Larbi of the University of East London for his invaluable assistance in compiling the State Profiles which appear as an Appendix to Chapter 9 on Federalism and the states.

Alan Grant and Edward Ashbee

1

Economy and society

This chapter surveys US economic and social trends. It considers:

- the long-term economic position of the United States;
- the character of the 'Goldilocks economy' that emerged in the late 1990s;
- the negative features of the contemporary economy;
- cultural change and the process of 'remoralisation'.

The long-term economic position

The US dominated the world economy in the decades that followed the Second World War. It owed its position to steady technological progress, the scale of its natural resources, and the shattering of rival nations by war. Although countries such as Japan and Germany had become formidable economic powers by the 1960s, the US remained well ahead. Even in 1990, American firms accounted for 23 per cent of world industrial output.

As other countries began to catch up, a number of commentators started to talk of American decline. There were suggestions that the US was following in the footsteps of earlier great powers and had overreached itself. It would be eclipsed, as a political, economic, and military power, by others. Although there were some hopes of renewed prosperity in the mid and late 1980s, and President Reagan's 1984 campaign commercials proclaimed that it was 'morning again in America', the recession of the early 1990s – in which unemployment rose to 7.5 per cent – gave added impetus to those who stressed the country's economic weaknesses. Commentators pointed to the long-term decline of traditional industries such as iron and steel. The process of **globalisation**, and initiatives such as the **North American Free Trade Agreement** (NAFTA) of 1993 (which phased out trade barriers between the US, Canada and Mexico), led to fears that there would be an influx of cheap imports and substantial job losses. There was opposition to NAFTA from the

---

Box 1.1
Reading economic statistics

A country's economic performance is reflected in different sets of statistics. Unemployment is measured as a proportion of the overall labour force. 'Growth' refers to the extent to which national income and output (gross domestic product) changes over a twelve-month period. It is regarded as the principal measure of a nation's economic success or failure. A minus figure shows that the country produced less than in the preceding year and is in recession. The term 'inflation' is used to describe a sustained and general rise in prices. It is measured using a weighted 'basket' of goods and services known as the consumer price index (CPI). The current account balance shows the difference between the value of imports and exports. The calculation includes goods, services, transfers, and IPD (interest, profits and dividends). A minus indicates a current account deficit. In other words, more has been imported than exported. As the 1990s progressed, the size of the deficit was a growing source of concern. Much of it reflected US demand for manufactured goods from abroad.

---

labour unions, their allies within the Democratic Party and some on the conservative right. They asserted the need for **protectionism**.

Other economic problems also gave rise to concern. Ross Perot, the Texan billionaire who contested the 1992 and 1996 presidential elections, highlighted the scale of the federal government's **budget deficit**. From 1970 onwards, the US federal government had spent much more than it gained in taxation. The borrowing that was required to fund this was, it was said, fuelling the national debt and 'crowding out' private sector investment. American **productivity** growth also attracted the attention of critical observers. It lagged behind that of competitor nations in both Europe and the Far East. In the long term, it seemed, the US would be priced out of world markets by industrial rivals.

The Goldilocks economy

However, despite the pessimism of these claims, suggestions that the US economy was mired in long-term decline lost much of their credibility as the 1990s progressed. As Table 1.1 shows, the recession of the early 1990s gave way to a sustained boom. By the closing months of 1999 there was a 4.2 per cent annualised growth rate and the proportion of the work force who were jobless had fallen to the level of unemployment that economists had tradition-

Table 1.1   *Economic indicators, 1985–2000*

	Unemployment (%)	Economic growth (%)	Inflation (%)	Current balance ($ million)
1985	7.2	3.8	3.6	−118,155
1990	5.6	1.8	5.4	−78,965
1991	6.8	−0.5	4.2	−3,747
1992	7.5	3.0	3.0	−48,515
1993	6.9	2.7	3.0	−82,523
1994	6.1	4.0	2.6	−118,244
1995	5.6	2.7	2.8	−109,898
1996	5.4	3.6	3.0	−120,937
1997	4.9	4.4	2.3	−139,809
1998	4.4	4.4	1.6	−217,457
1999	4.2	4.2	2.2	−324,364
2000	4.0	4.1	3.4	−444,667

Sources: adapted from Executive Office of the President – Council of Economic Advisers, *Economic Report of the President, Transmitted to the Congress, January 2001*, Washington DC, US Government Printing Office, w3.access.gpo.gov/eop/, Bureau of Labor Statistics, *Employment Status of the Civilian Noninstitutional Population, 1938 to date*, ftp://ftp.bls.gov/pub/special.requests/lf/aat1.txt and Bureau of Labor Statistics, *Consumer Price Index: December 2000*, ftp://146.142.4.23/pub/news.release/cpi.txt and Bureau of Economic Analysis, Balance of Payments and Related Data, www.bea.doc.gov/bea/di1.htm.

ally predicted would trigger increased inflation. Against this background, there was growing talk of a 'Goldilocks economy'. Like the porridge in the children's story, the US economy appeared to be neither too 'hot' nor too 'cold'. It had successfully avoided the dangers of both 'overheating', (excessive consumer demand leading to inflation) and a recession which would have brought unemployment in its wake. Other commentators went further and spoke of a 'new paradigm' or framework in which the traditional assumptions made by economists about growth, employment and inflation had lost their earlier validity.

Sustained economic growth had political consequences. It helped President Clinton's bid to win re-election in November 1996. It also changed the character of public policy debate. Tax revenue rises during periods of prosperity. Although the federal government budget was in a substantial deficit during the recession of the early 1990s and in its aftermath, it moved out of deficit and into surplus as the decade progressed. Whereas deficit reduction had been a pivotal political issue for much of the 1980s and in the early 1990s, later debates turned to the use of the surplus. Some argued for increased government spending on, for example, Medicare – the system of health care assistance for the elderly – while others (principally Republicans) called for substantial tax reductions. The budget figures drawn up by the Office of Management and

Table 1.2   *The federal government budget, 1990–2000 ($ billion)*

Year	Budget	Year	Budget
1990	−221,194	1995	−163,899
1991	−269,359	1996	−107,450
1992	−290,402	1997	−21,940
1993	−255,013	1998	69,246
1994	−203,104	1999	124,414
		2000	166,690[1]

Note:
1 Projected.
Source: adapted from J.W. Wright, *The New York Times Almanac 2001*, New York, Penguin, 2000, 137.

the Budget (OMB) shown in Table 1.2 are in billions of dollars. A minus indicates a deficit.

The emergence of the 'Goldilocks economy' requires explanation. Some say that there has simply been a cyclical upswing. Prosperity, they assert, will inevitably be followed by a prolonged downswing. Others emphasise that the US economy is now less dependent on oil, making it more resistant to the 'supply-side shocks' that arose in earlier decades from war or sudden increases in the world price of basic commodities.

However, those who speak of a 'new paradigm' suggest that there has been a more fundamental long-term shift in the character of the US economy. They point to three principal developments. Firstly, there has been a significant increase in **productivity** growth. A given level of resources now allows more to be produced. For about a quarter of a century after the Second World War, productivity grew at about 2.7 per cent a year. From 1973, however, the rate of growth slowed to approximately 1.5 per cent. There was then a rise – as Table 1.3 illustrates – to almost 3 per cent in the mid-1990s. Much of the

Table 1.3   *Productivity growth, non-farm businesses, 1990–99 (%)*

Year	Growth rate	Year	Growth rate
1990	1.1	1995	1.0
1991	1.6	1996	2.7
1992	4.1	1997	2.0
1993	0.1	1998	2.8
1994	1.3	1999	2.9

Source: adapted from Bureau of Labor Statistics, 146.142.4.24/cgi-bin/surveymost. The figures are also included in the *Economic Report of the President, February 2000*, Washington DC, US Government Printing Office, w3.access.gpo/usbudget/fy2001/sheets/b_48.xls.

increase can be attributed to technological change, a process symbolised by the personal computer and the internet.

Secondly, competition between firms has intensified. There are three principal reasons for this.

- Trade barriers, such as tariffs and quotas, which formerly sheltered some industries from international competition, have been lowered.
- The end of the Cold War opened up new markets and freed up resources for non-military purposes.
- There has been a process of **deregulation** in, for example, transport and energy supply. New firms can enter markets where, previously, small numbers of companies had a stranglehold.

As a consequence of these changes, a significant proportion of firms are now forced by competitive pressures to offer the consumer ever-improving products and services at the lowest possible price. Companies must utilise new technology if they are to survive. They cannot pay wage increases that significantly exceed the rate of **productivity** growth.

Thirdly, the US has an increasingly flexible labour force. In contrast with some European countries, the labour unions have traditionally always been weak. However, as Table 1.4 shows, the proportion of the work force belonging to unions or associations has fallen further.

The comparative weakness of the unions has allowed the increasing casualisation of the labour market. A growing number of jobs are part-time, short-term or organised through agencies. Home-based 'out-working' has boomed. These changes in the character of the work force allow companies to reduce their labour costs. At the same time, large-scale immigration has averted some of the dangers traditionally posed by labour shortages.

Table 1.4   *Labour union membership (as a percentage of the total work force)*

Year	%	Year	%
1983	20.1	1993	15.8
1985	18.0	1995	14.9
1987	17.0	1997	14.1
1989	16.4	1998	13.9
1991	16.1	1999	13.9

Sources: adapted from R.J. Alsop (ed.), *The Wall Street Journal Almanac 1999*, New York, Ballantine Books, 1998, 248, and Bureau of Labor Statistics, *Work Force Statistics from the Current Population Survey, table* 1: 'Union Affiliation of Employed Wage and Salary Workers by Selected Characteristics', stats.bls.gov/news/release/union2.to1.htm.

Table 1.5	*Average hourly private sector earnings (1982 dollars), 1970–2000*

Year	Earnings ($)	Year	Earnings ($)
1970	8.03	1995	7.39
1975	8.12	1996	7.43
1980	7.78	1997	7.55
1985	7.77	1998	7.75
1990	7.52	1999	7.88
		2000	7.91

Sources: adapted from *Economic Report of the President, Transmitted to the Congress, February 1999*, Washington DC, US Government Printing Office, 1999, 382, and Bureau of Labor Statistics, National Employment, Hours and Earnings, //146.142.4.24/cgi-bin/surveymost.

Negative features of the economy

Although the growth of a flexible labour force was a boon for companies and contributed to the creation of almost 22 million new jobs over the course of the 1990s, liberal and radical observers emphasise the negative consequences of casualisation. Many Americans have seen only a limited long-term improvement in their overall standard of living. This is evident, firstly, in surveys of real wages such as those shown in Table 1.5.

The figures have been adjusted so that they are in constant 1982 dollars. If they had been left unaltered as the sums that were actually paid in all the different years, there would appear to have been a dramatic increase in wage levels. However, this would be misleading. Much of the rise can be attributed to inflation, a rise in almost all prices. It is important – if valid comparisons are to be made between different years – to look at incomes in terms of what can be purchased. This is their real value.

Furthermore, the figures in Table 1.5 are an average. They conceal continuing disparities and inequalities between whites, blacks and those of Hispanic origin. Although there is a higher proportion of two-earner families in the African-American and Hispanic-American communities, their overall household income has lagged behind white earnings. Again, the figures in Table 1.6 have been adjusted so that they are shown in constant dollars.

Standards of living should not, however, be defined in terms of income levels alone. The overall quality of the lives that individuals lead should also be considered. Those commentators who emphasise the more negative features of the American 'economic miracle' point to the increasing number of hours that Americans work during each week. Some of the rise can be attributed to growing female participation in the labour force. However, many low-paid workers have had to take on a second or even a third job. This, critics

Table 1.6   *Real median household income, 1985–99 (constant 1999 dollars)*

Year	White (non-Hispanic)	Black	Hispanic origin
1985	39,433	22,945	27,042
1990	40,719	23,806	28,463
1991	39,538	23,005	27,756
1992	39,530	22,271	26,833
1993	39,399	22,520	26,386
1994	39,487	23,638	26,329
1995	40,642	24,479	24,990
1996	41,185	24,934	26,446
1997	42,119	26,002	27,640
1998	43,376	25,911	28,956
1999	44,366	27,910	30,735

Source: adapted from US Bureau of the Census, *Historical Income Tables – Households*,
www.census.gov/hhes/income/histinc/h05.html.

Table 1.7   *Average hours of work (per week), 1973–97*

Year	Hours
1973	40.6
1980	46.9
1989	48.7
1994	50.7
1997	50.8

Source: adapted from R.J. Alsop (ed.), *The Wall Street Journal Almanac 1999*, New York,
Ballantine Books, 1999, 231.

assert, has profoundly harmful consequences for family life, child care responsibilities, and leisure time. Table 1.7 shows the median number of hours worked in a week.

As 2000 came to a close there were signs of an economic slowdown. Growth projections were scaled back. A number of well known companies warned of reduced profits and some retailers reported disappointing earnings. There were fears that rising oil prices would have consequences for other industries. Over half the American public own stocks and there is a danger that a fall in stock prices could have a significant impact on consumer spending. Even if a downturn is avoided – and much will depend upon the handling of monetary policy by the Federal Reserve – talk of a new paradigm will lose much of its former credibility.

Cultural change and 'remoralisation'

Alongside economic changes, there have also been cultural shifts. The early and middle years of the 1990s were marked by prophecies of decline. There were claims that family life was being eroded. Self-reliance and individualism were being displaced by welfare dependence. The cities, it was said, had been disfigured by rising crime and the emergence of an entrenched **underclass**. Robert Bork, whom President Reagan unsuccessfully nominated to the US Supreme Court bench, asserted that the US was 'slouching towards Gomorrah'. William J. Bennett, an influential conservative who served as Chairman of the National Endowment for the Humanities, Secretary of Education under President Reagan, and 'drugs tsar' in the Bush administration, spoke in similarly apocalyptic terms:

> Current trends in out-of-wedlock births, crime, drug use, family decomposition, and educational decline, as well as a host of other social pathologies, are incompatible with the continuation of American society as we know it. If these things continue, the republic as we know it will cease to be. The trends are dangerous and they are potentially catastrophic. (Bennett 1994: 556)

These fears found echoes beyond the conservative camp. Cornel West, a black social commentator, talked about the decline of neighbourhood and the 'gangsterisation of culture' (West 1999: 11). Robert Putnam pointed to the demise of civic networks and organisations (1996). Individuals were, he argued, increasingly isolated and alone.

For some, these fears were confirmed as the decade progressed. William Bennett regarded the degree of support that President Clinton attracted during the 1998–99 impeachment crisis, and the apparent unwillingness of the American public to condemn marital infidelity, as unambiguous evidence of declining moral standards. He dubbed it the 'death of outrage' (1998). However, paradoxically, despite commentaries such as these, the 1990s were a period in which many of the most widely cited indices of social and moral decline changed direction. In place of the cultural anarchy that some envisaged, traditional values appear to have, at least partially, reasserted themselves.

Firstly, although they appear to have reached a plateau in 2000, crime levels fell from 1992 onwards. In the US crime is recorded in two ways. The Federal Bureau of Investigation (FBI) collects figures from police forces and law enforcement agencies across the country. These are known as Uniform Crime Reports (UCR) and are shown in Table 1.8. However, there are difficulties with these statistics. Many local and state forces and agencies have different reporting periods. States have their own laws, and definitions and categorisations of particular crimes therefore vary between the states. Furthermore, crimes – particularly those committed in the poorest neighbourhoods – often go unreported. For these reasons, the National Crime Victimization Survey (NCVS) was established in 1973. This is based on interviews with representative

Table 1.8   *Violent crimes recorded by the police, 1985–99*

Year	No.	Year	No.
1985	1,126,700	1994	1,605,600
1990	1,556,800	1995	1,549,900
1991	1,632,700	1996	1,444,600
1992	1,657,300	1997	1,405,200
1993	1,648,100	1998	1,319,800
		1999	1,130,700

Source: adapted from Bureau of Justice Statistics, *Four Measures of Serious Violent Crime*, www.ojp.usdoj.gov/bjs/glance/4meastbl.txt.

samples of the population. In contrast with the FBI figures, it suggests a much higher rate of criminality. For example, the NCVS recorded 8.1 million violent crimes in 1998. Nevertheless, both the FBI and the NCVS record a fall during the 1990s.

Different explanations for the fall in the crime rate have been offered. They include the increased employment opportunities that have arisen as a consequence of economic growth, changing patterns of drug use, and shifting demographic trends. There are, proportionately, fewer young men in American society. This is the grouping most likely to commit serious criminal offences. Intensive policing and the **zero tolerance** policing methods pursued by figures such as the Mayor of New York, Rudolph Giuliani, may also have played a role. Furthermore, many lawbreakers – who might have committed further offences – have been removed from society. This has particularly affected the African-American communities. Twenty-eight and a half per cent of black males are likely to be imprisoned at some point in their lives. The corresponding figure for whites is only 2.5 per cent (Wright 1999: 328).

Table 1.9 records the numbers sentenced to a year or more and held in either jail or prison. In contrast with prisons, jails are locally administered institutions. They generally hold those serving relatively short terms of incarceration.

Table 1.9   *The jail and prison population, 1985–99*

Year	Inmates	Year	Inmates
1985	502,507	1997	1,242,153
1990	773,919	1998	1,300,573
1995	1,125,874	1999	1,366,721

Sources: adapted from J.W. Wright (ed.), *The New York Times Almanac 2000*, New York, Penguin, 1999, 326, and J.W. Wright (ed.), *The New York Times Almanac 2001*, New York, Penguin, 2000, 310.

Alongside the fall in crime rates, there has been a shift in the character of popular attitudes. Young people, sometimes dubbed 'Generation X', are significantly more culturally conservative than the 'baby boomers' (those born in the aftermath of the Second World War and symbolised by President Clinton himself) were at a corresponding age (Leo 1999). As a consequence, the cultural climate at universities and colleges appears to be marked by increasing restraint. Surveys of opinion among new students revealed, for example, that approval of casual sex fell from 51.9 per cent in 1987 to 39.6 per cent in 1998. This, the *National Catholic Reporter* noted, was a record low (12 February 1999). 'Family values' have re-emerged in other ways. Although the divorce rate, the number of divorces taking place within a particular year per thousand people, grew dramatically in the 1960s and 1970s, it fell – as Table 1.10 indicates – during the 1980s and 1990s. Similarly, the abortion rate, a source of bitter political controversy, has also begun to fall (Table 1.11).

There have been parallel shifts in other forms of social and cultural behaviour. The proportions of high school seniors telling interviewers that they had used marijuana, cocaine or alcohol during the preceding thirty days fell significantly during the 1980s and 1990s (Table 1.12).

The process of 'remoralisation' has been evident in other ways. A growing number of popular radio talk shows such as *Call Dr Laura* offer a message

Table 1.10   *Divorce (per thousand people), 1985–98*

Year	‰	Year	‰
1985	5.0	1996	4.3
1990	4.7	1997	4.3
1995	4.4	1998	4.2

Source: adapted from J.W. Wright (ed.), *The New York Times Almanac 2000*, New York, Penguin, 1999, 295.

Table 1.11   *Reported abortions, 1980–97*

Year	No.
1980	1,297,606
1990	1,429,577
1995	1,210,883
1996	1,221,585
1997	1,184,758

Sources: adapted from J.W. Wright (ed.), *The New York Times Almanac 2000*, New York, Penguin, 1999, 386, and J.W. Wright (ed.), *The New York Times Almanac 2001*, New York, Penguin, 2000, 370.

Table 1.12   *Use of selected substances, 1985–99*

Year	Marijuana	Cocaine	Alcohol
1985	25.7	6.7	65.9
1990	14.0	1.9	57.1
1995	21.2	1.8	51.3
1997	23.7	2.3	52.7
1998	22.8	2.4	52.0
1999	23.1	2.6	51.0

Sources: adapted from J.W. Wright (ed.), *The New York Times Almanac 2000*, New York, Penguin, 1999, 397, and National Center for Health Statistics, *Use of Selected Substances by High School Seniors and Eighth-graders, According to Sex and Race: United States, Selected Years 1980–99*, www.cdc.gov/nchs/products/pubs/pubd/hus/tables/2000/00hus063.pdf.

based on responsibility rather than 'indulgence'. The 1995 Million Man March, organised by the radical black nationalist leader Louis Farrakhan, was a 'day of atonement'. It stressed the responsibility of men to their wives and children. The evangelical Christian movement Promise Keepers similarly called on men to pay much more attention to their duties (Fukuyama 1999b: 272– 3). Survey evidence also suggests that the US is still a nation 'under God'. In a survey of middle-class communities, 44 per cent reported attending a religious service at least once a week. The corresponding figures for France and Britain were 10 per cent and 14 per cent respectively. Eighty-two per cent of the American population describe themselves as 'religious' (Wolfe 1998: 129).

These trends have led some to talk of 'remoralisation'. American society is said to be regaining a sense of morality. The scale of the changes during the 1990s should, however, be placed in perspective. There has been a shift rather than a counter-revolution. For example, church attendance does not seem to have risen. It may also be, as Charles Murray observes, that the decline in the number of divorces – which has to be set against a rapid rise between the 1960s and early 1980s – reflects, to some extent at least, a decline in the popularity of marriage.

Furthermore, although some social statistics have begun to move in changed directions, the indices of decline remain at very high levels. For example, while the rate of growth of illegitimate births has slowed up, the proportion of births outside marriage is still the highest in the Western world. Why are the figures so high? In part, they reflect a shift in behaviour among married couples. They are having fewer children and the proportion of births to unmarried women has inevitably risen as a consequence. However, other reasons should also be cited. Some conservative commentators – most notably Charles Murray in his book *Losing Ground* – attributed illegitimacy to welfare provision – which, they assert, until it was reformed in 1996 allowed mothers to live on government-funded assistance. There has also been a decline in the number

Table 1.13   *Single motherhood, 1985–96*

Year	%	Year	%
1985	22.0	1993	31.0
1990	28.0	1994	32.6
1991	29.5	1995	32.2
1992	30.1	1996	32.4

Source: adapted from R.J. Alsop (ed.), *The Wall Street Journal Almanac 1999*, New York, Ballantine Books, 1999, 548.

of 'marriageable' men living in many inner-city neighbourhoods because of economic restructuring and the decline of traditional industries. Others point to changing social attitudes. Marriage is less highly valued. Furthermore, some professional women now have independent financial means and can raise children independently. Increasing numbers of couples also now live together instead of marrying. Table 1.13 shows the proportion (or percentage) of total births that are to unmarried women.

The concept of 'remoralisation' should also be qualified in another way. Some attitudes have become more liberal. The values associated with the 're-ligious right' have not been fully embraced. The proportion of the population regarding homosexuality as 'an acceptable lifestyle' rose from 38 per cent in June 1992 to 50 per cent in February 1999. Cohabitation has become institu-tionalised – contributing, perhaps, to the fall in the number of divorces – and the proportion of Americans condemning premarital sex has fallen. It was 36 per cent in 1972 but by 1996 had dropped to 24 per cent.

The scale of the changes should, then, be qualified. They do, nevertheless, require explanation. Some commentators have seen the growing emphasis on sexual fidelity as a lagged reaction to the threat posed by the HIV virus. The fall in the numbers on welfare can be attributed to a buoyant economy, which has led to an increase in entry-level jobs, and welfare reform. In August 1996 Congress and President Clinton ended welfare provision for those with depend-ent children as a federal entitlement. In its place they brought in Temporary Aid to Needy Families (TANF). Assistance is limited to a maximum of five years during an individual's lifetime, although some states have restricted it to as little as twenty-one months (Albelda 1998: 15). No able-bodied adult can receive assistance for more than a two-year period at any one time. Fur-thermore, states have been given the option of denying welfare to unwed parents under eighteen and to those who had further children while on wel-fare. Many who were welfare recipients have now joined the labour market. The Act's supporters maintain that employment encourages self-reliance and provides 'structure and dignity to family life . . .' (Murray 1999).

There has, however, also been a much broader and more general explana-tion of 'remoralisation'. In *The Great Disruption* Francis Fukuyama, a noted

Box 1.2
Race and ethnicity

As the 1990s progressed, many felt that the US was becoming a more divided society. Statistics continued to reveal large disparities in terms of education, occupation and income. In the Los Angeles riots of April 1992 blacks and Hispanics seemed pitted against whites and Asian-Americans. The acquittal of O.J. Simpson on murder charges was greeted with enthusiasm by many blacks and with incredulity by whites. The political influence of Louis Farrakhan – the radical black nationalist leader who organised the 1995 Million Man March – also highlighted the scale of the racial divide. Although he has widespread support within the black communities, whites have reacted against the antisemitism and bigotry that is associated with Farrakhan's organisation, the Nation of Islam. The racial divide has also been intensified by a growing backlash against school and college courses based on **multiculturalism**, and by increasingly visible opposition to **affirmative action**. Although there is not unqualified support for 'preferences' within the Hispanic and black communities, many saw the elimination or scaling down of affirmative action programmes as an assertion of white interests and an attack upon minority interests.

The 1990s were also marked by another shift. The long-term impact of immigration and differential birth rates began to become visible in states such as Texas, California, Illinois and New York. The Hispanic population, in particular, has grown at a rapid rate and preliminary reports from the 2000 census suggest that Hispanics are about to displace African-Americans as the country's largest minority grouping. These population shifts have led the Bureau of the Census to predict that the US will cease to be a white majority nation during the latter half of

The US population, by race and Hispanic origin, 1990–2050 (projected percentage shares)

Year	Black	White	American Indian, Eskimo, Aleut	Hispanic	Asian and Pacific Islander
1990	11.8	75.6	0.7	9.0	2.8
2000	12.2	71.8	0.7	11.4	3.9
2030	13.1	60.5	0.8	18.9	6.6
2050	13.6	52.8	0.9	24.5	8.2

Source: adapted from R.J. Alsop (ed.), *The Wall Street Journal Almanac 1999*, New York, Ballantine Books, 1999, 542.

the twenty-first century. Such projections have fuelled charges that it faces the prospect of **Balkanisation**.

For others, predictions of race wars or **Balkanisation** are exaggerated and alarmist. They emphasise that although the Hispanic (or Latino) population will grow in size it is a diverse ethnic bloc and many within it are assimilated Americans. They also stress the progress that the minorities have made since segregation – the system in the southern states by which blacks were confined to separate and unequal jobs and facilities – came to an end when measures such as the 1964 Civil Rights Act were passed. By 1997 6.9 per cent of executive, administrative and managerial posts were held by blacks (Alsop 1998: 241). They also emphasise the extent to which there are shared values across American society. As Jennifer Hochschild has shown, even poor blacks subscribe to the American dream – the belief that everyone can, with sufficient effort, 'make it' – and be successful (Hochschild 1995: 72).

social commentator, argued that the changes represented the beginnings of a reassertion of moral traditionalism. The 1960s – with their stress on personal and sexual 'liberation' and demands for constraints to be removed – constituted an attempt to reject natural and rational ways of living. This, Fukuyama asserts, had very damaging consequences for those involved, those dependent upon them, and society generally. However, individuals are, he stresses, essentially rational:

> Norms governing the behavior of both men and women with respect to families changed dramatically after the 1960s . . . But parents will also have a strong natural interest in the well-being of their children. If it can be demonstrated to them that their behavior is seriously injuring the life chances of their offspring, they are likely to behave rationally and to want to alter that behavior in ways that help their children. (1999b: 273)

This, according to Fukuyama, was happening during the 1990s. As he concludes, 'there is good reason to believe that society has begun a process of "remoralizing" itself and walking back from the cultural abyss it faced' (1999a).

Glossary

affirmative action   Affirmative action was the subject of intense debate during the 1990s. Although affirmative action programmes take both 'soft' and 'hard' forms, their purpose is to increase the representation of women and minorities on educational courses, in management positions, and in occupations where they have been traditionally underrepresented.

'Soft' forms of affirmative action attempt to encourage minority applicants by, for example, placing job advertisements in particular newspapers. 'Harder' types of affirmative action rest on the use of 'quotas' or 'preferences' by which fixed proportions of course places or vacancies are allocated to minorities, even though they may be less qualified than other applicants. Such programmes gave rise to widespread resentment. Many white men, in particular, felt that their interests were being threatened. There were also black commentators – such as Shelby Steele, whose book *The Content of our Character* was published in 1990 – who felt that affirmative action devalued the status of qualifications and posts that were attained and reinforced feelings of inferiority to whites within the minority communities.

In November 1996 the voters of California passed Proposition 209, which brought affirmative action to an end in California's education system and public services. For his part, President Clinton took a 'mend it, don't end it' approach and called for a modification of programmes. However, affirmative action programmes are still pursued by many large companies that see them as a means of winning or maintaining a market share for their products among minorities.

Balkanisation   Those who talk of Balkanisation suggest that the US is fragmenting and breaking apart. They are drawing a comparison with the countries of the former Yugoslavia. The term has been used to describe the emergence of distinct and separate identities based on a range of factors including gender and sexual orientation. However, it principally refers to race and ethnicity. Mass immigration, the continuing divide between blacks and whites, and the failure of traditional assimilative mechanisms, have divided cities such as Los Angeles into a patchwork of linguistic and cultural enclaves. In response to these claims, critics point to the beliefs and values that unite Americans.

the budget deficit   From 1970 until 1998 the US federal government spent much more than it gained from taxation. The borrowing that was required to fund this spending added to the long-term national debt and led to increased interest rates, which, in turn, 'crowded out' private sector investment.

After rising dramatically in the 1980s – partly because of tax reductions and increased military expenditure – the deficit fell in the 1990s and turned into a surplus. This may be attributed principally to the growth in tax revenue during a period of prosperity and cutbacks in government expenditure.

deregulation   Deregulation – a conservative policy – is the reduction of laws and regulations governing companies. It exposes businesses to intensified competition by lowering the barriers to entry into a particular sector of the economy.

globalisation   Companies increasingly operate on an international basis. The components of finished goods are produced in a number of different countries. Investment funds move across continents. Consumers buy goods from around the world. Culture – music, film, literature – is also increasingly taking a worldwide form and being marketed across the globe. There are fears that, as a consequence of globalisation, nations will lose their identity, worldwide companies will increasingly operate beyond the control of individual governments, and that they will always seek out the lowest labour costs, leading to dislocation and unemployment in 'First World' countries such as the US.

multiculturalism   The school and college curriculum traditionally concentrated on those who have been dubbed 'dead white European males'. Multiculturalism has sought to broaden – in some cases displace – such courses with an emphasis on the history and culture of minorities. This, proponents argue, affects students from the minorities. As Thomas Sobol's report on education in New York stated:

> African Americans, Asian Americans, Puerto Rican / Latinos and Native Americans have all been the victims of an intellectual and educational oppression that has characterized the culture and institutions of the United States and the European American world for centuries. Negative characterizations and the absence of positive references have a terribly damaging effect on the psyche of young people of African, Asian, Latino and Native American descent. (Quoted in Glazer 1997: 23–4)

Multiculturalism has become institutionalised within the curriculum. As Nathan Glazer, a veteran sociologist and neo-conservative, asserts, 'We are all multi-culturalists now.' However, critics assert that multiculturalism is a form of 'political correctness' that often distorts historical and literary realities. It also, they argue, encourages minorities to see themselves as passive 'victims', acts as a barrier to the assimilation of newcomers to the US, and contributes to the process of **Balkanisation**.

North American Free Trade Agreement   The North American Free Trade Agreement (NAFTA) progressively eliminates tariff barriers between the US, Canada, and Mexico over a fifteen-year period. It was agreed by Congress in 1993. There are fears that US industry will be undercut by Mexican companies, which have much lower labour costs, and that American firms will – for the same reason – relocate south of the border.

productivity   Productivity refers to the efficiency of the economy. It is a measure of the relationship between inputs and outputs. Increasing productivity allows companies to produce at a lower cost. They can thereby become more competitive, sell goods and services at a lower price, and – with appropriate marketing strategies – gain a greater share of the market. It also enables companies to pay their employees a higher wage. Economists attach particular importance to the rate at which productivity is growing.

protectionism   Although the overwhelming majority of economists and most politicians favour free trade, a minority – including many labour union leaders – call for the imposition of tariffs (taxes on imports), quotas and other trade barriers. Such measures will, proponents claim, lead consumers to buy goods produced in their own country rather than imports and will lead to increased production and employment. They vigorously opposed NAFTA. Opponents assert that protectionism shelters inefficient and outdated industries from competition. Trade barriers retard economic growth.

underclass   The 'underclass' refers to those mired in poverty. The term has become synonymous with the inner cities, unemployment, gang warfare, and teenage pregnancies. African-Americans and the ethnic minorities are overrepresented in its ranks. Liberals argue that those in the underclass (although it is a term they generally do not use) are 'locked' into disadvantage. They cannot escape because of racial discrimination, inadequate education, and the demands of modern industry, which has little use for unskilled labour. Conservatives tend to assert that those in the underclass are tied to a culture that makes them unemployable. They must be encouraged to change their behaviour.

zero tolerance   Sometimes known as the 'broken windows' policy, it owed much to James Q. Wilson from the University of California at Los Angeles. He emphasised the way in which graffiti, neglect, small-scale acts of antisocial behaviour, and broken windows created an atmosphere in a particular neighbourhood that encouraged violent crime to take root. If the police addressed these low-level problems, he argued, they would begin to reduce serious criminality. This approach to policing was particularly influential in New York.

Resources

References and further reading

Albelda, R. (1998), 'What Welfare Reform has Wrought', *Dollars and Sense*, 15, 15–17.

Alsop, R.J. (ed.) (1998), *The Wall Street Journal Almanac 1999*, New York, Ballantine Books.

Ashbee, E.G.C. (2000), 'The politics of "Balkanisation"', in A. Grant (ed.), *American Politics: 2000 and Beyond*, Aldershot, Ashgate.

Bennett, W.J. (1994), 'A Strategy for Transforming America's Culture: Friendships in the Good', *Vital Speeches*, 60:18, 556–62.

Bennett, W.J. (1998), *The Death of Outrage: Bill Clinton and the Assault on American Ideals*, New York, Touchstone.

Executive Office of the President – Council of Economic Advisers, *Economic Report of the President, Transmitted to the Congress, January 2001, Transmitted to the Congress, February 2000*, Washington DC, US Government Printing Office, w3.access.gpo.gov/eop/.

Fukuyama, F. (1999a), 'Cheer up, Conservatives!', *Wall Street Journal*, 11 February, A26.

Fukuyama, F. (1999b), *The Great Disruption: Human Nature and the Reconstitution of Social Order*, New York, The Free Press.

Glazer, N. (1997), *We are all Multiculturalists Now*, Cambridge MA: Harvard University Press.

Hochschild, J.L. (1995), *Facing up to the American Dream: Race, Class, and the Soul of the Nation*, Princeton NJ, Princeton University Press.

Leo, J. (1999), 'The Joy of Sexual Values', *US News and World Report*, 1 March, 13.

Murray, C (1999), 'And Now for the Bad News', *Wall Street Journal*, 2 February, A22.

Putnam, R.D. (1996), 'The Strange Disappearance of Civic America', *American Prospect*, 24, 34–48.

West, C. (1999), 'The Moral Obligations of Living in a Democratic Society', in D. Batsone and E. Mendieta (eds), *The Good Citizen*, New York, Routledge.

Wolfe, A. (1998), *One Nation, After All*, New York, Penguin.

Wright, J.W. (ed.) (1999), *The New York Times Almanac 2000*, New York, Penguin.

Websites

Bureau of the Census   www.census.gov
   The Bureau of the Census publishes the *Statistical Abstract of the United States*. This is an annual summary of key statistics about the US. It can be obtained in print form

but it can also be downloaded. The *Statistical Abstract* includes details of population distribution, the labour force, the position of minorities, crime, educational attainment, income and wealth.

The Bureau of the Census website also offers access to *Fedstats*. This allows the user to search for statistical information from about seventy different federal government agencies. These include, for example, the Equal Employment Opportunity Commission, the National Center for Education Statistics, and the Environmental Protection Agency.

Bureau of Economic Analysis   www.bea.doc.gov/

The Bureau of Economic Analysis (BEA) provides data about the US economy. It includes rates of growth and the balance of payments. There is also coverage of the different regions.

Bureau of Justice Statistics   www.ojp.usdoj.gov/bjs

The Bureau of Justice Statistics website offers detailed information and data on crime and apprehension rates. *Key Facts at a Glance* provides a useful summary.

Bureau of Labor Statistics   www.stats.bls.gov

The Bureau of Labor Statistics provides information about the American labour force. The data include earnings, hours, prices, and productivity. Its contents include a survey of the economy 'at a glance', information about employment and industry in the different regions, the position of the labour unions, inflation, and productivity figures. The Bureau also tracks health and safety issues.

Congressional Budget Office   www.cbo.gov

Congress has its own specialist staff who draw up economic forecasts and budget projections. These often differ from those offered by the executive branch.

Council of Economic Advisers   www.whitehouse.gov/WH/EOP/CEA/html/

The Council of Economic Advisers (CEA) is a component part of the Executive Office of the President. It draws up the annual *Economic Report of the President*. This is submitted to Congress and is published in both print form and on the CEA's web pages.

National Center for Health Statistics   www.cdc.gov/nchs/

The NCHS website includes data on marriages and divorces, pregnancies, drug use and other social statistics.

2

The US Constitution

This chapter examines the seven Articles and twenty-seven amendments that form the US Constitution. It considers:

- the background against which the Constitution was written;
- the principles underpinning the Constitution;
- the most significant features of the Constitution;
- the context within which the amendments were introduced and ratified.

A constitution can be defined as a country's 'fundamental' or 'basic' law in so far as all other forms of law are subordinate to it. Although the US Constitution prohibited the manufacture and sale of alcohol between 1920 and 1933, most Western constitutions confine themselves to determining the functions, powers and responsibilities of the constituent branches of government and the relationship between them. Nearly all constitutions also set out the rights, and in some cases the duties, of the individual citizen.

The writing of the Constitution

The US Constitution was written and agreed upon by the 'founding fathers' or 'framers' during the summer months of 1787. It is now the world's longest-surviving codified constitution. In contrast with Britain's uncodified constitution, which rests upon traditions, conventions and certain laws to which particular importance is assigned, it is a single document.

The thirteen former colonies that broke free from British rule and established the United States had initially created a loose association known as the Confederation. It rested on decentralised authority and, although there was a legislature (Congress), there was neither a president nor an executive branch. The states insisted upon maintaining their autonomy. As the 1781 Articles of Confederation asserted: 'each state retains its sovereignty, freedom and independence'. The loose character of the Confederation made it weak and vulnerable to the expansionist ambitions of foreign powers. There was, furthermore, a danger of fragmentation. In the absence of more centralised structures, regional and sectional interests could always pull the country apart. There were incipient tensions between the northern and southern states. Others simply resented the imposition of government authority. The calling of a constitutional convention in 1787 and the drafting of the US Constitution were a response to these weaknesses.

Constitutional principles

The '**founding fathers**' who wrote the Constitution established legislative, executive and judicial branches of government. The two houses of Congress – the House of Representatives and the Senate – form the national legislature. The executive branch is headed by the president and, today, consists of both his personal aides (organised in the Executive Office of the President) and a byzantine structure of departments, agencies, and bureaux. The federal courts – headed by the US Supreme Court – constitute the judicial branch of government.

Some observers argue that the founding fathers intended that Congress should have primacy. For example, Garry Wills emphasises that:

- Congress alone can remove office-holders from the other two branches through the process of **impeachment**.
- Congress decides upon the structure of the courts and the number of judges who serve on each of them.
- Congress has the right to decide upon the structure and organisation of executive branch departments (Wills 1999: 83–90).

However, despite the powers that were assigned to Congress, the political system was to be governed by a **separation of powers** between the presidency, Congress and the Supreme Court. They are often described as the executive, legislative and judicial branches of government, although Richard Neustadt has talked, rather more accurately, of separated institutions sharing executive, legislative, and judicial powers.

Why was power separated? The founding fathers, it is argued, feared that the concentration of power in one branch of government might lead to the assumption of unchecked or, indeed, unlimited power by one individual or a single institution. The Constitution therefore established that each branch of government would limit – or check – the powers assigned to the other branches. In James Madison's words, 'ambition must be made to counteract ambition'. The Constitution's admirers assert that the system of **checks and balances** imposes constraints upon the national government. These prevent 'big government' and ensure that the liberties of the individual and the rights of the states are respected. However, critics assert that because decision-making involves separate branches of government, US politics has often been characterised by periods of enforced inaction – or **gridlock**.

Alongside the **separation of powers**, the Constitution had two other defining principles.

- It placed constraints on **popular sovereignty**. In contrast to the French revolution and the hopes of radicals who talked about government as an expression of the popular will, the 'framers' ensured that the Constitution struck a deliberate balance between public pressures, demands and opinions and the judgement and wisdom of experienced legislators who would, to some extent, be insulated from the pressures of the public arena.
- It rested on **federalism**. The character and extent of 'states' rights' have, however, been the subject of extensive controversy. Some, including President Reagan, have portrayed the US as a compact between the states. This implies that the states have far-reaching rights that cannot be abrogated. Others argue the American people as a whole have **sovereignty**. From this perspective, the rights of the states are much more limited and the constraints placed upon the states in the Constitution are of particular importance.

The Constitution of the United States

We the people of the United States, in order to form a more perfect Union, establish Justice, insure domestic Tranquillity, provide for the common defence, promote the general Welfare, and secure the Blessing of Liberty to ourselves and our Posterity, do ordain and establish this CONSTITUTION for the United States of America.

In the preamble, the founding fathers looked back to the weaknesses of the Confederation and stated that they sought to build a complete or 'more perfect Union'. This goal, and the constitutional mechanisms through which it would be achieved, became the subject of intense debate within the thirteen states. The Constitution's backers had to overcome strident opposition from the 'Antifederalists' who feared that the creation of a national government represented a threat to the liberties of both individual citizens and the states.

Article I

Article I outlines the structure and character of Congress.

Section 1

All legislative Powers herein granted shall be vested in a Congress of the United States which shall consist of a Senate and House of Representatives.

Congress – the legislative (law-making) branch of government – is to be bicameral (or divided into two chambers).

Section 2

The House of Representatives shall be composed of Members chosen every second Year by the People of the several States, and the Electors in each State shall have the Qualifications requisite for Electors of the most numerous Branch of the State Legislature.

No Person shall be a Representative who shall not have attained to the age of twenty five Years, and been seven Years a Citizen of the United States, and who shall not, US when elected, be an Inhabitant of that State in which he shall be chosen.

Representatives and direct Taxes shall be apportioned among the several States which may be included within this Union, according to their respective Numbers, which shall be determined by adding to the whole Number of free Persons, including those bound to Service for a Term of Years, and excluding Indians not taxed, three fifths of all other Persons. The actual Enumeration shall be made within three Years after the first Meeting of the Congress of the United States, and within every subsequent Term of ten Years, in such Manner as they shall by Law direct. The Number of Representatives shall not exceed one for every thirty Thousand, but each State shall have at Least one Representative; and until such enumeration shall be made, the State of New Hampshire shall be entitled to chuse three, Massachusetts eight, Rhode-Island and Providence Plantations one, Connecticut five, New-York six, New Jersey four, Pennsylvania eight, Delaware one, Maryland six, Virginia ten, North Carolina five, South Carolina five, and Georgia three.

When vacancies happen in the Representation from any State, the Executive Authority thereof shall issue Writs of Election to fill such Vacancies.

The House of Representatives shall chuse their Speaker and other Officers; and shall have the sole Power of Impeachment.

Section 2 establishes the defining characteristics of the House of Representatives.

The frequency of elections   Elections are to be held every two years. The House is, as a consequence, sensitive to shifts and changes in popular opinion.

Eligibility rules   Members of the House have to be at least twenty-five years old, a US citizen for at least seven years, and must live in the state that they are seeking to represent. These requirements are lower than those needed by those seeking a seat in the Senate. This adds to the House's role as the chamber that is more closely tied and responsive to the immediate demands and wishes of the people.

The basis of representation   Representation in the House is based upon a state's population. Every state is to have at least one representative, and each member of the House was originally not to represent more than 30,000. Today, however, each representative speaks on behalf of about 625,000 people (Chapter 3).

In the original Constitution, this included 'free Persons' and indentured servants who – in exchange for their passage from Europe – were bound to work for a particular master for a given number of years. Unless taxed, native Americans were not included in the calculation. Slaves were, however, partially included. The southern states were fearful of being politically outnumbered by representatives from the north. A formula was agreed whereby slaves – who were largely held in the south – were counted as three-fifths of a person.

These provisions of the Constitution required the introduction of a census, and Section 2 specified that such a census would be held every ten years. A process of **reapportionment** takes place following each census and the recording of population shifts.

Officers The House can decide upon its own officers, including a Speaker.

The powers of the House The House is assigned 'the sole Power of Impeachment'. It alone can 'charge' the president, federal judges and other public officials with offences that demand their removal from office. If an individual is impeached by the House, the trial takes place in the Senate.

Section 3

The Senate of the United States shall be composed of two Senators from each State, chosen by the Legislature thereof, for six Years; and each Senator shall have one Vote.

Immediately after they shall be assembled in Consequence of the first Election, they shall be divided as equally as may be into three Classes. The Seats of the Senators of the first Class shall be vacated at the Expiration of the second Year, of the second Class at the Expiration of the fourth Year, and of the third Class at the Expiration of the sixth Year, so that one third may be chosen every second Year; and if Vacancies happen by Resignation, or otherwise, during the Recess of the Legislature of any State, the Executive thereof may make temporary Appointments until the next Meeting of the Legislature, which shall then fill such Vacancies.

No Person shall be a Senator who shall not have attained to the Age of thirty Years, and been nine Years a Citizen of the United States, and who shall not, when elected, be an Inhabitant of that State for which he shall be chosen.

The Vice President of the United States shall be President of the Senate but shall have no Vote, unless they be equally divided.

The Senate shall chuse their other Officers, and also a President pro tempore, in the Absence of the Vice President, or when he shall exercise the Office of President of the United States.

The Senate shall have the sole Power to try all Impeachments. When sitting for that Purpose, they shall be on Oath or Affirmation.

When the President of the United States is tried the Chief Justice shall preside: And no Person shall be convicted without the Concurrence of two thirds of the Members present.

Judgment in Cases of Impeachment shall not extend further than to removal from Office, and disqualification to hold and enjoy any Office of honor, Trust or

Profit under the United States: but the Party convicted shall nevertheless be liable and subject to Indictment, Trial, Judgment and Punishment, according to Law.

Section 3 establishes the defining characteristics of the US Senate.

The frequency of elections   Senators are subject to election every six years. These elections are staggered so that a third of the Senate end their term of office every two years. In contrast with the House of Representatives, senators are thereby 'insulated' from short-term shifts and changes in public opinion. These provisions were intended to ensure that that the Senate constituted, as James Madison, (one of the most influential of the Constitution's 'Framers' and the fourth US president), put it, the stable 'anchor' of Congress. It would offer an accumulation of experience, or what has been termed, an 'institutional memory' (Wills 1999: 74).

Eligibility rules   Senators must be at least thirty years old, a US citizen for nine years, and live in the state for which they are seeking election.

The basis of representation   There are two senators for each state, regardless of its population. This provided an assured role for the states in the process of government and offered some protection for the smaller states. Originally, senators were chosen by state legislatures. Under the Seventeenth Amendment of 1913, however, they became subject to popular election.

Officers   Although the vice-president is to serve as 'president of the Senate', the Constitution allows the Senate itself to appoint a 'president pro-tempore'. In practice, the vice-president only chairs the Senate on ceremonial occasions or in circumstances when the vice-president might cast a tie-breaking vote.

Impeachment   All **impeachment** trials are to be held in the Senate, and the senators constitute – in effect – a jury. If the president is subject to an impeachment trial, the proceedings are chaired by the Chief Justice, although his powers are circumscribed. Conviction – which leads to removal from office and disqualification from office-holding – requires a two-thirds majority.

Section 4

The Times, Places and Manner of holding Elections for Senators and Representatives, shall be prescribed in each State by the Legislature thereof; but the Congress may at any time by Law make or alter such Regulations, except as to the Places of chusing Senators.

   The Congress shall assemble at least once in every Year, and such Meeting shall be on the first Monday in December, unless they shall by Law appoint a different Day.

The Constitution again sought to balance out the powers of the national government with the prerogatives (or rights) of the individual states. The states were allowed to determine the 'Times, Places and Manner of holding Elections' for senators and Representatives. However, Congress was also permitted to pass laws or issue regulations laying out the timing and manner (but not the place) of elections.

Section 5

> Each House shall be the Judge of the Elections, Returns and Qualifications of its own Members, and a Majority of each shall constitute a Quorum to do Business; but a smaller Number may adjourn from day to day, and may be authorized to compel the Attendance of absent Members, in such Manner, and under such Penalties as each House may provide.
>
> Each House may determine the Rules of its Proceedings, punish its Members for disorderly Behaviour, and, with the Concurrence of two thirds, expel a Member.
>
> Each House shall keep a Journal of its Proceedings, and from time to time publish the same, excepting such Parts as may in their Judgment require Secrecy; and the Yeas and Nays of the Members of either House on any question shall, at the Desire of one fifth of those Present, be entered on the Journal.
>
> Neither House, during the Session of Congress, shall, without the Consent of the other, adjourn for more than three days, nor to any other Place than that in which the two Houses shall be sitting.

Section 5 outlines some of the other powers that the Constitution assigns to both chambers of Congress. They can determine for themselves the results of disputed elections. They may also impose penalties on those who fail to attend, and – if there is a two-thirds majority – expel a member. Furthermore, if a fifth of those in attendance request it, the names of those voting for and against particular measures are to be recorded.

Section 6

> The Senators and Representatives shall receive a Compensation for their Services, to be ascertained by Law, and paid out of the Treasury of the United States. They shall in all Cases, except Treason, Felony and Breach of the Peace, be privileged from Arrest during their Attendance at the Session of their respective Houses, and in going to and returning from the same; and for any Speech or Debate in either House, they shall not be questioned in any other Place.
>
> No Senator or Representative shall, during the Time for which he was elected, be appointed to any civil Office under the Authority of the United States, which shall have been created, or the Emoluments whereof shall have been encreased during such time; and no Person holding any Office under the United States, shall be a Member of either House during his Continuance in Office.

Section 6 includes provisions that are intended to maintain the separation of powers between the legislative and executive branches of government. Although an exception is made for those who join the armed forces, serving members of Congress cannot be appointed to positions within the executive branch.

Section 7

All Bills for raising Revenue shall originate in the House of Representatives; but the Senate may propose or concur with amendments as on other Bills.

Every Bill which shall have passed the House of Representatives and the Senate, shall, before it become a law, be presented to the President of the United States: If he approve he shall sign it, but if not he shall return it, with his Objections to that House in which it shall have originated, who shall enter the Objections at large on their Journal, and proceed to reconsider it. If after such Reconsideration two thirds of that House shall agree to pass the Bill, it shall be sent, together with the Objections, to the other House, by which it shall likewise be reconsidered, and if approved by two thirds of that House, it shall become a Law. But in all such Cases the Votes of both Houses shall be determined by Yeas and Nays, and the Names of the Persons voting for and against the Bill shall be entered on the Journal of each House respectively. If any Bill shall not be returned by the President within ten Days (Sundays excepted) after it shall have been presented to him, the Same shall be a Law, in like Manner as if he had signed it, unless the Congress by their Adjournment prevent its Return, in which Case it shall not be a Law

Every Order, Resolution, or Vote to which the Concurrence of the Senate and House of Representatives may be necessary (except on a question of Adjournment) shall be presented to the President of the United States; and before the Same shall take Effect, shall be approved by him, or being disapproved by him, shall be repassed by two thirds of the Senate and House of Representatives, according to the Rules and Limitations prescribed in the Case of a Bill.

Section 7 begins by asserting that Bills changing the level or system of taxation are to begin the legislative process in the House. The House was given this responsibility – one of the few prerogatives assigned to it – because it was, at that time, the only directly elected chamber and therefore more representative of the popular will. As Thomas Jefferson noted, it was a 'fundamental principle that the people are not to be taxed but by representatives chosen immediately by themselves' (quoted in Wills 1999: 75). Budgetary legislation must, however, be considered by the Senate in the same way as all other legislation. The Senate has, in contrast, a number of specified constitutional responsibilities.

However, the greater part of Section 7 considers the circumstances in which the president can veto (or stop) legislation adopted by Congress. Once a Bill – a proposed law – has been passed in an agreed and identical form by the House and the Senate, it must be put to the president. In most circumstances, the president has two options. He can:

- sign it, thus allowing the Bill to become law;
- veto the measure. If he chooses to do this, the Bill is sent back within ten days to the chamber where it was first considered. The president is required to issue a veto message outlining the reasons for his decision.

However, the procedures laid down in the Constitution establish an elaborate system of checks and balances. If both houses of Congress vote again to back the Bill – and it gains a two-thirds majority in both houses – the measure becomes law despite the president's objections. The names of those voting for and against are to be recorded.

The Constitution did, however, allow the president a further option in certain circumstances. Although Section 7 stated that if he neither returned the Bill nor signed it within ten days, it would still pass into law, it also established that if Congress adjourned during this period, the Bill would not become law. This has become known as the pocket veto. In practice, legislation is often only agreed by Congress towards the end of its sittings, and this has allowed successive presidents to use the pocket veto on a regular basis. Some doubt has, however, arisen about the meaning of the word 'adjournment' in this context.

Section 8

The Congress shall have Power To lay and collect Taxes, Duties, Imposts and Excises, to pay the Debts and provide for the common Defence and general Welfare of the United States; but all Duties, Imposts and Excises shall be uniform throughout the United States;

To borrow Money on the credit of the United States;

To regulate Commerce with foreign Nations, and among the several States, and with the Indian Tribes;

To establish a uniform Rule of Naturalization, and uniform Laws on the subject of Bankruptcies throughout the United States;

To coin Money, regulate the Value thereof, and of foreign Coin, and fix the Standard of Weights and Measures;

To provide for the Punishment of counterfeiting the Securities and current Coin of the United States;

To establish Post Offices and post Roads;

To promote the Progress of Science and useful Arts, by securing for limited Times to Authors and Inventors the exclusive Right to their respective Writings and Discoveries;

To constitute Tribunals inferior to the supreme Court;

To define and punish Piracies and Felonies committed on the high Seas, and Offences against the Law of Nations;

To declare War, grant Letters of Marque and Reprisal, and make Rules concerning Captures on Land and Water;

To raise and support Armies, but no Appropriation of Money to that Use shall be for a longer Term than two Years;

To provide and maintain a Navy;

To make Rules for the Government and Regulation of the land and naval Forces;

To provide for calling forth the Militia to execute the Laws of the Union, suppress Insurrections and repeal Invasions;

To provide for organizing, arming, and disciplining, the Militia, and for governing such Part of them as may be employed in the Service of the United States, reserving to the States respectively, the Appointment of the Officers, and the Authority of training the Militia according to the discipline prescribed by Congress;

To exercise exclusive Legislation in all Cases whatsoever, over such District (not exceeding ten Miles square) as may, by Cession of Particular States, and the Acceptance of Congress, become the Seat of the Government of the United States, and to exercise like Authority over all Places purchased by the Consent of the Legislature of the State in which the Same shall be, for the Erection of Forts, Magazines, Arsenals, dock-Yards and other needful Buildings; – And

To make all Laws which shall be necessary and proper for carrying into Execution the foregoing Powers and all other Powers vested by this Constitution in the Government of the United States, or in any Department or Officer thereof.

Section 8 assigns a number of specific powers and responsibilities to Congress. These are known as **enumerated powers**. Many were intended to establish a national framework for economic activity, ensure the integrity of the US as a nation, and prevent its dissolution through sectional division or the ambitions of foreign powers. The enumerated powers thereby assert the rights of Congress and impose constraints upon the states.

The Constitution specifies, for example, that only Congress can declare war and that duties (taxes imposed upon foreign goods) must be uniform throughout the US. The states are barred from placing trade barriers against each other or individual trade arrangements with other countries.

However, Section 8 also included words and phrases that have a more elusive meaning. They have subsequently proved a basis for an expansion of congressional authority, the emergence of **implied powers**, and the subject of extensive constitutional argument. Congress was, for example, to 'regulate Commerce . . . among the several States'. The 'interstate commerce' clause, as it has become known, established that businesses crossing state lines could be subject to regulation by Congress. Industrialisation, a growing division of labour, the transport revolution and mass marketing dramatically extended the number of companies to which the clause could be applied. It became the basis of government intervention and regulation in both the economy and society more generally.

Similarly, Section 8 concluded by empowering Congress to 'make all Laws which shall be necessary and proper for carrying into Execution the foregoing Powers . . .' The 'necessary and proper' clause also has a loose and elastic character. In *McCulloch v. Maryland* (1819) the US Supreme Court ruled on the basis of the 'necessary and proper' clause that Congress had the authority to create a national bank, even though it was not specified in the Constitution.

Section 9

The Migration or Importation of such Persons as any of the States now existing shall think proper to admit, shall not be prohibited by the Congress prior to the Year one thousand eight hundred and eight, but a Tax or duty may be imposed on such Importation, not exceeding ten dollars for each Person.

The Privilege of the Writ of Habeas Corpus shall not be suspended, unless when in Cases or Rebellion or Invasion the public Safety may require it.

No Bill of Attainder or ex post facto Law shall be passed.

No Capitation, or other direct, Tax shall be laid, unless in Proportion to the Census of Enumeration herein before directed to be taken.

No Tax or Duty shall be laid on Articles exported from any State.

No Preference shall be given by any Regulation of Commerce or Revenue to the Ports of one State over those of another: nor shall Vessels bound to, or from, one State, be obliged to enter, clear or pay Duties in another.

No Money shall be drawn from the Treasury, but in Consequence of Appropriations made by Law; and a regular Statement and Account of the Receipts and Expenditures of all public Money shall be published from time to time.

No Title of Nobility shall be granted by the United States: And no Person holding any Office of Profit or Trust under them, shall, without the Consent of the Congress, accept of any present, Emolument, Office, or Title, of any kind whatever, from any King, Prince or foreign State.

Section 9 prevents the states raising economic barriers against each other. It allowed habeas corpus (which offered protection against arbitrary arrest) to be suspended in times of crisis. President Abraham Lincoln cited this during the Civil War. Furthermore, in a rejection of European aristocratic tradition, 'no title of nobility' was to be allowed.

Section 10

No State shall enter into any Treaty, Alliance, or Confederation; grant Letters of Marque and Reprisal; coin Money; emit Bills of Credit; make any Thing but gold and silver Coin a Tender in Payment of Debts; pass any Bill of Attainder, ex post facto Law, or Law impairing the Obligation of Contracts, or grant any Title of Nobility.

No State shall, without the Consent of the Congress, lay any Imposts or Duties on Imports or Exports, except what may be absolutely necessary for executing it's inspection Laws: and the net Produce of all Duties and Imposts, laid by any State on Imports or Exports, shall be for the Use of the Treasury of the United States; and all such Laws shall be subject to the Revision and Controul of the Congress.

No State shall, without the Consent of Congress, lay any Duty of Tonnage, keep Troops, or Ships of War in time of Peace, enter into any Agreement or Compact with another State, or with a foreign Power, or engage in War, unless actually invaded, or in such imminent Danger as will not admit of delay.

The last section of Article I reinforced the Constitution's commitment to the creation of a unified country by placing further and specific constraints on the individual states. They were prohibited from entering into diplomatic agreements with other nations, creating their own currencies, curtailing the requirements and obligations created by contracts, and granting 'any Title of Nobility'. Neither could they impose trade barriers or maintain their own armed forces without authorisation by Congress.

Article II

Article II lays down the powers and responsibilities of the presidency.

Section 1

The executive Power shall be vested in a President of the United States of America. He shall hold his Office during the Term of four Years, and, together with the Vice President, chosen for the same Term, be elected, as follows:

Each State shall appoint, in such Manner as the Legislature thereof may direct, a Number of Electors, equal to the whole Number of Senators and Representatives to which the State may be entitled in the Congress: but no Senator or Representative, or Person holding an Office of Trust or Profit under the United States, shall be appointed an Elector.

The Electors shall meet in their respective States, and vote by Ballot for two Persons, of whom one at least shall not be an Inhabitant of the same State with themselves. And they shall make a List of all the Persons voted for, and of the Number of Votes for each; which List they shall sign and certify, and transmit sealed to the Seat of the Government of the United States, directed to the President of the Senate. The President of the Senate shall, in the Presence of the Senate and House of Representatives, open all the Certificates, and the Votes shall then be counted. The Person having the greatest Number of Votes shall be the President, if such Number be a Majority of the whole Number of Electors appointed; and if there be more than one who have such Majority, and have an equal Number of Votes, then the House of Representatives shall immediately chuse by Ballot one of them for President; and if no Person have a Majority, then from the five highest on the List the said House shall in like Manner chuse the President. But in chusing the President, the Votes shall be taken by States, the Representatives from each State having one Vote; a quorum for this Purpose shall consist of a Member or Members from two thirds of the States, and a Majority of all the States shall be necessary to a Choice. In every Case, after the Choice of the President, the Person having the greatest Number of Votes of the Electors shall be the Vice President. But if there should remain two or more who have equal Votes, the Senate shall chuse from them by Ballot the Vice President.

The Congress may determine the Time of chusing the Electors, and the Day on which they shall give their Votes; which Day shall be the same throughout the United States.

No Person except a natural born Citizen, or a Citizen of the United States, at the time of the Adoption of this Constitution, shall be eligible to the Office of President; neither shall any person be eligible to that Office who shall not have attained to the Age of thirty five Years, and been fourteen Years a Resident within the United States.

In Case of the Removal of the President from Office, or of his Death, Resignation, or Inability to discharge the Powers and Duties of the said Office, the Same shall devolve on the Vice President, and the Congress may by Law provide for the Case of Removal, Death, Resignation or Inability, both of the President and Vice President, declaring what Officer shall then act as President, and such Officer shall act accordingly, until the Disability be removed, or a President shall be elected.

The President shall, at stated Times, receive for his Services, a Compensation, which shall neither be encreased nor diminished during the Period for which he shall have been elected, and he shall not receive within that Period any other Emolument from the United States, or any of them.

Before he enter on the Execution of his Office, he shall take the following Oath or Affirmation: 'I do solemnly swear (or affirm) that I will faithfully execute the Office of President of the United States, and will to the best of my Ability, preserve, protect and defend the Constitution of the United States.'

Section 1 established the process by which presidents are elected.

The president's term of office   The president, and the vice-president, serve fixed four-year terms.

The system of election   The Constitution proposed an Electoral College. Each state is allocated a given number of Electors, reflecting its representation in Congress. The Constitution permits state legislatures to determine how such Electors are chosen.

The Electors would elect the president. To be elected, a candidate had to receive more than half the Electors' votes. If no candidate gained this, the process of election would be passed to the House of Representatives. However, for this purpose alone, each state delegation in the House was to have only one vote. In the early years of the US the runner-up in the contest was to serve as vice-president.

Eligibility rules   The Constitution specifies that the president must be at least 35 years old, resident in the US for fourteen years, and 'a natural born Citizen' (born in the US, its territories, or among its personnel serving overseas).

The role of the vice-president   Section 1 also laid down that if the president died, was removed from office, or was otherwise unable to undertake his responsibilities, 'the powers and duties of the said office' are transferred to the vice-president.

There is some ambiguity about this clause. It was uncertain whether the vice-president assumed the presidency in such circumstances or merely undertook the powers and responsibilities of the presidency. The position of the vice-president was later clarified by the Twentieth and Twenty-fifth Amendments.

The oath of office   An incoming president must, on assuming office, take the oath specified in Section I. This is, except in times of crisis, undertaken at the inauguration ceremony.

Section 2

> The President shall be Commander in Chief of the Army and Navy of the United States, and of the Militia of the several States, when called into the actual Service of the United States; he may require the Opinion, in writing, of the principal Officer in each of the executive Departments, upon any Subject relating to the Duties of their respective Offices, and he shall have Power to Grant Reprieves and Pardons for Offences against the United States, except in Cases of Impeachment.
>
> He shall have Power, by and with the Advice and Consent of the Senate, to make Treaties, provided two thirds of the Senators present concur; and he shall nominate, and by and with the Advice and Consent of the Senate, shall appoint Ambassadors, other public Ministers and Consuls, Judges of the supreme Court, and all other Officers of the United States, whose Appointments are not herein otherwise provided for, and which shall be established by Law: but the Congress may by Law vest the Appointment of such inferior Officers, as they think proper, in the President alone, in the Courts of Law, or in the Heads of Departments.
>
> The President shall have Power to fill up all Vacancies that may happen during the Recess of the Senate, by granting Commissions which shall expire at the End of their next Session.

Section 2 considers the powers that are assigned to the president. He is to be commander-in-chief of the armed forces and commander-in-chief of the state militias, allowing him to 'federalise' (or take control of) the national guard. The president can also grant reprieves and pardons, conclude treaties with other nations, and appoint public officials, including those who serve in the executive departments, Supreme Court judges and ambassadors. He can make temporary 'recess appointments' to government posts without those nominated being subject to confirmation by the Senate.

Section 3

> He shall from time to time give to the Congress Information on the State of the Union, and recommend to their Consideration such Measures as he shall judge necessary and expedient; he may, on extraordinary Occasions, convene both Houses, or either of them, and in Case of Disagreement between them, with Respect to the Time of Adjournment, he may adjourn them to such Time as he shall think proper; he shall receive Ambassadors and other public Ministers; he shall take Care that the Laws be faithfully executed, and shall Commission all the Officers of the United States.

Section 3 laid down the president's role as 'chief legislator'. It was, however, a responsibility only established in its contemporary form by President

Franklin Roosevelt. From 1933 onwards, presidents have been expected to put forward legislative programmes and they are judged, at least in part, on their ability to secure congressional backing for their proposals. Roosevelt revived the tradition of giving an annual State of the Union address to both houses of Congress and it has since become an institutionalised component of American political life. Section 3 also laid down that the president should ensure that the laws 'be faithfully executed' or implemented. This provision established the president in his role as 'chief executive'.

Section 4

> The President, Vice President and all Civil Officers of the United States, shall be removed from Office on Impeachment for and Conviction of, Treason, Bribery, or other high Crimes and Misdemeanors.

President Andrew Johnson was impeached in 1868 – following his removal of an official – but the Senate failed, by one vote, to remove him from office. In 1974 Richard Nixon resigned once impeachment proceedings had been initiated in the House of Representatives. In 1998–99 Bill Clinton was impeached on charges of perjury and obstruction of justice, tried by the Senate, but acquitted.

Article III

Article III considers the role of the US Supreme Court.

Section 1

> The judicial Power of the United States, shall be vested in one supreme Court, and in such inferior Courts as the Congress may from time to time ordain and establish. The Judges, both of the supreme and inferior Courts, shall hold their Offices during good Behaviour, and shall, at stated Times, receive for their Services, a Compensation, which shall not be diminished during their Continuance in Office.

Article III established the US Supreme Court. In contrast, however, with the carefully crafted eligibility and election rules laid down to govern the other two branches of government, its consideration of the Supreme Court was loosely worded. There was, for example, no attempt to specify the number of judges who should sit on the Court bench. The number of federal courts, and their structure, were left to congressional discretion.

Section 1 did, however, specify that, subject to 'good Behaviour', judges could not be removed from the federal courts. So as to further protect them from political pressures, it also required that their salaries could not be reduced.

Section 2

> The judicial Power shall extend to all Cases, in Law and Equity, arising under this Constitution, the Laws of the United States, and Treaties made, or which shall be made, under their Authority; – to all Cases affecting Ambassadors, other public ministers and Consuls; – to all Cases of admiralty and maritime Jurisdiction; – to Controversies to which the United States shall be a Party; – to Controversies between two or more States; – between a State and Citizens of another State; – between Citizens of different States; – between Citizens of the same State claiming Lands under Grants of different States, and between a State, or the Citizens thereof, and foreign States, Citizens or Subjects.
>
> In all Cases affecting Ambassadors, other public Ministers and Consuls, and those in which a State shall be Party, the supreme Court shall have original Jurisdiction. In all the other Cases before mentioned, the supreme Court shall have appellate Jurisdiction, both as to Law and Fact, with such Exceptions, and under such Regulations as the Congress shall make.
>
> The Trial of all Crimes, except in Cases of Impeachment, shall be by Jury; and such Trial shall be held in the State where the said Crimes shall have been committed; but when not committed within any State, the Trial shall be at such Place or Places as the Congress may by Law have directed.

Section 2 established the jurisdiction of the federal courts. It included the right to make rulings in cases resting on interpretations of federal law. This led to the Court – in 1803 – to assert that it could decide upon the constitutionality of all federal laws and government actions. This is called **judicial review**.

The US Supreme Court was to have 'original jurisdiction' in certain cases, such as disputes between individual states. This allows such cases to be initiated in the Supreme Court itself. In other instances, it was to have appellate jurisdiction. It would act as the highest court of appeal.

Section 3

> Treason against the United States, shall consist only in levying War against them, or in adhering to their Enemies, giving them Aid and Comfort. No Person shall be convicted of Treason unless on the Testimony of two Witnesses to the same overt Act, or on Confession in open Court.
>
> The Congress shall have Power to declare the Punishment of Treason, but no Attainder of Treason shall work Corruption of Blood, or Forfeiture except during the Life of the Person attainted.

Article IV

Article IV considers the relationship between the individual states and provides certain guarantees to them.

Section 1

Full Faith and Credit shall be given in each State to the public Acts, Records, and judicial Proceedings of every other State. And the Congress may by general Laws prescribe the Manner in which such Acts, Records and Proceedings shall be proved, and the Effect thereof.

Each state must respect the laws and court rulings of other states. Individuals cannot evade responsibilities by moving to another state.

Section 2

The Citizens of each State shall be entitled to all Privileges and Immunities of Citizens in the several States.

A Person charged in any State with Treason, Felony, or other Crime, who shall flee from Justice, and be found in another State, shall on Demand of the executive Authority of the State from which he fled, be delivered up, to be removed to the State having Jurisdiction of the Crime

No Person held to Service or Labour in one State, under the Laws thereof, escaping into another, shall, in Consequence of any Law or Regulation therein, be discharged from such Service or Labour, but shall be delivered up on Claim of the Party to whom such Service or Labour may be due.

Section 2 was intended to ensure that offenders could not gain refuge by crossing state lines. Each state has a responsibility to send back – or extradite – individuals who face charges in another part of the US. The original Constitution also included a stipulation that fugitive slaves and indentured servants (who were bound to a master for a specified period of time) must be returned to their owners and masters. This clause was increasingly challenged during the first half of the nineteenth century. Opinion in the northern states began to turn against slavery while the south insisted upon the return of runaways.

Section 3

New States may be admitted by the Congress into this Union; but no new State shall be formed or erected within the Jurisdiction of any other State; nor any State be formed by the Junction of two or more States, or Parts of States, without the Consent of the Legislatures of the States concerned as well as of the Congress.

The Congress shall have Power to dispose of and make all needful Rules and Regulations respecting the Territory or other Property belonging to the United States; and nothing in this Constitution shall be so construed as to Prejudice any Claims of the United States, or of any particular State.

The rights of the states include a constitutional assurance that a state's territorial boundaries will be respected. Section 3 also assigned Congress the authority to govern the US territories that have not become states.

Section 4

> The United States shall guarantee to every State in this Union a Republican Form
> of Government, and shall protect each of them against Invasion; and on Ap-
> plication of the Legislature, or of the Executive (when the Legislature cannot be
> convened) against domestic Violence.

The US authorities were to defend the individual states against both invasion and – when requested by the state authorities – 'domestic Violence'.

Article V

Article V lays down the methods by which the US Constitution can be amended.

> The Congress, whenever two thirds of both Houses shall deem it necessary, shall
> propose Amendments to this Constitution, or, on the Application of the Legis-
> latures of two thirds of the several States, shall call a Convention for proposing
> Amendments, which, in either Case, shall be valid to all Intents and Purposes, as
> Part of this Constitution, when ratified by the Legislatures of three fourths of the
> several States, or by Conventions in three fourths thereof, as the one or the other
> Mode of Ratification may be proposed by the Congress; Provided that no Amend-
> ment which may be made prior to the Year One thousand eight hundred and
> eight shall in any Manner affect the first and fourth Clauses in the Ninth Section
> of the first Article; and that no State, without its Consent, shall be deprived of its
> equal Suffrage in the Senate.

As constitutions represent the basic law of a country, amendments and
changes generally require the assent of a supermajority. Proposals to amend
the US Constitution can be put forward only by either:

- a two-thirds majority in both houses of Congress;
- or a constitutional convention called by the legislatures of two-thirds of the
  states.

To be ratified, and thereby become incorporated within the Constitution, all
amendments must be agreed upon by:

- three-quarters of the state legislatures;
- or by constitutional conventions in three-quarters of the states.

Only twenty-seven amendments have been passed since the Constitution
was written. The first ten – the **Bill of Rights** – were added to the Constitution
in 1791. The failure to adopt further amendments reflects, in part, the difficulties that arise in gaining the backing of three-quarters of the states for
particular measures. The process was intended to ensure that all amendments
reflected a widespread consensus rather than the wishes of a mere 'faction'. It

also, however, reflects the role of the Supreme Court in adapting the Constitution so as to reflect changing conditions and circumstances.

Article VI

Article VI places constraints upon the states by asserting the supremacy of US law over state law.

> All Debts contracted and Engagements entered into, before the Adoption of this Constitution, shall be as valid against the United States under this Constitution, as under the Confederation.
>
> This Constitution, and the Laws of the United States which shall be made in Pursuance thereof; and all Treaties made, or which shall be made, under the Authority of the United States, shall be the supreme Law of the Land; and the Judges in every State shall be bound thereby, any Thing in the Constitution or Laws of any state to the Contrary notwithstanding.
>
> The Senators and Representatives before mentioned, and the Members of the several State Legislatures, and all executive and judicial Officers, both of the United States and of the several States, shall be bound by Oath or Affirmation, to support this Constitution; but no religious Test shall ever be required as a Qualification to any Office or public Trust under the United States.

Article VI confirmed and reinforced the integrity of the US as a sovereign country – rather than a mere association of states – and the authority of the national government. It specified that the Constitution, federal law, and treaties concluded by the US with foreign powers were to be 'the supreme Law of the Land'. It is often cited by those who stress the limited and conditional character of 'states' rights'.

Article VI also introduced a separation between church and state. There were, even in the late eighteenth century, many different Christian denominations in the American states. Despite their deep religious convictions, the **founding fathers** believed that an 'established' or official church would prove divisive.

Article VII

Article VII establishes the requirements for acceptance – or ratification – of the Constitution.

> The Ratification of the Conventions of nine States, shall be sufficient for the Establishment of this Constitution between the States so ratifying the same. Done in Convention by the Unanimous Consent of the States present the Seventeenth Day of September in the Year of our Lord one thousand seven hundred and Eighty seven and of the Independence of the United States of America the Twelfth. In witness whereof We have hereunto subscribed our Names.

The Constitution required that nine of the thirteen states endorse the Constitution if it was to be accepted as a basis for national government. The **founding fathers** did not insist that the people, (although only limited numbers of white men had the vote in most states at this time) voted on the document.

The character of the ratification process gave rise to intense and bitter dispute.

- Many within the southern states, most notably John C. Calhoun of South Carolina, claimed that the Constitution was a compact between states. Individual states remained sovereign. They could therefore refuse to implement – or nullify – legislation passed by Congress. They also had the right to leave – or secede from – the US.
- Others, such as Daniel Webster of Massachusetts took a different view. They regarded the Constitution – and the institutions founded on the basis of it – as representative of the American people as a whole. States could, from this perspective, take legal action or seek a constitutional amendment but they no right of either nullification or secession.

These conflicting interpretations of the Constitution led to the nullification crisis of 1832–33, when South Carolina refused to adopt a national tax on imports – or tariff. Following a threat of military force by President Andrew Jackson, South Carolina backed down. However, the dispute foreshadowed the Civil War of 1861–65. The war began when the southern states seceded from the US and sought to establish the Confederate states as an independent nation. The victory of the north ensured that Webster's 'national' interpretation of the Constitution has subsequently held sway.

Amendments

There was, initially, considerable opposition to the adoption of a **Bill of Rights** among some of the **founding fathers**. Many felt that the Constitution was, in itself, sufficient and the further codification of rights might cut across the sovereignty of government. However, ten amendments – constituting the **Bill of Rights** – were added to the Constitution in 1791. The impetus for the amendments had four principal sources.

- It was a concession to the fears of the **Anti-federalists**. Indeed, had the Bill not been promised, the Constitution would probably not have been ratified by a number of the states. The **Anti-federalists** were concerned that the Constitution would – unless modified – lead to a process of centralisation and the imposition of elite rule.
- There were bitter memories of colonial rule. The British had – both before and during the war of independence – denied individual liberties. Under

Box 2.1
Unequal rights

Although the Bill of Rights appeared to echo the Declaration of Independence's universal language and seemed to rest on 'inalienable' and natural rights, such rights were extended only to relatively few among the US population. Native Americans were not afforded citizenship and were instead governed by laws and treaties that denied them their lands and independence. In the south, African-Americans were held as slaves until 1865 and were, for a further hundred years, subject to institution-alised injustices and arbitrary procedures.

the 1765 Stamp Act, for example, the British Parliament imposed taxes on business and legal documents. Attempts to enforce the measure by force led to arbitrary searches and raids on homes.

- The spirit of the age drew on notions of 'natural rights'. These, it was said, were derived from moral principles or endowed by God. They pre-dated the formation of governments. John Locke's conception of natural rights – put forward in his *Treatises of Civil Government* – is said, in particular, to have influenced the **founding fathers**.
- Some Americans looked back to the traditions of English common law. Although placed in jeopardy by tyrannical English rulers, common law had traditionally enshrined the rights of the 'freeborn Englishman'.

In offering assurances and safeguards to both citizens and the individual states, the provisions included in the **Bill of Rights** placed restraints upon the federal government. Indeed, the US Supreme Court ruled in 1833 (*Barron v. Baltimore*) that they did not circumscribe the actions of the states. However, the passage of the Fourteenth Amendment and the changing character of public attitudes led the Court to 'nationalise' the amendments by asserting that they also applied to the state governments.

The First Amendment

Congress shall make no law respecting an establishment of religion, or prohibiting the free exercise thereof; or abridging the freedom of speech, or of the press; or the right of the people peaceably to assemble, and to petition the Government for a redress of grievances.

The First Amendment establishes some of the most basic rights and freedoms. The first ten words are known as the Establishment Clause. According to

Thomas Jefferson, they were to create a 'wall of separation between Church and State'. The US Supreme Court ruled (in *Engel v. Vitale*, 1962) that the clause prevented prayer and other forms of religious worship in the public schools. This, however, still left some matters unresolved. Should, for example, student-led prayer be forbidden? Is a simple moment of silence at the beginning of the school day legitimate?

The First Amendment also sought to protect the 'free exercise' of religion. However, both the meaning of 'religion' and extent to which it should be protected have been the subjects of legal dispute. Should, for example, children be exempt from laws requiring compulsory schooling if it is in breach of their religious traditions? Can polygamy – by which a man takes a number of wives – be accepted if it has a religious foundation?

The assurance of 'freedom of speech' in the First Amendment has also provoked controversy. Although it has been accepted that 'speech' incorporates other mediums of expression (including the internet), the Supreme Court has at times regarded some forms of speech as constitutionally unprotected. It has allowed restrictions on forms of speech that might incite violence or could be considered subversive.

The Second Amendment

> A well-regulated Militia being necessary to the security of a free State, the right of the people to keep and bear Arms shall not be infringed.

For supporters of 'gun rights' such as the National Rifle Association, the Second Amendment offers the people an unfettered right of gun ownership. This, they argue, is a safeguard against the tyranny that could emerge if the national government is granted a monopoly hold on the use of force. For others, the second clause in the amendment is conditional upon the first. There is a right to 'bear arms' only within the context of a professional militia formed by a state government.

The Third Amendment

> No Soldier shall, in time of peace, be quartered in any house without the consent of the Owner, nor in time of war but in a manner to be prescribed by law.

The Third Amendment prohibited the forcible accommodation of troops in homes. During the War of Independence the British had forced colonists to house soldiers. However, despite the inclusion of this provision in the **Bill of Rights**, its implications remain undefined because it has not been subject to **judicial review**. It has, however, been cited by some legal scholars and justices as – alongside the Ninth Amendment – a partial basis for an implied constitutional 'right of privacy'. Government, it is said, should respect the private life of citizens. Some matters – including, some assert, contraception and abortion – are not a matter for legislation and must be left to personal discretion.

The Fourth Amendment

> The right of the people to be secure in their persons, houses, papers, and effects, against unreasonable searches and seizures, shall not be violated, and no Warrants shall issue but upon probable cause supported by Oath or affirmation, and particularly describing the place to be searched, and the persons or things to be seized.

The Fourth Amendment imposed limits on right of the authorities to search houses and belongings. The scope of the amendment has been progressively expanded so that it is now understood to prohibit the detention of individuals beyond forty-eight hours and restraints on the use of electronic surveillance. Under the amendment such steps require 'probable cause'. This is the reasonable suspicion that an individual has committed an unlawful act. In *Mapp v. Ohio* (1961), the Supreme Court ruled that evidence gained in the course of an 'unreasonable' search was not admissible in court. In April 2000 (*US v. Bond*), the Court concluded that the random feeling of bags by federal agents searching for drugs on a bus was a breach of the amendment.

The Fifth Amendment

> No person shall be held for a capital, or otherwise infamous crime unless on a presentment or indictment of a Grand Jury, except in cases arising in the land or naval forces, or in the Militia, when in actual service in time of War or public danger; nor shall any person be subject for the same offense to be twice put in jeopardy of life or limb; nor shall be compelled in any criminal case to be a witness against himself, nor be deprived of life, liberty, or property, without due process of law; nor shall private property be taken for public use without just compensation.

The Fifth Amendment confirmed the role of the 'grand jury' – which determines whether there is sufficient evidence to warrant an individual being brought to trial – in the American judicial system. It also afforded suspects the right to refuse to answer questions that might be self-incriminatory and established that the accused must be granted a formal trial.

The codification of the grand jury's role extended the role of citizens in the judicial process and thereby created a further obstacle to arbitrary detention or prejudicial treatment by the authorities. The provision against self-incrimination was extended in *Miranda v. Arizona* (1966) when the Supreme Court ruled that questioning or confession evidence obtained without suspects being warned that they have a right of access to a lawyer and to remain silent was inadmissible in court proceedings.

The Sixth Amendment

> In all criminal prosecutions, the accused shall enjoy the right to a speedy and
> public trial, by an impartial jury of the state and district wherein the crime shall
> have been committed, which district shall have been previously ascertained by
> law, and be informed of the nature and cause of the accusation; to be confronted
> with the witnesses against him; to have compulsory process of obtaining wit-
> nesses in his favor, and to have the Assistance of Counsel for his defense.

The Sixth Amendment laid down fair and recognised procedures for criminal trials. Its inclusion in the **Bill of Rights** was a reaction to the incidence
of arbitrary arrest and imprisonment without trial that had become associated with British rule. Its assurance of a right to legal representation led the
US Supreme Court to require the appointment of paid defence lawyers for
defendants unable to pay legal fees in both federal and state trials (*Gideon v.
Wainwright*, 1963).

The Seventh Amendment

> In suits at common law, where the value in controversy shall exceed twenty
> dollars, the right of trial by jury shall be preserved, and no fact tried by a jury,
> shall be otherwise re-examined in any Court of the United States, than according
> to the rules of the common law.

The Seventh Amendment placed the jury at the heart of the American
judicial process by ensuring that it had a place in **civil law** as well as in
criminal cases. This provision applies to cases tried under federal but not state
law.

The Eighth Amendment

> Excessive bail shall not be required, nor excessive fines imposed, nor cruel and
> unusual punishments inflicted.

The amendment stipulates that punishments or the requirements imposed
upon suspects before they are brought to trial must be proportionate to the
offence. In *Solem v. Helm* (1983), for example, the Supreme Court ruled on the
basis of the Eighth Amendment that a life sentence without parole for a seventh nonviolent offence was unconstitutional. Some have asserted that the
amendment also requires that punishment should be related to individual
circumstances and societal definitions of subjective terms such as 'cruel'. This,
however, has provoked controversy. The character of the arguments became
evident in the Supreme Court's deliberations on the death penalty. In *Furman
v. Georgia* (1972) some liberal justices such as Thurgood Marshall claimed
that the death penalty was inherently 'cruel and unusual'. The US had changed

since the late eighteenth century, and capital punishment had no place in an advanced society. Other justices saw the way in which some defendants were sentenced to death while others escaped with a lesser punishment through a process of plea bargaining or the skills of their lawyers as arbitrary and therefore, in this sense, both 'cruel and unusual'. Those who upheld the legitimacy of the death penalty argued that Constitution assumed its existence and that it had played a part in judicial procedures throughout American history.

The Ninth Amendment

> The enumeration in the Constitution of certain rights shall not be construed to deny or disparage others retained by the people.

The Ninth Amendment suggests that the people have other rights apart from those specified in either the **Bill of Rights** or the original constitution. It was added so as to emphasise that the rights of citizens are not restricted to those identified in the amendments. Alongside the Third Amendment, it has been cited as a basis for implied rights. In *Griswold v. Connecticut* (1965), a state law prohibiting the use of contraception was struck down by the Supreme Court as a breach of the 'right of privacy'. In writing the majority opinion Justice William O. Douglas asserted that the Ninth Amendment contributed to the existence of 'penumbras' or shadows in the Constitution that took its meaning far beyond specific words.

The Tenth Amendment

> The powers not delegated to the United States by the Constitution, nor prohibited by it to the states, are reserved to the States respectively, or to the people.

The Tenth Amendment is the cornerstone of 'states' rights'. It establishes that if a particular course of action by the states is not prohibited under the Constitution, or if the right to undertake an act is not assigned to the national government by the Constitution, then either the states or the population of the US have that power. The amendment underpinned the concept of dual federalism in which the national government played only a limited role and there was a clear division between the powers exercised by the national government and those that were the responsibility of state governments.

However, the wording of the amendment allowed a process of centralisation during the two centuries that followed its ratification.

- In drawing up the amendment Congress decided not to include the word 'expressly' before 'delegated'. If the powers held by the national government had been more strictly circumscribed, the constitutional position of states would have been strengthened.

- Despite the amendment, the national government can require states to comply with federal laws if they are rooted in the powers constitutionally assigned to it. As James Madison put it, 'If the power was not given, Congress could not exercise it; if given, they might exercise it, although it should interfere with the laws, or even the Constitutions of the States.' Successive Supreme Court rulings have, through their interpretation of particular constitutional provisions – such as the 'necessary and proper' clause in Article I, Section 8 – expanded the scope of the powers assigned to the national government.

However, although these considerations are important, the Tenth Amendment still plays a role in structuring federal–state relationships. Although the national government may use financial or other incentives, it cannot compel the states to undertake their own responsibilities in particular ways. Furthermore, during the 1990s, the US Supreme Court – with some notable exceptions – became more conscious of the 'etiquette of federalism' enshrined in the Tenth Amendment.

The Eleventh Amendment (1795)

> The judicial power of the United States shall not be construed to extend to any suit in law or equity, commenced or prosecuted against one of the United States by Citizens of another State, or by Citizens or Subjects of any Foreign State.

The Eleventh Amendment was added as a guarantee that a state would never again be brought to a federal court by a private citizen or a foreign citizen. This followed the case of *Chisholm v. Georgia* (1793) when the Supreme Court had ruled for two South Carolina citizens who had sued the state of Georgia on behalf of a British creditor to recover confiscated property. However, citizens can sue states in the state courts if they are deprived of their rights under the Constitution or federal laws, and states can appeal such cases to the federal courts. The Supreme Court made a number of decisions in the late 1990s citing the Eleventh Amendment (see Box 9.2).

The Twelfth Amendment (1804)

> The Electors shall meet in their respective States and vote by ballot for President and Vice-President, one of whom, at least, shall not be an inhabitant of the same State with themselves; they shall name in their ballots the person voted for as President, and in distinct ballots the person voted for as Vice-President, and they shall make distinct lists of all persons voted for as President, and of all persons voted for as Vice-President, and of the number of votes for each, which lists they shall sign and certify, and transmit sealed to the seat of the government of the United States, directed to the President of the Senate; – The President of the Senate shall, in the presence of the Senate and House of Representatives, open all the

certificates and the votes shall then be counted; – the person having the greatest number of votes for President, shall be the President, if such number be a majority of the whole number of electors appointed; and if no person have such majority, then from the persons having the highest numbers not exceeding three on the list of those voted for as President, the House of Representatives shall choose immediately, by ballot, the President. But in choosing the President, the votes shall be taken by states, the representation from each state having one vote; a quorum for this purpose shall consist of a member or members from two-thirds of the states, and a majority of all the states shall be necessary to a choice. And if the House of Representatives shall not choose a President whenever the right of choice shall devolve upon them, before the fourth day of March next following, then the Vice-President shall act as President, as in the case of the death or other constitutional disability of the President. The person having the greatest number of votes as Vice-President, shall be the Vice-President, if such number be a majority of the whole number of electors appointed, and if no person have a majority, then from the two highest numbers on the list, the Senate shall choose the Vice-President; a quorum for the purpose shall consist of two-thirds of the whole number of Senators, and a majority of the whole number shall be necessary to a choice. But no person constitutionally ineligible to the office of President shall be eligible to that of Vice-President of the United States.

The original procedure set out in Article II, section 1, for the election of the president and vice-president meant that the candidate with most votes became president and the runner-up would be vice-president. However, in 1800 the election resulted in a tie because Thomas Jefferson and his vice-presidential running mate, Aaron Burr, although members of the same party, each received the same number of Electoral College votes. The election was therefore thrown into the House of Representatives but it took thirty-six ballots in the chamber before Jefferson was finally chosen as president. This amendment changed the procedure so that in future there would be separate ballots for president and vice-president.

The Thirteenth Amendment (1865)

Section 1   Neither slavery nor involuntary servitude, except as a punishment for crime whereof the party shall have been duly convicted, shall exist within the United States, or any place subject to their jurisdiction.

Section 2   Congress shall have the power to enforce this article by appropriate legislation.

The Thirteenth Amendment was the first of three passed as a result of the Civil War. Its purpose was to free the slaves and complete the abolition of slavery in the US. Lincoln's Emancipation Proclamation – which was made during the war – applied to areas under Confederate control and therefore did not, in itself, free any slaves.

The Fourteenth Amendment (1868)

Section 1   All persons born or naturalized in the United States, and subject to the jurisdiction thereof, are citizens of the United States and of the State wherein they reside. No State shall make or enforce any law which shall abridge the privileges or immunities of citizens of the United States; nor shall any State deprive any person of life, liberty, or property, without due process of law; nor deny to any person within its jurisdiction the equal protection of the laws.

Section 2   Representatives shall be apportioned among the several states according to their respective numbers, counting the whole number of persons in each state, excluding Indians not taxed. But when the right to vote at any election for the choice of electors for President and Vice President of the United States, Representatives in Congress, the Executive and Judicial officers of a State, or the members of the Legislature thereof, is denied to any of the male inhabitants of such State, being twenty-one years of age, and citizens of the United States, or in any way abridged, except for participation in rebellion, or other crime, the basis of representation therein shall be reduced in the proportion which the number of such male citizens shall bear to the whole number of male citizens twenty-one years of age in such state.

Section 3   No person shall be a Senator or Representative in Congress, or elector of President and Vice President, or hold any office, civil or military, under the United States, or under any State, who, having previously taken an oath, as a member of Congress, or as an officer of the United States, or as a member of any State legislature, or as an executive or judicial officer of any State, to support the Constitution of the United States, shall have engaged in insurrection or rebellion against the same, or given aid or comfort to the enemies thereof. But Congress may by a vote of two-thirds of each House, remove such disability.

Section 4   The validity of the public debt of the United States, authorized by law, including debts incurred for payment of pensions and bounties for services in suppressing insurrection or rebellion, shall not be questioned. But neither the United States nor any State shall assume or pay any debt or obligation incurred in aid of insurrection or rebellion against the United States, or any claim for the loss or emancipation of any slave; but all such debts, obligations and claims shall be held illegal and void.

Section 5   The Congress shall have power to enforce, by appropriate legislation, the provisions of this article.

The Fourteenth Amendment was adopted in order to make the former slaves full citizens. Section 1 says that no state shall deprive any person of 'life, liberty or property without due process of law'. This clause has been used by the Supreme Court to protect the rights of citizens against the powers of the state in a broad range of cases. The section also includes the provision that states may not deny any person the 'equal protection of the laws'. This phrase has been used as the basis of challenges to unfair and discriminatory practices, and the Supreme Court found segregation by race to be unconstitutional in

Brown v. Board of Education (1954). It also required states to reapportion their electoral boundaries in *Baker v. Carr* (1962) and both of these decisions rested on the Fourteenth Amendment's 'equal protection' provision.

Section 3 banned former state or federal government officials who had acted in support of the Confederacy during the Civil War from holding public office again. It limited the president's ability to pardon those persons. Congress removed this 'disability' in 1898.

The Fifteenth Amendment (1870)

Section 1   The right of citizens of the United States to vote shall not be denied or abridged by the United States or any State on account of race, color, or previous condition of servitude.

Section 2   The Congress shall have the power to enforce this article by appropriate legislation.

This amendment barred the federal or state governments from denying people the right to vote because of race or colour or because they had previously been slaves. However, it did not prevent some states in practice disenfranchising blacks by the use of restrictive voting requirements such as literacy tests.

The Sixteenth Amendment (1913)

The Congress shall have power to lay and collect taxes on incomes, from whatever source derived, without apportionment among the several States, and without regard to any census or enumeration.

Forty-three years elapsed between the passage of the Fifteenth and Sixteenth Amendments. The latter allows Congress to raise revenue by imposing a graduated tax on individual incomes. At the same time it does not have to distribute the money so obtained to the states on the basis of population. In 1913 it was thought this tax would be temporary and mainly for use in time of war. However, it has become the main source of revenue for the federal government and provided the resources to pay for its greatly expanded domestic roles during the twentieth century.

The Seventeenth Amendment (1913)

The Senate of the United States shall be composed of two Senators from each State, elected by the people thereof, for six years; and each Senator shall have one vote. The electors in each State shall have the qualifications requisite for electors of the most numerous branch of the State legislatures.

When vacancies happen in the representation of any State in the Senate, the executive authority of such State shall issue writs of election to fill such vacancies:

Provided, That the legislature of any State may empower the executive thereof to make temporary appointments until the people fill the vacancies by election as the legislature may direct.

This amendment shall not be construed as to affect the election or term of any Senator chosen before it becomes valid as part of the Constitution.

This amendment reflected the demands in the early twentieth century for more democratic government. It modifies parts of Article I, Section 3, that related to the election of senators. Until that time they had been indirectly elected in so far as they were chosen by state legislatures which themselves were elected by the people of the state. The state legislatures saw their senators as 'ambassadors' representing the interests of the state and its government. The Seventeenth Amendment provided for the direct election of senators by the voters (or 'electors' as the amendment describes them). In doing so, it weakened the link between the US Congress and the state legislatures. When a vacancy occurs, for example by death or resignation, the state may fill the post either by a special election or by the governor appointing someone to take the seat until the next election.

The Eighteenth Amendment (1919)

Section 1 After one year from the ratification of this article the manufacture, sale, or transportation of intoxicating liquors within, the importation thereof into, or the exportation thereof from the United States and all territory subject to the jurisdiction thereof for beverage purposes is hereby prohibited.

Section 2 The Congress and the several States shall have concurrent power to enforce this article by appropriate legislation.

Section 3 This article shall be inoperative unless it shall have been ratified as an amendment to the Constitution by the legislatures of the several States, as provided in the Constitution, within seven years from the date of the submission hereof to the states by the Congress.

This amendment made it illegal to manufacture, sell or transport alcoholic beverages in the US. This attempt at Prohibition ultimately failed through lack of public support and the amendment was repealed in 1933 by the passage of the Twenty-first Amendment. However, its effects included the widespread defiance of the law by otherwise law-abiding citizens and the rise of organised crime that moved in to meet the demand for illegal liquor.

The Nineteenth Amendment (1920)

The right of citizens of the United States to vote shall not be denied or abridged by the United States or any State on account of sex.

Congress shall have power to enforce this article by appropriate legislation.

Although in many states women were allowed to vote before the Nineteenth Amendment was passed, this amendment provided a constitutional guarantee of women's right to vote. It came into effect in time for women to vote in the 1920 presidential election.

The Twentieth Amendment (1933)

Section 1   The terms of the President and Vice President shall end at noon on the 20th day of January, and the terms of Senators and Representatives at noon on the 3d day of January, of the years in which such terms would have ended if this article had not been ratified; and the terms of their successors shall then begin.

Section 2   The Congress shall assemble at least once in every year, and such meeting shall begin at noon on the 3d day of January, unless they shall by law appoint a different day.

Section 3   If, at the time fixed for the beginning of the term of the President, the President elect shall have died, the Vice President elect shall become President. If a President shall not have been chosen before the time fixed for the beginning of his term, or if the President elect shall have failed to qualify, then the Vice President elect shall act as President until a President shall have qualified; and the Congress may by law provide for the case wherein neither a President elect nor a Vice President elect shall have qualified, declaring who shall then act as President, or the manner in which one who is to act shall be selected, and such person shall act accordingly until a President or Vice President shall have qualified.

Section 4   The Congress may by law provide for the case of the death of any of the persons from whom the House of Representatives may choose a President whenever the right of choice shall have devolved upon them, and for the case of the death of any of the persons from whom the Senate may choose a Vice President whenever the right of choice shall have devolved upon them.

Section 5   Sections 1 and 2 shall take effect on the 15th day of October following the ratification of this article.

Section 6   This article shall be inoperative unless it shall have been ratified as an amendment to the Constitution by the legislatures of three-fourths of the several States within seven years from the date of its submission.

The Twentieth Amendment alters the dates when the president, vice-president and Congress start their terms. Prior to the amendment there was a four-month gap between the elections in November and the presidential inauguration day on 4 March. A president or Congressman who was defeated in the election would therefore stay in office but, having been injured by the voters, would be like a 'lame duck', unable to act effectively. The starting date for the presidential and vice-presidential terms was therefore moved to 20 January (leaving sufficient time for a transition between administrations) and the new Congress was to begin on 3 January.

Section 3 allows Congress to determine who should be president if the president elect and vice-president elect die before they take up office or fail to quality for the office.

The Twenty-first Amendment (1933)

Section 1   The eighteenth article of amendment to the Constitution of the United States is hereby repealed.

Section 2   The transportation or importation into any State, territory, or possession of the United States for delivery or use therein of intoxicating liquors, in violation of the laws thereof, is hereby prohibited.

Section 3   This article shall be inoperative unless it shall have been ratified as an amendment to the Constitution by conventions in the several States, as provided in the Constitution, within seven years from the date of submission hereof to the States by Congress.

The Twenty-first Amendment repealed the Eighteenth Amendment's constitutional support for prohibition but it did not make alcohol legal everywhere. States were allowed to choose whether they wished to remain 'dry' and some did so for a number of years after 1933. There are still some 'dry' counties in the US where alcoholic beverages are illegal.

The Twenty-second Amendment (1951)

Section 1   No person shall be elected to the office of the President more than twice, and no person who has held the office of President, or acted as President, for more than two years of a term to which some other person was elected President shall be elected to the office of the President more than once. But this article shall not apply to any person holding the office of President when this article was proposed by the Congress, and shall not prevent any person who may be holding the office of President, or acting as President, during the term within which this article becomes operative from holding the office of President or acting as President during the remainder of such term.

Section 2   This article shall be inoperative unless it shall have been ratified as an amendment to the Constitution by the legislatures of three-fourths of the several states within seven years from the date of its submission to the States by the Congress.

The Twenty-second Amendment introduced term limits for the presidency. No person may serve more than two elected four-year terms in the office. However, if a president has succeeded to the office after the halfway point of a term in which another president was originally elected, then that president can serve for more than eight years but not exceed ten. For example, Lyndon Johnson became president in November 1963 after the assassination of President John Kennedy who took office in January 1961. Johnson was therefore eligible to seek a second full term in his own right in 1968 but decided not to do so.

The amendment was passed after President Franklin Roosevelt broke the unwritten understanding that presidents serve only two terms which had been complied with by all holders of the office since George Washington. Roosevelt not only served three full terms but was also elected to a fourth in 1944. However, he died in office the next year. Critics argued that there are dangers of a president becoming over powerful if he stays in office too long; the American distrust of authority and the dangers of concentration of power ensured support for the amendment even though Roosevelt had generally been a popular president.

The Twenty-third Amendment (1961)

Section 1   The District constituting the seat of government of the United States shall appoint in such manner as the Congress may direct:

A number of electors of President and Vice President equal to the whole number of Senators and Representatives in Congress to which the District would be entitled if it were a state, but in no event more than the least populous State; they shall be in addition to those appointed by the States, but they shall be considered, for the purposes of the election of President and Vice President, to be electors appointed by a state; and they shall meet in the District and perform such duties as provided by the twelfth article of amendment.

Section 2   The Congress shall have power to enforce this article by appropriate legislation.

The Twenty-third Amendment gives citizens living in Washington DC the right to vote in presidential elections, which they did for the first time in 1964. The District of Columbia now has three Electoral College votes, whereas before this amendment it had none. At the time of its adoption the capital had a population of 800,000, which was greater than thirteen states.

The Twenty-fourth Amendment (1964)

Section 1   The right of citizens of the United States to vote in any primary or other election for President or Vice President, the electors for President or Vice President, or for Senator or Representative in Congress, shall not be denied or abridged by the United States, or any State by reason of failure to pay any poll tax or other tax.

Section 2   The Congress shall have power to enforce this article by appropriate legislation.

The Twenty-fourth Amendment abolished the poll tax (a tax collected equally from each person as a tax per head) as qualification for voting in federal elections. It applied only to five southern states that still imposed such a tax. Originally it had been used as a device to prevent blacks (and some poor whites) from voting.

The Twenty-fifth Amendment (1967)

Section 1   In case of the removal of the President from office or of his death or resignation, the Vice President shall become President.

Section 2   Whenever there is a vacancy in the office of the Vice President, the President shall nominate a Vice President who shall take office upon confirmation by a majority vote of both Houses of Congress.

Section 3   Whenever the President transmits to the President pro tempore of the Senate and the Speaker of the House of Representatives his written declaration that he is unable to discharge the powers and duties of his office, and until he transmits to them a written declaration to the contrary, such powers and duties shall be discharged by the Vice President as Acting President.

Section 4   The Congress shall have power to enforce this article by appropriate legislation. Whenever the Vice President and a majority of either the principal officers of the executive departments or of such other body as Congress may by law provide, transmit to the President pro tempore of the Senate and the Speaker of the House of Representatives their written declaration that the President is unable to discharge the powers and duties of his office, the Vice President shall immediately assume the powers and duties of the office as Acting President.

Thereafter, when the President transmits to the President pro tempore of the Senate and the Speaker of the House of Representatives his written declaration that no inability exists, he shall resume the powers and duties of his office unless the Vice President and a majority of either the principal officers of the executive department or of such other body as Congress may by law provide, transmit within four days to the President pro tempore of the Senate and the Speaker of the House of Representatives their written declaration that the President is unable to discharge the powers and duties of his office. Thereupon Congress shall decide the issue, assembling within forty-eight hours for that purpose if not in session. If the Congress, within twenty-one days after receipt of the latter written declaration, or, if Congress is not in session, within twenty-one days after Congress is required to assemble, determines by two-thirds vote of both Houses that the President is unable to discharge the powers and duties of his office, the Vice President shall continue to discharge the same as Acting President; otherwise, the President shall resume the powers and duties of his office.

The Twenty-fifth Amendment was ratified in 1967 following concerns about presidential succession in the light of President Eisenhower's heart attack in 1955 and the assassination of President Kennedy in 1963. After Kennedy's death, Lyndon Johnson became president but there was no vice president; the next in line for succession would have been the elderly Speaker of the House of Representatives.

Section 2 requires that if the office of vice president becomes vacant for any reason the president must nominate someone to fill the post. The person will become vice president upon confirmation by majorities in both houses of Congress. This provision was used in 1973 when President Nixon nominated Gerald Ford to the post when Vice-President Agnew resigned. In 1974 when Nixon himself was forced to resign over the Watergate scandal, Ford became president and he then filled the vice presidential vacancy with Nelson Rockefeller.

Sections 3 and 4 define the circumstances under which the vice-president may take over the leadership of the country in the event of the mental or physical illness or disability of the president. In 1985 President Reagan invoked the provision in Section 3 when he handed over power to Vice-President George Bush for eight hours while undergoing surgery.

The Twenty-sixth Amendment (1971)

Section 1   The right of citizens of the United States, who are eighteen years of age or older, to vote shall not be denied or abridged by the United States or any State on account of age.

Section 2   Congress shall have the power to enforce this article by appropriate legislation.

The Twenty-sixth Amendment gave persons eighteen years or older the right to vote in all elections, whether they be federal, state or local. This amendment was ratified by the states within three months of being proposed by Congress and came into effect in time for the 1972 elections.

The Twenty-seventh Amendment (1992)

No law varying the compensation for the services of the Senators and Representatives shall take effect, until an election of Representatives shall have intervened.

The amendment requires that members of the national legislature should face the voters in an election before any increase in congressional pay which they may have passed comes into effect. It is intended to make members cautious about the level of pay awards they grant themselves. It was finally ratified in 1992 following a public outcry at a large legislative salary increase. The amendment is unusual in that it was first proposed in 1789 but until 1978 only eight states had ratified it.

Interest in the amendment was resurrected following the disputed pay award and, although there was some constitutional debate as to whether a proposal that took 200 years to complete the ratification process was valid, and represented the 'contemporaneous consensus' required by the Supreme Court, Congress accepted its legitimacy.

Glossary

Anti-federalists Most Anti-federalists sought to maintain the Articles of Confederation that had governed America since 1781. They feared that the US Constitution placed excessive power in the hands of the national government. James Monroe of Virginia spoke of the dangers that the Constitution entailed: 'never grant to Rulers an atom of power that is not most clearly and indispensably necessary for the safety and wellbeing of Society' (quoted in Morris 1986: 59).

Bill of Rights A Bill of Rights defines the rights and liberties of the people. It thereby places constraints upon the powers of government. The US Bill of Rights – which also extends rights to the individual states – is entrenched in the first ten amendments to the Constitution. Its provisions include freedom of speech, constraints upon the searching of homes, and the right to 'a speedy and public trial'. It was ratified in 1791.

checks and balances Checks and balances are limits – or constraints – that are placed upon a particular branch of government. Congress can, for example, check the powers of the president by refusing to confirm a nomination that he puts forward or by failing to ratify a treaty that he has concluded with another country. Checks and balances ensure limited government, although it can also be argued that they prevent effective decision making and thereby contribute to **gridlock**.

civil law Civil law governs disputes between private citizens or groups, in contrast to criminal law.

enumerated powers These are the specific powers assigned to Congress in Article I of the Constitution. A distinction can be drawn between enumerated powers and the **implied powers** that were not stated explicitly but, the Supreme Court later established, stemmed from particular phrases and words in both the original Constitution and the later amendments.

federalism A system of government under which powers are shared between a national government and individual states. See Chapter 9.

founding fathers The 'founding fathers' or 'framers' of the Constitution were those who attended the 1787 constitutional convention in Philadelphia. After prolonged debate, they drew up the US Constitution. Their numbers included figures such as James Madison, Benjamin Franklin, Alexander Hamilton and George Washington.

gridlock The concept of 'gridlock' is drawn from a parallel with traffic conditions in many American cities. Decision making, it has been argued, is impeded by the **separation of powers**. The branches of government are elected at different times, responsive to different pressures, and sometimes have conflicting goals. In such circumstances, proposals for legislative reform can always be blocked. The failure of attempts to reform health care provision is sometimes cited as an example of gridlock.

impeachment The decision to put a public official – not excluding the president – on trial. Specific charges are brought and, if convicted, the individual is removed from office. Under the US Constitution the House of Representatives can bring forward an impeachment and the Senate conducts a trial. If the president is the subject of proceedings, the Chief Justice presides. Two presidents have been impeached (Andrew Johnson and Bill Clinton), but both were acquitted by the Senate.

implied powers The US Supreme Court asserted in *McCulloch v. Maryland* (1819) that the Constitution included implied powers. In contrast to **enumerated powers**, they were not explicitly stated but, nonetheless, still constituted the law of the land.

judicial review   The right of the federal courts to rule on the constitutionality of a law or governmental action. See Chapter 5.

popular sovereignty   Popular **sovereignty** is rule by the people.

reapportionment   The numbers allocated to each state in the House of Representatives – and the Electoral College – are based on the size of that state's population. A census is conducted every ten years so as to record the changes in the distribution of the US population. There has been a long-term shift from states in the north-east and around the Great Lakes to the south and west. After the 2000 census, Arizona, Florida, Georgia and Texas gained two further congressional seats. A further four states, including California, gained one additional seat. Correspondingly, ten states – including New York and Illinois – lost representation. Following reapportionment, a process of redistricting – whereby congressional districts are redrawn – takes place within the affected states.

Despite these changes, overall representation in the House of Representatives remains at 435. The figure was set by the 1929 Apportionment Act.

separation of powers   The separation of powers between the legislative, executive and judicial branches of government was seen as a bulwark against overbearing government and tyranny. Furthermore, it ensures that the process of government allows popular participation but also draws on the 'wisdom' of those – such as Supreme Court justices – who are largely 'insulated' from the unchecked feelings of the people. The separation of powers is, however, incomplete. A system of **checks and balances** ensures that each branch of government has a role – through, for example, the confirmation of presidential appointments – in the work of the other branches. Furthermore, some observers emphasise the 'sharing' of powers. Each of the three branches, they assert, plays a legislative, executive and judicial role.

sovereignty   Power and the ability to rule over a particular territory.

Resources

References and further reading

Boorstin, D.J. (2000), *The Americans: The National Experience*, London, Phoenix Press.

Elazar, D.J. (1988), *The American Constitutional Tradition*, Lincoln NE, University of Nebraska Press.

Mitchell, R. (1994), *CQ's Guide to the US Constitution*, Washington DC, Congressional Quarterly.

Morris, R.B. (1986), *The Framing of the Federal Constitution*, Washington DC, National Park Service.

Wills, G. (1999), *A Necessary Evil: A History of American Distrust of Government*, New York, Simon & Schuster.

Websites

American Civil Liberties Union   www.aclu.org
   The ACLU is a liberal-oriented pressure group and it has pursued large numbers of cases in court.

The Constitution of the United States of America   www.access.gpo.gov/congress/senate/constitution/toc.html

   This website is maintained by the Congressional Research Service.

Findlaw   www.findlaw.com

   Findlaw offers a searchable index of constitutional provisions and US Supreme Court rulings.

The US Constitution Resource Centre Index   tcnbp.com/index1.htm

   The website includes links to on-line resources about the Constitution.

The US Constitution Search   www.law.emory.edu/FEDERAL/usconser.html

   This website allows searches for particular concepts or cases.

3

Congress

This chapter analyses the working of the US Congress at the beginning of the twenty-first century. It examines:

- how and why the membership of the legislature has become more diverse;
- how power over policy making and activity within Congress have changed in recent times;
- how partisanship within Congress has increased;
- the causes and consequences of divided party control of the legislative and executive branches.

The 1990s were a period of major change and upheaval for the Congress. As an institution its membership became more diverse, there was a shift in the distribution of power over policy making on Capitol Hill, congressional politics became more partisan and polarised and relations between the national legislature and the presidency were significantly affected by divided party control of the two branches for all but two years (1993–95) in the decade. At the same time **incumbent** members of the legislature continued to dominate congressional elections with the majority facing weak or token opposition to their re-election. These trends have continued into the early years of the new century.

Membership of Congress

The membership of Congress became more diverse during the 1990s, with substantial increases in the numbers of women, African-Americans and Hispanics, as Table 3.1 shows. However, despite these trends, Congress remains overwhelmingly male and white at the beginning of the twenty-first century.

Female membership of the House stood at fifty-nine in the 107th Congress (2001–02), compared with the twenty-five who were elected to the 101st

Table 3.1   *Membership of Congress by gender and minority status*

Congress	Female	African-American	Hispanic
House of Representatives			
96th (1979–80)	16	16	6
99th (1985–86)	22	19	11
101st (1989–90)	25	23	11
102nd (1991–92)	29	25	10
103rd (1993–94)	48	38	17
104th (1995–96)	49	39	18
105th (1997–98)	51	37	18
106th (1999–2000)	56	39	20
107th (2001–02)	59	36	19
Senate			
96th (1979–80)	1	0	0
99th (1985–86)	2	0	0
101st (1989–90)	2	0	0
102nd (1991–92)	2	0	0
103rd (1993–94)	6	1	0
104th (1995–96)	8	1	0
105th (1997–98)	9	1	0
106th (1999–2000)	9	0	0
107th (2001–02)	13	0	0

Source: *Congressional Quarterly Almanacs*, various dates.

Congress (1989–90). This constitutes just under 14 per cent of the total membership, whereas women make up approximately 51 per cent of the population. The big jump happened as a result of the 1992 elections – the so-called 'Year of the Woman'. The parties (particularly the Democrats) have encouraged female candidates to run, a political action committee, Emily's List, was formed to channel money into their campaigns and in the early 1990s a larger number of incumbents than usual decided to retire as public dissatisfaction with Congress increased. This last factor is very significant because female candidates have succeeded mainly by replacing male incumbents who have stood down, thus creating open races. For example, in 1998 the six new women members in the House all won open seats. In the Senate the number of women increased from two to nine during the decade in the 100 member chamber and following the 2000 elections there was a record number of thirteen female senators. As recently as the 95th Congress (1977–78) there were no female senators at all.

Table 3.2   *Apportionment of membership in the House of Representatives,*
1950–2000

State	1950	1960	1970	1980	1990	2000	Change 1950–2000
Alabama	9	8	7	7	7	7	−2
Alaska	1	1	1	1	1	1	0
Arizona	2	3	4	5	6	8	+6
Arkansas	6	4	4	4	4	4	−2
California	30	38	43	45	52	53	+23
Colorado	4	4	5	6	6	7	+1
Connecticut	6	6	6	6	6	5	−1
Delaware	1	1	1	1	1	1	0
Florida	8	12	15	19	23	25	+17
Georgia	10	10	10	10	11	13	+3
Hawaii	1	2	2	2	2	2	+1
Idaho	2	2	2	2	2	2	0
Illinois	25	24	24	22	20	19	−6
Indiana	11	11	11	10	10	9	−2
Iowa	8	7	6	6	5	5	−3
Kansas	6	5	5	5	4	4	−2
Kentucky	8	7	7	7	6	6	−2
Louisiana	8	8	8	8	7	7	−1
Maine	3	2	2	2	2	2	−1
Maryland	7	8	8	8	8	8	+1
Massachusetts	14	12	12	11	10	10	−4
Michigan	18	19	19	18	16	15	−3
Minnesota	9	8	8	8	8	8	−1
Mississippi	6	5	5	5	5	4	−2
Missouri	11	10	10	9	9	9	−2
Montana	2	2	2	2	1	1	−1
Nebraska	4	3	3	3	3	3	−1
Nevada	1	1	1	2	2	3	+2
New Hampshire	2	2	2	2	2	2	0
New Jersey	14	15	15	14	13	13	−1
New Mexico	2	2	2	3	3	3	+1
New York	43	41	39	34	31	29	−14
North Carolina	12	11	11	11	12	13	+1
North Dakota	2	2	1	1	1	1	−1
Ohio	23	24	23	21	19	18	−5
Oklahoma	6	6	6	6	6	5	−1
Oregon	4	4	4	5	5	5	+1
Pennsylvania	30	27	25	23	21	19	−11
Rhode Island	2	2	2	2	2	2	0
South Carolina	6	6	6	6	6	6	0
South Dakota	2	2	2	1	1	1	−1
Tennessee	9	9	8	9	9	9	0

Table 3.2   (*cont'd*)

State	1950	1960	1970	1980	1990	2000	Change 1950–2000
Texas	22	23	24	27	30	32	+10
Utah	2	2	2	3	3	3	+1
Vermont	1	1	1	1	1	1	0
Virginia	10	10	10	10	11	11	+1
Washington	7	7	7	8	9	9	+2
West Virginia	6	5	4	4	3	3	−3
Wisconsin	10	10	9	9	9	8	−2
Wyoming	1	1	1	1	1	1	0
Apportionment ratio (000)	345	410	469	521	574	625	

Note: apportionment effective with congressional elections held two years after census.
Sources: adapted from Harold W. Stanley and Richard G. Niemi, *Vital Statistics on American Politics 1997–98*, Washington DC, Congressional Quarterly Press, 1998, 193–4; 2000 census figures (US Census Bureau).

African-American membership of the House rose from twenty-three to thirty-nine during the 1990s. In 2001 there were thirty-six black members, which constitutes 8 per cent of the total membership, compared with 12.7 per cent of the US population as a whole. Again the 1992 elections saw the most significant shift but the key factor here was the adoption in a number of states of majority–minority districts. This form of affirmative action was encouraged by the Justice Department as a way of increasing the number of minority members in Congress. When state legislatures draw up new congressional district boundaries following the diennial census, those with a history of race discrimination in voting procedures are obliged to submit their plans to the federal government for approval. Majority–minority districts involve drawing electoral boundaries in such a way as to ensure that at least some of the constituencies contain a majority of African-American voters, rather than have them spread around so that their political influence is diluted. As a result, in 1992 additional African-American members were elected from the newly created majority–minority districts. In the mid-1990s the Supreme Court declared that the redistricting plans in Georgia, Texas and North Carolina and the majority–minority districts they contained were unconstitutional because they subordinated traditional redistricting principles such as maintaining the integrity of recognisable communities to the overriding factor of the race of electors. This led to the creation of districts which had unusual, even bizarre, shapes. Despite the fact that as a result of the Court decision some of these districts disappeared in subsequent elections, African-American members mostly retained their seats and their total has remained stable since 1993. However, there has not been an African-American in the Senate since Carol Moseley-Braun (D. Illinois) – the first ever African-American woman senator – lost her seat in the 1998 elections.

The number of Hispanic members in the House increased from eleven to twenty during the 1990s and stood at nineteen in 2001 (4 per cent of the total); Hispanics comprise approximately 12–13 per cent of the total US population, according to the 2000 census.

Table 3.2 shows the number of seats that each state has in the House of Representatives as a result of reapportionment following the diennial census. The total number of seats has remained the same at 435 since 1910 (except for the period immediately following Alaska and Hawaii's admittance to the Union, when the number was temporarily increased by two in the late 1950s), despite a huge increase in the US population. This has meant the average district in 1910 contained 281,000 voters while in the 1990s the figure was 574,000 and, following the 2000 census, approximately 625,000.

After each census a reapportionment of seats takes place to reflect the growth or decline in the population of the states. Over the period shown in this table there have been major shifts in representation, mostly reflecting the growth of population in regions such as the west and the south, including the 'Sunbelt' in particular and the relative and in some cases absolute decline in the number of residents in the north-east and Midwest, especially the so-called 'Rustbelt' states with declining, traditional heavy industries. These changes inevitably affect the political influence of the different states and regions within the House. On the other hand, the Senate continues to represent all states equally regardless of population. This means that half the seats in the Senate are elected by 15 per cent of the US population and it is estimated by some experts that on the basis of continuing demographic trends around 1–5 per cent of the people could command a majority in the upper chamber by 2050.

Congressional organisation and activity

Traditionally power over policy making was decentralised so that congressional committees developed proposals in their specialist areas and committee chairmen took the lead in promoting them in the legislative process. After reforms in the 1970s power was devolved even further, with sub-committees of the main standing committees playing an increasingly important role. The elected party leaders were mainly responsible for organisational matters, such as arranging the scheduling of Bills in their respective chambers and building party support for the proposals emerging from committees. However, the post-reform era saw a strengthening of the party leaders' role. Very large omnibus Bills covering many subjects were considered by a number of committees and the party leadership played a key role in negotiating agreements between committee chairmen. Divided party control in the Reagan–Bush era

(1981–93) meant that Democrats in Congress gave their leaders more powers to bargain over budgets and legislation with the White House and also expected them to represent the party to the public. Therefore, by the mid-1990s, a shift in power from committees and their chairmen to party leaders had already taken place (Sinclair 1992: 93).

The sweeping electoral success of the Republican Party in the November 1994 mid-term elections heralded a new era in congressional history. The Democrats had been the majority party in the House of Representatives for forty years and had become used to doing things their own way, with little consideration for the minority. The new Republican majority led by Speaker Newt Gingrich was determined to make radical changes in the way the House did its business and in the type of policies it promoted. In the Senate the Republicans had been the majority in the period 1981–87 and neither had the same level of ideological fervour as their House colleagues nor saw themselves as an oppressed minority, but even here a number of important procedural reforms took place.

The high point of the 'Republican revolution' was in 1995 when Gingrich, fresh from leading his party to a momentous victory, managed to gain the support of a remarkably unified Republican **caucus** in passing through the House all but one of the major proposals in the *Contract with America* campaign manifesto. The new Speaker also instituted a range of important changes in House rules and procedures which strengthened the powers of the party leadership and significantly weakened the roles of committees and their chairmen and went much further than under his Democratic predecessors.

Gingrich and his allies attempted to institute a system of party government in the House whereby the committee chairmen were accountable to the party leadership and the majority caucus for delivering the party's election programme. (See Grant 1995, 1997: 65–73 for more detailed surveys.) Among the changes made in the 104th Congress (1995–96) were:

- The Speaker effectively decided who the committee chairmen would be, and Gingrich ignored claims of seniority which would normally have been decisive in determining who was selected.
- Chairmen were in future to be limited to six years in the job so that they could not become autonomous and powerful leaders in their own right as had happened in the past. (The Speaker agreed to accept an eight-year limit for himself.)
- Sub-committees were to be brought more strictly under the control of their parent committees.
- The number of major committees was reduced by three and twenty-five sub-committees were abolished while the number of committees and sub-committees members could serve on was reduced.
- The Speaker regularly set up task forces made up of chosen party members to consider issues and make legislative proposals as a way of bypassing the committee system altogether.

However, House Republicans were disappointed that many of their *Contract* Bills foundered in the Senate (despite a Republican majority there) or were vetoed by President Clinton. The 1995–96 budget crisis, which led to a temporary shutdown of the federal government, weakened Gingrich's personal authority and members began increasingly to criticise his leadership and the centralisation of power he had initiated. Recognition by members that by-passing the committees with their specialist knowledge and understanding of issues had resulted in the leadership sometimes bringing Bills to the floor which later caused political trouble led to a counter-trend in the late 1990s whereby committees again took a more important role in the initiation and processing of legislation. Gingrich was obliged to replace his Speakers' Advisory Group with a wider twenty-member leadership group and Republican committee chairmen became more confident and assertive. Occasionally this led to conflicts between the party leadership and the chairmen; sometimes the hard-line rank-and-file conservative members, especially the **freshmen** members, criticised their leadership for compromising and not insisting on what they saw as the majority view of the party caucus. Indeed, a frequently rebellious **caucus** has acted as a major constraint on the establishment of strong party leadership, except for the period immediately after the 1994 elections.

The attempt by Gingrich to institute a party government system in the House could be said to have ultimately failed because it took insufficient account of the checks and balances inherent in Congress and the wider American political system, the countervailing pressures on members (particularly from their constituencies and the need to get re-elected) and the small party majorities which the Republicans had to work with, particularly after the 1996 and 1998 elections. The disappointing electoral results in 1998 led to Gingrich being forced to resign. When Robert Livingston announced, as the House began to consider voting on the impeachment of President Clinton, that he had committed adultery on a number of occasions and would not run for the speakership, the mantle fell to the deputy whip, Dennis Hastert. The new Speaker's approach was one of being a conciliator and consensus builder rather than the visionary role Gingrich saw for himself. Hastert reverted to a more traditional party leadership style (similar to Gingrich's successor, Tom Foley) with an emphasis on mastering legislative procedures, being present in the chamber, organising his party and deferring to committee chairmen on the details of policy; a 'return to regular order' as John E. Owens describes it (2000: 54). This meant a reaction to but not a complete reversal of the Gingrich era and the re-establishment of the *status quo* before 1995; term limits for chairmen, which came into effect after the 2000 elections, for example, prevented the consolidation of power which many long-term Democratic chairmen enjoyed, with the Republican majority having to find new chairmen for thirteen committees. Speaker Hastert introduced a new system of selecting committee chairmen for the 107th Congress, rejecting both the traditional seniority system and the approach under Gingrich where the Speaker effectively

Box 3.1
The leaders of Congress

Newt Gingrich, House Speaker 1995–98

Newt Gingrich was born in 1943 and, after teaching history at a college in Georgia, was elected to represent a House district covering suburban Atlanta in 1978. He earned a reputation as one of a new breed of young Republican members who sought to confront the long-standing Democratic majority in House and provide a vigorous opposition, highlighting ideological differences between the parties. This was in contrast to the more traditional approach of Minority Leader Robert Michel, who emphasised bipartisanship, seeking compromises with the majority group. When Michel announced his retirement Gingrich became the heir apparent and led his party to a momentous victory in the 1994 mid-term elections.

Gingrich was installed as Speaker and carried the gratitude and support of a party which had been the minority for forty years. He piloted all but one of the proposals in the party's manifesto, the *Contract with America*, through the House and instituted a more centralised form of party government in the chamber during 1995. However, Gingrich's hold on his party weakened over the next three years. His own public approval ratings sank as low as 17 per cent as congressional Republicans were blamed for the budget crisis which resulted in temporary closure of government offices in the winter of 1995–96. He was reprimanded by the House after an investigation into political fund-raising activities and faced growing criticism within the caucus. Following the 1998 mid-term elections, when the Republicans' House majority was reduced, Gingrich resigned as Speaker when it became clear that there would be a formal challenge to his leadership. Gingrich was hailed as the most powerful Speaker in modern times but this turned out to be very short-lived.

Trent Lott, Senate Majority Leader 1996–2001

Trent Lott was born in 1941 and, having practised law and served as an administrative assistant to a Democratic congressman in Washington, was himself elected to the House in 1972 as a Republican. He served sixteen years in the House, becoming a conservative ally of Newt Gingrich. In 1998 he gave up a safe seat to win election as Mississippi's junior senator. He rose quickly in the leadership of the Senate Republicans, becoming conference secretary after the 1992 election and majority whip two years later. In the election for whip Lott beat the incumbent

Alan Simpson, who had the backing of Majority Leader Robert Dole, by twenty-seven to twenty-six. Lott won the support of most of the younger conservative members elected in 1992 and 1994. When Dole surprisingly announced in May 1996, during his presidential campaign, that he would retire from the Senate in June, Lott was the obvious successor and he defeated his fellow Mississippian, Thad Cochran, forty-four to eight.

With Dole's defeat in the presidential race and Gingrich facing ethics charges, Lott suddenly became the most visible Republican in Congress. Although a strong conservative, Lott established a reputation for working well with the Minority Leader, Tom Daschle, and was solicitous to Republican party moderates whose support the leadership often needed on key votes. He lost his position as Majority Leader in June 2001 when, following the defection of the Republican James Jeffords, who become an independent, the Democrats took control of the Senate and Tom Daschle replaced him.

Dennis Hastert, House Speaker 1998–

Born in 1942, Dennis Hastert was brought up on a farm in Illinois and after graduation became a high school teacher for sixteen years. He served in the state legislature from 1980 to 1986, before his election to the US House of Representatives. Although he had a conservative voting record he was not seen as a close ally of Newt Gingrich; he worked to get Tom DeLay of Texas elected as majority whip in 1994 and when successful was named as DeLay's chief deputy. He was given considerable credit by Gingrich for helping to secure the passage of the *Contract with America* Bills through the House and was increasingly looked to by other leaders to help Republicans reach consensus and negotiate on difficult issues with the Democrats.

Until December 1998 Hastert was well known and respected by fellow legislators but virtually unknown to the public. Following the November 1998 election disappointment, Gingrich announced his resignation, triggering off challenges to almost everyone in the leadership with the notable exception of DeLay. Hastert was urged by many members to challenge Majority Leader Dick Armey. Hastert had pledged to support Armey, and when Armey refused to release him from his pledge Hastert said no despite the fact that he had a good chance of winning. When Speaker-designate Bob Livingston announced his retirement on 19 December, Gingrich urged Hastert to fill the breach, telling him he was the only person who could keep the factionalised GOP caucus together. In the event Hastert was elected unopposed by House Republicans. Although seen by many as a stopgap Speaker, Hastert earned praise for his work in the 106th Congress, where he took on the more traditional roles of the Speaker which Gingrich had to a large extent ignored.

chose the chairmen. The Republican House Steering Committee made up of twenty-five members representing the GOP leadership and the rank-and file membership had the crucial role of interviewing candidates for each post. Twenty-nine members put themselves forward for the thirteen chairmanships and the Steering Committee, after a six-hour meeting, decided which should be proposed for confirmation by the full Republican Conference. Ultimately seniority did not prevail in a number of cases. Some outgoing chairmen retired from the House while others became chairmen of other committees or sub-committees.

Across the Capitol, Republican senators also took steps, albeit not so radical, to strengthen the hands of their party leaders and caucus and weaken the power of committee chairmen by instituting a six-year limit and the intro- duction of secret ballots for chairmen as well as the adoption of a formal legislative agenda and party positions on issues. However, the public and media interest in the House of Representatives under Gingrich's leadership distracted attention from an important factor in congressional politics. As Tim Hames notes, it is the Senate that is the real 'centrepiece' of the American legislative machine in the modern era (Hames 2000: 78). This is because the balance in the upper chamber can determine what happens to proposals supported by the majority party in the House, as was clearly demonstrated with the *Contract* legislation. Because of the requirement that sixty votes are necessary to pass a **cloture** motion and bring a Bill to a vote, a reasonably united min- ority party with forty-one or more seats can either block a Bill or force the majority to compromise and accept amendments to its proposals.

Table 3.3 provides a statistical picture of congressional activity during the 1990s. The legislative process has been likened to an obstacle race where thousands of contestants start the race but very few actually finish the course successfully. This is demonstrated by comparing the number of Bills and resolutions introduced and the number of laws enacted in the period of a Congress. Any Bill must pass through the process (including presidential action on the Bill) within the two years of a Congress. Not surprisingly, the table shows more Bills are enacted in the second session of each Congress, as members complete their consideration and there is pressure to pass legislation before the next congressional elections.

Table 3.4 shows the changes in committee activity during the 1990s. It demonstrates the reduction in the number of committees and sub-committees made by the Republicans when they took over the control of Congress in 1995, reversing the trend of the previous twenty years towards decentra- lised committees operating principally through sub-committees. The table also shows that as rank-and-file Republicans wanted more influence in the legislative process the number of sub-committees, full committee seats, sub- committee seats, the mean size of full committees and the mean number of full and sub-committee assignments all increased between 1995 and 1999.

Table 3.3 *Congressional activity, 1990–99*

	1990	1991	1992	1993	1994	1995	1996	1997	1998	1999
Days in session										
Senate	138	158	129	153	138	211	132	153	143	162
House	134	154	123	142	123	168	122	132	119	137
Time in session (hours)										
Senate	1,250	1,201	1,091	1,270	1,244	1,839	1,037	1,093	1,095	1,184
House	939	939	857	982	905	1,525	919	1,004	999	1,125
Average length of daily session (hours)										
Senate	9.1	7.6	8.5	8.3	9.0	8.7	7.9	7.1	7.7	7.3
House	7.0	6.1	7.0	6.9	7.4	9.1	7.5	7.6	8.4	8.2
Public laws enacted										
	410	243	347	210	255	88	245	153	241	144[1]

Table 3.3 (cont'd)

	1999	1998	1997	1996	1995	1994	1993	1992	1991	1990
Bills/resolutions introduced										
Senate	2,352	1,321	1,839	860	1,801	999	2,178	1,544	2,701	1,636
House	4,241	2,253	3,662	1,899	3,430	2,104	4,543	2,714	5,057	2,769
Total	6,593	3,574	5,501	2,759	5,231	3,103	6,721	4,258	7,758	4,405
Recorded votes										
Senate	374	314	298	306	613	329	395	270	280	326
House[2]	611	547	640	455	885	507	615	488	444	536
Total	985	861	938	761	1,498	836	1,010	758	724	862
Vetoes										
	5	5	3[3]	6	11	0	0	21[4]	4[4]	11

Notes:
1 As of 10 December, 1999.
2 Includes quorum calls.
3 Does not include line-item vetoes.
4 Includes pocket vetoes.
Source: *Congressional Quarterly Weekly*, 11 December 1999, 2986.

Box 3.2
Congressional committees, their chairmen and sub-committees in the 107th Congress, 2001–02

Senate

The chairmen in italics are those Republicans in office between January and June 2001. The names next to them are those senators who took over from June 2001; with the exception of James Jeffords, the former Republican who became an independent, they are all Democrats.

Agriculture, Nutrition and Forestry Ch: *Richard Lugar (Indiana)*, Tom Harkin (Iowa)
Subs (4): Forestry, Conservation and Rural Revitalisation; Marketing, Inspection and Product Promotion; Production and Price Competitiveness; Research, Nutrition and General Legislation.

Appropriations Ch: *Ted Stevens (Alaska)*, Robert Byrd (West Virginia)
Subs (13): Agriculture, Rural Development and Related Agencies; Commerce, Justice, State and Judiciary; Defense; District of Columbia; Energy and Water Development; Foreign Operations; Interior; Labor, Health and Human Services, Education; Legislative Branch; Military Construction; Transportation; Treasury and General Government; VA, HUD, Independent Agencies.

Armed Services Ch: *John Warner (Virginia)*, Carl Levin (Michigan)
Subs (6): Airland; Emergency Threats and Capabilities; Personnel; Readiness and Management Support; Sea Power; Strategic.

Banking, Housing and Urban Affairs Ch: *Phil Gramm (Texas)*, Paul Sarbanes (Maryland)
Subs (5): Economic Policy; Financial Institutions; Housing and Transportation; International Trade and Finance; Securities.

Budget Ch: *Pete Domenici (New Mexico)*, Kent Conrad (North Dakota)
No subs

Commerce, Science, and Transportation Ch: *John McCain (Arizona)*, Ernest Hollings (South Carolina)
Subs (7): Aviation; Communications; Consumer Affairs, Foreign Commerce and Tourism; Manufacturing and Competitiveness; Oceans and Fisheries; Science, Technology and Space; Surface Transportation and Merchant Marine.

Energy and Natural Resources Ch: *Frank Murkowski (Alaska)*, Jeff Bingaman (New Mexico)
Subs (4): Energy Research, Development, Production and Regulation; Forests and Public Land Management; National Parks, Historic Preservation and Recreation; Water and Power.

Environment and Public Works Ch: *Bob Smith (New Hampshire)*, James Jeffords (Vermont)
Subs (4): Clean Air, Wetlands, Private Property and Climate Change; Fisheries, Wildlife and Drinking Water; Superfund, Toxics, Risk and Waste Management; Transportation, Infrastructure and Nuclear Safety.

Finance Ch: *Chuck Grassley (Iowa)*, Max Baucus (Montana)
Subs (5): Health Care; International Trade; Long-Term Growth and Debt Reduction; Social Security and Family Policy; Taxation and IRS Oversight.

Foreign Relations Ch: *Jesse Helms (North Carolina)*, Joseph Biden (Delaware)
Subs (7): African Affairs; East Asian and Pacific Affairs; European Affairs; International Economic Policy, Export and Trade Promotion; International Operations and Terrorism; Near Eastern and South Asian Affairs; Western Hemisphere, Peace Corps, and Narcotics Affairs.

Governmental Affairs Ch: *Fred Thompson (Tennessee)*, Joseph Lieberman (Connecticut)
Subs (3): International Security, Proliferation and Federal Services; Oversight of Government Management, Restructuring and the District of Columbia; Permanent Sub-Committees on Investigations.

Judiciary Ch: *Orrin Hatch (Utah)*, Patrick Leahy (Vermont)
Subs (6): Administrative Oversight and the Courts; Antitrust, Business Rights and Competition; Constitution, Federalism and Property Rights; Immigration; Technology, Terrorism and Government Information; Youth Violence.

Health, Education, Labor and Pensions Ch: *James Jeffords (Vermont)*, Edward Kennedy (Massachusetts)
Subs (4): Aging; Children and Families; Employment, Safety and Training; Public Health.

Rules and Administration Ch: *Mitch McConnell (Kentucky)*, Christopher Dodd (Connecticut)
No subs

Small Business and Entrepreneurship   Ch: *Christopher Bond* (*Missouri*), John Kerry (Massachusetts)
No Subs

Veterans' Affairs   Ch: *Arlen Specter* (*Pennsylvania*), John Rockefeller (West Virginia)
No Subs

Special, Select and other
Select Committee on Intelligence Ch: *Richard Shelby* (*Alabama*), Bob Graham (Florida)
Select Committee on Ethics   Ch: *Pat Roberts* (*Kansas*), Harry Reid (Nevada)
Indian Affairs Committee   Ch: *Ben Nighthorse Campbell* (*Colorado*), Daniel Inouye (Hawaii)
Special Committee on Aging   Ch: *Larry Craig* (*Idaho*), John Breaux (Louisiana)

House of Representatives

All Chairmen are Republicans

Agriculture   Ch: Larry Combest (Texas)
Subs (5):   Department Operations, Oversight, Nutrition and Forestry; General Farm Commodities, and Risk Management; Livestock and Horticulture; Speciality Crops and Foreign Agriculture Programs; Conservation, Credit, Rural Development and Research.

Appropriations   Ch: Bill Young (Florida)
Subs (13):   Agriculture, Rural Development, Food and Drug Administration and Related Agencies; Commerce, Justice, State and Judiciary; Defense; District of Columbia; Energy and Water Development; Foreign Operations, Export Financing and Related Programs; Interior; Labor, Health and Human Services, and Education; Legislature; Military Construction; Transportation; Treasury, Postal Service and General Government; VA, HUD and Independent Agencies.

Armed Services   Ch: Bob Stump (Arizona)
Subs (5):   Military Installations and Facilities; Military Personnel; Military Procurement; Military Readiness; Military Research and Development

Budget   Ch: Jim Nussle (Iowa)
No Subs

Energy and Commerce   Ch: W.J. 'Billy' Tauzin (Louisiana)
Subs (5):   Commerce, Trade, and Consumer Protection; Energy and Air
            Quality; Environment and Hazardous Materials; Health; Over-
            sight and Investigations; Telecommunications.

Education and the Workforce   Ch: John Boehner (Ohio)
Subs (5):   Employer–Employee Relations; Workforce Protections; Edu-
            cation Reform; Twenty-first Century Competitiveness; Select
            Education.

Financial Services   Ch: Michael Oxley (Ohio)
Subs (6):   Housing and Community Opportunity; Financial Institutions
            and Consumer Credit; Capital Markets, Insurance and Gov-
            ernment Sponsored Enterprises; Oversight and Investigations;
            Domestic Monetary Policy, Technology, and Economic
            Growth; International Monetary Policy and Trade.

Government Reform   Ch: Dan Burton (Indiana)
Subs (8):   Census; Civil Service; Criminal Justice, Drug Policy and
            Human Resources; District of Columbia; Government Man-
            agement, Information and Technology; National Economic
            Growth, Natural Resources and Regulatory Affairs; National
            Security, Veterans' Affairs and International Relations; Postal
            Service.

House Administration   Ch: Robert Ney (Ohio)
No Subs

International Relations   Ch: Henry Hyde (Illinois)
Subs (5):   International Operations and Human Rights; International
            Economic Policy and Trade; Africa; Western Hemisphere;
            Asia and the Pacific.

Judiciary   Ch: F. James Sensenbrenner Jr (Wisconsin)
Subs (5):   Commercial and Administrative Law; Constitution; Courts
            and Intellectual Property; Crime; Immigration and Claims.

Resources   Ch: James Hansen (Utah)
Subs (5):   National Parks, Recreation and Public Lands; Fisheries, Con-
            servation, Wildlife and Oceans; Water and Power; Energy
            and Mineral Resources; Forests and Forest Health.

Rules   Ch: David Dreier (California)
Subs (2):   Legislative and Budget Process; Technology and the House.

Science   Ch: Sherwood Boehlert (New York)
Subs (4):   Research; Energy; Space and Aeronautics; Environment, Technology, and Standards.

Small Business   Ch: Donald Manzullo (Illinois)
Subs (4):   Workforce, Benefits and Empowerment; Regulatory Reform and Oversight; Tax, Finance and Exports; Rural Enterprises and Agricultural Policy.

Standards of Official Conduct   Ch: Joel Hefley (Colorado)
No Subs

Transportation and Infrastructure   Ch: Don Young (Alaska)
Subs (6):   Aviation; Coast Guard and Marine Transportation; Economic Development, Public Buildings and Emergency Management; Highways and Transit; Railroads; Water.

Veterans' Affairs   Ch: Christopher Smith (New Jersey)
Subs (3):   Health; Benefits; Oversight and Investigations.

Ways and Means   Ch: Bill Thomas (California)
Subs (6):   Trade; Oversight; Health; Social Security; Human Resources; Select Revenue Measures.

Joint Committees of Senate and House

Joint Committee on the Library
Joint Economic Committee
Joint Committee on Taxation

Box 3.2 lists the standing committees of the House of Representatives and the Senate in the 107th Congress (2000–01) as well as their chairmen and sub-committees. After the 2000 elections the Republicans retained control of the Senate even though there was a fifty–fifty split on party lines. Republican vice-president Dick Cheney, as President of the Senate, would have a casting vote in the event of a tied vote. The committee chairmen were therefore all Republicans until the moderate Republican senator James Jeffords of Vermont announced in May 2001 that he was leaving the party and would sit as an independent. This resulted in the Democrats having a fifty to forty-nine majority over the Republicans, and all the chairmanships were subsequently changed, putting Democratic members in charge, with the exception of the Environment and Public Works Committee, where Jeffords was rewarded with the post.

Table 3.4   *Changes in House and Senate Committee activity, 102nd–106th Congress*

	102nd (1991–92)	103rd (1993–94)	104th (1995–96)	105th (1997–98)	106th (1999–2000)
House of Representatives					
No. of full committees	27	23	20	20	20
No. of full committee seats	827	870	812	803	835
Mean size of full committees	37.9	38.6	39.2	40.1	41.8
Largest committee membership	68	62	62	73	75
Committee assignments per majority member	1.98	2.11	1.89	1.96	2.05
Total majority committee seats	528	545	435	445	458
% of majority with at least two full committee assignments	98	99	99	100	96.7
No. of sub-committees	149	117	84	86	89
Mean No. of subcommittee assignments	4.0	3.7	2.9	3.2	3.4
Senate					
No. of full committees	20	20	20	20	20
No. of full committee seats	343	362	350	355	370
Mean size of full committees	17.6	17.7	16.7	17.8	18.5
Largest committee membership	29	29	28	28	28
Committee assignments per majority member	3.50	3.63	3.64	3.56	3.60
Total majority committee seats	196	203	193	196	198
Mean No. of full committee assignments	4.0	4.0	3.8	3.8	3.4
No. of sub-committees	87	86	68	68	69
Mean No. of sub-committee assignments	7.4	7.8	6.2	6.5	6.76

Note: House full committees include the Select Committee on Intelligence, which, like the standing committees, reports legislation. Senate committees include select committees. All data pertain to assignments and party affiliations at the beginning of each Congress.
Sources: *Congressional Quarterly Weekly Report*, various dates. Taken from John E. Owens, 'Congress after the "Revolution": the Continuing Problems of Governance in a Partisan Era' in Alan Grant (ed.), *American Politics: 2000 and Beyond*, Aldershot, Ashgate, 2000, 48.

Partisanship

The shifts in the balance of power within Congress have taken place during an era of increasingly partisan politics. Intense party-line voting became the norm in the 1990s, peaking in 1995 when a majority of Republicans voted against a majority of Democrats 73 per cent of the time in the House and 69 per cent in the Senate. This has been accompanied by more polarised parties, an often bitterly rancorous atmosphere and personal invective becoming commonplace. Although political parties in the country may have declined in many respects as organisations, the drop in partisanship in the electorate which began in the 1960s came to a halt in the late 1970s and has been reversed. What is more, there was an increasingly sharp polarisation of views between the respective parties' activists who play a key role in the selection of party candidates and are more likely to vote in primary elections. Partisanship has been exacerbated by the narrow party majorities of the late 1990s, particularly in the House, with its two-year cycle of elections. Low electoral participation overall, especially in mid-term elections, means that it is crucial for a party to ensure a high turnout from its core constituencies and most committed supporters. Parties in Congress have therefore often taken stands on issues with this in mind rather than seeking common ground with their opponents.

The parties have become more homogeneous as Democratic support among white southerners has declined and the Republicans made major gains in the south. The effect has been that in Congress the Democratic Party has become more urban-based and liberal and the Republican Party's balance geographically has shifted to the west and south and has become more conservative ideologically. What is more, partisanship has been reinforced by ideologically based pressure groups on the right and left who exert influence on members through their ability to raise large amounts of money for electoral campaigns and demand loyalty to their cause in return, making it more difficult for lawmakers to strike compromises and make deals in the legislative process. As John E. Owens comments, 'The contemporary Congress is truly a partisan institution and the contemporary era is truly a partisan one' (Owens 2000: 29).

Although some aspects of partisanship in congressional politics are difficult or impossible to measure in statistical terms, for example the level of personal attacks in debates, we can gain an impression of what has been happening by examining the figures published each year by *Congressional Quarterly* based on their analyses of congressional roll call votes. Table 3.5 shows the percentage of all recorded votes in which a majority of voting Democrats opposed a majority of voting Republicans. This in itself may be seen as a relatively weak measure of partisanship, especially when compared with a parliamentary system such as the United Kingdom where the vast majority of divisions are based on the main parties going into separate lobbies. However, we can see that, based on this measure, 1995 (the year when the Republicans' *Contract* legislation was being pushed through the House and being considered by the Senate) was the high point in terms of the percentage of partisan votes, and that the 1990s generally saw more such votes than earlier decades.

However, floor votes do not tell the complete story, and partisan fighting occurs in committee battles, conflicts within **conference committees** and in

Companion to American government

Table 3.5   *Percentage of partisan roll call votes, 1956–99*

Year	House	Senate	Year	House	Senate	Year	House	Senate	Year	House	Senate
1956	44	53	1967	36	35	1978	33	45	1989	55	35
1957	59	36	1968	35	32	1979	47	47	1990	49	54
1958	40	44	1969	31	36	1980	38	46	1991	55	49
1959	55	48	1970	27	35	1981	37	48	1992	64	53
1960	53	37	1971	38	42	1982	36	43	1993	65	67
1961	50	62	1972	27	36	1983	56	44	1994	62	52
1962	46	41	1973	42	40	1984	47	40	1995	73	69
1963	49	47	1974	29	44	1985	61	50	1996	56	62
1964	55	36	1975	48	48	1986	57	52	1997	50	50
1965	52	42	1976	36	37	1987	64	41	1998	56	56
1966	41	50	1977	42	42	1988	47	42	1999	47	63
									2000	43	49

Note: figures show the percentage of roll call votes on which a majority of voting Democrats opposed a majority of voting Republicans.
Source: *Congressional Quarterly Weekly,* 11 December 1999, 2994, and 6 January 2001, 68.

relations between Congress and the White House that are not reflected in these figures. In 1999 the rate of partisan voting in the House declined to a relatively modest 47 per cent, even though most observers predicted that the atmosphere following the impeachment trial of President Clinton would be even more vituperative than normal. (See Box 3.3.). This may be partially explained by the Republican leaders being reluctant to push their agenda to a vote on a number of partisan issues because they lacked a sufficient majority

---

Box 3.3
The parties and impeachment

The attempt to impeach and convict President Clinton at the end of 1998 and the beginning of 1999 followed publication of the Starr report. Kenneth Starr had been appointed as an independent counsel to investigate allegations of financial impropriety by both Bill and Hillary Clinton in their home state of Arkansas (the so-called Whitewater scandal). His inquiry broadened out so as to incorporate claims that the president had lied under oath, obstructed justice and abused his position so as to hide the nature of his relationship with Monica Lewinsky, who had been employed on a short-term placement – an internship – in the White House.

Under the US Constitution the House of Representatives determines whether or not a president should be impeached. In December 1998 the

House of Representatives debated four articles of impeachment. Article I, alleging that the president had committed perjury, passed 228 to 206. Article III asserted that concealing the affair with Monica Lewinsky had been an obstruction of justice. It was adopted by 221 votes to 212. Following impeachment, there was, as the Constitution requires, a trial before the Senate, which act as a 'jury'. The Chief Justice acted as presiding officer. Conviction requires a two-thirds majority. In the event, Article I was defeated and Article III divided the Senate equally (fifty–fifty).

Whereas the impeachment proceedings against Richard Nixon in 1974 had a largely bipartisan character, the 1998–99 crisis was a much more partisan affair. Republicans overwhelmingly backed both impeachment in the House of Representatives and the subsequent attempt to convict the president in the Senate. In contrast, almost all Democrats opposed both stages of the process. As the table indicates, very few members of Congress crossed party lines. For many observers, Congress's handling of the affair illustrates the continuing significance of partisanship in the legislature.

Votes in the House of Representatives on the Articles of Impeachment,
19 December 1998

	No. of Republicans who opposed	No. of Democrats who backed
Article I (perjury)	5	5
Article III (obstruction of justice)	12	5

The president was not impeached on Articles II and IV.

Votes in the US Senate on the Articles of Impeachment,
12 February 1999

	No. of Republicans who opposed conviction	No. of Democrats who backed conviction
Article I (perjury)	9	0
Article III (concealing evidence – obstruction of justice)	4	0

Source: adapted from Michael Barone and Grant Ujifusi, *The Almanac of American Politics 2000*, Washington DC, National Journal, 1999, 20–3.

Companion to American government

Table 3.6 *Party unity in Congress, 1965–2000 (%)*

Year	Republicans	Democrats	Year	Republicans	Democrats
1965	70	69	1983	74	76
1966	67	61	1984	72	74
1967	71	66	1985	75	79
1968	63	57	1986	71	78
1969	62	62	1987	74	81
1970	59	57	1988	73	79
1971	66	62	1989	73	81
1972	64	57	1990	74	81
1973	68	68	1991	78	81
1974	62	63	1992	79	79
1975	70	69	1993	84	85
1976	66	65	1994	83	83
1977	70	67	1995	91	80
1978	67	64	1996	87	80
1979	72	69	1997	88	82
1980	70	68	1998	86	83
1981	76	69	1999	86	84
1982	71	72	2000	87	83

Note: the scores indicate the average percentage of Democratic and Republican members in both houses who voted with the majority of their own party in votes that divided the parties. Source: *Congressional Quarterly Weekly*, 6 January 2001, 67.

to ensure passage, while a number of measures were passed overwhelmingly on final floor votes but were the subject of intense partisan battles in earlier stages of the legislative process. In 2000 the number of partisan votes actually fell to its lowest for eighteen years in the House, although political scientists still noted the strength of partisanship in the chamber. ('Votes Belie Partisan Intensity', *Congressional Quarterly Weekly*, 6 January 2001, 56–7.)

Table 3.6 shows the average party unity score in Congress since 1964. This demonstrates the percentage of party unity votes on which members voted in agreement with the majority of their party. We can clearly see that the trend has been for these scores to rise in the 1990s compared with earlier decades. Scores in the 80–90 per cent range were unknown in the period until the last decade. Again, the high point was the Republican House members' 91 per cent recorded in 1995. The shifts in membership of the parties in Congress, and in particular the decline of Democratic Party conservatives in the south and of Republican Party moderates in the north, have been a major contributory factor to enhanced party cohesion in Congress.

Divided party control

The separation of powers system has always allowed the possibility of different parties controlling the executive and one or both of the two houses of Congress. In recent times this has become the norm rather than the exception. Since 1952 sixteen of the twenty-five presidential and mid-term elections have resulted in divided control; since 1980 all but the 1992 and 2000 elections have led to this situation. In the past split control was usually the result of mid-term election losses by the president's party in Congress, but recently this has been just as likely to happen in presidential election years, such as 1988 and 1996. Even though the modern experience of unified control under Carter and Clinton (1993–95) shows the difficulties of governing even when the president has a majority of his own party in both houses of Congress, divided party control produces even greater challenges, especially in an era of breakdown of consensus and more polarised and ideologically consistent parties.

Political scientists differ over how far divided control is harmful to the US system of government. James Sundquist, for example, says that it exacerbates the institutional tensions inherent in the separation of powers and provides an electoral incentive for one branch to work for the failure of the branch held by the other party (Sundquist 1988–89: 613–35). Others have pointed to the lack of clear accountability, with both sides claiming credit for successes and blaming the other for failures. At its worst it can lead to 'gridlock', with frequent use of the presidential veto and refusal by Congress to act on presidential proposals. This also leads to a decline in public trust in government and politicians.

Others, such as David Mayhew, have disputed this analysis and pointed out that there are often productive legislative periods under divided control where both parties see the need to compromise and they have incentives to show the voters their achievements (Mayhew 1991). The results may be nearer to what the average voter wants if the ideologues on both sides are forced to bargain.

One impact of divided control has been that Congress has tended to use its oversight powers of the executive branch in an increasingly partisan way. Investigations into presidential and executive branch misbehaviour have increased and have also led to the frequent appointment of independent counsels since 1978. The Starr inquiry and the Clinton impeachment trial were the ultimate culmination of this process, with the consequent poisoning of the political atmosphere both between the president and the Republicans in Congress and between the parties on Capitol Hill during the 105th (1997–98) and 106th Congresses (1999–2000).

Table 3.7 demonstrates the incidence of divided party control, whether one or both houses of the legislature were of a different party from the president, and whether this happened in mid-term or presidential election years. In the nineteenth century it can be seen that split control normally involved one

Table 3.7   *Divided party control of the presidency and Congress*

President and year	Type of split control		Time split control occurred	
	Both houses	One house	Presidential election	Mid-term
Buchanan (D) 1858	–	•(H)	–	•
Grant (R) 1874	–	•(H)	–	•
Hayes (R) 1876	–	•(H)	•	–
Hayes (R) 1878	•	–	–	•
Garfield (R) 1880	–	•(S)[1]	•	–
Arthur (R) 1882	–	•(H)	–	•
Cleveland (D) 1884	–	•(S)	•	–
Cleveland (D) 1886	–	•(S)	–	•
Harrison (R) 1890	–	•(H)	–	•
Cleveland (D) 1894	•	–	–	•
Taft (R) 1910	–	•(H)	–	•
Wilson (D) 1918	•	–	–	•
Hoover (R) 1930	–	•(H)[2]	–	•
Truman (D) 1946	•	–	–	•
Eisenhower (R) 1954	•	–	–	•
Eisenhower (R) 1956	•	–	•	–
Eisenhower (R) 1958	•	–	–	•
Nixon (R) 1968	•	–	•	–
Nixon (R) 1970	•	–	–	•
Nixon (R) 1972	•	–	•	–
Ford (R) 1974	•	–	–	•
Reagan (R) 1980	–	•(H)	•	–
Reagan (R) 1982	–	•(H)	–	•
Reagan (R) 1984	–	•(H)	•	–
Reagan (R) 1986	•	–	–	•
Bush (R) 1988	•	–	•	–
Bush (R) 1990	•	–	–	•
Clinton (D) 1994	•	–	–	•
Clinton (D) 1996	•	–	•	–
Clinton (D) 1998	•	–	–	•
Bush (R) 2001	–	•(S)[3]	•	–

Notes:
1 The situation following the 1880 election was extraordinary. The Senate was split evenly: thirty-seven Democrats, thirty-seven Republicans, two independents. After much manoeuvring and two Republican resignations, the Democrats appointed the officers and the Republicans organised the committees.
2 The Republicans, in fact, won a majority of House seats (218–216), but by the time the Congress first met a sufficient number had died to permit the Democrats to organise the House.
3 The 2000 elections left the Senate evenly divided on party lines, but the Republicans retained control, with Vice-president Cheney having the casting vote in the event of a tie. With the defection in June 2001 of Senator James Jeffords, who became an independent, control of the chamber switched to the Democrats.

Sources: Adapted from Charles O. Jones, *The Presidency in a Separated System*, Washington DC, Brookings Institution, 1994, 13; data in Harold W. Stanley and Richard G. Niemi, *Vital Statistics on American Politics*, third edition Washington DC, Congressional Quarterly Press, 1992, table 3–17.

house and occurred mostly as a result of mid-term reverses for the president's party. In the first half of the twentieth century divided party control was relatively rare and only twice (in 1918 and 1946) involved both houses, again as a result of mid-term elections. In the latter half of the century the table shows that split control happened frequently, was likely to involve both houses being of a different party from the president (except for six years in the Reagan era when his party controlled the Senate and after June 2001, when the Senate changed from Republican to Democratic control) and was just as likely to happen in presidential election years as mid-term.

In mid-term elections during the twentieth century the presidential party has lost an average of thirty-two House seats and almost four Senate seats. In 1998 President Clinton's Democratic Party defied this historical trend by winning five additional seats in the House and holding its own in the Senate. Table 3.8 shows the number of seats gained and lost by the president's party in mid-term elections since 1934 and the occasions when this led to or continued a period of divided party control of the two branches of government.

Table 3.8   *Mid-term fortunes of presidential parties, 1934–98*

Year	President	Seats gained or lost		Split control presidency and Congress
		House	Senate	
1934	Roosevelt (D)	+9	+10	
1938	Roosevelt (D)	−71	−6	
1942	Roosevelt (D)	−55	−9	
1946	Roosevelt–Truman (D)	−45	−12	•
1950	Truman (D)	−29	−6	
1954	Eisenhower (R)	−18	−1	•
1958	Eisenhower (R)	−48	−13	•
1962	Kennedy (D)	−4	+3	
1966	Johnson (D)	−47	−4	
1970	Nixon (R)	−12	+2	•
1974	Nixon–Ford (R)	−48	−5	•
1978	Carter (D)	−15	−3	
1982	Reagan (R)	−26	+1	•(H)
1986	Reagan (R)	−5	−8	•
1990	Bush (R)	−8	−1	•
1994	Clinton (D)	−52	−8	•
1998	Clinton (D)	+5	0	•

Notes: where divided party control is indicated it involved both houses of Congress in every year except 1982, when the Senate remained under the control of the president's party.
Source: adapted from Roger H. Davidson and Walter J. Oleszek, *Congress and its Members*, Washington DC, Congressional Quarterly Press, 2000, 112.

Explanations for the phenomenon of divided party control tend to centre around the willingness of many Americans to 'split their ticket' when voting for their congressional representatives and the president. It appears that many voters are happy with divided control and want to reinforce the checks and balances of the constitutional system by preventing one party or person having too much power.

Table 3.9 shows the percentage of voters who split their ticket when voting by supporting different parties for the presidency and their House district, and for the House and Senate. It appears that split-ticket voting reached its peak in the 1972 presidential election, when Richard Nixon was re-elected with a

Table 3.9   *Split-ticket voting, 1952–96 (%)*

Year	President–House	Senate–House
1952	13	9
1954		–
1956	16	10
1958		10
1960	14	9
1962		–
1964	14	18
1966		21
1968	17	21
1970		20
1972	30	22
1974		24
1976	25	23
1978		35
1980	28	31
1982		24
1984	25	20
1986		28
1988	25	27
1990		25
1992	22	25
1994		24
1996	18	19

Note: – indicates not available. Entries are the percentages of voters who 'split' their tickets by supporting candidates of different parties for the offices indicated. Those who cast ballots for other than Democratic and Republican candidates are excluded in presidential and congressional calculations.

Source: Harold W. Stanley and Richard G. Niemi, *Vital Statistics on American Politics 1997–98*, Washington DC, Congressional Quarterly Press, 1998, 129. Calculated by the editors from National Election Studies data, Ann Arbor MI, Center for Political Studies, University of Michigan.

landslide victory but the Democrats retained control of Congress, and remained at levels around 30 per cent in the period leading up to Reagan's election in 1980. During the 1990s approximately a quarter of those voting split their ticket, although in 1996 this fell below 20 per cent. Voters' willingness to do this is clearly related to levels of partisan identification and the relative strength or weakness with which voters relate to a particular party (see Chapter 7). A feature of split-ticket voting is the number of House districts carried by a House candidate of one party and a presidential candidate of another. This is shown in Table 3.10, where it can be seen that, in Nixon and Reagan's re-election

Table 3.10   *Split district outcomes: presidential and House voting, 1900–96*

Year	Total No. of districts[1]	No. of districts with split results[2]	% of total
1900	295	10	3.4
1904	310	5	1.6
1908	314	21	6.7
1912	333	84	25.2
1916	333	35	10.5
1920	344	11	3.2
1924	356	42	11.8
1928	359	68	18.9
1932	355	50	14.1
1936	361	51	14.1
1940	362	53	14.6
1944	367	41	11.2
1948	422	90	21.3
1952	435	84	19.3
1956	435	130	29.9
1960	437	114	26.1
1964	435	145	33.3
1968	435	139	32.0
1972	435	192	44.1
1976	435	124	28.5
1980	435	143	32.8
1984	435	196	45.0
1988	435	148	34.0
1992	435	100	23.0
1996	435	111	25.5

1 Before 1952 complete data are not available on every congressional district.
2 Congressional districts carried by a presidential candidate of one party and a House candidate of another party.
Sources: Norman J. Ornstein *et al.* (eds), *Vital Statistics on Congress, 1993–94*, Washington DC, Congressional Quarterly, 1994, 64; *Congressional Quarterly Weekly Report*, 1997, 862.
Harold W. Stanley and Richard G. Niemi, *Vital Statistics on American Politics, 1997–98*, Washington DC, Congressional Quarterly Press, 1998, 42.

years of 1972 and 1984, 44–5 per cent of House districts had split results
in this way. In the first half of the century it was normal for 80–90 per cent
of districts to be won by House members and presidential candidates of the
same party.

Glossary

advice and consent   The Constitution gives the Senate the power to advise the
president and give consent to proposed treaties and presidential appointments. In
the early days of the Republic the Senate was a relatively small body of twenty-six
members, distinguished citizens elected by the state legislatures to represent their
states who might well be seen as a suitable group to offer counsel to the president. Since that time the Senate has become a directly elected body as a result of
the Sixteenth Amendment, ratified in 1913, and as the US grew from thirteen to
fifty states became a much larger body with 100 members. The Senate's power of
advice and consent over foreign treaties and appointments remains very important,
and party politics often play a significant role in the Senate's deliberations and
decisions. For example, in 1999 the Senate rejected the Comprehensive Test Ban
Treaty and delayed consideration of many of President Clinton's appointments
because the majority felt some of his proposed federal judges were too liberal in their
views.

caucus   Within Congress a caucus is a group of members who meet on a regular
basis to plan strategy, make decisions and elect leaders. The two main parties in
both houses have caucuses (or conferences, as they are also known) and in recent
times these bodies have become more important in deciding policies which they
hope members will support, although party discipline in Congress is relatively weak
compared with parties in parliamentary systems. They also determine the party
leaderships for each house, and leaders subsequently have to retain the confidence
of their party caucuses. Members may also join other bipartisan caucuses set up on
the basis of race, region or interest and these may act as internal pressure groups
within Congress pushing for specific policies and priorities. Examples include the Congressional Black Caucus, the Congressional Sunbelt Caucus and the Congressional
Steel Caucus. In 1995 the House Republicans caused an outcry by withdrawing
financial support and office space from twenty-eight such caucuses (known as
legislative service organisations), saying that they could continue to meet but without public funding.

cloture   In the Senate cloture is the closing of debate or ending of a **filibuster** by a
required three-fifths vote, that is, sixty senators supporting the motion, thereby
allowing a Bill to be voted on. In practice this will mean that on a controversial
measure supporters will need to find sixty members to back the proposal rather than
a simple majority, as opponents will be able to block the Bill if they can muster forty-
one votes. In the late 1990s, for example, supporters of campaign finance reform
Bills had fifty-two or fifty-three senators voting for cloture but they fell seven or
eight votes short of the sixty necessary and the Bills failed in the Senate. The last
time a party had more than sixty members in the Senate was in 1977–78 and
therefore the Majority Leader must often find some members of the minority to

support his party's legislative proposals to ensure their passage. As partisanship has increased this has become more problematic but it tends to encourage a somewhat more bipartisan approach than in the House, where a simple majority is all that is required to secure a vote. The Senate has traditionally been seen as one of the checks and balances in the US system that protects minority rights, but members only deployed filibusters on rare occasions. In recent times their use has increased to further partisan opposition to the majority's party's legislative proposals.

conference committee   A conference committee is one that is made up of members of both houses and whose job is to iron out any differences that appear in the House and Senate versions of a Bill and recommend one version to the two houses for final approval. Members will be chosen from the original standing committees that considered the Bills. For legislation to pass Congress it must be passed in identical form by the two chambers. No amendments are allowed to a conference report and therefore members will be faced with a clear choice of passing or rejecting the Bill. It is rare for either house to reject the conference committee's compromise version.

continuing resolution   This is legislation providing continued funding for a federal government department or programme, usually at the level provided in the previous fiscal year. It is used when Congress has failed to pass the necessary appropriations Bill for the new fiscal year beginning 1 October, a quite common occurrence, given the complexities of the congressional appropriations process, partisan differences and divided control of the executive and legislative branches. Failure to agree a continuing resolution can lead to a budget crisis and the temporary closure of departments and agencies.

filibuster   The word comes from the Spanish word meaning 'pirate' and is used to describe a time-delaying tactic used by a legislative minority in an effort to prevent a vote on a Bill. Strict limits on the length of speeches in the House of Representatives mean the tactic cannot really be used in the chamber, but in the Senate there are no such restrictions and filibusters and threats of filibuster have become part of the normal political process. A senator does not have to speak continuously; he or she can yield to a colleague, to ask a question, for example, without losing the floor. Senator Strom Thurmond of South Carolina holds the record for the longest individual filibuster, when his speech against the Civil Rights Act of 1957 lasted a total of twenty-four hours and eighteen minutes. (Also see **cloture**.)

freshmen   Freshmen are the new intake of members at the beginning of each congressional session (as in universities, where freshmen are first-year students). The term includes both male and female members. Often this 'class' of members assumes an identity of its own and freshmen members of a particular party may meet together as a group, partly to increase their influence within the **caucus**. New members in the past often felt relatively powerless, given the traditional importance of the **seniority** system within Congress for determining committee assignments and leadership positions. In the 1970s freshmen House members in the Democratic caucus played an important role in passing procedural reforms that weakened the position of chairmen and the role of seniority. In the 104th Congress the seventy-three Republican freshmen (mostly hard-line conservatives and only seven with any experience of government at all) played an important role in supporting the Gingrich 'revolution', although many later accused him of 'selling out' and being weak when he was forced to compromise with Senate leaders and President Clinton.

incumbent   Incumbent members of Congress are the current holders of the office. Most members seek and gain re-election easily and serve for a large number of terms, thus building up their **seniority** within the legislature.

pork-barrel   Pork-barrel legislation is that which favours the district of a particular legislator by providing for the funding of public works or other projects such as defence contracts, which will bring some economic advantage to the district. In doing so the member hopes that it will help him politically with his electorate. Members may use their influence on committees or with leaders and chairmen to win such favours and it is one of many advantages that **incumbent** legislators enjoy which potential challengers do not at election time. Membership of certain committees such as the House Transportation and Infrastructure Committee (which, according to its website, 'builds America') provides ample opportunities for 'pork-barrel' politics, even when Republican conservatives, who are supposed to abhor unnecessary or wasteful public spending, are in control of Congress.

ranking member   The member of the majority political party on a committee who is first in seniority after the chairman. The ranking minority party member of a committee plays an important role as spokesman for the opposition party but also has to work closely with the chairman to expedite committee business. If there is a change of party control after an election it is likely that the ranking minority member will take over as chairman of the committee.

rider   A rider is a provision that is added to a Bill so it may 'ride' to approval on the strength of the Bill. Riders are often attached to appropriations Bills. A rider may have no relation to the basic subject of the Bill it is riding on, although the House of Representatives has a strict 'germaneness' rule which means that such provisions must have a bearing on and are pertinent to the Bill.

senatorial courtesy   The process by which the president consults senators of his own party when making an appointment to one of the states (for example, federal district judges), thus helping to secure confirmation of the appointment by the Senate. This results from the Senate's tradition of honouring any objections by senators of the president's party to appointments in the states of those senators.

seniority   The seniority system gives priority or status to an individual on the basis of his length of service in an organisation. The seniority system has played an important role in Congress in determining the relative influence of members. Seniority within a chamber as a whole is important in terms of the allocation of committee assignments, while seniority within a committee traditionally determined who became chairman. This meant that the member of the majority party with the longest unbroken record of service on the committee automatically became the chairman. Reforms in the 1970s weakened the principle so that, for example, in the House the Democratic majority caucus agreed to elect the chairmen at the beginning of each session. Although this resulted in the vast majority of cases in the most senior member being elected there were a few examples of the system being bypassed or the chairmen losing their position to members lower down in the pecking order. In 1995 Newt Gingrich, as the new Speaker, relied heavily on the seniority principle in his choice of committee chairmen but in some cases bypassed the ranking members on committees from the previous Congress. In the Senate the Republican Conference decided to hold secret ballots when committee members vote for chairmen, thereby allowing alternative candidates to be supported without fear of retribution from the chairman if the effort failed.

Resources

References and further reading

Davidson, R.H. and W.J. Oleszek (2000), *Congress and its Members*, Washington DC, Congressional Quarterly Press.
Fiorina, M. (1992), 'An Era of Divided Government', in G. Peele, C.J. Bailey and B. Cain (eds), *Developments in American Politics*, Basingstoke, Macmillan.
Grant, A. (1995), 'Legislative Careerism and the Term Limitation Movement', in A. Grant (ed.), *Contemporary American Politics*, Aldershot, Dartmouth.
Grant, A. (1995), 'The New Republican Congress', *Talking Politics*, 7.3, 195–202.
Grant, A. (1997), *The American Political Process*, Aldershot, Ashgate, chapter 2.
Hames, T. (2000), 'Presidential Power and the Clinton Presidency', in A. Grant (ed.), *American Politics: 2000 and Beyond*, Aldershot, Ashgate.
Mayhew, D.R. (1991), *Divided we Govern*, New Haven CT, Yale University Press.
McSweeney, D. and J.E. Owens (1998), *The Republican Takeover of Congress*, Basingstoke, Macmillan; New York, St Martin's Press.
Owens, J.E. (2000), 'Congress after the 'Revolution': the Continuing Problems of Governance in a Partisan Era', in A. Grant (ed.), *American Politics: 2000 and Beyond*, Aldershot, Ashgate.
Sinclair, B. (1992), 'House Majority Leadership in an Era of Legislative Constraint', in R. Davidson, *The Postreform Congress*, New York, St Martin's Press.
Sundquist, J.L. (1988–9), 'Needed: a Political Theory for the New Era of Coalition Government in the United States', *Political Science Quarterly*, 103, 613–35.
Thurber, J.A. and R.H. Davidson (eds) (1995), *Remaking Congress: Change and Stability in the 1990s*, Washington DC, Congressional Quarterly Press.

Websites

The Library of Congress   www.thomas.loc.gov/
The Library of Congress site, named after Thomas Jefferson, provides detailed information on legislation, including summaries and texts of bills, the Congressional Record, details on roll call votes as well as links to the Senate and House websites.

The Senate   www.senate.gov
The Senate website includes home pages for individual senators and committees, details on schedules of meetings and the latest progress on legislation. The committee pages include information on the membership and chairmen, subcommittees and jurisdictions. There are pages relating to the history and constitutional powers of the Senate, ways of contacting senators and a virtual tour of Capitol Hill.

The House of Representatives   www.house.gov
The House website provides similar information about the House as the Senate site described above.

Roll Call   www.rollcall.com
Roll call is the newspaper read by those who work on Capitol Hill and provides news and analysis of congressional politics.

Keele University Politics Department   www.keele.ac.uk/depts/por/usbase.htm
Keele University's website provides links with a wide range of organisations that provide news and analysis of congressional politics. They include newspapers such as the *Washington Post* and public interest groups such as Common Cause and Congress Watch.

4

The president and the executive branch

This chapter examines the presidency and the role of the executive branch of government. It surveys:

- the powers granted to the president and the constraints imposed upon him by the US Constitution;
- the growth of presidential power and the reasons for it;
- the character of the 'imperial presidency';
- the limits to presidential authority, particularly those that emerged in the aftermath of the Vietnam War and the Watergate crisis;
- the ways in which the power of the president is dependent upon public opinion, party relationships, and the skills of the office holder.

The powers of the president

The presidency often seems, particularly in periods of international crisis, to be synonymous with the entire apparatus of government. However, the position of the president, and the character of his relationship with the other branches of government, is subject to intense debate and disagreement.

The power of the presidency stems, in part, from the specific responsibilities assigned to the office by the US Constitution. Those who wrote the Constitution established that the president was to be **commander-in-chief**. He would head the executive branch, nominate senior public officials, including federal judges, and conclude **treaties** between the US and other nations. The Constitution also allowed the president to **veto** legislation passed by the two houses of Congress.

However, the framers also imposed constraints. Although the president was given authority over the armed forces – enabling the country to respond promptly to surprise attacks – the right to declare war was assigned to Congress alone. Since its founding, the US has issued only five declarations of war, as follows.

Box 4.1
The nature of the office

Presidents serve four-year terms of office and, under the Twenty-second Amendment to the US Constitution (1951), are limited to two such terms. Unless a presidency begins because of death or resignation (and the vice-president has therefore assumed the office), a presidential term commences on 20 January in the year following a presidential election. Most presidents previously served as state governors, vice-president (VP), or were in Congress. Their original occupation may therefore be of only limited significance.

Presidents, elections, periods of office, and backgrounds, 1952–2000

President	Party	Election(s)	Tenure	Previous political office
Dwight D. Eisenhower	R	1952 1956	1953–61	
John F. Kennedy	D	1960	1961–63	Senate
Lyndon B. Johnson	D	1964	1963–69	VP
Richard M. Nixon	R	1968 1972	1969–74	VP (1953–61)
Gerald R. Ford	R		1974–77	VP
Jimmy Carter	D	1976	1977–81	Governor
Ronald Reagan	R	1980 1984	1981–89	Governor
George Bush	R	1988	1989–93	VP
William J. Clinton	D	1992 1996	1993–2001	Governor
George W. Bush	R	2000	2001–	Governor

1812   Britain
1846   Mexico
1898   Spain
1917   Germany
1941   Japan

The Constitution also established other checks and balances. Presidential appointments and treaties had to be ratified by the Senate. Indeed, the founding fathers stipulated that treaties would require a two-thirds majority. Similarly, a veto could be overridden if there was a two-thirds majority in both houses of

Congress. Furthermore, the Constitution was structured around federalism. The powers of government were divided up between the national government and the individual states, placing further restrictions upon a president's freedom of action.

The growth of presidential power

However, despite the carefully crafted character of the Constitution, the role of the presidency has grown since 1789, when the first US president, George Washington, took office. Many observers suggest that, as a consequence, the separation of powers has been undermined and eroded. Twelve broad reasons for the growth of presidential power can be identified.

1.   Particular presidential styles or decisions by individual presidents set precedents that would be followed by their successors. Their actions enlarged the scope of the office and changed expectations about its nature. Norman C. Thomas and Joseph A. Pika point to the role of figures such as Abraham Lincoln in the Civil War and Franklin D. Roosevelt during the New Deal – the economic recovery programme of the 1930s – and the Second World War (Thomas and Pika 1997: 26–30).

2.   The president's constitutional role as commander-in-chief enabled him to dispatch US forces across the world without seeking a formal declaration of

---

Box 4.2
President Franklin D. Roosevelt (Democrat: 1933–45)

F.D.R. is the only president to have served more than two terms of office, (subsequently prohibited by Amendment XXII). He was elected four times. He is remembered for both domestic and foreign policy achievements. Roosevelt took office during the depression that followed the Wall Street crash, and the country's eventual economic recovery is attributed to the programme of public works and legislative reforms known as the New Deal. Following the Japanese attack on US naval forces at Pearl Harbor in December 1941, Roosevelt led the US through the Second World War, and with the other Allied leaders – Winston Churchill and Joseph Stalin – began to map out the future of Europe. Roosevelt died in April 1945, just weeks before the end of the war in Europe. Although Roosevelt was subsequently praised for his political skill, his critics have been harsh in their judgements. The New Deal, it is said, ushered in an era of 'big government'. In foreign affairs too many concessions were made to the totalitarian ambitions of the Soviet Union.

war from Congress. Although Congress retained the 'power of the purse', and could, where it disagreed with the president's objectives, threaten the withdrawal of funding, its options were otherwise limited. Although there have only been five declarations of war, American forces have been ordered into action abroad on over a hundred occasions (Pfiffner 2000: 176).

3.   The US was, by 1945, a world 'superpower'. In the post-war era it led the Western allies in their efforts to 'contain' the spread of communism. Increasingly, US intervention was expected and anticipated in troublespots across the globe. America served as the world's 'policeman'. At the same time, the nature of war was transformed by the stationing of American forces around the world, by missile technology and by the creation of a nuclear arsenal. In the atomic age, military and strategic decisions had to be made within a matter of minutes. These developments had profound consequences for the nature of the presidency, and the incumbent's roles as commander-in-chief and chief diplomat dramatically increased in importance.

4.   There has frequently been, Stephen R. Weissman has asserted, a 'culture of deference' within Congress. By this he means there is 'a distinct set of norms, beliefs, customs and institutions, that confine it to the margins of power' (Weissman 1995: 17). Because of this, Congress has repeatedly bowed to presidential leadership, particularly in foreign policy matters. Where legislation has been passed that appears to restrict executive actions, it has been rendered ineffective by unclear and imprecise wording. Although the number of research and advisory staff serving members of Congress grew until the mid-1990s, few foreign policy specialists have been employed.

5.   Although US Supreme Court rulings (Box 4.3) have, at times, reined in presidential power, some of the court's judgements – particularly those affecting the president's foreign and defence policy role – have enlarged the scope of the office.

6.   Although the Constitution stipulates that **treaties** are subject to Senate ratification, successive presidents have circumvented this by drawing up **executive agreements** with the heads of foreign governments. These have sometimes had far-reaching international implications (Box 4.4). Futhermore, as Table 4.1 illustrates, the number of agreements dwarfs the treaties that have been concluded. However, executive agreements do not have the legitimacy of treaties and may not necessarily be maintained by subsequent presidents.

7.   The size of the organisational apparatus serving the president has grown. The modern presidency does not consist of one individual, but instead involves a large number of aides, decision makers and administrators. Although there was some shrinkage during the 1990s, the **Executive Office of the President** (EOP) – the president's personal staff – has expanded in terms of both size and authority (Table 4.2).

Box 4.3
**Examples of Supreme Court rulings that have bolstered
presidential power**

United States v. Belmont (1937)

In 1933 an **executive agreement** had established diplomatic relations
between the US and the USSR. Soviet assets in the US were to be used
to pay Americans for losses they had incurred when the Bolsheviks
had taken power in 1917. New York refused to comply, arguing that its
state laws prohibited it. The US Supreme Court ruled that executive
agreements, like treaties, supersede state laws (*Congressional Quarterly*
1997: 126).

United States v. Curtiss-Wright Export Corporation (1936)

By a seven-to-one majority, the Court upheld a 1934 Act allowing the
president to embargo arms shipments to foreign combatants in a South
American war. Justice George Sutherland asserted that the president
was 'the sole organ of the federal government in . . . international relations' (*Congressional Quarterly* 1997: 126).

Box 4.4
Examples of executive agreements

1940 President Franklin Roosevelt and Winston Churchill, the British
 Prime Minister, agreed a 'swap' by which Britain gained fifty
 US destroyers in exchange for the use of British naval bases. It
 provided desperately needed aid for Britain at a critical stage of
 the war.

1973 North Vietnam and the US ended the fighting and agreed to
 exchange prisoners.

1981 The US reached agreement with Israel on a plan for strategic
 co-operation.

Sources: adapted from Jack C. Plano and Milton Greenberg, *The American Political Dictionary*, Fort Worth TX, Holt Rinehart & Winston, 1989, 168–69, and
Norman C. Thomas and Joseph A. Pika, *The Politics of the Presidency*, Washington DC, Congressional Quarterly Press, 1997, 419.

Table 4.1   *Treaties and executive agreements*

President	Executive agreements	Treaties
Kennedy	813	36
Johnson	1,083	67
Nixon	1,317	93
Ford	666	26
Carter	1,476	79
Reagan	2,840	125
Bush	1,350	67
Clinton (until 1996)	1,137	97

Source: adapted from Harold W. Stanley and Richard G. Niemi, *Vital Statistics on American Politics 1997–1998*, Washington DC, Congressional Quarterly Press, 1998, 327. Varying definitions of 'executive agreements' make these numbers approximate.

Table 4.2   *The Executive Office of the President*

Year	White House Office	Office of Management and Budget	National Security Council	Total Executive Office
1990	391	568	60	1,729
1992	392	553	62	1,869
1994	381	544	49	1,577
1996	387	527	43	1,582

Source: adapted from H.W. Stanley and R.G. Niemi, *Vital Statistics on American Politics 1997–1998*, Washington DC, Congressional Quarterly Press, 1998, 247.

8.   The power of **veto** allows the president to prevent to prevent legislation he opposes becoming law. Although the Constitution permits Congress to override a veto, it is, in practice, very difficult to muster the two-thirds majorities in both houses required under the Constitution. Indeed, only two of the vetoes imposed by President Clinton were overridden. The veto can, however, also be used as a political bargaining tool. Despite the Republicans' control of Congress, President Clinton was able to use the threat of a veto so as to win funding for the programmes he favoured. These included education, children's insurance, and child care provision. Table 4.3 shows the total number of vetoes and **pocket vetoes** imposed by presidents from Kennedy onwards.

9.   The legislation passed by Congress can often be broad in scope and the character of its implementation depends upon decisions made by the executive branch. Furthermore, as W. Craig Bledsoe, Christopher J. Bosso and Mark J. Rosso note:

Table 4.3 *The use of the presidential veto*

President	Total no. of vetoes	Annual average
Kennedy	21	7.00
Johnson	30	5.00
Nixon	43	7.17
Ford	66	22.00
Carter	31	7.75
Reagan	78	9.75
Bush	44	11.00
Clinton	37	4.63

Source: adapted from Victoria Allred, 'Versatility with the Veto', *Congressional Quarterly Weekly Report*, 20 January 2001, 175–7.

> Even when Congress is reasonably precise in its instructions to the executive branch . . . there are often policy contradictions, unforeseen circumstances, or technical considerations that require executive branch officials to exercise their judgement in implementing legislative intent. (*Congressional Quarterly* 1997: 42)

10.   Certain laws passed by Congress added to the president's powers. For example, the 1946 Employment Act created the Council of Economic Advisers (CEA) within the Executive Office of the President and empowered the president to 'use all practicable means . . . to promote maximum employment, production, and purchasing power' (quoted in Ragsdale 1998: 255).

11.   Some critics assert that successive presidents have increased the scope of the office by circumventing the provisions of the Constitution. For example, although the president's appointments to senior government positions require Senate confirmation, he can make **recess appointments**. These are made while Congress is in recess and are temporary. Nonetheless, the individual appointed can serve until the end of the next congressional session. Furthermore, such a move puts Congress in a defensive position. If the nominee is not confirmed, the senators are removing an individual from a post that she or he already occupies. From 1949 onwards a number of black judges – including Thurgood Marshall, who eventually served on the Supreme Court – were placed on the federal courts as recess appointments so as to pose difficulties for the opponents of integration. Just weeks before he left office, President Clinton made a recess appointment by placing Roger Gregory on the US Court of Appeals (Fourth Circuit). The president can, furthermore, issue **executive orders**. His ability to do so is derived from the authority bestowed upon him by the Constitution and laws that have been passed by Congress. Although there has been a long-term decline in the number of orders issued, many have had far-reaching political, economic or social importance (Table 4.4 and Box 4.5).

Table 4.4   *Executive orders*

President	No. of orders	Average per year
Kennedy	228	76.00
Johnson	316	63.20
Nixon	355	63.39
Ford	152	63.33
Carter	311	77.75
Reagan	409	51.13
Bush	165	41.25
Clinton	364	45.50

Source: adapted from Congressional Quarterly, *Powers of the Presidency*, Washington DC, Congressional Quarterly Press, 1997, 41, and National Archives and Records Administration, *Federal Register – Executive Orders*, www.nara.gov/fedreg/eo.html#top.

Box 4.5
Examples of executive orders

President	Date		Executive order
Roosevelt	1942	9,066	Forcible relocation of Japanese-Americans from the west coast
Truman	1948	9,981	Desegregation of the armed forces
Kennedy	1963	11,063	Prohibition of racial discrimination in housing subsidised by the federal government

Source: adapted from Congressional Quarterly, *Powers of the Presidency*, Washington DC, Congressional Quarterly Press, 1997, 45.

---

12.   The modern presidency has also acquired emergency powers. They were rationalised and codified by the 1976 National Emergencies Act, which was passed during the post-**Watergate** period. The Act stated that, if an emergency is declared, the president must specify the laws under which powers are being exercised. The emergency is automatically terminated after a year unless he notifies Congress to the contrary. The president's emergency powers include:

- the restriction of travel to particular countries;
- the restriction of movement within the US;
- the suspension of *habeas corpus* – which prevents arbitrary arrest;
- the ability to declare martial law;
- the ability to order the stockpiling of strategically important materials;
- the fixing of wages and prices;
- the withholding of sensitive information.

(Sources: adapted from Congressional Quarterly, *Powers of the Presidency*, (1997) 50, and Plano and Greenberg (1989), 282.)

Box 4.6
The presidential Cabinet

At first sight, it may appear that the president's Cabinet can play a role in bringing the work of the administration and the federal bureaucracy together. However, it plays only a limited and essentially advisory role. There are five reasons for this:

- Its membership has traditionally been loose. Alongside the secretaries who head departments, the Cabinet also includes other figures brought in at the president's discretion.
- Under President Clinton the Cabinet became too large and unwieldy. He accorded Cabinet-level rank to eleven other officials, including his chief of staff, the Director of the Office of Management and Budget (OMB), and the US Trade Representative. When these numbers are added to the fourteen Cabinet secretaries, the Cabinet had a total of twenty-five members (Pfiffner 2000: 111).
- Cabinet secretaries serve only for relatively short periods of time. Between 1945 and 1995 secretaries of state (responsible for foreign relations) and secretaries of commerce served, on average, only thirty-eight and twenty-eight months respectively.
- In contrast to the British Cabinet, who are MPs or peers, members of the US Cabinet hold no position of political influence apart from that assigned to them by the president.
- Presidents are often fearful that Cabinet secretaries are drawn too closely to their departments and associated interest groups. From the president's perspective, their loyalty is often suspect.

Policy decisions are not generally made by the Cabinet. Instead, matters will be resolved by small, informal groupings or on a bilateral basis between the president and the appropriate Cabinet official. In his study of the early years of the Clinton presidency Pfiffner suggests that the relatively large membership of both the Cabinet and other policy groups such as the National Security Council shifted the locus of decision making to less formal arenas: 'Actual policy deliberations were most often conducted in informal subsets of the groups' members along with the staffs of the groups who actually did most of the policy development work' (Pfiffner 2000: 111).

The 'imperial presidency'

By the early 1970s the US was governed by what Arthur M. Schlesinger Jr, a distinguished historian, described as an 'imperial presidency'. The growth of presidential power – captured by Schlesinger in his celebrated phrase – was symbolised by US involvement in the **Vietnam War**. Despite the intensity of the conflict – which led to the loss of 58,000 American lives and embroiled neighbouring countries – there was never a declaration of war. President Lyndon Johnson and Richard Nixon's only authority was the Gulf of Tonkin resolution, passed by Congress in 1964, which backed retaliatory action in response to an alleged attack on American vessels by North Vietnamese forces.

Although the eventual defeat of US forces in Vietnam led to a reassertion of congressional authority and changed the character of warfare, subsequent presidents have also ordered military intervention overseas. The Reagan administration, for example, sent ground troops into the Caribbean island of Grenada (1983) and launched air strikes against Libya (1986). With the exception of Operation Desert Storm in 1991, when a vote was held in both chambers, Congress played only a marginal role in these episodes.

Box 4.7
Examples of the presidential use of force, 1980–99

Carter

1980   There was an unsuccessful military attempt to free hostages held in Iran by students (who had acted with the backing of the Iranian government)

Reagan

1981   Military advisers were sent to El Salvador in support of attempts to defeat radical insurgents

1981   US planes shot down Libyan jets

1982   US forces were stationed in the Lebanon so as to assist the Palestine Liberation Organisation's withdrawal from the country

1983   US forces were sent into the Caribbean island of Grenada. The mission was ostensibly aimed at protecting American students living on the island, but – in reality – sought to remove the ruling leftist regime

1986 There were air strikes against Libya following alleged Libyan involvement in a terrorist bombing

Bush Sr

1989 US troops were sent to Panama so as to bring its president, Manuel Noriega, to trial in the US on drug trafficking charges. He was later convicted and imprisoned
1991 President Bush sought a vote in both the Senate and the House, and won congressional backing for the war to retake Kuwait from the Iraqis. Following this, US and allied forces launched Operation Desert Storm

Clinton

1993 There was US Air Force action against the Bosnian Serbs in support of UN peacekeeping operations
1993 Inheriting a US presence in Somalia, the president used the armed forces to protect humanitarian relief efforts from powerful warlords
1993 Missile attacks on Iraq were authorised following evidence of an Iraqi plot to assassinate former President Bush
1994 US troops were stationed in Haiti as part of an operation to reinstate the country's elected president, Jean-Bertrand Aristide
1995–96 There were US-led airstrikes against the Bosnian Serbs. Following the Dayton (Ohio) peace accord, US troops were sent to Bosnia as part of a multinational force so as to enforce the agreement
1998 There were further air attacks on Iraq in response to alleged violations of the agreement that brought the 1991 Gulf War to an end
1999 US forces played a leading part in NATO air attacks on Serbia. Once Serbian forces had withdrawn from Kosovo, the province was policed by NATO forces

Bush Jr

2001 There were US and British air strikes against Iraq following the targeting of Western planes by the Iraqis in the 'no fly' zones

Source: adapted from Lyn Ragsdale, *Vital Statistics on the Presidency*, Washington DC, Congressional Quarterly Press, 1998, 330–1.

As the 1960s and early 1970s progressed, the domestic powers of the presidency also appeared to have largely escaped the constraints that are imposed by a system of constitutional checks and balances. In *The Imperial Presidency* (1974) Arthur M. Schlesinger made six principal charges against the Nixon administration:

- It had, he said, pursued a policy of **impoundment** by which funds allocated by Congress for a particular purpose were not spent.
- It enforced the law selectively, choosing, for example, not to enforce parts of the Civil Rights Act that would cut off federal funding to school districts discriminating against minority students (Schlesinger 1974: 240–1).
- The president's aides in the **Executive Office of the President**, particularly figures such as John Erhlichman and H.R. Haldeman, wielded much more power than the Cabinet officials who headed the federal departments such as Defense and the Treasury. Haldeman is said to have used his position as White House chief-of-staff to ensure that very few individuals had access to the president.
- The administration had used government agencies to pursue personal vendettas and silence critics.
- **Executive privilege** was being invoked to prevent congressional scrutiny of executive actions.
- Presidential **press conferences**, allowing reporters to ask critical questions, were being displaced by television addresses to the nation.

Limits and constraints

There have, however, always been those who, despite Schlesinger's claims, have emphasised the constraints imposed upon a president. On leaving office President Lyndon Johnson (1963–69) warned his successor:

> Before you get to the presidency, you think you can do anything. You think you're the most powerful leader since God. But when you get in that tall chair, as you're gonna find out, Mr President, you can't count on people. You'll find your hands tied and people cussin' you. (Quoted in MacGregor *et al.* 1999: 104)

Why, from this perspective, is presidential power so limited? Firstly, the Constitution specifies that treaties require a two-thirds majority in the Senate if they are to be ratified. A number of treaties – most notably the Versailles Treaty of 1919 – failed to gain this. Some recent examples are shown in Box 4.8. This, however, provides only a partial picture. There have also been instances where **treaties** have been abandoned in committee or withdrawn by the president when defeat appeared probable. For example, in 1980, following the Soviet occupation of Afghanistan, President Carter withdrew the Strategic Arms Limitation Treaty (SALT II) that he had concluded with the USSR.

Box 4.8
Examples since 1945 of treaties *not* ratified by the Senate

26 May 1960	Law of the Sea Convention	49–30
8 March 1983	Montreal Aviation Protocol	50–42
13 October 1999	Comprehensive Nuclear Test Ban Treaty	48–51

Source: adapted from Michael Nelson (ed.), *Congressional Quarterly's Guide to Congress*, Washington DC, Congressional Quarterly Press, 2000, 203.

Similarly, although the president's powers of appointment include senior officials in the government bureaucracy, federal judges and ambassadors, he cannot be assured of congressional support for his nominations. The Constitution requires that his nominees have to be confirmed by a simple majority in the Senate. That chamber considers between 90,000 and 170,000 nominations to both civilian and military posts during each Congress (a two-year period).

Confirmation is generally a routine process. However, the Senate has rejected some nominations and others have been withdrawn by the White House once it became clear that rejection was probable. Some of these are listed in Box 4.9. The Senate has also used prolonged delay in considering nominations as a tactic when relations with the White House are poor.

Box 4.9
Unsuccessful nominations

Baird, Zoe

Zoe Baird was put forward by President Clinton in 1993 to head the Justice Department as his first Attorney General. The nomination was withdrawn following revelations that she had employed an illegal immigrant as a nanny for her children. The administration's critics talked of 'Nannygate'.

Bork, Robert

Robert H. Bork was nominated to the US Supreme Court by President Reagan in 1987. He was a conservative 'strict constructionist' who opposed the legal reasoning that underpinned rulings such as *Roe v. Wade* (1973). Roe, he asserted, came 'out of nowhere in the Constitution'. 'Pro-choice' and liberal organisations campaigned vigorously against his confirmation, and he was rejected by forty-two votes to fifty-eight. From then on, Presidents Reagan and Bush pursued a more carefully crafted appointments strategy. Only one overt conservative, Clarence Thomas, was put forward. Civil liberties and liberal organisations found it more difficult to oppose Thomas because he was an African-American.

Carswell, G. Harrold

Harrold Carswell of Florida was nominated to the Supreme Court bench in early 1970 following Clement Haynesworth's rejection by the Senate (see below). The nomination was opposed by liberal and black interest groups, who regarded his rulings in civil rights cases as discriminatory. There were, furthermore, claims that Carswell was unqualified to serve on the Court (Thomas and Pika 1997: 302). Carswell's nomination was rejected by the Senate (51–45) in April 1970.

Chavez, Linda

Linda Chavez was nominated by George W. Bush to be Secretary of Labour. In an echo of 'Nannygate' eight years earlier, she had to withdraw following claims that an illegal immigrant had lived in her home and performed various household duties.

Fortas, Abraham (Abe)

In 1968 President Lyndon Johnson nominated Abe Fortas as Chief Justice in place of Earl Warren, who had announced his retirement. There were claims that Fortas had, at times, behaved unethically, that he was personally too close to the President, and many in the Senate saw the nomination as a partisan attempt to deny the next president (who would take office in January 1969) the opportunity to put forward a nominee of his own choice and thereby shape the character of the Court.

Guinier, Lani

In June 1993 President Clinton nominated Lani Guinier as Assistant Attorney General for Civil Rights. Opponents publicised some of her writings that included calls for the introduction of cumulative voting systems. These, she argued, would lead to greater minority representation. Sections of the press claimed that she was an extreme radical and dubbed her the 'quota queen'. Amidst controversy, Clinton withdrew the nomination.

Haynesworth, Clement

Clement Haynesworth Jr, a federal court of appeal judge from South Carolina, was nominated by President Nixon to the Supreme Court bench in 1969. His nomination attracted opposition from black organisations and the labour unions. Alongside claims that Haynesworth's rulings revealed prejudice, it was alleged that he had presided over cases in which he had a personal financial stake (Thomas and Pika 1997: 302). His nomination was rejected (45–55).

Reynolds, William Bradford

In 1985 the Senate refused to confirm Reynolds as Associate Attorney General, following claims that, when responsible for the civil rights division, he had failed to pursue cases of alleged discrimination with sufficient vigour.

Tower, John

President Bush's initial appointments on assuming the presidency included John Tower as Secretary of Defense. He was rejected by the Senate (47–53) in March 1989 following allegations about his private life and suggestions that he had an inappropriately close relationship with companies seeking contracts from the Pentagon.

Weld, William

William F. Weld had served as the Republican governor of Massachusetts. Like some other north-eastern Republicans, he combined economic conservatism with a degree of cultural liberalism. In 1997 President Clinton nominated him US ambassador to Mexico. Despite Weld's Republican credentials, there was vigorous opposition to the nomination, led by Senator Jesse Helms, the Foreign Relations Committee chairman. After five months of argument, which highlighted deep divisions within the Republican Party, it became clear that the nomination would not be accepted by the Senate, and Weld withdrew his name.

Wood, Kimba

Judge Kimba Wood was President Clinton's second nominee for the post of Attorney General following the withdrawal of Zoe Baird (see above). However, her nomination also had to be withdrawn once it became clear that she too had employed illegal immigrants as nannies for her children.

Table 4.5 *Federal civilian employment, executive departments and selected agencies, 1990 and 1998*

Dept or agency	1990	1998
Executive branch (total)	3,067,167	2,789,495
State	25,288	24,713
Treasury	158,655	140,873
Defense	1,034,152	717,901
Justice	83,932	122,759
Interior	77,679	72,434
Agriculture	122,594	105,664
Commerce	69,920	50,041
Labor	17,727	15,894
Health and Human Services	123,959	59,813
Housing and Urban Development	13,596	10,063
Transportation	67,364	64,859
Energy	17,731	16,156
Education	4,771	4,677
Veterans' Affairs	248,174	240,398
Environmental Protection Agency	17,123	18,787
Federal Communications Commission	1,778	1,988

Source: adapted from US Census Bureau, *Statistical Abstract of the United States 1999*, Washington DC, US Census Bureau, 1999, 363.

Although often dubbed 'chief executive', the president is, thirdly, constrained by the bureaucracy. Although there was a drop in numbers during the 1990s (Table 4.5), the federal government still employs almost 3 million civil servants, and the departments, commissions and agencies in which they work have a labyrinthine structure. The loyalties of bureaucrats are torn between the White House, Congress and particular interest groups. Some critics have talked of 'iron triangles' bringing together agencies, sectional groupings and congressional committees. They are bound together by self-interest and are often resistant to external pressure or direction.

Furthermore, the president cannot – by law – issue instructions to sections of the federal bureaucracy. Many independent regulatory commissions (IRCs) are *quasi-judicial* bodies. Their role includes the making of judgements about the imposition of federal regulations. Similarly, the president cannot instruct the Federal Reserve's board of governors – the 'Fed' – about the setting of monetary policy. It alone determines the US interest rate.

The president is limited, fourthly, by the role of Congress as the national legislature. Although the president has the power of veto, law-making can often be a battle of wills between the White House and Congress. There are particular tensions around the passage of the annual budget that sets taxation and government spending levels for the following year.

Table 4.6   *Presidential victories in Congress: Congressional Quarterly ratings (%)*

President	Tenure	House of Representatives, average	Senate, average	House and Senate, average
Kennedy	1961–63	83.7	85.2	84.6
Johnson	1963–69	85.9	79.7	82.2
Nixon	1969–74	68.2	61.5	64.3
Ford	1974–77	51.0	65.0	58.3
Carter	1977–81	73.1	79.7	76.6
Reagan	1981–89	45.6	77.9	62.2
Bush	1989–93	40.2	65.6	51.8
Clinton	1993	87.2	85.4	86.4
	1994	87.2	85.5	86.4
	1995	26.3	49.0	36.2
	1996	53.2	57.6	55.1
	1997	38.7	71.4	53.6
	1998	36.6	67.0	50.6
	1999	35.4	42.2	37.8
	2000	49.3	65.0	55.0

Sources: adapted from Norman J. Ornstein, Thomas E. Mann and Michael J. Malbin, *Vital Statistics on Congress 1999–2000*, Washington DC, AEI Press, 2000, 197; *Congressional Quarterly Weekly*, 11 December 1999, 2971–72, and 6 January 2001, 61–3.

Congressional Quarterly Weekly – an influential Washington periodical – has drawn up ratings by which a president's successes in his relationship with Congress can be recorded. The *Congressional Quarterly* ratings, which are shown in Table 4.6, measure the proportion of formal – or *roll-call* – votes in which Congress backs the position on an issue that has been adopted by the president. A high score can be considered a success for a president. Conversely, a low score is regarded as a failure. There are, however, some methodological difficulties. *Congressional Quarterly* ratings are confined to roll-call votes, and do not, therefore, consider matters resolved on a voice votes. Some policy proposals are killed in committee rather than on the floor of the House or Senate. The administration may not take a formal position on an issue if defeat is considered likely. They also assign an equal weighting to all issues regardless of their importance. Furthermore, comparisons between *Congressional Quarterly* scores for the two houses of Congress can also be misleading. In many cases, different amendments will have been offered. The votes that are being compared will have involved different issues.

Lastly, although the US Supreme Court has, at times, enlarged the presidency, its power of judicial review has enabled it, when an appropriate case has been brought, to rule on the constitutionality of a president's actions. Some of the Court's rulings have significantly circumscribed a president's freedom of action (Box 4.10). The 1952 *Youngstown* judgement declared that President

Box 4.10
US Supreme Court rulings and the presidency

Clinton v. Jones (1997)

The Supreme Court unanimously ruled that a president can – despite the responsibilities and burdens of the office – be the subject of civil litigation. The case was brought by Paula Jones, who alleged that Bill Clinton had, while serving as Governor of Arkansas, sexually harassed her (Alsop 1997: 13–14).

Schechter v. United States (1935)

In the *Schechter* case the Supreme Court declared the National Industrial Recovery Act – part of President Franklin Roosevelt's New Deal – unconstitutional.

United States v. Butler (1936)

The *Butler* ruling struck down the Agriculture Adjustment Act of 1933. The Act was another important part of the New Deal. Following the *Schechter* and *Butler* rulings, Roosevelt sought to enlarge the Court by adding to the nine judges who sit on the bench. Although denied, the 'court packing' plan was an attempt to change its political character.

United States v. Richard M. Nixon (1974)

The Court ruled unanimously that the powers accorded to the presidency, and its right to confidentiality – 'executive privilege' – did not permit President Nixon to withhold tape recordings of his discussions with aides in the Oval Office. The decision circumscribed presidential authority and led directly to Nixon's resignation.

Youngstown Sheet & Tube Company v. Sawyer (1952)

Faced by a threatened strike during the Korean War, President Harry Truman issued an executive order putting the steelworks under federal government control. The Court ruled that Truman had acted unconstitutionally. Congress, the Court noted, had rejected giving the executive branch such powers. The president's actions were an attempt to assume a legislative role and were therefore *ultra vires*.

Truman's take-over of a strike-hit steel mill had been unconstitutional. In *US v. Nixon* (1974) the Court ruled that **executive privilege** did not allow the president to withhold recordings of his conversations. Following the Court decision in the *Jones* case (1997), President Clinton found that he could not evade civil charges because of the demands of his office.

After Vietnam and Watergate

There are other limits on the presidency apart from those imposed by the Constitution and the evolution of judicial review. Military defeat in Vietnam and the **Watergate** crisis shrank the authority of the Oval Office. A series of legislative measures, most notably the War Powers Act (1973) and the Budget and Impoundment Control Act (1974), were passed by Congress (Box 4.11). Although observers disagree about their long-term significance, they have, at the least, reshaped and modified presidential actions.

Other developments also played a part in curbing the growth of presidential power.

- The mass media traditionally approached the presidency with a sense of deference and respect. There were, for example, unwritten rules forbidding the taking of photographs or the publication of stories showing Franklin Roosevelt's disability and John F. Kennedy's sexual liaisons. The code was abandoned during the late 1960s and early 1970s. All aspects of the presidency became subject to intense scrutiny, and investigative reporting by the *Washington Post* played a pivotal role in bringing the Nixon administration to an end. The growth of dedicated twenty-four-hour news channels and of the internet during the 1990s placed further pressures on the White House.
- The level and scale of congressional oversight of the executive branch also grew from the 1970s onwards. In 1961 only 8.2 per cent of congressional committee meetings and hearings were devoted to oversight. By 1983 this had risen to 25.2 per cent. Richard Armitage, Assistant Secretary of Defense for International Security Affairs during the Reagan years, was asked to testify before congressional committees over 150 times (Rose 1997: 40).
- As Gary L. Rose notes, Congress has also placed many more restrictions on federal government spending – or appropriations – Bills. It has given only temporary, rather than permanent, authorisation for projects. It has more closely specified how money is to be spent (Rose 1997: 41). At the same time, Congress has continued to include a **legislative veto** in some items of the legislation despite a 1983 ruling by the US Supreme Court declaring it unconstitutional (*Immigration and Naturalization Service v. Chadha*). A

Box 4.11
Statutory limits on the president's powers

Budget and Impoundment Control Act, 1974

The Act prevented the president impounding funds that had been allocated for a particular purpose by Congress. It established a budget committee in both houses of Congress and a structured framework for the budget-making process. It also created the Congressional Budget Office (CBO) as a counterweight to the Office of Management and the Budget (OMB) in the executive branch.

Case–Zablocki Act, 1972

The Act required the president to inform Congress of every foreign policy commitment that he makes. Prior to this, some executive agreements had been concluded in secrecy.

War Powers Act, 1973

'The President in every possible instance shall consult with Congress before introducing United States armed forces into situations where imminent involvement in hostilities is clearly indicated by the circumstances' (quoted in Lipsitz 1986: 345). Successive presidents have denied the legitimacy of the Act – asserting that it violated their constitutional position as commander-in-chief. Nonetheless, although Congress has been reluctant to demand the Act's implementation, the White House has broadly observed its provisions. Peacekeeping missions aside, military actions have been short-term and tied to well defined objectives. Troops have been withdrawn at an early opportunity. Congressional leaders have generally been informed as the attack was being mounted. At the beginning of 1991, just before hostilities began in the Gulf War with Iraq, President Bush asked for, and gained, backing in both houses of Congress.

legislative veto is a provision included in a law allowing Congress to review, delay or end the implementation of a particular measure.
- The nature of American society and politics is changing. Michael Barone argues that the era of big government, large-scale companies and other nationally organised institutions is over. The country is again becoming decentralised and individualistic. Decisions are being made at a micro-level.

Box 4.12
President John F. Kennedy (Democrat: 1961–63)

In the aftermath of his assassination, Kennedy – 'J.F.K.' – was portrayed in idealised terms. Both his administration and his family appeared to have a glamour hitherto lacking in American politics. He was – at forty-three – the youngest man to be elected to the White House. His handling of the Cuban missile crisis in October 1962, the subsequent creation of the Washington–Moscow 'hot line' and the 1963 Nuclear Test Ban Treaty have generally been portrayed as examples of measured statesmanship.

Subsequent 'revisionist' historians have, however, been much more critical of Kennedy's record. His pursuit of the presidency, they say, led him to become a Cold War 'hawk' during the late 1950s and to reach an unprincipled accommodation with party bosses and white southerners. His foreign policy record was marred by a botched attempt to invade Cuba (the Bay of Pigs venture) shortly after assuming the presidency. He bequeathed an increasingly large-scale US military presence in Vietnam to his successor.

Against this background, the president and the federal government as a whole can play only a limited role (Barone and Ujifusa 1999: 26). Others stress the process of globalisation, the influence of multinational corporations, and the determining role of the financial markets. These compel governments to pursue economic policies based upon minimal government intervention and the freeing-up of markets.

Factors shaping presidential authority

What should be said about the power and authority of the White House today? Although significant, the constraints imposed upon the president should not be exaggerated. The Reagan administration took military action initiatives in, for example, Grenada and Libya. Even the Clinton presidency, threatened by a hostile majority in both houses of Congress and humiliated by **impeachment** proceedings, was still able to assert its authority and initiate some, albeit small-scale, legislative changes.

In reality the authority of the presidency is not static or fixed. It depends upon a president's standing with the American public, the relationship between the parties, and his skills as a 'persuader'. Presidential power – and the

Table 4.7   *Presidential approval ratings, 1953–99 (%)*

President	Average	High	Low
Kennedy	70	83	56
Eisenhower	65	79	48
Bush	61	89	29
Clinton	60	73	37
Johnson	55	79	35
Reagan	53	65	35
Nixon	49	67	24
Ford	47	71	37
Carter	45	74	28

Source: adapted from Gallup Organization, *Poll Trends – Clinton Job Approval*, 2000,
<www.gallup.com/poll/trends/ptjobapp.asp>.

political opportunities open to him – depend, at least partially, upon his popularity. This may be in the wake of a successful policy venture or a period of sustained economic growth. In usual circumstances, an incoming president also enjoys a 'honeymoon' period during his first months in office. According to established models of attitudinal change, the 'honeymoon' is followed by a period of decline, although there is a partial recovery as a president's first term comes to an end.

The Gallup Organization began measuring the 'approval ratings' of successive presidents in the 1930s. Pollsters simply ask respondents, 'Do you approve or disapprove of the way [name of president] is handling his job as president?' Their findings are recorded in Table 4.7.

However, the assumption that public backing can transform a president's relationship with Congress has been challenged by Charles O. Jones. As he notes, 'High approval does not transform a president's program into law; declining approval does not suspend a policy momentum that has been building for months or years' (1994: 134). Although his popularity waned as the US became mired in Vietnam, President Lyndon Johnson had numerous successes as a legislator. Despite acclaim following military victory in the 1991 Gulf War, President Bush encountered significant difficulties in his dealings with Congress.

Other observers emphasise the tensions between parties. Since 1945 'divided government', in which the White House and Congress are under the control of different parties, has become common (Table 4.8; see also Chapter 3). This limits a president's freedom of action and his ability to bring about legislative change. 'Divided government' posed particular difficulties for President Clinton. Although the Democrats held the White House from January 1993 onwards, both houses of Congress had a Republican majority after the

Table 4.8   *The presidency and Congress: partisan control, 1961–2000*

Period	President	Congress
1961–69	Democrat	Democrat
1969–77	Republican	Democrat
1977–81	Democrat	Democrat
1981–87	Republican	Senate – R, House – D
1987–93	Republican	Democrat
1993–95	Democrat	Democrat
1995–2001	Democrat	Republican
2001–	Republican	Republican/Democrat[1]

Note:
1 Initially the Senate was divided equally and Republican control was only maintained
  through the use of the vice-president's casting vote. Following a defection from the
  Republican ranks, the Democrats took control in June 2001.
Source: adapted from N.C. Thomas and J.A. Pika, *The Politics of the Presidency*, Washington DC,
Congressional Quarterly Press, 1997, 209.

1994 mid-term elections. Nearly all the Republicans in the House of Representatives were, under Newt Gingrich's leadership, committed to an assert-
ively conservative agenda. Despite policy shifts by the president, relations
between the White House and Capitol Hill were bitterly acrimonious. The
federal government had to be closed down for periods following the failure of
the two branches to agree upon an annual government budget.

It should, however, be noted that unified government – in which both
branches are under the control the same party – does not necessarily offer an
assurance of presidential success. The US parties are loose federations rather
than disciplined organisations. In the late 1970s President Jimmy Carter had
to abandon some of his most important legislative proposals following opposition from fellow Democrats in Congress. Indeed, in a survey of Congress
between 1946 and 1990 David Mayhew asserts that 'it does not seem to make
all that much difference whether party control of American government
happens to be unified or divided' (quoted in Ashbee and Ashford 1999: 105).
However, such a conclusion may now need to be reassessed. As Chapter 7
notes, the parties became more cohesive and ideologically polarised during
the 1990s.

Persuasion

The strategies that a president, aided by the White House's Office of Congressional Relations, adopts are all-important. His authority rests, as Richard

---

Box 4.13
11 September and presidential power

The terrorist attacks on New York and Washington DC on 11 September 2001 shook the US to its foundations. After some initial confusion on the day itself, the Bush administration took the initiative in shaping and organising the American response. The president committed the country to a war against terrorism.

Against this background, there was a rallying around behind the president. Just over a week after the attacks, 91 per cent backed the president's handling of the crisis. In Congress, a resolution authorising the use of military force against all those involved in the attacks passed the Senate by 98–0 and the House by 420–1. The president's request for $20 billion in emergency funding was doubled by congressional leaders.

Over 600 people were held for questioning by the federal authorities. Proposals were also put forward to extend the covert surveillance of suspects. Furthermore, the administration issued an executive order allowing foreign terrorists to be tried by military tribunals rather than the courts. Proposals were put forward to re-organise the Immigration and Naturalization Service. The administration took steps that might, in other circumstances, have required congressional ratification. All of this added to presidential power. As the *Washington Post* recorded:

> The Sept. 11 terrorist attacks and the war in Afghanistan have dramatically accelerated a push by the Bush administration to strengthen presidential powers, giving President Bush a dominance over American government exceeding that of other post-Watergate presidents and rivaling even Franklin D. Roosevelt's command. (*Washington Post*, 20 November, 2001)

Neustadt noted in a celebrated phrase, on the 'power to persuade'. Presidents need to build coalitions of support in Congress, and in doing this, personal style is significant. Some have used formal occasions such as the annual **State of the Union address** to initiate reforming programmes. Lyndon Johnson cajoled legislators, and at times, as both admirers and detractors acknowledge, bullied those who dissented. He set the agenda and drew in members of Congress behind him. For his part, Ronald Reagan used public appeals, lobbying and bargaining. Others were, however, much less successful. Jimmy Carter presented Congress with numerous Bills in his first year of office. There was no sense of priorities. Furthermore, little was done to court or lobby influential members of Congress. Although both the White House and Congress were controlled by the Democrats, relations were poor.

Box 4.14
President Ronald Reagan (Republican: 1981–89)

As the 1980 presidential election approached, Reagan was treated harshly by liberal critics. They highlighted his age (sixty-nine) and his former career as a Hollywood film actor. However, he defeated an incumbent president (Jimmy Carter) and was re-elected by a landslide majority four years later. Reagan's supporters attribute America's economic recovery in the late 1980s to the tax reductions and policy of deregulation (sometimes dubbed 'Reaganomics') with which his administration is identified. They also point out that during Reagan's terms of office the US began to recover from the trauma of Vietnam and to reassert itself on the world stage. Some go further and assert that the Reagan administration's commitment to renewed arms spending and its willingness to support anti-communist forces in countries such as Afghanistan and Nicaragua led directly to the collapse of the Soviet bloc at the end of the 1980s. However, Reagan's critics emphasise the dramatic increase in the size and the scale of the federal government budget deficit during this period and the consequences of his 'hands off' style, which, it is said, contributed to the **Iran-Contra affair**.

Box 4.15
The role of the vice-president

The position of the vice-president has always lacked clarity. The vice-president assumes the presidency if the president dies or resigns. Beyond that, the original Constitution assigned him only one responsibility. He was to serve as president of the Senate. This is largely a formal position, but does, on occasion, have political significance. He has a casting vote in the event of a tie. This has given vice-presidents the opportunity to ensure that legislation is passed in a form sought by the White House.

Tie-breaking votes by the vice-president in his role
as president of the Senate

Lyndon B. Johnson 1961–63	0
Hubert H. Humphrey 1965–69	4
Spiro T. Agnew 1969–73	2
Gerald R. Ford 1973–74	0
Nelson A. Rockefeller 1974–77	0
Walter F. Mondale 1977–81	1

George Bush 1981–89   7
Dan Quayle 1989–93   0
Al Gore 1993–2001   4 (until September 1999)

(Sources: adapted from Michael Nelson, *Congressional Quarterly's Guide to Congress*, Washington DC, Congressional Quarterly Press, 2000, 134, and Bruce Wetterau, *Desktop Reference on American Government*, Washington DC, Congressional Quarterly Press, 1995, 77.)

The Twenty-fifth Amendment (1967) was introduced in the aftermath of the Kennedy assassination and added further responsibilities. The vice-president, along with a majority of Cabinet secretaries, may determine whether the president 'is unable to discharge the powers and duties of his office'. If this happens, the vice-president becomes acting president. Such circumstances have, however, never arisen. The vice-president also assumes the position if the president makes a declaration that he is, for some reason, unable to carry out his responsibilities. In July 1985 George Bush served as acting president for eight hours while President Reagan was in the operating theatre.

Other responsibilities and roles have evolved over time. From 1949 onwards the vice-president has been a statutory member of the National Security Council. He also attends Cabinet meetings. John Nance Garner (1933–41) and subsequent vice-presidents have often represented the US abroad. Richard Nixon, for example, made a number of high-profile visits to the USSR. George Bush made forty-one foreign trips as vice-president. Vice-presidents from Walter Mondale (1977–81) onwards have had offices in the West Wing of the White House. A number have also played a role in terms of legislative liaison, acting as envoys on behalf of the White House, and attempting to win over wavering members of Congress to a particular position. Although many vice-presidents were excluded from decision-making circles, some have found a place as advisers to the president. Al Gore (1993–2001) was a significant figure in the Clinton White House. Warren Christopher, Clinton's first Secretary of State, noted that Gore was 'relied on more heavily than any vice-president has ever been in the past' (quoted in MacGregor *et al.* 1999: 172).

Glossary

commander-in-chief The US Constitution states that the president 'shall be Commander in Chief of the Army and Navy of the United States' (Article II, section 2). Although the founding fathers balanced this by specifying that only Congress could declare war, presidents have, particularly since 1945, used their role as commander-in-chief to order US military intervention overseas. While abiding by its provisions, successive presidents have also denied the constitutional legitimacy of the 1973 War Powers Act which sought – in the aftermath of Vietnam – to ensure that the US was committed only to short-term military operations.

executive agreement(s)   An executive agreement is an agreement reached between the president and a foreign head of state or leader of government. Such agreements are not specifically provided for in the constitution, and, as such, do not require congressional ratification. Those who emphasise the power of the presidency assert that executive agreements have been used so as to circumvent the need for confirmation by the Senate.

In 1953–54 there were attempts, most notably by Senator John Bricker of Ohio, to require that presidents obtain congressional approval of executive agreements, but the proposal was narrowly defeated (*Congressional Quarterly* 1997: 142). However, the Case–Zablocki Act – which forced presidents to report all international agreements to Congress – was passed in 1972.

Executive Office of the President   The Executive Office of the President (EOP) was established in 1939. It consists of the president's personal aides and advisers. In contrast with those who have a formal position, heading government departments and agencies, relatively few of those in the EOP have to be confirmed by the Senate. They are answerable to the president alone.

The EOP grew rapidly in size. Under Kennedy it had – on average – 2,058 employees. In the Johnson era the EOP was used to co-ordinate and centralise the Great Society programmes and it expanded to 3,839. In the Nixon White House the total rose to 5,142. However, the **Watergate** scandal led to a reduction in the EOP's customary size. Reagan had – on average – only 1,557 EOP employees in his second term (Ragsdale 1998: 266–8). Since then EOP staffing has remained at approximately that level.

The EOP has a number of component parts, most notably the White House Office (which organises the president's day-to-day work), the Office of Management and the Budget, and the National Security Council.

The Office of Management and Budget (OMB) has a particularly important role. It is responsible for assembling annual budget plans from departments and agencies, and drawing them together in proposals that are submitted to Congress. The OMB also screens planned executive orders before they are sent to the president for signature. Similarly, proposals for changes in legislation by departments and agencies must be submitted to the OMB before they can be taken further. The OMB also examines Bills passed by Congress. The president is advised whether they should be signed or subjected to a veto. Lastly, the Reagan administration added to the OMB's responsibilities. The office now screens the rules and regulations issued by departments and agencies. Each must submit an 'impact analysis'.

executive orders   An executive order is an instruction or rule issued by the president. It has the force of law. Such orders can only, however, be issued in certain circumstances. Such orders must either be derived from the president's constitutional powers or based upon earlier legislation enacted by Congress.

executive privilege   This refers to 'the right of executive officials to refuse to appear before or to withhold information from a legislative committee or a court' (Plano and Greenberg 1989: 169). It was recognised for the first time only in the Supreme Court's 1974 decision in *US v. Richard M. Nixon*. The judgement also, however, imposed strict parameters on executive privilege by ruling that the president had to release tape recordings of his conversations in the White House to those investigating the Watergate scandal.

impeachment   The Constitution states that a president 'shall be removed from Office on Impeachment for, and Conviction of, Treason, Bribery, or other high Crimes and Misdemeanors.' (Article II, section 4). A president is impeached (committed for trial) by the House of Representatives, and tried by the Senate. If convicted, he is removed from office. The Chief Justice presides at impeachment trials, although his powers are circumscribed. President Andrew Johnson was impeached in 1868 – following his removal of an official – but the Senate failed, by one vote, to remove him from office. In 1974 Richard Nixon resigned once impeachment proceedings had been initiated in the House of Representatives. In 1998–99 Bill Clinton was impeached on charges of perjury and obstruction of justice, tried by the Senate, but acquitted.

impoundment   Impoundment was used by presidents from Thomas Jefferson onwards. In the twentieth century it was employed by Franklin Roosevelt, Truman, Eisenhower, Kennedy and Lyndon Johnson so as to control overall levels of federal government spending. However, Nixon not only impounded funds on a large scale. He withheld spending that had been allocated for purposes that the Democratic majority in Congress particularly valued. These included low-rent housing, mass transit, food stamps and medical research. Nixon's impoundment strategy constituted, Arthur M. Schlesinger charged, a **line-item veto** allowing the president to delete individual sections of an Act. However, Schlesinger maintained, there was no constitutional authority for this. The Budget and Impoundment Control Act, 1974, was adopted so that a future president's ability to take such steps could be reined in by Congress.

Iran-Contra affair   In November 1986 press reports revealed that President Reagan had authorised the selling of weaponry to Iran. Iran was a rigidly authoritarian Islamic state and was believed to be complicit in the holding of Western hostages in the Lebanon. It later transpired that some of the profits from these transactions were used to finance arms purchases for the Contras, although military aid to the Contras had been prohibited by Congress in the 1985 Boland Amendment. The Contras were a rightist guerilla army fighting the Nicaraguan government, which, at that time, was aligned with Cuba and the Soviet bloc. These operations were authorised within the Executive Office of the President by Admiral John Poindexter, the National Security Adviser, and his deputy, Lieutenant-colonel Oliver North.

line-item veto   In 1996 Congress introduced the line-item veto. It added to the president's powers by allowing him to delete individual items in expenditure Bills. Like a full or regular veto, it could be overridden only by a two-thirds majority in both houses of Congress. Following the passage of the Act, twelve items were deleted by President Clinton from legislation passed in 1997–98. However, in June 1998 (*Clinton v. City of New York*) the US Supreme Court declared that the line-item veto was unconstitutional. The Constitution allowed the president to sign or veto a Bill only in its entirety.

nomination   The president 'shall nominate, and by and with the Advice and Consent of the Senate, shall appoint Ambassadors, other public Ministers and Consuls, Judges of the supreme Court, and all other Officers of the United States' (Article II, section 2).

pocket vetoes   In the final days of a legislative session, Bills sent to the president for signature may simply die if he takes no action. There is, however, a lack of clarity about the precise time at which a proposed law can be subjected to a pocket veto. A federal court ruled, in a 1974 case brought by Senator Edward Kennedy, that its use is limited to adjournments *sine die*. These take place at the end of a two-year congressional session. However, both President Ford and President Bush continued the practice of imposing pocket vetoes at the beginning of a short-term holiday recess. Ford was overruled by a federal appeal court, but the issue will remain uncertain until a case is heard by the US Supreme Court. (See also **veto**.)

press conference   The press or news conference – in which the president meets reporters – has become an important part of the American political process. Whereas the British Prime Minister is subjected to regular questioning by the House of Commons, the president is not – because of the separation of powers – a member of Congress. There is therefore no equivalent of Prime Minister's Questions. The news conference offers the only opportunity for the president to be asked about his policies and actions. The relatively small number of news conferences held by President Nixon and President Reagan attracted considerable criticism from those who argued that their refusal to appear before reporters reduced the accountability of the presidency. The yearly average for recent presidents is listed below.

Kennedy	22
Johnson	26
Nixon (first term)	8
Nixon (second term)	5
Ford	19
Carter	15
Reagan (first term)	6
Reagan (second term)	5
Bush	33
Clinton (first term)	30

(Source: adapted from Lyn Ragsdale, *Vital Statistics on the Presidency: Washington to Clinton*, Washington DC, Congressional Quarterly Press, 1998, 170–1.)

recess appointments   These are appointments to positions within the administration, bureaucracy or federal judiciary that are made on a temporary basis while Congress is in recess. The post holder can serve until the end of the following session of Congress (up to ten or eleven months) without Senate confirmation.

State of the Union address   The president 'shall from time to time give to the Congress Information of the State of the Union, and recommend to their Consideration such Measures as he shall judge necessary and expedient' (Article II, section 3).

In 1913 President Woodrow Wilson revived a tradition established in the early years of the American republic by George Washington and John Adams and, instead of submitting a written report, appeared before Congress to give an address. The precedent was subsequently followed by all presidents.

The State of the Union address has, as Michael Nelson notes, 'become a key vehicle for expounding the president's annual legislative agenda and priorities' (Nelson 1989: 465). Presidents have generally focused on particular themes. In 1965 Lyndon Johnson emphasised the eradication of poverty and his vision of the US as a 'Great Society'. In 1995 Bill Clinton stressed the importance of making the federal government more efficient and accountable.

treaties   Treaties are formal agreements between two or more countries. For example, the 1949 North Atlantic Treaty was an agreement between the US, Canada and the countries of western Europe that a military attack on one member country would be regarded as an attack upon them all. However, the Constitution imposed constraints upon the president's role as 'chief diplomat' by requiring him to gain Senate ratification; he 'shall have Power, by and with the Advice and Consent of the Senate, to make Treaties, provided two-thirds of the Senators present concur' (Article II, Section 2). Presidents have often attempted to involve the Senate Foreign Relations Committee at an early stage when a treaty is under consideration, and senators may accompany the president when the treaty is signed.

triangulation   'Triangulation' was a political strategy adopted by President Clinton on the advice of Dick Morris. Morris, a close aide of the president, urged Clinton to come to terms with the Republican victories in the 1994 mid-term elections. The president, Morris asserted, had to respond by positioning himself between the Republican Party – led by Newt Gingrich in the House of Representatives and Bob Dole in the Senate – and the Democrats. In political terms, this meant that the White House should accept those Republican policies that had widespread popular backing – such as far-reaching welfare reform – but resist demands for budget reductions that did not have public support. On issues such as this the Republicans were to be portrayed as 'extremists'. 'Triangulation' was condemned by the president's liberal supporters, such as Robert Reich, the Labor Secretary, as an abandonment of principle. However, Clinton's re-election victory and his subsequently high approval ratings can, in part, be attributed to the strategy.

veto   The Constitution grants the president a veto power. He can prevent a measure passed by Congress becoming law by vetoing it. Under the provisions of Article I he has ten days within which either to sign a Bill – thereby passing it into law – or to return it to Congress with a **veto message** stating his objections. (See also **pocket veto**.)

   In some circumstances the imposition of a veto, or the threat of a veto, conveys the impression of firmness. As noted above, President Clinton used veto threats to gain legislative concessions from Congress. However, other observers regard it as evidence of weakness. It can mean that the president's attempts to use diplomacy, persuasion and coalition building have failed. Definitive conclusions are, however, difficult. A simple listing of veto numbers fails to distinguish between those issues that are of far-reaching significance and those that have little importance.

veto message   A statement of the president's objections to a Bill. It is sent to Congress when a Bill is vetoed.

Vietnam War   In 1954, following a war of independence against French colonial rule, Vietnam was divided between the north, under communist rule, and a Western-oriented south. However, the government of South Vietnam faced increasing opposition from the National Liberation Front (NLF or 'Vietcong'), guerilla forces backed by North Vietnam.

   US policy makers feared that if the south fell to the NLF, and Vietnam was reunited under a communist government, other countries in South-east Asia would fall – like a row of dominoes – to the communists. President Kennedy sent military advisers to back up the South Vietnamese forces. In 1964, following an alleged attack on US vessels in the Gulf of Tonkin, Congress responded to a request by President Lyndon Johnson and passed resolutions authorising measures to prevent further attacks. Although later criticised as a 'blank cheque' allowing almost any form of military action in South-east Asia, the resolutions were passed in the Senate by 98 votes to 2 and in the House by 416 to 0.

In these circumstances, US ground troops were committed to Vietnam. The war led to the loss of 58,000 American lives. Faced by increasing domestic opposition to the war effort and repeated military setbacks, American forces were eventually withdrawn. In April 1975 the South Vietnamese government collapsed. The NLF and North Vietnamese forces captured Saigon and Vietnam was, as the US had originally feared, reunited under communist rule.

Watergate   In June 1972, five months before the presidential election, police disturbed five men breaking into the offices of the Democratic National Committee in the Watergate building in Washington DC. They were carrying wiretapping and photographic equipment. Initial investigations revealed that there were personal connections between some of those arrested (three of whom were Cuban exiles), the Committee to Re-elect the President (CREEP), the Attorney General (John Mitchell) and the White House. As the months went on, reporters working for the *Washington Post* and a Senate committee uncovered further details about the Watergate break-in, the extent of other illegal activities that had been sanctioned from within the Nixon administration, and the subsequent attempts to conceal these from investigators. As President Nixon's own involvement in the cover-up became manifest, Archibold Cox, the special prosecutor who had been appointed, sought the tape-recordings of the president's conversations that had been routinely made in the Oval Office. Nixon dismissed Cox. However, in July 1974 the US Supreme Court (*US v. Richard M. Nixon*) ruled that the president must hand over the tapes. Shortly after this, the House of Representatives Judiciary Committee voted to recommend three articles of impeachment to the House as a whole. In the face of this and almost certain conviction in a senate trial, the president resigned on 9 August 1974.

Resources

References and further reading

Alsop, R.J. (ed.) (1997), *The Wall Street Journal Almanac 1998*, New York, Ballantyne.

Ashbee, E.G.C. and N.J. Ashford (1999), *US Politics Today*, Manchester, Manchester University Press.

Barone, M. and G. Ujifusa (1999), *Almanac of American Politics 2000*, Washington DC, National Journal.

Congressional Quarterly (1997), *Powers of the Presidency*, Washington DC, Congressional Quarterly Press.

Jones, C.O. (1994), *The Presidency in a Separated System*, Washington DC, Brookings Institution.

Lipsitz, L. (1986), *American Democracy*, New York, St Martin's Press.

MacGregor Burns, J. and G.J. Sorenson (1999), *Dead Center: Clinton–Gore Leadership and the Perils of Moderation*, New York, Scribner.

Nelson, M. (1989), *Congressional Quarterly's Guide to the Presidency*, Washington DC, Congressional Quarterly Press.

Nelson, M. (ed.) (2000), *Congressional Quarterly's Guide to the Presidency*, Washington DC, Congressional Quarterly Press.

Ornstein, N.J., T.E. Mann and M.J. Malbin (2000), *Vital Statistics on Congress 1999–2000*, Washington DC, AEI Press.

Pfiffner, J.P. (2000), *The Modern Presidency*, Boston MA, Bedford/St Martin's Press.

Plano, J.C. and M. Greenberg (1989), *The American Political Dictionary*, Fort Worth TX, Holt Rinehart & Winston.

Ragsdale, L. (1998), *Vital Statistics on the Presidency: Washington to Clinton*, Washington DC, Congressional Quarterly Press.

Rose, G.L. (1997), *The American Presidency under Seige*, Albany NY, State University of New York Press.

Schlesinger, A.M. (1974), *The Imperial Presidency*, London, Andre Deutsch.

Stanley, H.W. and R.G. Niemi (1998), *Vital Statistics on American Politics, 1997–98*, Washington DC, Congressional Quarterly Press.

Thomas, N.C. and J.A. Pika (1997), *The Politics of the Presidency*, Washington DC, Congressional Quarterly Press.

Weissman, S.R. (1995), *A Culture of Deference: Congress's Failure of Leadership in Foreign Policy*, New York, Basic Books.

Websites

The president and vice-president   www.whitehouse.gov
The White House website offers press releases and a 'virtual library', including policy statements, executive orders and commission reports. There are also reports and recommendations from the Executive Office of the President. These include materials from the Council of Economic Advisers (CEA) and the Office of Management and the Budget. The president can be emailed – president@whitehouse.gov.

Other websites
Further information about the president can be found on newspaper websites. For example, *New York Times*, www.nytimes.com; *Washington Post*, www.washingtonpost.com.

5

The US Supreme Court

This chapter surveys the judicial branch of government. It considers:

- the development and evolution of the Supreme Court;
- the concept of **judicial review**;
- the nature of **interpretivism** and its role in shaping the early history of the Court;
- the thinking and impact of the Warren and Burger courts (1953–86);
- the judicial and political character of the Rehnquist court (1986–).

The development and evolution of the Supreme Court

There are state and federal courts in the US. The overwhelming majority of cases – both criminal and civil – are heard in state courts and tried under state laws. However, although the federal courts consider only a small proportion of cases, they occupy a pivotal role. Indeed, the US Supreme Court – the highest of the federal courts – constitutes the third branch of government.

Despite the importance of the position that the Supreme Court has come to occupy, the US Constitution says relatively little about its purpose and structure. Article III consists of only three sections. They state that 'judicial power . . . shall be vested in one supreme Court and in such inferior Courts as the Congress may from time to time ordain and establish'. They also established that the Supreme Court would, almost always, play an appellate role. It hears appeals from 'inferior' federal courts and, in some instances, directly from state supreme courts. The Court only has **original jurisidiction**, and hears cases that have not have been initially considered by another court, in a small number of specified instances. Article III also established that federal judges were to be appointed by the president and confirmed by the Senate. Their term of office was to last until death or retirement, subject only to 'good behaviour'. So as to further insulate the judges from external pressures, their

Box 5.1
Supreme Court appointments

A president's nominations to the Supreme Court are among the most important appointments that he will make. There is every likelihood that those placed on the Court will continue to serve long after the president has left the White House. Justice William O. Douglas was nominated by President Franklin Roosevelt in 1935 and remained on the bench until 1975. However, a president's opportunity to make appointments depends upon the death or retirement of a serving justice and the willingness of the Senate to confirm his nominee. A president will generally appoint those with whom he has relatively close political associations in terms of both party affiliation and ideological outlook.

Presidential appointments to the Supreme Court, 1961–93

President	Party	Number of vacancies	Appointments from the president's party
Kennedy 1961–63	D	2	2
Johnson 1963–69	D	2	2
Nixon 1969–74	R	4	3
Ford 1974–77	R	1	1
Carter 1977–81	D	0	0
Reagan 1981–89	R	4	4
Bush 1989–93	R	2	2
Clinton 1993–2001	D	2	2

Sources: adapted from R.J. Alsop, *The Wall Street Journal Almanac 1999*, New York, Ballantine Books, 1998, 96–8, and Lyn Ragsdale, *Vital Statistics on the Presidency: Washington to Clinton*, Washington DC, Congressional Quarterly Press, 1998, 427–8.

salaries were not to be reduced. There was to be a Chief Justice (see Table 5.2), although his powers were largely undefined.

The absence of precision in Article III meant, as Robert McKeever notes, that the Supreme Court 'began its life as an institution with uncertain authority and relatively little prestige' (McKeever 1997: 50). The structure of the federal courts, the purpose of the judicial branch, and the role of the Chief Justice evolved through legislation and precedent. The 1789 Judiciary Act created the federal court system. The westward expansion of the US and a

Table 5.1   *The size of the Supreme Court since 1789*

No. of judges		No. of judges	
1789	6	1863	10
1807	7	1865	9
1837	9	1867	8
		1869 onwards	9

Source: adapted from K. Jost (ed.), *The Supreme Court A to Z*, Washington DC, Congressional Quarterly Press, 1998, 422–3.

growing population placed greater demands upon the federal and led to pressure for an increased number. By the end of the twentieth century there were (within the fifty states) eighty-nine US district courts – the lowest tier in the federal court structure – and twelve courts of appeal or 'circuit courts' (Wright 1999: 144).

The number of judges who serve on the Court (see Table 5.1) is determined by Congress. The 1789 Judiciary Act established a Court of six. The size of the Court varied because of attempts by Congress to deny particular presidents the opportunity to make appointments that would have changed the ideological character of the Court. The Court's size has been fixed at nine since 1869, although, in 1937, President Franklin Roosevelt put forward the **court packing plan** in response to Court rulings striking down New Deal legislation.

The role of the Chief Justice progressively took shape over the two centuries that followed the founding of the US. He is regarded as *primus inter pares* (first among equals). He presides both at open sessions of the Court and at closed conferences and determines who should write the opinion if he is in the majority when a particular case has been considered. He also has other roles. At inauguration ceremonies he administers the oath of office. He presides over presidential impeachment trials in the US Senate. He is also chairman of the Judicial Conference of the US. This studies and reviews the rules of practice governing the entire judicial system. The Chief Justice has, furthermore, sometimes been asked to undertake other responsibilities. Following the assassination of President John F. Kennedy in November 1963, Chief Justice Earl Warren presided over the commission that investigated the shooting.

In almost every instance the Court itself determines which cases it will hear. This is the granting of review or *certiorari* ('cert'). Friday afternoons are set aside for discussion of these matters. The Chief Justice prepares an initial 'discuss list' of cases that the Court will hear, but under the **rule of four**, if four justices vote to hear the case, 'cert' is granted. Robert McKeever notes that the law clerks, who assist each of the justices, may play a role in the process (1997: 78–9).

Table 5.2   *Chief Justices, 1789–*

Incumbent	Dates served	Appointed by President
John Jay	1789–95	Washington
John Rutledge	1795[1]	Washington
Oliver Ellsworth	1796–1800	Washington
John Marshall	1801–35	Adams
Roger B. Taney	1836–64	Jackson
Salmon P. Chase	1864–73	Lincoln
Morrison R. Waite	1874–88	Grant
Melville W. Fuller	1888–1910	Cleveland
Edward D. White	1910–21	Taft
William Howard Taft	1921–30	Harding
Charles Evans Hughes	1930–41	Hoover
Harlan Fiske Stone	1941–46	Roosevelt
Fred M. Vinson	1946–53	Truman
Earl Warren	1953–69[2]	Eisenhower
Warren E. Burger	1969–86	Nixon
William H. Rehnquist	1986–	Reagan

Notes:
1 Presided during a recess, but not confirmed by Senate.
2 Appointed in a recess and confirmed by the Senate in 1954.
Source: adapted from R.J. Alsop (ed.), *The Wall Street Journal Almanac 1998*, New York, Ballantine Books, 1998, 120–1.

Judicial review

What is the Court's role and purpose? The Constitution stated that the federal courts were to consider cases 'arising under this Constitution' and some other matters. However, the precise meaning of these words was not specified. *Marbury v. Madison* (1803) offered clarification. In the *Marbury* case, the Court declared that the Court could undertake **judicial review**. The US Constitution was 'the fundamental and paramount law of the nation', and therefore 'an act of the legislature repugnant to the constitution is void'. In other words, the Supreme Court could invalidate – or 'strike down' – a law (passed by Congress and signed by the president) or an action undertaken by the executive branch of government, if it considered it to be unconstitutional. Seven years later, in *Fletcher v. Peck* (1810), the Court extended the scope of judicial review and assumed the right to rule on the constitutionality of state laws.

Its judgements are more or less definitive. As Chief Justice William Rehnquist bluntly put it: 'Congress may not supersede our decisions interpreting and applying the Constitution' (quoted in Rosen 2000: 17). A Supreme Court ruling can be overturned only through an amendment of the Constitution. An amendment must be proposed either by two-thirds of the Senate and the House of Representatives or through a convention called by two-thirds of the states. It then requires the assent of three-quarters of the states. Because of the requirement for a supermajority only twenty-seven amendments have been passed since 1787.

The power of the federal judiciary also grew for another reason. Through its rulings the Court – in effect – added to the Constitution, thereby enlarging the scope of its decision making. In *McCulloch v. Maryland* (1819) the Court was faced by the question of whether the government had the authority to establish a national bank. Such a step was not among the 'enumerated' powers of Congress specified in Article I of the Constitution. The Court noted, however, that the Constitution assigned Congress the right 'to make all Laws which shall be necessary and proper for carrying into Execution the foregoing Powers . . .' (Article I, Section 8). On the basis of the phrase 'necessary and proper', the Court ruled that the national government had a range of 'implied powers' alongside the powers that had been formally listed in the Constitution.

Interpretivism and the early Court

Against the background of growing self-assertion by the Court, different legal philosophies emerged. Although the concept of 'implied powers' was accepted, and the Court played a pivotal role in consolidating the powers of the national government, the doctrines that held sway for much of the nineteenth and early twentieth centuries stressed the limitations and constraints that, it was felt, the federal judiciary should impose upon itself. The Court adhered to interpretivist doctrines such as **strict constructionism** and **original intent**.

Interpretivism, which is closely allied with conservatism, asserts that the role of the judiciary should be limited and constrained. The consequences of a particular ruling are of no relevance. Instead the judges' task and purpose – in adjudicating upon a particular issue – are simply to interpret the meaning of the relevant constitutional article or amendment. Robert McKeever has described the way in which judges saw themselves: 'They were legal mechanics who did not make law or policy, but rather "discovered" law in the text of the Constitution and previous judicial decisions and then applied it to concrete cases' (McKeever 1997: 90).

Interpretivism has two implications. Firstly, its adherents deny the legitimacy of almost all rights that are not specified in the original Constitution or its later amendments. The arguments they adopt are evident in their opposition to *Roe v. Wade* (1973). In the *Roe* case the Court declared that abortion was a constitutional right. The judges' reasoning was based, in part, on a 'right to privacy' that Justice William O. Douglas had claimed, in an earlier judgement, could be drawn from the 'penumbras and emanations' – or nuances and implications – of the US Constitution. For their part, interpretivists reject the legitimacy of this reasoning and insist on a more literal reading of the Constitution. Secondly, the emphasis that interpretivists place upon the Constitution's wording almost always leads them to argue that Congress and the presidency – despite the early period in which the Court enlarged their

Box 5.2
The US Supreme Court and civil rights

The Supreme Court has been described as the guardian of individual and civil rights. Its role in the 'civil rights revolution' of the 1950s and 1960s is often emphasised. In the 1954 *Brown* case the Warren Court began the process of desegregating schools in the southern states. It declared that 'separate educational facilities are inherently unequal' (Bennett and Lane-Clark 1989: 19). A decade later, the rights of criminal suspects were extended by the *Gideon* and *Miranda* rulings. However, despite these judgements, critics assert that, for much of its history, the Court has colluded in the abrogation of rights.

In *Dred Scott v. Sanford* (1857) the Court invalidated the Missouri Compromise of 1820. This had excluded slavery from the northern states. In striking down the compromise the Court accepted the legitimacy of slavery and denied the rights of slaves to pursue cases in court. Forty years later, in *Plessy v. Ferguson* (1896), the Court accepted the constitutionality of segregation – the institutionalised separation of the races – on the pretext that public facilities would be 'separate but equal'. In reality African-Americans were consigned to a subordinate role across the southern states until the 1960s.

Despite the provisions of the Bill of Rights, the Court also accepted the denial of rights to other groups. In the Second World War (1941–45) 100,000 Japanese-Americans were interned in ten camps amidst fears that they might assist a Japanese invasion of the west coast. Until overturned by a later ruling, the Supreme Court declared that this was constitutional (*US v. Korematsu*).

In some instances, political minorities also felt that they were denied the protection offered under the Constitution. These fears were justified by the claim that the US faced a 'clear and present' danger. In 1919 Justice Oliver Wendell Holmes spelt out that there were, in particular, limits on the right to freedom of speech: 'When a nation is at war, many things that might be said in time of peace are such a hindrance to its effort that their utterance will not be endured . . . no court could regard them as protected by any constitutional right.'

The notion that national security took precedence over rights and liberties also led the Court to accept the constitutionality of restrictions on the activities of communists. In *Dennis v. US* (1951), for example, the Court upheld the Smith Act of 1940. This had made the teaching and advocacy of violent revolution unlawful.

Critics – particularly those associated with liberalism – also point to the record of the contemporary court. In *Bowers v. Hardwick* (1986) the Court ruled that the 'right to privacy' did not extend to homosexual relationships. This allowed states discretion in outlawing gay sexual activity. In 1997 the Court ruled that euthanasia ('mercy killing') did not constitute a constitutional right (*Washington v. Glucksberg*) (McKeever 2000: 141–2).

Box 5.3
The Supreme Court before 1954: significant rulings

Dred Scott v. Sanford (1857)

Although the Missouri Compromise of 1820 had confined slavery to the southern states, the Scott judgement denied slaves the opportunity to sue for liberty when travelling with their masters in 'free territory' and asserted, furthermore, that a slave, being mere property, could not be represented in court. The ruling is important both as an example of judicial review and as a factor that fuelled sectional tensions during the period preceding the Civil War. (Dred Scott was a slave owned by John Sanford. Sanford's name was misspelt 'Sandford' in the Court records.)

Fletcher v. Peck (1810)

In a ruling concerning the state of Georgia, the Court struck down a state law for the first time.

Gibbons v. Ogden (1824)

The ruling established a broad understanding of the Constitutions's interstate commerce clause. It interpreted 'commerce' (business and trade) as a reference to all forms of economic activity. Furthermore, as John Zvesper notes, 'this phrase extends federal power over commerce to any location within a state where a commercial activity affects other states' (McKeever *et al.* 1999: 59).

Gitlow v. New York (1925)

This ruling established that the states, as well as the federal government, must respect the guarantees of free speech and freedom of the press offered by the First Amendment. The decision marked the adoption of the **incorporation doctrine**.

Although the Court had ruled in 1833 (*Barron v. Baltimore*) that the Bill of Rights limited the federal government alone, and did not therefore apply to the states, later rulings largely abandoned this. They cited the Fourteenth Amendment (1868) and drew on its injunction against state attempts to 'deprive any person of life, liberty, or property, without due process of law . . .'. 'Due process' was increasingly understood to mean that states must respect the basic liberties and freedoms offered in the Bill of Rights.

'Due process' has not only been used to 'nationalise' court procedures across the US and extend de facto civil rights. It also formed the constitutional basis of the Supreme Court's efforts (in cases such as *US v. Butler*) to rein in the New Deal and curtail the federal government's economic interventionism.

Marbury v. Madison (1803)

The Marbury judgement is widely regarded as the most significant that the Court has made. The case – a controversy about appointments to the federal courts – allowed the Supreme Court to establish that it could subject decisions made by the other branches of government to **judicial review**. As the Court later reiterated in the case of *United States v. Nixon*, its role is 'to say what the law is' (Plano and Greenberg 1989: 259).

McCulloch v. Maryland (1819)

The *McCulloch* ruling extended the powers of both the federal government and the federal judiciary. The Court asserted that the Constitution assigned implied as well as enumerated (or specifically identified) powers to the federal government. It cited the 'necessary and proper' clause in Article I, Section 8. Therefore, although it was not provided for in the precise wording of the Constitution, Congress did have the authority to establish and maintain a national bank and the states did not have the right to undermine it.

National Labor Relations Board v. Jones & Laughlin Steel Corporation (1937)

In the *Schechter* and *Butler* cases the Court struck down significant parts of the New Deal. However, in this ruling the Court accepted the constitutionality of other New Deal laws. These offered protection to labour unions and outlawed some 'unfair labor practices'. This, and some other judgements, represented a significant change in approach and a broader, more 'expansive' reading of the **interstate commerce clause**.

Plessy v. Ferguson (1896)

In the *Plessy* ruling the Court accepted that the southern states could legally segregate public facilities. Although a provision was attached that provision for the different races should be 'equal' as well as 'separate', the judgement offered a basis for institutionalised discrimination against black citizens.

Schechter Poultry Corporation v. United States (1935)

Sometimes known as the 'sick chickens case', the *Schechter* ruling struck down the National Industrial Recovery Act, an important New Deal programme. The Act had imposed federal government regulations on industry, and this, the Court argued, assigned excessive powers to the executive branch and infringed the rights of the individual states.

Youngstown Steel & Tube Company v. Sawyer (1952)

President Truman ordered a federal government take-over of strike-hit steel plants which he considered vital to the US war effort in Korea. The Court asserted that his powers as commander-in-chief did not extend to such large-scale confiscation of property.

Box 5.4

The president and the Supreme Court: the success rate of the Solicitor General as an *amicus curiae* in cases before the Supreme Court

The **Solicitor General** represents the executive branch in cases brought before the courts. His *amicus curiae* briefs represent the administration's viewpoint. Although his 'success rate' has fallen dramatically, and may simply represent shared thinking rather than a victory for his or her persuasive skills, the Solicitor General still plays an important role in shaping judicial decision making.

Solicitor General's success rate

President	% of cases won	President	% of cases won
Kennedy	87.5	Carter	65.1
Johnson	82.9	Reagan	67.5
Nixon	70.9	Bush	75.8
Ford	71.1	Clinton (1993)	44.4

Source: adapted from *Congressional Quarterly's Guide to Congress*, Washington DC, Congressional Quarterly Press, 2000, 443.

---

powers – had only limited authority. For this reason, the Supreme Court asserted that much of the New Deal, President Franklin Roosevelt's economic programme, was unconstitutional. Congress, the Court declared, in rulings such as *Schechter v. United States* (1935) and *United States v. Butler* (1936), had exceeded its powers. Eight laws were invalidated within two years.

The Warren and Burger Courts

Roosevelt responded to the Court's challenge with the **court packing plan**. He proposed that additional judges would be appointed to balance out each justice who had reached the age of seventy. The Court would have a maximum of fifteen judges. Although the plan had to be abandoned, it did prompt a change of direction by the Supreme Court. Subsequent New Deal legislation – including the National Labor Relations Act and the Social Security Act – was upheld.

Non-interpretivist approaches to the Constitution such as **loose constructionism** slowly took hold in the aftermath of the Court's confrontations with President Roosevelt. The Constitution, it was said by a growing number of twentieth-century judges and legal scholars, could not be understood in terms of its exact wording. Nor – despite the claims of those who talked of discerning **original intent** – could the courts turn to the ideas of those who wrote the Constitution and its later amendments. The intricacies of their thinking could never be discerned and nor is it necessarily relevant to later circumstances. Instead, as Justice William Brennan put it, 'We current justices read the Constitution in the only way that we can: as twentieth-century Americans' (quoted in McKeever *et al.* 1999: 377).

What were the implications of **non-interpretivism**? It was increasingly suggested that phrases such as 'cruel and unusual punishments', which were prohibited under the Eighth Amendment, had to be understood differently from the way in which they were regarded in 1791, when floggings and executions were commonplace. The courts, it was said, should assess the consequences of particular judgements and the degree to which they corresponded with broad constitutional principles. Non-interpretivist methodology was evident, for example, when the Burger Court suspended the death penalty in *Furman v. Georgia* (1972). Although the individual judges used different forms of reasoning, the Court based its ruling on the disproportionate impact that the penalty had on different socio-economic groupings. African-Americans and those from a poor background were much more likely to be found on Death Row than whites or the affluent. In terms of outcome, the Court asserted, the application of the death penalty was 'unusual' (Amendment VIII). It also denied citizens the 'equal protection of laws' (Amendment XIV). As Justice Potter Stewart put it: 'The Eighth and Fourteenth Amendments cannot tolerate the infliction of a sentence of death under legal systems that permit this unique penalty to be so wantonly and freakishly imposed' (quoted in McKeever 1995b: 60).

Non-interpretivism – with its emphasis upon *outcome* rather than the formal wording of the Constitution – led the Court towards liberalism. Many of its judgements called for mechanisms that would ensure greater social equality. At the same time, their implementation depended upon federal government intervention. Furthermore, **non-interpretivism** was associated with **judicial activism**. The Court became increasingly assertive in promulgating its goals and establishing its place within the American system of government. As Robert McKeever notes, the Court, rather than Congress or the presidency, led: 'the fight for progressive change in public policy on matters such as race and sex equality, abortion, political and religious dissent, censorship and the rights of the criminally accused' (McKeever 1995a: 25).

By the mid-twentieth century **non-interpretivism** was in the ascendant. It was reflected in a succession of pivotal Court judgements, most notably those reached when Earl Warren and Warren E. Burger served as Chief Justices (1953–86). In *Brown v. Board of Education of Topeka* (1954) the Court ruled that racially segregated schooling was unconstitutional. Other rulings also had a far-reaching impact. *Gideon v. Wainwright* (1963) laid down that all defendants in state as well as federal trials had a constitutional right to an attorney. *Miranda v. Arizona* (1966) established that criminal suspects must be read their rights on arrest if confession evidence was to be admissible in court proceedings. In *Swann v. Charlotte-Mecklenburg Board of Education* (1971) the Court addressed '*de facto* segregation' – the continued existence of predominantly black, white or Hispanic schools – and mandated the busing of school students across cities so that there was a greater degree of racial balance within each school. In *Roe v. Wade* (1973) the Court declared that women had a constitutional right to an abortion. Many of these judgements rested on reinterpretations of the different amendments to the Constitution, most notably those identified in Box 5.6.

However, the picture is not entirely straightforward. Although the Warren and Burger Courts (1953–86) were characterised by both non-interpretivism and judicial activism, there were a number of contrary rulings. Just four years after declaring all existing death penalty laws unconstitutional the Court reinstated capital punishment (*Gregg v. Georgia*). In the *Bakke* case it permitted affirmative action – the use of racial and gender 'preferences' to ensure a more mixed student body or work force – only in limited and circumscribed cirumstances.

There are four reasons for these apparent inconsistencies. Firstly, the Court is not a political institution, and judicial reasoning has a logic and rationale that differ from those followed in a legislature. Secondly, other considerations than ideology and philosophy play a part in moulding judicial rulings. The thinking of the Court is, in part, shaped by *stare decisis* and the constitutional arguments submitted in *amicus curiae* briefs. Thirdly, both Presidents Nixon and Reagan sought to change the character of the Court by appointing judges committed to more interpretivist philosophies. Although their nominees sometimes took a more cautious approach than these presidents might have wished, the atmosphere on the bench began to change. Lastly, public opinion shifted rightward during the 1970s and early 1980s, and the Court seems to have responded.

Box 5.5
The Warren and Burger Courts: significant rulings

Baker v. Carr (1962)

The Court ruled that the districts used as a basis for elections to state legislatures must be drawn in an equitable way. The case marked a growing willingness by the Supreme Court to become involved in matters that had traditionally been a state prerogative.

Brown v. Board of Education, Topeka (1954)

The *Brown* ruling represented a repudiation of the 'separate but equal' doctrine established in *Plessy v. Ferguson*. The Court argued that by consigning black children to a separate (although nominally equal) education the southern states were inculcating in them a sense of inferiority. African-Americans were being denied 'the equal protection of the laws' required by the Fourteenth Amendment. Although the *Brown* ruling provoked widespread white resistance, it also contributed to the growth of the civil rights movement and paved the way for the desegregation of public schools.

Engel v. Vitale (1962)

The First Amendment's requirement that 'Congress shall make no law respecting an establishment of religion' ('the Establishment clause') led the Court to invalidate the saying of prayers in government funded schools. The decision was followed a year later by *Abington School District v. Schempp*, which struck down state laws requiring a Bible reading at the beginning of the school day.

Furman v. Georgia (1972)

By a five to four majority the Court struck down all existing death penalty laws. Two of the justices in the majority were opposed to the use of capital punishment in any circumstances. They considered it 'cruel and unusual' and therefore prohibited under the Eighth Amendment. Two others based their arguments on the way in which the death penalty was imposed. Only a very small proportion of those convicted of murder were executed. Capital punishment was imposed in some circumstances but not others. Those that faced the executioner were disproportionately African-American, poor, had been poorly defended in court, or were simply unlucky. As Justice Potter Stewart put it, capital punishment was 'wantonly and freakishly imposed'. For Justice Byron White, the penalty was 'pointless and needless'. Four years later – in *Gregg v. Georgia* (1976) – states were again allowed to impose the death penalty.

Gideon v. Wainwright (1963)

Citing the Sixth Amendment, the Court ruled that the states would have to pay to ensure legal representation for those on low incomes who were defendants in felony cases.

Gregg v. Georgia (1976)

In the aftermath of the *Furman* ruling, many of the states rewrote their death penalty laws. They sought to ensure that there were institutionalised procedures and that the imposition of capital punishment became less arbitrary. The *Gregg* ruling accepted the constitutionality of these revised statutes. This seeming *volte-face* is sometimes regarded as a concession by the Court to public opinion, which has always backed the death penalty by a substantial majority.

Since 1976 the death penalty has been used increasingly widely in some states, most notably Texas and Virginia. Despite doubts about the guilt of some executed, and claims that African-Americans are still much more likely to be executed, the Supreme Court has resisted challenges to the practice and has restricted the grounds for appeal.

Griswold v. Connecticut (1965)

The Court struck down a state law prohibiting the use of contraception. The ruling was based on a 'right to privacy' that Justice William O. Douglas asserted could be found in the 'emanations' and 'penumbras' of the Bill of Rights. The judgement is an example of **loose constructionism** and served as the basis of the later *Roe* ruling.

Immigration and Naturalization Service v. Chadha (1983)

In the *Chadha* case the Court asserted that the 'legislative veto' was unconstitutional. Many Acts, passed from 1932 onwards, included provisions requiring the executive branch to seek authorisation from Congress before undertaking particular actions or enforcing regulations. Such a procedure, the Court argued, violated the separation of powers.

Miranda v. Arizona (1966)

The Court established that criminal suspects must be advised of their rights. If confession evidence was otherwise obtained, it was to be inadmissible in legal proceedings.

Roe v. Wade (1973)

The *Roe* ruling established abortion as a constitutional right. State laws restricting it were admissible only within the final three months of a pregnancy. Despite significant public backing, there was widespread opposition to the judgement, particularly from those associated with the Christian right. It led to the greater politicisation of Court appointments, and subsequent nominees have been closely questioned about their attitude to abortion.

Swann v. Charlotte-Mecklenburg Board of Education (1971)

Although the *Brown* ruling eventually led to the abandonment of *de jure* segregation (which was imposed under state law), '*de facto* segregation' remained. States and school districts proved unco-operative. Furthermore, the neighbourhoods that schools served were divided by race. As a consequence, the schools that served those neighbourhoods were either predominantly black or white. *Swann* sanctioned the busing of pupils across cities so as to ensure a racial mix in every school.

United States v. Nixon (1974)

During the later stages of the Watergate drama it was revealed that President Nixon had ordered the tape recording of his own discussions in the White House. The Court ruled that he must release these to investigators seeking to establish his role in the scandal. Nixon claimed that his conversations with aides were covered by 'executive privilege'. This was, however, rejected in a unanimous Court ruling.

University of California Regents v. Bakke (1978)

In the *Bakke* case the Court considered the constitutionality of affirmative action. Although the Court rejected the use of racial quotas, it did accept that race could be 'a factor' in recruitment policies for both college courses and employment. This created a constitutional basis for affirmative action during the 1980s.

Box 5.6
Constitutional provisions most subject to litigation, 1953–92

Amendment XIV

'nor shall any State deprive any person of life, liberty, or property, with-out the due process of law . . .'

Amendment XIV

'nor shall any State . . . deny to any person within its jurisdiction the equal protection of the laws.'

Amendment I

'Congress shall make no law . . . abridging the freedom of speech, or of the press; or the right of the people peaceably to assemble . . .'

Source: adapted from R.J. McKeever, *The United States Supreme Court: A Political and Legal Analysis*, Manchester, Manchester University Press, 1997, 9.

The Rehnquist Court

From the 1980s onwards, however, the Court began to change markedly. In a conscious effort to change its ideological character, Presidents Reagan and Bush nominated conservative jurists, most notably Antonin Scalia and Clarence Thomas, to the Supreme Court bench. On Warren Burger's retire-ment in 1986, William H. Rehnquist, another conservative who had served as an associate justice since 1971, was elevated to the post of Chief Justice.

As a consequence of these appointments the Court's centre of gravity has shifted. Some have argued that the Court's rulings have been characterised by growing reliance on **interpretivism** and an increasing sense of **judicial restraint**. For example, the number of cases that the Court was prepared to consider during each **term** fell from the mid-1980s onwards (see Table 5.4). Furthermore, fewer federal and state laws were struck down in the 1990s than in earlier decades (Table 5.5). As Joan Biskupic has noted, 'Gone is the self-consciously loud voice the Court once spoke with, boldly stating its position and calling upon the people and other institutions of government to follow' (Biskupic 2000).

However, others counter suggestions that the Court's behaviour has been characterised by judicial restraint. They assert that, although the Court has

Table 5.3   *The ideological composition of the Supreme Court, 2000*

Justice	Judicial philosophy	Appointed by President	Year appointed	Senate vote
William H. Rehnquist	Conservative	Reagan	1986[1]	65–33
John Paul Stevens	Liberal	Ford	1975	98–0
Sandra Day O'Connor	Centre-right	Reagan	1981	99–0
Antonin Scalia	Conservative	Reagan	1986	98–0
Anthony Kennedy	Centre-right	Reagan	1988	90–0
David H. Souter	Centre	Bush	1990	90–9
Clarence Thomas	Conservative	Bush	1991	52–48
Ruth Bader Ginsburg	Centre-liberal	Clinton	1993	96–3
Stephen B. Breyer	Centre-liberal	Clinton	1994	87–9

Note:
1 Rehnquist had served as all associate justice since 1971, when he was first appointed by
   President Nixon.
Sources: adapted from H.W. Stanley and R.G. Niemi, *Vital Statistics on American Politics
1997–1998*, Washington DC, Congressional Quarterly Press, 1998, 268, and K. Jost (ed.),
The Supreme Court A to Z, Washington DC, Congressional Quarterly Press, 1998, 531.

Table 5.4   *The Supreme Court case load, 1980–97*

Year	Cases submitted	Cases heard
1980	5,144	154
1985	5,158	171
1990	6,316	125
1995	7,565	90
1996	7,602	90
1997	7,692	96
1998	8,083	90

Source: adapted from J.W. Wright (ed.), *The New York Times Almanac 2001*, New York,
Penguin, 2000, 126.

Table 5.5   *Laws declared unconstitutional by the Supreme Court, 1960–96*

Decade	Federal	State and local
1960–69	16	149
1970–79	20	193
1980–89	16	162
1990–96	10	45

Source: adapted from H.W. Stanley and R.G. Niemi, *Vital Statistics on American Politics
1997–1998*, Washington DC, Congressional Quarterly Press, 1998, 282.

Box 5.7
**Federal laws held to be unconstitutional by the Rehnquist Court:
some examples**

Flag Protection Act, 1989

Following the Court's ruling in *Texas v. Johnson* – allowing the burning
of the US flag as a protected form of free expression – Congress responded
to public anxieties by passing a federal law outlawing desecration of the
stars and stripes. In *US v. Eichman* (1990) the Court followed the precedent
established in the *Johnson* case and ruled that the Act conflicted with
the First Amendment's guarantee of free speech.

Gun-free School Zones Act, 1990

The Act made it a federal offence knowingly to possess firearms within
a school zone. However, the Court ruled in *US v. Lopez* (1995) that
Congress had exceeded its constitutional powers in passing the Act.
Congress had drawn its authority for the measure from the interstate
commerce clause of the Constitution. This gives Congress the right to
make laws regulating business and trade that cross state lines. As the
twentieth century progressed, the clause was used as a basis for legislation extending the role of the federal government on a broad range of
matters. However, the Court ruled that gun control constituted too broad
a reading of the clause.

Cable Television Consumer Protection and Competition Act, 1992

The Act required companies offering cable television to block or separate out 'indecent' programming. The Court ruled in *Denver Area
Educational Television Consortium v. Federal Communications Commission*
(1996) that companies could not be compelled in this way because such
a requirement violated the First Amendment.

Source: adapted from J. Bisupic and E. Witt, *Congressional Quarterly's Guide to
the US Supreme Court*, Washington DC, Congressional Quarterly Press, 1997.

changed in terms of its ideological character, it is still playing an overtly
political role. The contemporary Court has not, they note, shrunk from chal-
lenging the authority of the legislative and executive branches of government.
Indeed, Jeffrey Rosen compares the Rehnquist and Warren Courts, arguing
that both sought the aggrandisement of judicial power: 'Both combine haughty

declarations of judicial supremacy with contempt for the competing views of the political branches' (Rosen 2000: 16).

Furthermore, for the Court's critics, the conservative majority has substituted its own prejudices for the rule of law. From this perspective, the five to four ruling in *Bush v. Gore* (2000) exemplified these trends (see below). Although the Court's supporters argue that the judgement simply applied the Fourteenth Amendment's requirement for the 'equal protection of the law' to the process of recounting votes in Florida, critics assert that it was an overtly political decision that handed the presidency to the Republicans. As John Paul Stevens – who was, ironically, a Republican appointee – remarked in a dissenting opinion that was also signed by Stephen Breyer and Ruth Bader Ginsburg:

> One thing, however, is certain. Although we may never know with complete certainty the identity of the winner of this year's Presidential election, the identity of the loser is perfectly clear. It is the nation's confidence in the judge as an impartial guardian of the rule of law. (Greenhouse 2000)

However, although the term 'conservative' is helpful as a shorthand description of the Rehnquist court, the political character of the bench is not as clear-cut as the designation implies. Its conservatism has been tempered by four factors.

- Justices serve until death or retirement and, therefore, the composition of the Court reflects the politics of past presidents. At the beginning of the 1990s liberals such as Thurgood Marshall and Harry A. Blackmun were still on the bench.
- Although Reagan and Bush appointed some committed conservatives, they also nominated Sandra Day O'Connor, Anthony Kennedy and David Souter, who, although broadly conservative, came to adopt a more moderate approach. They became 'swing' votes on the Court bench. In *Bush v. Gore* O'Connor and Kennedy sided with the conservative bloc whereas Souter joined forces with the liberal grouping on the Court.
- The Senate – which must under the Constitution ratify presidential appointments – rejected the nomination of Judge Robert H. Bork in 1987. Bork is a forceful figure and would almost certainly have acted as an organising focus for judicial conservatives.
- The election of President Clinton halted the trend towards strict constructionism. He appointed Ruth Bader Ginsburg (1993) and Stephen G. Breyer (1994). Although not liberals in the tradition of the Warren Court, their commitment to a moderate form of liberalism acts as a counterweight to the conservatism of Rehnquist, Scalia and Thomas.

Although majorities and minorities shift between judgements and categorisations are, by definition, oversimplifications, the contemporary Court is loosely divided between different groupings. Each represents a third of the Court's membership. There are consistent conservatives such as Scalia, moderate conservatives such as Souter, and moderate liberals such as Breyer (see Table 5.3). The Rehnquist Court reflects these tensions. Its conservatism is evident, for example, in the rulings that have constrained the authority of Washington DC. *United States v. Lopez* (1995) struck down the 1990 Gun-free School Zones Act. In passing the law, which prohibited the carrying of firearms within the vicinity of schools, Congress drew its authority from a clause in Article I, Section 8, of the Constitution. This empowered Congress to regulate 'Commerce . . . among the several states'. From the nineteenth century onwards the interstate commerce clause, as it became known, had provided the basis for an increasing number of federal government laws and regulations. In the *Lopez* case the Court, however, ruled that the clause could not be interpreted in such a broad and elastic way. As Rehnquist himself stated, in writing the majority opinion: 'if we were to accept the government's arguments, we are hard pressed to [think of] any activity by an individual that Congress is without power to regulate' (quoted in Bennett 1996: 27).

Subsequent rulings such as *Alden v. Maine* (1999), which limited the right of individuals to sue states for non-compliance with federal standards, further tilted the balance of power towards the states (Policy.com 1999). The Rehnquist Court has also circumscribed the use of affirmative action and minority 'set-asides', whereby a fixed proportion of federal, state or local government contracts are awarded to minority-owned companies. *Richmond v. Croson* (1989) disallowed set-asides in industries where there was no convincing evidence of sustained discrimination. *Adarand v. Pena* (1995) circumscribed the use of affirmative action programmes by the federal government.

However, other rulings disappointed conservatives. In 1999, for example, the Court maintained national standards by declaring that states must give equal welfare benefits to new residents. It also extended the responsibilities of school boards by ruling that they can be sued if they fail to respond to the harassment of students by other students. In *US v. Bond* (2000) the Court prohibited federal agents from feeling the bags of bus passengers so as to

---

Box 5.8
The Rehnquist Court: significant rulings

Agostini v. Felton (1997)

Although the Warren and Burger courts insisted that the First Amendment required a strict separation of church and state, the *Agostini* ruling reversed an earlier Court judgement by allowing federally funded schoolteachers to provide remedial assistance to students attending church-run schools.

Bowers v. Hardwick (1986)

The Court argued that the 'right to privacy' established in the *Griswold* case does not extend to gay sex. States can, therefore, make their own laws governing homosexual relationships.

Bush v. Gore (2000)

Following the presidential election, and the bitter dispute about the votes cast in Florida, the Court cited the Fourteenth Amendment and ruled that the manual recount of votes that had been undertaken in some counties represented a form of unequal treatment, since the validity of those votes rested, at times, on a subjective assessment of a 'chad' (or punched hole in the voting card). Five of the justices also asserted that shortage of time precluded further recounts. The ruling ended Al Gore's hopes of securing the presidency and was seen by many of his supporters as an overtly political ruling.

Clinton v. Jones (1997)

In a unanimous decision the Court rejected claims that a sitting president should, because of the pressures imposed by the office, be protected from civil actions brought by other citizens. This opened the way for Paula Jones to seek damages from President Clinton, who, she alleged, had sexually harassed her while he was serving as Governor of Arkansas.

Clinton v. New York City (1998)

By a six to three majority the Court struck down the line-item veto. This had allowed the president to delete individuals items of expenditure from Bills passed by Congress. The Court asserted, however, that the president must either accept or veto a Bill in its entirety.

Kansas v. Hendricks (1997)

A number of rulings by the Rehnquist Court allowed states greater latitude in determining their response to law-and-order problems. The *Kansas* ruling permitted states to pass legislation requiring the confinement of sex offenders in mental hospitals after they had served a term of imprisonment.

Lee v. Weisman (1992)

Although conservatives had hoped that the judicial branch would look again at the relationship between church and state and begin to take down the 'wall' that the Warren court had built between them, the Court ruled that the saying of prayers at a high school graduation ceremony was unconstitutional.

Planned Parenthood of Southeastern Pennsylvania v. Casey (1992)

The Court majority reaffirmed the 'essential holding' of the Roe judgement, but reined in the availability of abortion. The ruling allowed states to impose a twenty-four-hour waiting period on those seeking an abortion and to require that minors must have the consent of a parent or judge.

Reno v. American Civil Liberties Union (1997)

The Court struck down the Communications Decency Act, which had prohibited 'indecent' and 'patently offensive' material on the internet. It was argued that the Act lacked precision and thereby infringed First Amendment rights.

Texas v. Johnson (1989)

Despite its broadly conservative character, the Rehnquist Court ruled that the burning of the US flag (the 'stars and stripes') represented a form of protected speech under the First Amendment and was, therefore, a constitutional right.

Washington v. Glucksberg (1997)

The Court declared that euthanasia ('mercy killing' or 'physician-assisted suicide') was not a constitutional right. The issue was thereby left to the individual states.

Webster v. Reproductive Health Services (1989)

By a five to four majority the Court upheld a Missouri state law prohibiting the use of public facilities or employees in the performance of an abortion.

Table 5.6   *Confirmation battles, 1968–*

Date	Nominee	President	Action
1968	Abe Fortas	Johnson	Withdrawn
1968	Homer Thornberry	Johnson	Not acted upon
1969	Clement F. Haynsworth Jr	Nixon	Rejected (45–55)
1970	G. Harrold Carswell	Nixon	Rejected (45–51)
1987	Robert H. Bork	Reagan	Rejected (42–58)
1987	Douglas Ginsburg	Reagan	Withdrawn

Note: between 1789 and 2000 there have been 148 nominations to the Court. In total, twenty-eight of them failed.
Source: adapted from *Congressional Quarterly's Guide to Congress*, Washington DC, Congressional Quarterly Press, 2000, 286.

check for drugs or other illegal items. The practice, the judges asserted by a seven to two majority, contravened the Fourth Amendment's prohibition of 'unreasonable searches and seizures'.

The Court also failed to meet the hopes of those who campaigned against abortion. Instead of being overturned *Roe* was merely modified. In *Webster v. Reproductive Health Services* (1989) the Court upheld a Missouri law, thereby allowing individual states to prohibit the use of state facilities for abortions 'not necessary to the save the life of the mother'. In *Planned Parenthood of Southeastern Pennsylvania v. Casey* (1992) the Court agreed to permit the imposition of waiting periods and parental notification laws. It did not, however, end abortion as a constitutional right, and the basic framework established by *Roe v. Wade* remained broadly intact.

Through its rulings from 1954 onwards the Court placed itself at the heart of the American political process. Appointments – particularly when there has been a fine balance between contending philosophies or amidst the partisan battles of the 1990s – became subject to increasing controversy and politicisation (see Table 5.6). In particular, although most nominees are reluctant to be drawn during Senate Judiciary Committee hearings, the 1973 ruling made abortion a 'litmus test' of judicial appointments.

During the 1980s and 1990s two clashes between the White House and the Senate led to particularly bitter acrimony. In 1987 Robert Bork was rejected by the Democratic majority because he was an uncompromising conservative who would have changed the ideological character of the Court. Clarence Thomas was only the second African-American to be nominated. However, his nomination (1991), already controversial because of his conservatism, provoked intense debate once allegations of sexual harassment became public. After about ninety witnesses had been called to appear before the Senate Judiciary Committee, he was confirmed by only fifty-two votes to forty-eight.

Earlier nominees failed to secure a place on the Court for other reasons. Abe Fortas withdrew and Clement Haynesworth was rejected because of ethics charges. G. Harrold Carswell, a southerner, was on record as an opponent of racial integration.

Glossary

amicus curiae   An *amicus curiae* brief is used by those who, although not a party to litigation, wish to express a view about the case and the judgement that, they believe, should be reached. Such briefs are generally filed by individuals, interest groups, members of Congress, the administration (through the **Solicitor-General**) and state governments.

appellant   An appellant is the person bringing forward an appeal from a lower court.

appellate jurisdiction   In most circumstances the Supreme Court has only appellate jurisdiction. This means that it reviews cases initially considered in a lower court.

Attorney General   The Attorney General is the chief legal officer of the US. She or he is a member of the Cabinet and responsible for the work of the Department of Justice. This includes the administration and application of federal law. The Attorney General also plays a role in screening those nominated to the federal courts.

certiorari, **writ of**   A writ of *certiorari* is an order issued by the Supreme Court requiring a lower court to prepare a record of a particular case so that it can be subjected to **judicial review**. A petition for 'cert' must explain the constitutional grounds on which it is based. It cannot simply claim that the lower court made an erroneous decision. The Supreme Court issues 'cert' in only a small number of cases. Its decisions about the cases to be heard are governed by the **rule of four**.

class action   A class action is a lawsuit brought by one or more persons on behalf of others who have been similarly affected by a particular issue. There was a substantial growth in class action cases from the 1940s onwards.

court packing plan   In 1937 President Franklin Roosevelt proposed that for each Supreme Court judge aged over seventy, a further justice should be appointed. There would be a maximum of fifteen on the bench. Roosevelt's initiative was widely interpreted as a response to Court rulings such as *US v. Butler* that had struck down parts of the New Deal. Roosevelt backed down in the face of widespread opposition. The plan may, however, have played a role in shifting attitudes. From then onwards the Court accepted the constitutionality of the New Deal.

docket   *See* trial docket.

due process   The Fifth and Fourteenth Amendments to the Constitution were written so as to protect citizens against arbitrary or tyrannical government. In practice they impose limits on the actions of the police and prosecutors. The phrase 'due process of law' has also, at times, been used to buttress *laissez-faire* doctrines by protecting the owners of industry from government interventionism (McKeever 1997: 5–6).

incorporation doctrine   From the 1920s onwards (in cases such as *Gitlow v. New York*) the Court asserted that most of the guarantees enshrined in the Bill of Rights not only bound the federal government but also applied to the state governments.

interpretivism   Interpretivism is an approach to judicial decision making that embraces **strict constructionism** (or textualism), intentionalism (the discerning of

original intent) and inferentialism. All three emphasise the importance of understanding the original meaning of the Constitution and those who wrote it. Inferentialism permits some latitude in this process and allows the courts to 'infer powers and rights from the structures and relationships created by the Constitution' (McKeever 1995b: 30).

interstate commerce clause　The interstate commerce clause is in Article I, Section 8, of the Constitution. It gave Congress the power to 'regulate commerce . . . among the several States'. In 1824 *Gibbons v. Ogden* established a relatively broad understanding of 'commerce'. However, the Court struck down later attempts to regulate business activities such as the 1916 Federal Child Labor Act. In 1937 the Court changed its attitude and permitted an enlargement of the federal government's economic role and the use of the clause as an instrument of social policy. This approach was maintained until the Rehnquist Court began to take a more restrictive attitude in cases such as *US v. Lopez* (1995).

judicial activism　Judicial activism emphasises the position of the federal courts as a co-equal branch of government. The Supreme Court, it is said, has a particular responsibility to minorities who may be neglected, or subjected to oppression, by majoritarian legislatures.

judicial restraint　The concept of judicial restraint emphasises the limits that the courts should place upon their own role. They should, in most circumstances, defer to the elected branches of government. According to rules laid down by Justice Louis D. Brandeis in 1936, the Court would interpret a statute so as to avoid ruling it unconstitutional 'even if a serious doubt of constitutionality is raised' (Witt 1993: 216). Brandeis's approach was echoed in 2000 by Anthony Kennedy, a member of the Rehnquist court:

> Do I make policy? Was I appointed for life to go around answering these great questions and suggesting answers to the Congress? That's not our function . . . it's very dangerous for people who are not elected, who have lifetime positions, to begin taking public stances on issues that political branches of government must wrestle with. (Biskupic 2000)

Judicial restraint also extends to the rules that the federal courts apply to their own proceedings. Its advocates insist upon respect for principles such as **standing**.

Belief in judicial restraint has, since the 1950s, been associated with conservatism. Those on the right reacted against the activism of the Warren and Burger courts, arguing that the elected branches of government were being usurped by appointed judges. However, in the 1930s, when the Court overturned parts of President Roosevelt's New Deal, it was Roosevelt's backers who questioned the legitimacy of the Court's actions and called upon it to play a less assertive role.

judicial review　The principle of judicial review was first established in *Marbury v. Madison*. The Supreme Court has the right to assess the constitutionality of a law or an action undertaken by the executive and legislative of government.

jurisprudence　The study of the law, its application and place within particular societies.

loose constructionism　Loose constructionism is a form of **non-interpretivism**. It asserts that the courts should not be bound by attempts to discern the original meaning of particular words and phrases in the Constitution, but should instead apply the democratic principles and spirit of the Constitution to today's circumstances.

moot If an issue is declared moot, it is no longer of relevance. In *Roe v. Wade* (1973) lawyers acting for the state of Texas unsuccessfully sought to have the case declared moot because the plaintiff – who was seeking the right to an abortion – was no longer pregnant.

non-interpretivism Non-interpretivism is a broad term used to describe approaches to judicial decision making that reject attempts to discern the original meaning of particular words and phrases. These methodologies rest on the claim that the courts should, instead, apply the *spirit* of the Constitution to the modern age. It is said, furthermore, that because federal judges are insulated from the pressures imposed by periodic elections, they have a particular responsibility to draw on moral rather than narrowly judicial considerations. Non-interpretivists also assert that many of the concepts associated with the original Constititution have become outdated. It was written at a time when African-Americans, women, and the white poor were denied political or civil rights.

original jurisdiction The Supreme Court has original jurisdiction in a limited number of matters. In these instances it is the first court to hear a particular case.

rule of four If four of the Supreme Court justices agree that a case deserves review, it will be listed for consideration. The Court does not generally give reasons why a particular case is either heard or rejected.

Solicitor General The Solicitor General represents the administration before the Court. He may, for example, ask for particular cases that had been heard before a lower court to be reviewed. Although – as Box 5.4 shows – there has been a marked decline, the Solicitor General still appears to have significant influence. For example, between 1984 and 1989, 76 per cent of government petitions for *certiorari* were granted (Witt 1993: 384). He also submits *amicus curiae* briefs on behalf of the administration.

standing An individual bringing a case must – unless a **class action** suit is being brought – have personally suffered because of the law or action that is under consideration.

stare decisis In literal terms, *stare decisis* means 'let the decision stand'. The doctrine suggest that courts should follow precedents established by earlier judgements. For example, the 1973 *Roe* ruling built upon the 'right to privacy' established in the 1965 *Griswold* case. Although it is a factor in shaping the decisions made by the Supreme Court, there are always other considerations. Precedents are sometimes overturned. *Brown v. Board of Education* (1954), which declared the segregation of public schooling to be unconstitutional, was a repudiation of the 1896 *Plessy* judgement.

strict constructionism Strict constructionism is closely allied with the doctrine of **original intent**. Both are forms of **interpretivism**. They suggest that judges should base their rulings upon historical enquiry. Strict constructionism or textualism:

> places primary emphasis upon the words of the clause and attempts to identify their 'plain meaning'; that is, the meaning that would have been given to the clause by 'the normal speaker of English' at the time of its adoption. (McKeever 1995b: 30)

Strict constructionism and other interpretivist approaches are associated with conservatives such as Robert Bork, whom President Reagan unsuccessfully nominated to the US Supreme Court in 1987, and Edwin Meese, who served as Reagan's Attorney General. In the modern age, interpretivism has been tied to **judicial restraint**.

term   The Supreme Court term runs from October to June.

trial docket   A list – or calendar – of cases to be considered by the Court. Almost all the cases that are listed will have been chosen by the justices themselves. (See also **rule of four**.)

Resources

References and further reading

Bennett, A.J. (1996) *American Government and Politics 1996*, Godalming, published by the author.

Bennett, A.J. and P. Lane-Clark (1989), *Themes in the Relationship between the Constitution of the USA and the Supreme Court*, Todmordon, Altair.

Biskupic, J. (2000), 'The Rehnquist Court: Justices want to be known as Jurists, not Activists', *Washington Post*, 9 January, B03.

Biskupic, J., and E. Witt (1997), *Congressional Quarterly's Guide to the US Supreme Court*, Washington DC, Congressional Quarterly Press.

Greenhouse, L. (2000), 'By single vote, Justices end recount, blocking Gore after five-week struggle', *New York Times*, 13 December.

Jost, K. (ed.) (1998), *The Supreme Court A to Z*, Washington DC, Congressional Quarterly Press.

McKeever, R.J. (1995a), 'All quiet on the US judicial front', *Politics Review*, 4:4, 25–7.

McKeever, R.J. (1995b), *Raw Judicial Power? The Supreme Court and American Society*, Manchester, Manchester University Press.

McKeever, R.J. (1997), *The United States Supreme Court: A Political and Legal Analysis*, Manchester, Manchester University Press.

McKeever, R.J. (2000), 'The Supreme Court in a post-Civil Rights Era', in A. Grant (ed.), *American Politics: 2000 and Beyond*, Aldershot, Ashgate.

McKeever, R.J., J. Zvesper and R. Maidment (1999), *Politics USA*, Harlow, Prentice-Hall.

Plano, J.C., and M. Greenberg (1989), *The American Political Dictionary*, Fort Worth TX, Holt Rinehart & Winston.

Rosen, J. (2000), 'Pride and prejudice', *New Republic*, 10 and 17 July, 4,460 and 4,461, 16–18.

Stanley, H.W., and R.G. Niemi (1998), *Vital Statistics on American Politics, 1997–98*, Washington DC, Congressional Quarterly Press.

Witt, E. (1993), *Congressional Quarterly's Guide to the US Supreme Court*, Washington DC, Congressional Quarterly Press.

Wright, J.W. (1999), *The New York Times Almanac 2000*, New York, Penguin.

Websites

The US Supreme Court   www.supremecourtus. gov
The Supreme Court has its own website. It offers information about the Court's background and history, the rules governing its procedures, and its calendar.

Oyez Oyez Oyez   oyez.nwu.edu
This is a Northwestern University site. It includes a virtual tour of the Court buildings, answers to Frequently Asked Questions (FAQs) and information about the nine justices. A CD-ROM (*The Supreme Court's Greatest Hits CD-ROM*) which includes recordings of oral arguments can be ordered from Northwestern University Press.

Cornell Legal Information Institute   supct.law.cornell.edu/supct
The Cornell website provides the full text of rulings from May 1990 onwards and about 600 historic judgements such as the *Roe*, *Bakke* and *Griswold* rulings. Cornell University has also issued a CD-ROM of rulings from 1794 onwards.

Findlaw   www.findlaw.com/casecode/supreme.html
This website offers the full text of all rulings since 1893 together with links to other sites, including the Office of the Solicitor General. There are, additionally, message boards allowing open discussion of cases and trends.

The New York Times   www.nytimes.com/library/politics/scotus/index-scotus.html
The *New York Times Guide to the Supreme Court* includes reports on cases, a search facility and links with other sites. Questions about the Supreme Court (which should contain 'Supreme Court Q & A' in the subject line) can be e-mailed to the *New York Times* at scotuswb@nytimes.com.

Policy.com   www.policy.com
Policy.com covers a broad range of topics, but these include surveys of particular rulings and broad judicial trends.

6

Pressure groups

This chapter surveys pressure group politics in the United States. It examines:

- why there has been a substantial growth in such activity in recent decades;
- the significant changes in the types of groups that exist and the ways in which they seek to influence policy making;
- which groups wield most influence in Washington;
- the growth of lobbying and how lobbyists spend their time;
- the working of political action committees and the ways they seek influence through financial contributions to election campaigns.

The US political system has always been open to the influence of pressure groups. Since its inception it has provided a positive and welcoming environment in which organisations promoting a diverse range of interests and causes can develop and flourish. The political culture has encouraged **pluralism** and group politics as legitimate forms of democratic expression. The decentralised nature of American government, based on the separation of powers and federalism, has provided a multiplicity of **access points** which allow groups to influence policy making. The relative weakness of political parties as national organisations and in terms of cohesion and discipline within Congress has also created opportunities for pressure groups' participation in both the electoral process and the formulation of legislation.

The growth of pressure group activity

During the 1960s and 1970s there was a substantial growth in pressure group activity resulting in what has been described as a 'veritable explosion in the number of groups lobbying in Washington' (Cigler and Loomis 1995: 10). The growing complexity of American society, characterised by economic specialisation and greater diversity among the population, has been fundamental to group proliferation. Increased government intervention, in the New Deal period of the 1930s, the Great Society programmes of the 1960s and the expansion of regulation in areas such as the environment, civil rights and consumer protection, meant that a growing number of groups were affected by government policies and began to have a stake in decisions made in Congress, the executive branch and the courts. This resulted, for example, in the number of business corporations with offices in Washington increasing tenfold in the period between 1961 and 1982 (Salisbury 1990: 204–5). Greater affluence and a more highly educated population have transformed social relations, creating both rising expectations and feelings of entitlement. The development of a post-industrial society has resulted in the satisfaction of material needs for many Americans and the opening up of opportunities for involvement in 'quality of life' issues and the promotion of a bewildering array of political causes.

Political scientists have suggested that there have been significant changes in the American pressure group universe as a result of these developments:

- Until the 1970s three major economic interests were seen as dominant in Washington: business, organised labour and agriculture. As far as business is concerned, while it is still extremely important, the number of organisations claiming to speak for corporate interests has grown considerably. The **peak associations** such as the National Association of Manufacturers and the US Chamber of Commerce have been joined by the Business Round Table, representing the largest corporations, the National Federation of Independent Business, speaking for smaller businesses, as well as a huge range of **trade associations** and individual companies. The trade unions have been in decline, with membership falling from 25.4 per cent of the work force in 1970 to 14.5 per cent in 1996, mostly concentrated in northern industrial states and in the public sector. The political influence of the agriculture lobby has declined as the number of people working in agriculture has fallen remorselessly (McKay 1992: 24–5).

- There has been a proliferation of new **interest groups**, based on highly specialised concerns. As David McKay notes:

  There was a time . . . when medicine broadly defined was represented by the American Medical Association (AMA). Today the AMA is just one of dozens of groups representing medical interests organised on the basis of occupation (doctors, nurses, paramedics), medical specialism, service delivery system (clinics, general practice, hospitals) and the employers and insurance companies which pay for and underwrite most medical care in America. (McKay 1992: 24; see Box 6.1)

- There has been a huge rise in the number of **promotional** or **cause groups**, including many **single-issue** groups, campaigning over questions such as abortion, gun control and legislative term limits.

Box 6.1
Examples of interest groups involved in health policy

Organisation	Membership
Health care providers	
American Medical Association	Physicians
American Academy of Family Physicians	Family physicians
American Podiatric Medical Association	Podiatrists
American Academy of Ophthalmology	Ophthalmologists
American Dental Association	Dentists
American Chiropractic Association	Chiropractors
American Nurses' Association	Nurses
American Occupational Therapy Association	Occupational therapists
American Hospital Association	Hospitals and hospital administrators
Catholic Hospital Association	Catholic hospitals
Federation of American Health Systems	For-profit hospitals
American Health Care Association	Nursing homes and hospitals providing long-term care
Medical Rehabilitation Education Foundation	Rehabilitation hospitals and professional organisations
National Association of Psychiatric Health Systems	Private psychiatric hospitals
Health insurance companies	
Health Insurance Association of America (HIAA)	Small, medium and large insurance companies
National Association of Health Underwriters	Insurance agents
Association of Independent Insurance Agents of America	Insurance agents
Pharmaceutical and medical equipment manufacturers	
Pharmaceutical Manufacturers' Association	Pharmaceutical companies
Health Industry Manufacturers' Association	Medical equipment manufacturing companies
Employers	
National Federation of Independent Business	Small businesses
Business	
Chamber of Commerce	Small and large businesses
National Association of Manufacturers	Manufacturing firms of all sizes

Source: adapted from Frank L. Davis, 'Interest Groups and Policymaking', in G. Peele, C.J. Bailey, B. Cain and B.G. Peters (eds), *Developments in American Politics 2*, Basingstoke, Macmillan, 1994, 88–9.

- The US has also witnessed an increased number of **public interest** groups such as Common Cause and Ralph Nader-inspired organisations, specialising in areas such as consumer and environmental protection, as well as a range of **citizens' groups.**
- The number of **think tanks** and **policy institutes,** such as the Heritage Foundation, the American Enterprise Institute and the Progressive Policy Institute, has multiplied, bringing a range of new ideas and approaches to the political debate in Washington. Whereas well established think tanks such as the Hoover Institution and the Brookings Institution had discernible political leanings, to the right and liberal left respectively, their work was essentially scholarly and serious. In recent times many think tanks have become more ideological and partisan and concerned with issue advocacy (Reilly 1998: 173–5).
- There has been a substantial growth in the number of institutions, such as universities, public bodies, state and local governments, as well as foreign governments, opening offices in Washington to promote their interests with the federal government.
- A notable increase in the amount of pressure group activity in state capitals has also taken place, particularly since moves to devolve more decision making from Washington to the states in areas such as welfare policy have taken effect.
- Since the 1960s and 1970s the development of a range of new **social movements** has taken place. These are broad-based networks of groups which seek radical change in society and are often based on a cultural as well as political identity. Examples include the women's movement, based on the growth of feminist ideas, and the gay rights movement, as well as counter-movements such as the New Christian Right.

All these changes have tended to create a more complex and, at the same time, more open policy-making process. Members of Congress, executive agencies and bureaucrats are likely to be lobbied by a much wider range of interests and groups than in the past. It is rare to hear talk nowadays of an agency being 'captured' by a particular interest group. The opening up of congressional committees to public and media scrutiny in the 1970s made it much more difficult for legislators to do deals with special interests without anyone noticing.

Pressure group methods

Pressure groups themselves have become increasingly sophisticated in the ways they seek to influence the political process. Innovations in technology have opened up new opportunities. For example, the internet can now be used as a way of publicising a group's aims and recruiting new supporters as well as as a method of mobilising its membership on behalf of a cause. New electronic methods of communication can be utilised to bombard legislators with targeted mailings from the organisation's supporters. Many groups seek to energise grass-roots support in the home districts or states of individual legislators to complement their more traditional lobbying activities in Washington. There are specialist companies which can be hired by pressure groups to identify and then recruit influential individuals (such as business or community leaders) in particular constituencies who will put the organisation's message across direct to policy makers.

Many pressure groups are also active at election time. The number of **political action committees** or PACs which are established to channel groups' financial contributions into individual candidates' campaigns increased dramatically in the 1980s, while some groups offer other forms of help such as endorsements, campaign workers and office and administrative support. Some PACs spend money on **independent expenditures** (amounting to $21 million in 1999–2000) mostly on advertising in support of or in opposition to particular candidates but which must not, by law, be co-ordinated with the official candidate campaigns.

Other pressure groups have increasingly used **issue advertising** in the run-up to elections whereby they can spend money unregulated by campaign finance laws. These commercials can support or attack a legislator's record in office or his stand on a particular issue but cannot directly call for the election or defeat of a particular candidate. 'Issue ads' may also be used to mobilise public opinion on a matter before Congress; perhaps the most well known examples were the 'Harry and Louise' commercials paid for by the Health Insurance Association of America in 1994. Harry and Louise were supposed to be a couple reading the Clinton plan and discovering how their health care would deteriorate. The ads played a significant part in forcing President Clinton to abandon his health care proposals by portraying them as an expensive and bureaucratic nightmare that would restrict patients' choice of doctors.

Pressure groups and influence in Washington

What factors affect the degree of influence pressure groups wield in the American political system and why are some organisations more successful than others in achieving their goals? Many different variables are significant: the size of the group in terms of membership, how members are distributed geographically, how many of them are active and how united and committed they are to the organisation; the resources available to a group in its campaigning; the political skills of its leadership; the nature of its objectives and the level of opposition and how well organised it is are just some of the most important. As the number of pressure groups has increased in Washington and in state capitals the competition to be heard and to maintain the attention and interest of policy makers has become more intense.

In order to ascertain which are the most influential pressure groups in the US, *Fortune*, the business magazine, has since 1997 carried out an annual survey. In 2001, for example, every member of Congress, Capitol Hill staffers, senior White House aides, professional lobbyists and top-ranking officers of the largest lobbying firms in Washington DC were sent a questionnaire and asked to assess on a scale of 0 to 100 the political strength of eighty-seven trade associations, trade unions and other interest groups. Based on the responses, a list of 'the power twenty-five' was assembled (see Table 6.1). Although there are, of course, fluctuations year by year there is remarkable

Table 6.1   *Washington's most powerful pressure groups*

Ranking 2001	Association	Ranking 1999
1	National Rifle Association of America	2
2	American Association of Retired Persons	1
3	National Federation of Independent Business	3
4	American Israel Public Affairs Committee	4
5	American Association of Trial Lawyers	6
6	AFL-CIO	5
7	Chamber of Commerce of the United States of America	7
8	National Beer Wholesalers' Association	19
9	National Association of Realtors	15
10	National Association of Manufacturers	14
11	National Association of Home Builders of the USA	16
12	American Medical Association	13
13	American Hospital Association	31
14	National Education Association of the United States	9
15	National Farm Bureau Federation	21
16	Motion Picture Association of America	17
17	National Association of Broadcasters	20
18	National Right to Life Committee	8
19	Health Insurance Association of America	25
20	National Restaurant Association	10
21	National Governors' Association	12
22	Recording Industry Association of America	40
23	American Bankers' Association	11
24	Pharmaceutical Research and Manufacturers of America	28
25	International Brotherhood of Teamsters	23

Note: surveys were carried out in 1997–99 and 2001 but not in 2000.
Source: *Fortune* 'The Power Twenty-five' survey, 28 May 2001.

consistency over the three years of the surveys in terms of the most powerful pressure groups: only six groups (the American Association of Retired Persons, the National Rifle Association, the National Federation of Independent Business, the American Israel Public Affairs Committee, the AFL-CIO and the Association of Trial Lawyers of America) have featured in the top five in the period. The AARP was voted the most influential group in each year from 1997 to 1999. Perhaps this is not surprising, given the fact that it is, next to the Roman Catholic church, the nation's largest organisation, with approximately half of all Americans over fifty years old being members. Millions of them are politic-ally active and can be readily mobilised when issues affecting the elderly are being debated in Washington. However, in 2001 the AARP was beaten to the top position by the National Rifle Association, a far more partisan organisation, which saw its reputation enhanced by having one of its supporters, George W. Bush, in the White House.

Influence can also be gained or lost as a group's reputation is enhanced by factors such as a particularly successful lobbying operation or damaged by internal divisions. Christian Coalition, for example, was ranked seventh in the first two surveys but fell to thirty-fifth in 1999 and sixty-fifth in 2001, after the departure of its charismatic executive director, Ralph Reed, a shake-up in its internal management and other well publicised troubles (Durham 2000).

Box 6.2
Examples of leading pressure groups

National Rifle Association (NRA)

The NRA was formed in 1871, and today has almost 3 million members. It developed as a group to promote shooting sports and marksmanship but has become best known for its political activities. It defends the right of citizens, under the Second Amendment of the Constitution, to 'bear arms' and seeks to counter attempts at gun control at national, state or local level. The NRA argues that law-abiding citizens should be able to defend themselves by being armed against criminals and that private gun ownership provides a safeguard against an over-powerful and potentially autocratic government.

In 1975 the NRA established the Institute for Legislative Action as its lobbying arm. It employs over seventy members of staff and seven full-time lobbyists on Capitol Hill. It has also set up a political action committee, the NRA Political Victory Fund, which in 1997–98 was the thirteenth largest donor in the mid-term elections. It donates principally to Republican and conservative candidates who profess sympathy with its support for Second Amendment rights. It is generally felt to have been a very significant influence in the defeat of attempts to tighten gun control laws.

In recent years it has been criticised as increasingly extreme in its views and a number of prominent members resigned, including former president George Bush. With a high-profile president of its own in the person of the actor Charlton Heston, the NRA is continually in the news. Its membership of 4.3 million gun owners and its annual budget of $200 million, including $35 million for political campaigns mean that it has far more resources than opponents such as Hand Gun Control Inc. Grass-roots opposition to its views was demonstrated in 2000 by the 'Million Mom March', a demonstration by women in Washington, following a number of shooting tragedies involving schoolchildren.

American Association of Retired Persons (AARP)

The AARP is the largest pressure group in the US, with 34.8 million members. It was founded in 1958 by a retired teacher, Dr Ethel Percy Andrus, and its role is to represent the interests of 'midlife and older persons'. Membership is open to anyone aged fifty or over, whether working or retired, and, as subscriptions are cheap (only $10 a year), many Americans join the organisation to receive its bi-monthly magazine and benefits such as discounted insurance and travel.

The Association supports research into gerontology (the aging process) and its Research Information Center and Public Policy Institute bring information on issues affecting the elderly to the attention of government, the media and the public.

The AARP has a twenty-one-member board of directors and a twenty-five member National Legislative Council which develops policy. The Council holds regular forums throughout the country to obtain the views of ordinary members. The organisation has a very effective lobbying operation run by its Federal Affairs Department and it is renowned for its ability to mobilise its members, ensuring that elected members know the group's views when they are considering issues affecting the elderly.

Large and influential though it may be, the AARP faces competition from the National Council of Senior Citizens, the National Council to Preserve Social Security on the left, and the Seniors' Coalition, the Sixty-plus Association and the United Seniors' Alliance on the right of the political spectrum.

National Federation of Independent Business (NFIB)

Founded in 1943, NFIB was created to give small and independent businesses a voice in public policy making. It today represents over 600,000 business owners who together employ more than 7 million people and has a budget of some $22 million. It claims to use balloting of members rather than a steering committee or board of directors as a way of determining its policies and ensuring they reflect the opinions of its grass roots. During the 1990s it changed from being a significant but relatively low-profile organisation to one that became 'a powerful political force . . . (with) close ties to, and influence upon, the Republican Party, and a reputation founded on its ability to combine traditional and newer lobbying tactics' (Reilly 1998: 165).

The NFIB has a strongly conservative ideology and opposes what it sees as costly and burdensome regulations on business. Unlike business organisations which represent large corporations, many of whom benefit from government contracts, tax breaks and subsidies, the NFIB's membership is opposed to 'the corporate welfare state'. For this reason the organisation is ideologically compatible with the conservative wing of the Republican Party, which took over control of Congress following the 1994 mid-term elections, and its representatives took part in regular legislative strategy meetings with the House Republican leadership.

American Israel Public Affairs Committee

The AIPAC, which was founded in 1951, has established itself as the leading pressure group on behalf of Israel and the most influential organisation lobbying on foreign policy in Washington. AIPAC is an umbrella organisation and many groups that support it, such as the American Jewish Congress and the Anti-Defamation League of B'Nai B'rith, have their own representatives on Capitol Hill. It has a total membership of over 55,000.

AIPAC's objectives are to advance Israel's security and prosperity. This involves supporting US foreign aid to Israel and maintaining its position as the single largest beneficiary of America's financial support. AIPAC also represents Israeli interests on Middle East issues, for example by opposing arms sales to Arab states.

Despite its acronym, AIPAC is not a political action committee and does not give directly to congressional candidates, although it can be influential in advising pro-Israeli contributors where to donate their money. AIPAC finds its natural support among the 6 million American Jews and the legislators from those states, mainly in the north-east, which have the highest concentrations of Jewish voters. However, it also benefits from generally sympathetic support for Israel's interests within successive US administrations and the general public.

American Federation of Labor–Congress of Industrial Organizations (AFL–CIO)

The AFL-CIO was established in 1955 as a result of a merger between the American Federation of Labor, a craft union federation representing skilled workers founded in 1886, and the Congress of Industrial Organisations, an alliance of mass industrial unions set up in 1935. It is a peak association representing the interests of organised labour, with over 13 million members, although some of the most powerful unions such as the Teamsters (truckers) are not members. The AFL-CIO has carried out its political roles principally through a body called the Committee on Political Education (COPE).

The influence of the trade unions declined in comparison with their heyday in the period from the Great Depression to the 1960s. Union membership as a percentage of the work force declined along with the nation's heavy industries, and manufacturing firms relocated from the north-east and Midwest to the anti-union Sunbelt states. While private sector unionism contracted, those unions in the public sector, such as the American Federation of State, County and Municipal Employees and the National Education Association, the main teachers' organisation, grew rapidly. Trade union influence within the Democratic Party also declined as other minority groups mobilised from the late 1960s on.

The AFL-CIO has seen some revival in its influence in recent years, particularly since the election in 1995 of its new president, John Sweeney, who was seen as a reformer committed to modernising the union movement. The AFL-CIO is still seen as a powerful pressure group because of labour's overall membership, the large number of paid organisers and its financial resources. It has been very active in recent elections in supporting Democratic candidates and helping the party take back the control of Congress it lost in 1994. In 1996 the AFL-CIO spent over $35 million on an advertising campaign targeted at defeating vulnerable Republican freshmen, with mixed results. In the 1998 mid-term elections it reverted to the more traditional tactic of seeking to mobilise trade union members and their families to vote, and this appeared to be a significant factor in reducing the Republicans' House majority in the 106th Congress. Union households comprised 22 per cent of those voting in 1998, compared with 14 per cent in 1994.

Table 6.2   *Numbers of registered lobbyists in Washington DC*

1997	14,946
1998	18,590
1999	20,512

Note: figures are those registered on 30 September 1997, 30 September 1998 and 15 June 1999, according to the Senate Office of Public Records, as required by the Lobbying Disclosure Act of 1995.
Source: Center for Responsive Politics, Influence Inc: Lobbyists' Spending in Washington 1999, http://www.opensecrets.org/pubs/lobby98/index.htm.

Lobbying

The *Fortune* surveys also indicated the importance of lobbying (for example, compared with the level of political donations to candidates) in exerting influence with policy makers. There was a marked increase in the number of lobbying firms and lobbyists in Washington in the 1980s and 1990s. Table 6.2 shows the growth in the number of registered lobbyists since 1997, when the new Lobbying Disclosure Act of 1995 came into effect. The Act defines lobbyists as individuals who:

- spend at least 20 per cent of their time for a particular client on lobbying activities;
- have multiple contacts with legislative staff, members of Congress or high-level executive branch officials;
- work for a client paying more than $5,000 over six months for that service.

Additionally, an organisation employing its own in-house lobbyists must register once expenses exceed $20,500 for a semi-annual period. Since all criteria must be met to be considered a lobbyist, some people who make money from lobbying can avoid registering. Lobbyists file reports twice a year with the Senate's Office of Public Records and the House's Legislative Resource Centre.

Expenditure on lobbying activities in 1998 was $1.42 billion, an increase of 13 per cent on the previous year, while the number of registered lobbyists jumped 37 per cent between September 1997 and June 1999. The number of organisations that reported spending more than $1 million during the year increased from forty-three in 1997 to 261 in 1998. Thirty-nine spent more than $5 million, nine over $10 million and three spent more than $20 million on lobbying activities (see Table 6.3). In all, there were more than thirty-eight registered lobbyists and $2.7 million in lobbying expenditures for every member of Congress, according to the Center for Responsive Politics, an independent watchdog body that monitors the use of money in politics.

Table 6.3   *Top spending organisations on lobbying, 1997–98*

Rank/Industry	1998 Lobbying expenditure ($)	1997 Lobbying expenditure ($)	Campaign contribs ($)	% to Dems	% to Repubs
1 British American Tobacco	25,190,000	4,060,000	938,971	12	88
2 Philip Morris	23,000,000	15,800,000	3,546,038	22	77
3 Bell Atlantic	21,260,000	15,672,840	2,129,743	33	67
4 Chamber of Commerce of the US	17,000,000	14,240,000	31,151	2	98
5 American Medical Assn.	16,820,000	17,280,000	2,701,907	30	70
6 Ford Motor Company	13,807,000	7,343,000	718,454	28	72
7 Business Roundtable	11,640,000	9,480,000	1,750	0	100
8 Edison Electric Institute	11,020,000	10,020,000	531,907	36	64
9 American Hospital Assn.	10,520,000	7,880,000	1,460,821	46	54
10 Blue Cross/Blue Shield	9,171,572	8,761,936	1,581,740	33	67
11 Citigroup	8,710,000	9,040,000	2,786,942	41	59
12 Boeing	8,440,000	10,020,000	1,653,838	37	63
13 General Motors	8,414,900	10,600,000	817,917	31	69
14 Pfizer	8,000,000	10,000,000	1,137,310	20	80
15 AT&T	7,740,000	7,800,000	2,122,971	39	61
16 Sprint Corp.	7,398,665	6,740,000	880,566	52	48
17 General Electric	7,280,000	7,220,000	1,130,312	43	56
18 Ameritech	7,254,000	6,800,000	902,266	39	61
19 American Council of Life Insurance	7,050,000	4,935,000	894,255	29	71
20 American International	6,940,000	3,400,000	754,315	46	54
21 National Cmte/Preserve Social Security	6,780,000	7,660,000	944,968	70	30
22 Lockheed Martin	6,600,880	3,600,000	1,582,001	34	66
23 Christian Coalition	6,380,000	7,980,000	252,500	0	100
24 Seniors Coalition	6,290,053	6,183,352	0	0	0
25 DaimlerChrysler	6,280,000	4,340,000	838,098	32	68

Note: figures include all reported payments made to lobbying firms and in-house expenses for lobbying activities, including those of subsidiaries and affiliates of these organisations. The table also includes the campaign contributions made to federal candidates and political parties.
Source: Center for Responsive Politics, Influence Inc: Lobbyists' Spending in Washington, 1999, http://www.opensecrets.org/pubs/lobby98/topspend.htm.

Table 6.3 lists the twenty-five organisations which spent most on lobbying activities in 1998, compares their spending with the previous year, as well as showing their campaign contributions and how they were split in terms of partisan support. The table shows that many of the top spenders are individual business corporations, as opposed to the trade associations which feature so strongly in the *Fortune* survey of powerful pressure groups.

Many trade associations focus on lobbying and leave direct campaign contributions to their member companies and organisations, a practice that accounts for the very limited or non-existent political donations of the Chamber of Commerce and Business Round Table in the table. Although some organisations are perpetual big spenders, there are fluctuations from year to year which are, not surprisingly, affected by the political agenda in Congress. This is best demonstrated by the fact that two tobacco companies head the 1998 list, with British American Tobacco markedly stepping up its lobbying activities compared with 1997. During 1998 Congress was considering legislation which would have introduced sweeping changes to the regulation of tobacco products. Faced with a legislative proposal that could fundamentally affect their industry, tobacco companies dramatically increased their lobbying and succeeded in persuading legislators to block the Bill promoted by Senator John McCain (R, Arizona). Interestingly the AARP (ranked as the most influential pressure group in the *Fortune* survey) was seventieth in terms of lobbying expenditure, with $3.7 million in 1998. All but two organisations on the list which made campaign contributions (Sprint Corporation and the National Committee to Preserve Social Security) weighted their donations strongly in favour of Republican candidates.

Table 6.4 sets out the sort of activities lobbyists undertake and how frequently they are involved in the different areas of their work. Robert Salisbury

Table 6.4   *How lobbyists spend their time*

Alerting client about issues	4.3
Developing policy or strategy	4.3
Maintaining relations with government	3.8
Making informal contacts with officials	3.7
Monitoring proposed changes in rules and laws	3.7
Providing information to officials	3.5
Preparing testimony or official comments	3.4
Commentary for press, public speaking	3.2
Mobilising grass roots support	3.0
Monitoring interest groups	2.8
Testifying	2.7
Drafting proposed legislation or regulations	2.7
Making contacts with opposition	2.6
Making contacts with allies	2.5
Resolving internal organisational disputes	2.5
Litigation	2.1
Arranging for political contributions	2.0
Working for amicus briefs	1.6

Note: the figures show the frequency of lobbyists' task performance (1 never; 5 regularly).
Source: R. Salisbury *et al.*, 'Iron Triangles: Similarities and Differences among the Legs', American Political Science Association Conference, September 1988, reported in R. Salisbury, 'The Paradox of Interest Groups in Washington: More Groups, Less Clout', in A. King, *The New American Political System*, Washington DC, AEI Press, 1990, 228.

has pointed out that in the increasingly complex world of interdependent interests and policies and with more and more groups seeking influence in the political process, it is often unclear what the real interests of organisations are. Therefore lobbyists have been obliged to spend more of their time and energy in gathering and analysing information and somewhat less than in the past in contacting officials and advocating policies (Salisbury 1990).

Political action committees

Political action committees were first established by trade unions in the 1940s because they were legally prohibited from spending money from their regular funds on supporting electoral candidates. They therefore set up special committees where donations from members could be pooled and passed on to candidates instead. Business organisations set up their own PAC in 1963 but it was not until after the passage of the Federal Election Campaign Act (FECA) in 1974 which officially sanctioned the idea of PACs that the huge growth in their number took off. This legislation, which was passed in the post-Watergate reform era, was intended to reduce the influence of very wealthy individuals, or 'fat cats', in elections. Under FECA individual donors can donate a maximum of $1,000 to individual campaigns, with a limit of $25,000 on all campaigns in a single year. PACs can donate up to $5,000 per campaign, but no overall limit was set on their total contributions. Therefore the law effectively favoured them in relation to individual gifts and made candidates more reliant on PACs.

These amounts have not been increased since 1974 and their value has been eroded by two-thirds as a result of inflation compared with when they were set. Following a ruling by the new Federal Election Commission in 1975 that the Sun Oil Company could form a PAC and that a business corporation could pay the PAC's administrative and overhead expenses as long as its direct political activities were paid for by a separate fund, any remaining doubts about the legitimacy of PACs were dispelled and the number of PACs soared, as is shown in Table 6.5. The number of PACs more than doubled during the 1980s, peaking in 1988 with 4,268, and in the 1990s stabilised at just under 4,000.

Corporate, labour and trade and professional associations all have PACs which are connected with the parent body and can raise money from their employees, shareholders or members. They do this by direct mail appeals, face-to-face solicitations for donations or, in the case of employees, through deductions from pay. The biggest growth in PACs has been among individual corporations setting up their own organisations so that today they outnumber trade unions' PACs by a ratio of five to one. Non-connected PACs have no parent body, are often ideological, with a clear political philosophy, or have been established to campaign on a single issue such as the National Right to Life PAC, the leading anti-abortion group. Unlike other PACs, they can appeal directly to the public at large for funds and do so through extensive direct mail operations.

Table 6.5   *PACs, by type, in selected years, 1974–2000*

Date	Corporate	Labor	Trade/ membership/ health	Non-connected	Co-operative	Corporations without stock	Total
1974	89	201	318[1]				608
1976	433	224	489[1]				1,146
1979	950	240	514	247	17	32	2,000
1982	1,469	380	649	723	47	103	3,371
1985	1,710	388	695	1,003	54	142	3,992
1988	1,816	354	786	1,115	59	138	4,268
1991	1,738	338	742	1,083	57	136	4,094
1994	1,660	333	792	980	53	136	3,954
1997	1,597	332	825	931	42	117	3,844
1998	1,567	321	821	935	39	115	3,798
1999	1,548	318	844	972	38	115	3,835
2000	1,545	317	860	1,026	41	118	3,907

Note:
1 1974–76: these numbers represent all other PACs; no further categorisation is available.
Source: Federal Election Commission, 'FEC Issues Semi-annual Federal PAC Count',
25 January 2001. Figures are those registered with FEC on 31 December in each year.

Table 6.6 demonstrates the total amounts contributed by the PACs to candidates for federal office in the twelve election cycles since 1977–78. PAC spending has tended to contribute around a quarter of the total spent by candidates on congressional campaigns. For example, in 1999–2000 overall spending by congressional candidates was $1,005.6 million, of which $245.4 million came from PACs. PACs have generally played a more significant role in House of Representatives elections than in those for the Senate, where candidates have larger constituencies with a more diverse range of wealthy individual donors. In 1999–2000 PACs gave $193.4 million to House campaigns, which constituted 32 per cent of overall receipts, whereas they contributed $51.9 million to Senate races, which accounted for only 12 per cent of the total. The table shows that PAC donations to Senate candidates have been stable in cash terms since 1985–86, while those for House candidates almost doubled in the same period. PACs play a minor role in presidential elections, where almost all the private money in the nominations process comes from individual donors, and they provide only 2 per cent of the total.

Table 6.7 breaks down the amounts PACs gave to candidates overall in the period 1997–99. It shows that over a third of the total number of PACs were inactive in the period in that they made no financial contributions to candidates at all. At the other extreme, a total of thirty-four gave over $1 million and a further fifty-seven more than $500,000. Overall the table shows that a relatively small number of PACs gave a large percentage of the total donated

Table 6.6 PAC contributions to candidates, 1977–78 to 1999–2000 ($ million)

	77–78	79–80	81–82	83–84	85–86	87–88	89–90	91–92	93–94	95–96	97–98	99–00
All federal candidates	35.2	60.2	87.6	113.0	139.8	159.2	159.1	188.9	189.6	217.8	219.9	259.8
Current candidates	34.1	55.2	83.6	105.3	132.7	151.1	149.7	179.4	179.6	203.9	206.8	247.9
Senate	9.7	17.3	22.5	29.7	45.3	45.7	41.2	51.2	47.2	45.6	48.1	51.9
House	24.4	37.9	61.1	75.7	87.4	102.2	108.5	127.4	132.4	155.8	158.7	193.4

Source: Federal Election Commission, 'PAC Activity Increases in 2000 Election Cycle', 31 May 2001.

Table 6.7　PACs, grouped by total contributions to candidates, 1997–99

	0	$1–$5,000	$5,001–$50,000	$50,001–$100,000	$100,001–$250,000	$250,001–$500,000	$500,001–$1 million	Over $1 million
No. of committees (total 4,599)	1,604	921	1,273	329	287	94	57	34
% of all committees (total 100%)	34.88	20.03	27.68	7.15	6.24	2.04	1.24	0.74

Source: Federal Election Commission, 'FEC Releases Information on PAC Activity for 1997–98', 8 June 1999.

Table 6.8　PAC contributions, by type of PAC and candidate office, 1999–2000 ($ million)

Contributor	No. of committees	Total contribution	Presidential	Senate	House
Corporate	1,365	91.5	1.7	26.8	63.1
Labor	236	51.6	0.06	7.4	44.0
Non-connected	670	37.3	0.4	9.5	27.4
Trade/membership health	662	71.8	0.4	15.7	55.7
Co-operative	37	2.4	0.02	0.4	1.9
Corporations without stock	94	5.2	0.07	1.4	3.8
Total	3,064	259.8	2.6	61.3	195.9

Source: Federal Election Commission, 'PAC Activity Increases in 2000 Election Cycle', 31 May 2001.

by such committees and 83 per cent of PACs gave money in the range of zero to $50,000 and therefore play a very limited role in the election process. When it comes to donating to individual campaigns relatively few PACs give the full $5,000 possible; for example, in the 1992 elections the average PAC donation was $1,600 and the most common contribution was $500. Candidates therefore have to raise money from a large number of PACs as well as individuals rather than become dependent on a small number of large donors.

Table 6.8 shows how the different types of PAC contributed to presidential, Senate and House candidates in 1999–2000. It also illustrates the fact that while business PACs vastly outnumber labour committees, trade unions are major contributors to campaigns, giving 56 per cent of the total donated by corporations. It also highlights the role played by trade and professional associations, which give 27.6 per cent of the overall total contributed by PACs.

Table 6.9   *PAC contributions, by candidate status, 1987–88 to 1999–2000*

Period	Incumbents	Challengers	Open seats
1987–88			
$ million	118.2	18.9	22.2
%	74	12	14
1989–90			
$ million	125.8	16.2	17.1
%	79	10	11
1991–92			
$ million	135.3	22.9	30.7
%	72	12	16
1993–94			
$ million	137.2	19.0	33.4
%	72	10	18
1995–96			
$ million	146.4	31.6	39.8
%	67	15	18
1997–98			
$ million	170.9	22.1	27.0
%	78	10	12
1999–2000			
$ million	195.4	27.5	36.9
%	75	11	14

Source: Federal Election Commission, 'PAC Activity Increases in 2000 Election Cycle',
31 May 2001.

PACs have regularly heavily weighted their contributions to the campaigns of congressional incumbents (see Table 6.9). For example, in 1999–2000 sitting members seeking re-election received 75 per cent of the total, while their opponents were given only 11 per cent. Candidates in open seats, where there was no incumbent on the ballot paper, received 14 per cent of PAC money. PACs generally have an 'access' strategy when deciding which campaigns to support. They wish to gain or maintain access to members of Congress who are important to them, such as party leaders, committee chairmen and members of committees which have jurisdiction in areas of interest to them. They hope that such contributions will enable their lobbyists to be given a hearing when members are debating legislation which is important to the group. Incumbents have many advantages when seeking re-election, of which greater ability to raise campaign funds is an important one. Generally, most PACs support incumbents not so much because they want them to win as because they expect them to do so (Grant 1995: 170–1).

As PACs are concerned to win the support of those in power and positions of influence, it is not surprising that the candidates of the majority party in Congress receive a higher percentage of donations than the minority.

Table 6.10   *PAC contributions to candidates, by party status, 1987–88 to 1999–2000*

	Senate		House	
Period	Democrat	Republican	Democrat	Republican
1987–88				
$ million	24.2	21.5	67.4	34.7
%	53	47	66	34
1989–90				
$ million	20.2	21.0	72.2	36.2
%	49	51	67	33
1991–92				
$ million	29.0	22.2	85.4	41.7
%	57	43	67	33
1993–94				
$ million	23.9	23.2	88.2	43.9
%	51	49	67	33
1995–96				
$ million	16.6	29.0	77.3	77.7
%	36	64	50	50
1997–98				
$ million	20.7	27.3	77.6	80.7
%	43	57	49	51
1999–2000				
$ million	23.9	37.4	99.2	96.2
%	39	61	51	49

Source: Federal Election Commission, 'PAC Activity Increases in 2000 Election Cycle',
31 May 2001.

Table 6.10 demonstrates that in the years up to 1995 the Democrats received the greater proportion of PAC donations in both Senate and House races. (In the House this regularly amounted to a two-to-one advantage in relation to the Republicans.) However, when the Republicans took over control of both houses of Congress after the 1994 mid-term elections the trend in the 1995–96 election cycle and subsequent years was a clear swing to the GOP, although in the House this led to an almost equal share of PAC donations with its Democratic opponents. The ideological non-connected PACs tend to have a marked preference for more conservative or liberal candidates and trade union PACs overwhelmingly back Democrats even after they were relegated to minority status. Business corporations and trade PACs have tended to be more pragmatic in their donation strategies, giving to Democrats when they were in power even when they mostly preferred the Republicans' more conservative pro-business policies. Given the small majorities the Republicans have had in the House, especially since 1996, many business and trade PACs have played safe by giving to Democrats as well as Republicans in the belief that control of the chamber could well swing back in the near future.

Many, but not all, pressure groups have established PACs so that they can contribute financially to campaigns for federal office. They see their PAC donations working in support of their lobbying activities in Washington DC. Table 6.11 lists the top twenty-five PACs in terms of the amounts given

Table 6.11   *Top PACs contributing to candidates, 1999–2000 ($ million)*

Name of PAC	Contributions to candidates
1 Realtors Political Action Committee	3.423
2 Association of Trial Lawyers of America PAC	2.656
3 American Federation of State, County and Municipal Employees – People Qualified	2.590
4 Dealers Election Action Committee of the National Automobile Dealers Association	2.498
5 Democrat Republican Independent Voter Education Committee	2.494
6 International Brotherhood of Electrical Workers Committee on Political Education	2.455
7 Machinists Non-partisan Political League	2.181
8 United Auto Workers Voluntary Community Action Program	2.155
9 American Medical Association Political Action Committee	1.942
10 Service Employees International Union Political Campaign Committee	1.887
11 National Beer Wholesalers' Association PAC	1.871
12 Build PAC of the National Association of Home Builders	1.822
13 Laborers' Political League–Laborers' International Union	1.792
14 United Parcel Service Inc PAC	1.755
15 United Food and Commercial Workers Active Ballot Club	1.734
16 National Education Association Fund for Children and Public Education	1.716
17 Carpenters' Legislative Improvement Committee/ United Brotherhood of Carpenters and Joiners	1.714
18 National Rifle Association Political Victory Fund	1.583
19 American Federation of Teachers Committee on Political Education	1.580
20 Committee on Letter Carriers Political Education/Letter Carriers Political Action Fund	1.530

Source: adapted from Federal Election Commission, 'Top Fifty PACs: Contributions to Candidates', 31 May 2001.

Box 6.3
Are pressure groups good for democracy?

The case for

- They represent the diverse range of interests and political ideas that exist in American society. By expressing these views they carry out the function of interest articulation and keep government in touch with opinion in the country.
- They complement the official system of representation in Congress by representing people of similar interests and views across geographical boundaries.
- They encourage political participation by their members, as well as educating them about political issues.
- They provide officials and legislators with information and expertise, as well as feedback about reaction in the country to government policies and proposals for legislation.
- They act as intermediaries between citizens and politicians in Washington, who are often distrusted by the public.
- The rise of promotional groups ensures that those sections of the population which are difficult to organise or lack resources manage to have their interests represented.

The case against

- There is a great inequality in the resources available to different pressure groups, allowing some to have disproportionate access and influence in the political system.
- Many interest groups use their position to selfishly promote the interests of their own members above the overall interest of society as a whole. The views and interests of the mass of the population are increasingly marginalised.
- The US political system's diffuseness and checks and balances provide advantages for those seeking to prevent legislative changes, even if they are supported by the majority of the public.
- Many pressure groups are not internally democratic and their leaders are not in practice accountable to the membership, let alone the general public.
- Pressure groups have managed to secure tax advantages, government subsidies and regulations favourable to their members at considerable cost to the nation's economic performance and to the ordinary taxpayer. To quote Steve Reilly, 'Organised interests often clog the arteries of the body politic' (Reilly 1998: 182).
- The methods used by pressure groups (such as electoral contributions) lead to the public believing that their government system is up for sale, increasing cynicism about politicians and the political process.
- The role of PACs in helping to finance campaigns has undermined and weakened political parties, which perform important functions in a democracy.

to congressional candidates in 1999–2000. It is instructive to compare this table with the lists of the most powerful pressure groups (Table 6.1) and the highest-spending groups on lobbying activities (Table 6.3). Interestingly, the American Association of Retired Persons has not felt the need to establish a PAC but, on the other hand, the Association of Trial Lawyers of America PAC was the second biggest spender, while the NRA's Political Victory Fund is ranked eighteenth.

Glossary

access points   Access points are those parts of the formal governmental structure which are open to influence by pressure groups. The decentralised and diffuse nature of American government created by federalism and the separation of powers has provided many opportunities for groups to make contact with policy makers who affect their particular interests. A pressure group seeks 'access' to make its case and be heard by those making decisions.

citizens' groups   Many federal laws have included requirements for citizen participation in order to oversee the activities of federal agencies and act as advocates on behalf of the public. This has spurred the rise of citizens' groups, which include neighbourhood associations, health care organisations and senior citizens' groups. The vast majority of such groups received outside funding, often from the federal government, in the initial stages of their development.

independent expenditure   The Federal Election Campaign Act and subsequent judicial decisions lay down that individuals, PACs and parties may support candidates for office by making independent expenditures on their behalf without any legal limits. Political advertising paid for by independent expenditures may expressly advocate the election or defeat of a candidate for federal office but must not be made with the co-operation of or in consultation with the supported candidate or his campaign staff.

interest groups   Interest groups are primarily self-interested and their goals are to protect, defend and promote the interests of their members. They tend to have a clearly defined clientele based on specific occupations, financial interests or industries. They frequently have considerable economic power and are often referred to disparagingly as 'special interests' by politicians and the media.

issue advertising   Pressure groups can pay for advertising in the media to promote their views on particular policy issues. They can also fund commercials which support or attack the views or voting record of a candidate on specific issues and, as long as they avoid expressly calling for the election or defeat of a candidate, the Supreme Court has determined that such advertising may not be regulated by campaign finance legislation.

peak associations   Peak associations are broad-based organisations which speak for a range of similar interests and may count other associations among their members. For example, the AFL-CIO as a peak association supports the interests of organised labour, while the National Association of Manufacturers represents many businesses across the country.

pluralism   Pluralism is a theory of government which emphasises the importance of competing groups in a democratic political system. Pluralist theorists argue that power is widely dispersed across society and that no single interest or group has a disproportionately influential position.

political action committees   A PAC is an organisation which is established by a pressure group to raise and then distribute campaign funds to candidates for political office. There are two types of PAC: the segregated fund type which is wholly accountable to its parent organisation and may not seek funds from the general public and the non-connected political committee which solicits money from the public, often by direct mail appeals.

promotional groups   Promotional groups are those attempting to secure political objectives which are in the interests of those other than themselves or are concerned with promoting a cause which, in their view, will be to the benefit of society as a whole.

public interest groups   A public interest group is one which seeks a collective good which will not selectively and materially benefit the membership of the organisation. Public interest groups operate in areas such as civil rights, consumer protection, animal rights and the reform of government.

single issue groups   A single issue group concentrates its attention on the achievement of one specific objective. Its members tend to be so strongly committed to the specific cause that they do not wish to be party to compromises or bargaining on the issue.

think tanks   Think tanks or policy institutes are research organisations which provide detailed analysis of policy options. Although they often have tax-exempt status which prevents them from directly campaigning and lobbying, their ideas have been influential in policy development in both the executive and the legislative branches. In recent times some think tanks have become increasingly ideological and partisan in nature.

trade associations   Trade associations are organisations that represent the interests of one industry. They constitute some of the most powerful groups in Washington, including the National Association of Realtors (estate agents), the National Restaurant Association and the Motion Picture Association of America.

Resources

References and further reading

Berry, J. (1989), *The Interest Group Society*, Glenview IL, Scott Foresman/Little Brown.

Cigler, A.J., and B.A. Loomis (1995), *Interest Group Politics*, Washington DC, Congressional Quarterly Press.

Durham, M. (2000), 'The Christian Right in American Politics', in A. Grant (ed.), *American Politics: 2000 and Beyond*, Aldershot, Ashgate.

Grant, A. (1995), 'Political Action Committees in American Politics', in A. Grant (ed.), *Contemporary American Politics*, Aldershot, Dartmouth.

Grant, A. (2001), 'Pressure Groups and PACs in the USA', *Politics Review*, February, 11–14.

Hrebener, R. (1997), *Interest Group Politics in America*, New York, Sharpe.

McKay, D. (1992), 'Interest Group Politics in the United States', *Politics Review*, April, 24–5.

McSweeney, D. (1997), 'Interest Groups American Style', *Politics Review*, September, 16–19.

Rauch, J. (1995), *Demisclerosis*, New York, Time Books.

Reilly, S. (1998), 'Interest Groups in National Politics', in G. Peele, C.J. Bailey, B. Cain and B.G. Peters (eds), *Developments in American Politics* 3, Basingstoke, Macmillan.

Sabato, L. (1985), *PAC Power: Inside the World of Political Action Committees*, New York, Norton.

Salisbury, R. (1990), 'The Paradox of Interest Groups in Washington: More Groups, Less Clout', in A. King (ed.), *The New American Political System*, Washington DC, AEI Press.

Wolpe, B.C., and B.J. Levine (1996), *Lobbying Congress*, Washington DC, Congressional Quarterly Press.

Websites

The Center for Responsive Politics   www.opensecrets.org
   The Center is a non-profit research group based in Washington DC which tracks the effect of money on elections and public policy. Its website provides a search facility to investigate financial details relating to individual politicians and donors. It also contains information about PACs and lobbying activities.

Policy News and Information Service   www.policy.com
   This website provides news and analysis of policy issues and links with organisations related to particular issue areas, as well as think tanks and advocacy groups.

Keele University Politics Department   www.keele.ac.uk/depts/por/usbase.htm
   Provides a comprehensive listing of websites related to American politics, including links with a wide range of pressure groups and other organisations.

Federal Election Commission   www.fec.gov
   The FEC website covers detailed information on campaign finance laws and regulations, press releases about FEC rulings and election expenditure. It gives information about political action committees and their contributions to candidates.

Pressure group websites   Almost all pressure groups, large and small, now have their own websites. Typically these cover information about the group's history, objectives and organisation, as well as news on issues of interest to them. There are also facilities to subscribe to the group as well as information on publications, services to members and, in some cases, on-line shopping. Some examples are:

   American Association of Retired Persons   www.aarp.org
   National Rifle Association   www.nra.org
   National Federation of Independent Business   www.nfib.com
   American Israel Public Affairs Committee   www.aipac.org
   AFL-CIO   www.afl-cio.org/home.htm
   US Term Limits   www.ustermlimits.org

7

Political parties

This chapter looks at the role of both major and minor parties in the American political process. It considers:

- the traditional roles played by the parties;
- the arguments put forward by those who talk of party decline;
- the 'party vitality' thesis;
- the minor parties and the obstacles that they face.

The traditional role of the parties

What role do the parties play in the political process? The distinguished historian, Arthur Schlesinger Jr, has argued that the parties traditionally provided a mechanism through which the work of the executive and legislative branches of government – deliberately divided by those who wrote the US Constitution – could be co-ordinated so as to allow effective decision making. The parties 'furnished the connective tissue essential to unity of administration' (1999: 259).

The parties also served other functions. Although now discredited, the 'machines', which dominated the parties in cities such as New York, Boston and Chicago – offering assistance and employment in return for political loyalty – drew individuals into the political process and bolstered participation. They:

- offered upward mobility to those otherwise excluded, because of class or ethnic prejudice, from the ladder of opportunity;
- acted as agencies of 'Americanisation', promoting American ideals and patterns of behaviour among newly arrived European immigrants.

The parties also made the work of Congress and the state legislatures manageable both by organising otherwise disparate individuals and by mediating between some of the different ethnic, regional and sectional groupings that made up the nation and bringing them into a process of compromise and co-operation.

Party decline

To some observers, it seems that when judged against these representations of the past, the US parties are now locked into a spiral of decline. To an extent, this was an inevitable consequence of assimilation – the incorporation of immigrants and minorities into the American mainstream – and the democratisation of society. As the children and grandchildren of immigrants moved up the economic ladder and left the urban neighbourhoods they no longer depended on the party machines for employment or assistance. Furthermore, the professional-isation of the federal civil service, which ensured that appointments were based largely on merit rather than on an individual's ties with the winning political party, weakened the parties by reducing their ability to dispense patronage.

However, many assert that the decline of the parties has gone beyond that. They have also lost many of the defining characteristics of parties across the world. Firstly, the growth of **primaries** and **caucuses** has undermined the parties' role in selecting candidates. Primaries – allowing the voting public to play a part in selecting the parties' election nominees – began in the Progressive era during the early years of the twentieth century. By 1960 they had become institutionalised both for candidates seeking their party's presidential nomination and for those standing for other public offices. Nevertheless, despite this, there are still significant differences between the state parties in the way they select the delegates who attend the parties' national conventions and formally pick the presidential candidate.

- While some state parties use **primaries**, others still hold **caucuses** or con-ventions. These are meetings requiring participation rather than the mere casting of a vote. (See Chapter 8 for a summary of the processes used in the 2000 election.)
- There are variations in terms of the franchise. Some state parties hold open primaries or caucuses in which all registered voters can participate. Other primaries and caucuses are 'closed' and the franchise is restricted to those who registered as party supporters. A small number of state parties offer modified open primaries or caucuses that allow those registered as Inde-pendents to vote in a Republican or Democratic contest. The different selec-tion processes are shown in Table 7.1. The figures include the District of Columbia but exclude US territories such as Puerto Rico.

There are also differences in the systems by which national convention delegates are allocated once the votes have been recorded (Table 7.2). For their part, the Democrats insist that although some state parties still formally

Table 7.1   *Open and closed primaries/caucuses, 2000*

Party	Open and modified open	Closed
Democrats	29	22
Republicans	32	19

Source: adapted from The Green Papers: Election 2000, www.thegreenpapers.com.

Table 7.2   *Systems of delegate allocation, 2000*

Party	Proportional	Winner-takes-all	Other
Democrats	40	0	11
Republican	10	26	15

Source: adapted from The Green Papers, *Primary, Caucus and Convention Results*, www.thegreenpapers.com/PCC/Tabul.htm.

assign delegates at state conventions, they all use a system of proportional representation. A candidate gaining at least 15 per cent of the popular vote in a state primary has to be awarded delegate representation at the convention (although the Democrats' selection process also includes unpledged or 'superdelegates' – chosen from amongst the party's leading public officials – who can vote for candidate of their choice). In contrast, the Republicans permit their state parties much greater leeway. They can, if they so decide, hold winner-takes-all primaries (although a number of state parties assign delegates on a winner-takes-all basis only if the winning candidate has received a majority of the votes) or, if a proportional system is used, set their own thresholds above which a candidate gains convention delegates. Other state parties still allow conventions to determine delegate allocation or hold loophole primaries that allow the appointment of delegates who may be 'unpledged' and are able to back a candidate other than the individual who topped the ballot.

The long-term shift towards systems of delegate selection that involve the electorate rather than party activists alone had important consequences. Firstly, the **national party conventions**, which are held in the summer months preceding a presidential election, and are attended by delegates chosen in the primaries who are generally bound to support the winner in their own state, have become largely a formality. They simply 'crown' the candidate who emerges victorious during the primary season. Secondly, the post-nomination stage of the election process that follows the national party conventions has become candidate-centred rather than party-based. Once nominated, candidates owe little to the party and feel free to disregard its **presidential platform.**

To an extent, the parties have also lost their role in funding candidates for public office. Legislative reforms in the 1970s placed restrictions on the direct contributions that the parties could make to their candidates' campaign funds. Presidential election candidates receive financial assistance from the taxpayer. Under the Federal Election Campaign Act, candidates seeking their party's nomination in the primaries and caucuses are eligible for matching funds. To qualify, they must raise $5,000 in each of twenty different states. Those who accept matching funds are then subject to overall expenditure limits. The presidential candidates eventually selected by the principal parties receive funding from the Federal Election Commission to cover their entire campaign. Furthermore, the parties' national conventions attract a large-scale subsidy (Table 7.3).

Party decline theorists assert that the parties have also been displaced as fund raisers in congressional as well as presidential elections. Their place has been taken by **political action committees** (PACs). Table 7.4 records PAC and

Table 7.3   *Taxpayer subsidies to presidential candidates, 1984–96 ($ million)*

Year	Primaries and caucuses	General election	National conventions
1984	36.1	80.8	16.2
1988	67.2	92.2	18.4
1992	41.8	110.4	22.0
1996	58.2	152.7	25.8

Source: adapted from William J. Keefe, *Parties, Politics, and Public Policy in America*, Washington DC, Congressional Quarterly Press, 1998, 164.

Table 7.4   *Funding for House and Senate candidates: the role of political action committees and parties, 1984–98 (% of total funding)*

Year	House		Senate	
	PACs	Parties	PACs	Parties
1984	36	7	18	6
1986	36	4	21	9
1988	40	4	22	9
1990	40	3	21	7
1992	36	5	21	13
1994	34	5	15	8
1996	33	4	17	9
1998	35	3	18	7

Source: adapted from Norman J. Ornstein, Thomas E. Mann and Michael J. Malbin, *Vital Statistics on Congress 1999–2000*, Washington DC, AEI Press, 2000, 93–101.

party contributions as a proportion of the funds collected by congressional candidates.

In contrast to European political parties, the US parties play only a marginal role in developing new policy options. Think tanks such as the Heritage Foundation and the Progressive Policy Institute have taken on much of this work. Furthermore, although the US parties have always been characterised by diversity, the ideological divide within each of the parties has become more pronounced. The Democrats are torn between traditionalists, who emphasise the need for 'big government', those identified with the politics of race and gender, and 'New Democrats' such as President Bill Clinton who accept some conservative policies and approaches. Among Republicans there are growing tensions between those in the north-eastern states and those in the south. Abortion is a particularly divisive issue. There are, furthermore, organised factions and groupings within each of the principal parties. Some of these are shown in Box 7.1.

Those who talk of party decline also suggest that partisanship – 'the sense of attachment or belonging that an individual feels for a political party' – is being eroded (Flanigan and Zingale 1998: 51). Table 7.5 shows that despite a very limited resurgence of partisanship as politics polarised between the

---

Box 7.1
Party groupings

Democratic Party: Democratic Leadership Council

The Democratic Leadership Council (DLC) was formed in the aftermath of the 1984 presidential election. It attempted to bring the party's elected officials together and co-ordinate their activities. It was ideologically moderate and sought to distance itself from the 'tax and spend' policies and calls for minority rights that had been the party's hallmarks since the 1970s.

In the wake of the Democrats' third successive presidential election defeat in 1988 the moderate character of the DLC became more pronounced and the Council began to act as a focus for 'New Democrats'. They accepted much of the Reagan revolution, and called for cuts in government spending, free trade, welfare reform, strong national defence, and adherence to 'the moral and cultural values that most Americans share' (quoted in Shafer 2000: 12). However, they remained distanced from most conservatives by backing gun control and supporting action for abortion rights (Baer 2000: 181). The DLC served as a base and provided a programme for Bill Clinton's 1992 compaign for the presidency. It also formed the Progressive Policy Institute, an associated 'think tank'.

Democratic Party: the Blue Dog Coalition

The Blue Dog Coalition brings together moderate and conservative Democrats in Congress. Its members, who are drawn principally from the south, are committed to low levels of government spending and a balanced budget, minimal government, and local decision making (Green and Shea 1999: 275). The group, which had a membership of twenty-four in 1996, meets weekly, has its own officers, and admits new members only on a vote. *Congressional Quarterly Weekly* suggested that the Coalition played a particularly important role during 1999. It broke with the majority of Democrats on four occasions, thereby changing the outcome of the vote. For example, members opposed both more restrictive laws on gun purchases and attempts to increase funding for the National Endowment for the Arts (Willis 1999).

Republican Party: the Tuesday Group

The Tuesday Group was formed by some Republican members of Congress so as to exchange information over lunch. Although market-oriented, it has a broadly moderate character. Its membership has taken a more liberal approach to the environment, gun control, abortion and civil rights than the Republican majority. The group is committed to working with moderate Democrats – a spirit of bipartisanship – wherever possible. It had fifty-four members in 1996, most of whom represented districts in the north-east and industrial Midwest (Green and Shea 1999: 273–9).

Republican Party: Ripon Society

The Ripon Society is a longer-established forum for Republican moderates. Although not organised as a grouping within Congress, it has a presence among party activists across the country. Its advisory board includes such figures as Senator Arlen Spector of Pennsylvania and Governor Christine Todd Whitman of New Jersey. The Ripon Society's goals include the internal reform of the party. It has, in particular, challenged those party rules which, they assert, lead to the overrepresentation of the smaller western and Midwestern states at the Republican Party's national conventions. If these rule changes were brought about, it would increase the strength of moderate forces within the party.

Table 7.5   *The strength of partisanship, 1952–98*

Year	Strong partisan	Weak partisan	Overall partisanship
1952	35	39	74
1956	36	37	73
1960	36	39	75
1964	38	38	79
1968	30	40	70
1972	25	39	64
1976	24	39	63
1980	26	37	63
1984	29	35	64
1988	31	32	63
1990	30	34	64
1992	29	32	61
1994	30	33	63
1996	30	34	64
1998	29	34	63

Source: adapted from *The NES Guide to Public Opinion and Electoral Behavior: Strength of Partisanship 1952–98*, www.umich.edu/~nes/nesguide/toptable/tab2a_3.htm.

parties in the Reagan years and again, to a much lesser extent, in the mid-1990s there has been a long-term decline in the proportion of party identifiers. The process – known as partisan **dealignment** – is evident in other ways. As William J. Keefe records, there has been a significant growth in the number who can be defined as 'independents'. They may either be 'pure' independents – who are uncommitted in terms of partisanship – or they may be independents who are loosely sympathetic – or *lean* – towards one party rather than another. In 1940 the figure was about one in five. By the 1970s it had risen to almost one in three. Surveys undertaken in the 1990s suggested that independents constituted between 32 per cent and 38 per cent of the electorate (Keefe 1998: 197). There has also been a growing sense of indifference or 'neutrality' towards the parties (Wattenberg 1991: 42). Martin P. Wattenberg notes that in 1952 only one in ten people had no feelings – either negative or positive – about the two major parties. By the 1990s the figure had tripled (Wattenberg 1997: 4–5).

Table 7.5 shows the percentage of the electorate who regard themselves either as 'strong' or 'weak' identifiers with either the Democratic or the Republican Party. It also adds the figures together so as to show overall partisanship. It includes findings from some mid-term as well as presidential elections in the 1990s.

How can partisan **dealignment** be explained?

Box 7.2
Minor parties

For some observers, Ross Perot's 1992 success in winning 19 per cent of the vote in the 1992 election appeared to represent the beginnings of a long-term change in the character of the party system. However, the suggestion has been countered. The minor parties face formidable obstacles (Box 7.3). Furthermore, although there have been challenges to the two major parties in the past, nearly all the new parties that were formed have either been confined to the political sidelines or have ended their days amid internal dissension.

Constitution Party

The Constitution Party was established in 1992 as the US Taxpayers' Party. It changed its name in 1999. The party seeks to restrict the federal government in Washington DC to its proper 'constitutional boundaries'. It is committed to the extensive decentralisation of political power. Despite the formidable difficulties that minor parties face, it was on the ballot in thirty-nine states in 1996.

Green parties

In contrast with some European nations, the Greens play only a marginal role in US politics. There are, however, two national organisations. The Greens/Green Party (USA) (GPUSA) was originally formed in 1984. Although it began as an environmental movement, it is also committed to a broad range of radical policies. These include the imposition of a 100 per cent rate of tax on the wealthiest sections of society and the break-up of companies with more than a 10 per cent market share. The Association of State Green Parties (ASGP), which was established in 1996 and has a more decentralised structure, emphasises themes such as non-violence, feminism, and sustainable forms of development.

In January 2000 an estimated seventy-three Greens held office in nineteen different states, although many of these were positions which were not contested on a party basis. Ralph Nader, who established himself as a campaigner against corporate interests in the 1970s, was backed by both organisations when he stood for the presidency in 1996 and 2000. He has, however, distanced himself from the more radical forms of Green politics, particularly those of the GPUSA.

Libertarian Party

The LP was founded in 1972. Although libertarians oppose government intervention in the personal lives of individuals (it supports the legalisation

of both drugs and prostitution), the party's support for *laissez-faire* and
the abolition of welfare provision places it within the conservative camp.
The party generally wins about 0.75 per cent of the vote.

Reform Party

The Reform Party emerged out of Ross Perot's 1992 independent bid
for the presidency. Perot ran for a second time as the Reform Party
candidate in 1996, although he gained only 8.4 per cent. In 1998
184 candidates ran for the Senate, the House of Representatives and
state offices on the party ticket. Jesse Ventura was elected Governor of
Minnesota.

The party is committed to making the federal government more
accountable to the people. It emphasises the importance of protecting
American jobs and businesses and calls for the repeal of the North American Free Trade Agreement and for restrictions on immigration.

As the 2000 election approached, there were major divisions within
the party. It had been joined by Pat Buchanan, a hard-line conservative
who left the Republicans so as to seek the Reform Party presidential
nomination. Buchanan's nationalism and cultural conservatism provoked dissent and contributed to Ventura's decision to withdraw from
the party's ranks. The party split into two distinct and separate factions
at its August 2000 national convention. The majority backed Buchanan
as presidential candidate. However, a significant minority supported John
Hagelin, the Natural Law Party's candidate.

The table below shows the minor party candidates who stood in 2000
and gained at least 50,000 votes. Five other candidates were on the
ballot in enough states to theoretically win the presidency by gaining
270 Electoral College votes.

*The popular vote for minor party candidates gaining at least 50,000 votes
in the 2000 presidential election*

Candidate	Party	Popular vote
Ralph Nader	Green	2,882,897
Pat Buchanan	Reform	448,920
Harry Browne	Libertarian	384,429
Howard Phillips	Constitution	98,020
John Hagelin	Natural Law	83,555

Source: adapted from the Federal Election Commission, *2000 Presidential Election
Results*, fecweb.fec.gov/pubrec/2000presgeresults.htm.

- The growth of higher education may have played a role. The electorate is said to have become more politically informed and therefore discerning. However, as Martin Wattenberg observes, increasing access to education has not led to greater knowledge and understanding of political institutions (Wattenberg 1998: 114–20).
- **Dealignment** has also been attributed to generational differences. Today's young people are said to have more detached attitudes than earlier age cohorts. However, the adoption of increasingly neutral attitudes is evident among all age groupings, including the elderly.
- As canvassing by party volunteers gave way to professionalised mechanisms such as television commercials and focus groups the parties lost the ranks of activists that once gave them a vigorous presence within precincts and neighbourhoods.
- Much of the mass media, which traditionally reinforced partisanship by adopting a particular stance and 'filtering' news so that it corresponded with that perspective, now has a broadly independent approach to the parties.

For those who talk in these terms, partisan **dealignment** and the other characteristics of party decline have had important repercussions.

- The electorate appear to be increasingly volatile. Issues and personalities are playing much more of a role. Voters are being drawn to particular candidates rather than party nominees. Elections therefore have greater unpredictability.
- Minor party and independent candidates have the opportunity to take a significant share of the poll.
- Voting in Congress has become individualistic and members are now much more subject to the pressures applied by lobbyists. This has allowed the 'buying' of congressional votes by outside interests. It has also made the process of building coalitions that allow the passage of legislation more difficult. There are now 535 separate voices in Congress that must be heard. This has contributed to 'gridlock' – impeding the progress of much-needed reforms, most notably health legislation. As David Broder notes: 'the governmental system is not working because the political parties are not working' (quoted in Wattenberg 1998: 2).
- Anthony King suggests that it is now more difficult – as a consequence of party decline – for those in Congress and the state legislatures to resist pressures and make decisions that may be unpopular but are, nonetheless, in the national interest:

> Lack of party cover in the United States means that elective officeholders find it hard to take tough decisions partly because they lack safety in numbers . . . congressmen and senators are always in danger of being picked off one by one. (King 1997)

- The parties traditionally acted as agencies of political socialisation and offered a link between the citizen and the political process, they encouraged political participation. The low level of turnout in US elections can be tied, it has been suggested, to the weakness of the party system.

Adaptation and renewal

The party decline thesis has, however, been vigorously contested. Paul S. Herrnson speaks of the parties' success in adapting to changing circumstances (1988: 121). Others go further and detect a process of revival or renewal.

Firstly, they argue, despite the attention that some independent and minor party presidential candidates have received, there has been no serious threat to Republican and Democratic pre-eminence. Although Ross Perot attracted

---

Box 7.3
The obstacles facing minor parties

- Interest group activity generally offers a much more effective focus for those seeking legislative change. The US political system has a significant number of 'access points' at both federal and state level. They can all be utilised by well organised groupings.
- Many states – such as Alaska, California, Connecticut, Hawaii, Indiana, Maine, New York – have restrictive laws making access to the ballot difficult for independents and minor parties (Collet and Wattenberg 1999: 244). Candidates must, for example, raise large numbers of signatures. In the 2000 election, for example, Ralph Nader, the Green candidate, was unable to secure a place on the ballot in seven states. In many instances these obstacles are not insurmountable, but they force minor parties to devote their energies and financial resources to ballot access. The principal parties can, in contrast, concentrate their efforts on campaigning.
- A large number of states allow 'straight ticket' voting. A voter can simply cast one vote backing a particular party's candidates in all the posts that it is contesting. Survey evidence suggests that this option discourages the voter from looking through the entire ballot and seeing that minor party candidates are standing for certain posts. As a consequence, minor party and independent candidates gain, on average, twice as many votes in districts that do not allow straight-ticket voting (Collet and Wattenberg 1999: 240).
- As the events following the 2000 election highlighted, presidential elections are decided in the Electoral College (see Chapter 8). Although some minor party candidates – whose votes were concentrated in the

- southern states – have been well represented in the College, those whose votes are dispersed across the nation gain few Electoral College votes (ECV). In 1992 Ross Perot received 19 per cent of the popular vote but no ECV.
- A significant proportion of minor parties have a 'fringe' character. Most Americans share basic political values such as a commitment to limited government, free market economics, and a strong sense of national purpose. Parties outside the national consensus – such as the Communist Party – have little prospect of success.
- The major parties have a quasi-public character. This has forced them to accept – whatever the wishes of the party leadership – all those who have sought election as candidates in the party primaries. For example, despite the feelings of the party leaderships, David Duke, a former Ku-Klux-Klan leader, contested the 1988 Democratic Party primaries and, in 1992, stood in the Republican primaries. The openings and opportunities that the system of primaries gives to independent campaigners undermine the rationale for the formation of alternative organisations and parties.
- Congressional elections are fought using the simple plurality or first-past-the-post system. Voters are unlikely to back a party unless it has a reasonable prospect of attracting more votes than any other party. However strongly they may sympathise with the minor party, they are concerned that their vote may be 'wasted'. In presidential elections the fear of wasting a vote usually leads to a fall in the level of support for minor party candidates as the election approaches. In September 1968, for example, George Wallace, the segregationist governor of Alabama who contested the presidency as the American Independent Party candidate, was attracting 21 per cent in the opinion polls. However, in the November election he only gained 13.4 per cent of the vote (Pfiffner 2000: 26–7).
- Modern election campaigns depend upon television commercials and direct mail. These are capital-intensive. Although some independent bids for the presidency – most notably Ross Perot's 1992 campaign – have had access to large-scale funding, most independents and minor parties have only limited financial resources.
- The federal campaign finance laws can assist minor parties if they gained over 5 per cent of the vote in the preceding presidential election. However, they can also constitute a barrier. Newly formed parties will gain nothing when funds are most needed and full funding is offered only to parties gaining at least 25 per cent in the preceding election. Furthermore, the Republican and Democratic national conventions attract a subsidy from the Federal Election Commission.

Table 7.6   *Party 'soft money' spending, 1992–2000 ($ million)*

Year	Democrats	Republicans
1992	32.8	46.2
1994	50.4	48.4
1996	121.8	149.6
1998	92.9	127.7
2000	243.1	244.4

Source: adapted from Norman J. Ornstein, Thomas E. Mann and Michael J. Malbin, *Vital Statistics on Congress 1999–2000*, Washington DC, AEI Press, 2000, 110 and *Congressional Quaterly Weekly*, 10 March 2001, 525.

19 per cent of the vote in 1992, his support was more than halved four years later. Only two independents served in Congress during the 1990s, and they were both, in practice, closely aligned with one of the principal parties.

Furthermore, despite taxpayer funding and PAC contributions in presidential and congressional elections, party organisations – most notably the national committees, the Senate and House committees – have been able to play an increasingly significant role in fund raising and campaigning on behalf of candidates by raising and spending **soft money**. This is generally donated by companies, labour unions and wealthy individuals. It is 'soft' because it circumvents the limits imposed by the Federal Election Campaign Act (FECA). Instead of being spent on direct assistance to a candidate, it is used by national and state party organisations for party building, issue advertisements, get-out-the-vote campaigns, and voter registration drives (see Chapter 8). Many observers assert, however, that there is a thin and blurred line between spending on these forms of activity and the promotion of a particular candidate. William J. Keefe has noted:

> Soft money found its way in huge quantities into the 1996 presidential race . . . through issue advocacy advertisements that supposedly were independent of the candidates' campaigns. Issue ads are legal . . . as long as they stop short of using words such as 'elect', 'vote for', or 'vote against' – even though an election message is clearly being conveyed. (Keefe 1998: 159–60)

There are also signs of greater party unity within Congress. In 1994 nearly all House Republican candidates signed up to a national platform, the *Contract with America*. Burdett A. Loomis has described the atmosphere in the House of Representatives following the GOP victories:

> the fragmenting elements of committees, caucuses, individual policy entrepreneurs, self-interested incumbents and particularistic interest groups proved weaker than a legislative party buoyed by long-awaited electoral success and a willingness to invest great power in its leaders. (Loomis 1998: 190)

Table 7.7   *Local party organisations, 1980–96*

Feature	1980		1992		1996	
	Reps	*Dems*	*Reps*	*Dems*	*Reps*	*Dems*
Has complete set of officers	81	90	92	94	96	95
Has formal annual budget	31	20	34	23	34	26
Distributes campaign literature	79	79	88	90	87	86
Arranges fund-raising events	68	71	74	76	76	74
Distributes posters or lawn signs	62	59	90	89	93	93
Conducts registration drives	45	56	39	50	34	45
Organises door-to-door canvassing	48	49	52	55	57	55

Source: adapted from John Frendreis and Alan R. Gitelson, 'Local Parties in the 1990s: Spokes in a Candidate-centered Wheel', in John C. Green and Daniel M. Shea (eds), *The State of the Parties: The Changing Role of Contemporary American Parties*, Lanham MD, Rowman & Littlefield, 1999, 138–9.

The aftermath of the 2000 presidential election revealed the degree to which partisanship is still a factor in US politics. During the bitter disputes that followed the vote, when the Florida result was contested, members of Congress were divided on party lines. Even conservative Democrats or those representing states that had voted for George Bush supported Al Gore's attempts to ensure that further recounts took place. Despite forecasts that there would be defections, there were few signs of fragmentation. Furthermore, a number of observers detect indications of a revival and renewal of the parties at a grass-roots level. After a period of decline, there are suggestions that activists are involved in campaigning work and in the rebuilding of party organisations. Table 7.7 shows that there is evidence to support this picture.

From this perspective, there has been – instead of **dealignment** – a degree of **realignment** between the parties. Whereas the Democrats were the hegemonic party from the 1930s, the Republicans have, at times, appeared predominant from the 1960s onwards. The GOP held the White House for twenty of the twenty-four years between 1969 and 1993. It gained control of both houses of Congress as a result of every election since 1994. In so far as there is evidence of *dealignment*, it may be a prelude to *realignment*. Established loyalties and attachments eventually break up as new problems and issues come to the fore. Shifts may begin at a state or regional level before they become evident across the entire country. Trends such as these were seen on the eve of the Civil War and in the prolonged recession that followed the Wall Street Crash of 1929. They heralded the creation of new party loyalties and a change of majority party. Those who talk of *realignment* or challenge the *dealignment* thesis emphasise three further points.

- From 1964 onwards the Democratic Party has held an unassailable position among blacks. In 1996 about 65 per cent of African-Americans regarded themselves as either 'weak' or 'strong' Democrats. If the figures for those who 'leant' towards the Democrats are added in, the total reached 81 per cent in 1996. (Abrahamson *et al.* 1999: 171.) Although, in the 2000 presidential election, George W. Bush made a sustained attempt to increase the Republican Party's share of the black vote, he won the support of only 8 per cent of the black electorate.

- Although there has been a growth in the proportion of the electorate describing themselves as 'independents', this is misleading. There are relatively few 'pure' independents. Instead, most 'lean' towards either the Democrats or the Republicans. Their voting behaviour is not increasingly volatile, but rather there are still strong and secure partisan loyalties. As Bruce E. Keith *et al.* noted in 1992:

  > They display an impressive tendency to vote for the candidate of the party they feel closer to; indeed, in presidential elections *they are generally more loyal to their party than weak partisans*. In seven of the ten presidential elections since 1952, Independent Democrats gave a higher proportion of their vote to the Democratic presidential candidate than did Weak Democrats . . . On average, since 1952, 89 per cent of Independent Republicans have voted for the Republican presidential candidate, compared to 87 per cent of Weak Republicans. (Keith *et al.* 1992: 65–6)

- As Table 7.8 shows, there has been a long-term shift among white voters (particularly men) from the Democrats to the Republicans in the southern states. White southerners were once so closely identified with the Democrats that the region was known as the 'solid south'. However, the Democrats were progressively abandoned as the party became associated with both radicalism and black activism. At the same time, the Republican

Table 7.8   *The southern white vote in presidential elections, 1976–2000*

Year	Democrat	Republican	Other
1976	47	52	
1980	35	61	
1984	28	71	
1988	32	67	
1992	34	49	18
1996	36	56	8
2000	31	66	1

Source: adapted from *New York Times*, 12 November 2000.

Table 7.9   *Partisan identification and independents, 1974–98*

Year	Strong and weak partisans	Independent or 'apolitical'
1974	61	18
1976	63	15
1978	60	16
1980	63	15
1982	68	13
1984	64	13
1986	65	14
1988	63	12
1990	64	12
1992	61	13
1994	63	12
1996	64	10
1998	63	12

Source: adapted from *The NES Guide to Public Opinion and Electoral Behavior*, Party Identification Seven-point Scale 1952–98, www.umich.edu/~nes/nesguide/toptable/tab2a_3.htm.

Party increasingly emphasised themes that found a resonance among significant numbers of whites such as welfare reform, law and order and opposition to 'forced' racial integration.

From this perspective, the 1980s and 1990s had a markedly partisan character. As the distrust and cynicism created by the Watergate scandal and Vietnam began to dissipate, and the Reagan administration began to redefine politics, the proportion of independents fell away. At the same time, the proportion of party identifiers remained stable and, at times, grew. Table 7.9 shows the proportion of the electorate who can be defined as either strong or weak partisans. The third column records the proportion of the electorate defining themselves – although they may have very different attitudes – as 'independents' or as 'apolitical'.

There are also suggestions that the major parties are gaining more polarised ideological identities and are thereby acquiring greater cohesiveness (Pfiffner 2000: 171). While there are some members of Congress, particularly in the north-eastern states, who have a relatively moderate approach to social and cultural issues, the GOP has lost its liberal wing – who were sometimes known as 'Rockefeller Republicans' – and has become a more conservative party. Similarly, although there are still differences among the Democrats, the party's centre of gravity shifted towards liberalism from the 1960s onwards, following the defection to the Republicans of white southerners – the

Table 7.10   *1996 national convention delegates' attitudes (%)*

Opinion	Democrats	Republicans
Government should do more to solve the nation's problems	76	4
Government should do more to promote traditional values	27	56
Abortion should be permitted in all cases	61	11
Favour a nationwide ban on assault weapons	91	34
Affirmative action programmes should be continued	81	9
Organised prayer should be permitted in public schools	20	57

Source: adapted from Gerald M. Pomper, 'Parliamentary Government in the United States?', in John C. Green and Daniel M. Shea (eds), *The State of the Parties: The Changing Role of Contemporary American Parties*, Lanham MD, Rowman & Littlefield, 1999, 264.

Democrats' most conservative and up to that time one of its most faithful constituencies. These trends are, to an extent, evident in the views of the activists who campaign for the parties and attend their national conventions as delegates. There are now significant differences between the parties both in terms of the policies they adopt and in the views of their most committed supporters. In 1996 there was a *CBS News/New York Times* survey of opinions among national convention delegates (Table 7.10).

The process of ideological demarcation and polarisation between the parties has been accompanied by other changes. The demise of the **party 'boss'** reinvigorated some urban parties. Successive Supreme Court rulings – such as *Cousins v. Wigoda* (1975), *Tashjian v. Republican Party of Connecticut* (1986) and *Colorado Republican Federal Campaign Committee v. Federal Election Commission* (1996) – strengthened party organisations and enabled them to play a more proactive political role. The parties should not necessarily be seen in terms of either 'decline' or 'revival', however. Instead the picture may be more complex. There is little evidence that the parties can rebuild themselves in the form that they adopted for much of the late nineteenth and twentieth centuries. The mass party, or, in John H. Aldrich's (1995) phrase, the 'party-in-the-electorate', has been undermined by modern technology and the increasingly capital-intensive character of campaigning. However, the parties have – in another way – been organisationally strengthened. They were, traditionally, loose confederations of state parties. However, national rules governing the selection of delegates to national conventions have been adopted. The number of staff employed by the Republican and Democratic national committees has grown dramatically. In 1972 the Democratic National Committee employed thirty people. By 1990 the number had grown to 130. For its part, the Republican National Committee also had a staff of only thirty in

Box 7.4
The national party conventions

Although the role of the parties' national conventions has been limited by the growth and subsequent institutionalisation of the primary system, a formal roll-call vote is almost always taken to determine the party's presidential nominee. The overall result is predetermined by the primaries. However, a spokesperson from each state party delegation reads out the allocation of votes and, depending upon the ways in which – under national and state party rules – the delegate votes reflect the popular vote, there will be some votes for defeated challengers.

Votes at the national party conventions in 2000

Republican Party		Democratic Party	
Bush	1,288	Bradley	369
Keyes	2	Gore	2,916
McCain	233		
Uncommitted	1		

Source: adapted from the *Washington Post*, washingtonpost.com/wosrv/politics/elections2000/primaries/democrats/apdelegates.htm.

1972. By the time of the 1984 presidential election there were 600. In 1990 the figure was 400 (Aldrich 1995: 257). The parties have also taken on a crucial role in the training of candidates and have co-ordinated national campaigns. Their congressional and senatorial campaign committees are playing a particularly vigorous role. As Aldrich concludes: 'They have become more truly national parties, better financed, more professionalized, and more institutionalized, with greater power to shape the actions of their state and local organizations' (Aldrich 1995: 260).

Glossary

Buckley v. Valeo (1976)   The US Supreme Court's ruling arose out of the 1974 amendments to the Federal Election Campaign Act. *Buckley* allowed unlimited spending by political action committees (PACs) provided such campaigns were organised on an independent basis and not working in conjunction with an election candidate. The net effect was to strengthen the position of PACs as a source of campaign finance and accelerate the trend to candidate-centred politics.

caucuses   Although most state parties hold primaries to select their candidates, some – particularly Democrats – still convene caucuses. In place of the more usual form of election, caucuses are meetings. Party supporters gather together, debate the merits of rival nominees, and then divide up on the basis of the individual they wish to support. The Iowa caucuses are among the first to be held in presidential election year. The result offers an early indication of a particular candidate's prospects. However, those who attend caucuses tend – to an even greater extent than primaries – to be strong party identifiers. They are therefore unrepresentative of those who may vote for a party in a general election. In 1988, for example, the Republican caucuses in Iowa were won by the Reverend Pat Robertson, a Christian fundamentalist.

Colorado Republican Federal Campaign Committee v. Federal Election Commission **(1996)** The US Supreme Court ruled that party spending on 'independent' election campaigning could not be limited. The judgement – which was based on the First Amendment's guarantees of free speech – placed parties in the same position as **political action committees.**

Contract with America   The *Contract with America* was a policy platform signed by 367 House Republican candidates in the run-up to the elections of November 1994. It consisted of ten Bills and eight changes in Congressional procedures. In contrast with the ambiguities that characterise many pre-election statements, the *Contract* was a clear assertion of conservative principle, reflecting the politics of Newt Gingrich, who became Speaker following the Republican victory, and his supporters.

The *Contract* included the 'Taking Back Our Streets Act', offering more rigorous law-and-order policies, the 'Fiscal Responsibility Act', a constitutional amendment imposing a balanced budget or restrictions on tax increases, a line-item veto, enabling a president to eliminate individual spending items from a Bill, and the 'Personal Responsibility Act' which would prohibit welfare assistance to mothers under the age of eighteen and tie the provision of welfare for others to work requirements (Gillespie and Schellhas 1994: 8–10).

The *Contract* has been portrayed as a nationalising of US politics. Congressional candidates traditionally campaigned on the basis of district concerns or their own philosophies and politics. It can also be seen as a shift towards a parliamentary form of government: a political system – such as that in the United Kingdom – based on a structured party system in which a majority party is said to have a mandate from the electorate. A mandate not only legitimises government actions, it also provides a basis upon which the majority party is judged and held accountable at subsequent elections. If this is to happen, however, the majority party must act together. Parliamentary systems depend upon relatively tight and enforceable systems of party discipline. There is little scope for mavericks and rebels who persistently defy the party whips.

However, the overall significance of the *Contract* should not be overstated. It represented only a commitment that the ten Bills would be brought forward and voted upon within the first hundred days of the 104th Congress. In contrast with the manifestoes issued by parliamentary parties, there was no promise to support the measures. Nor should the *Contract* be seen as the reason why the Republicans won a majority in Congress in 1994. The initiative was confined to those standing in House elections. It was not embraced by senatorial candidates. Furthermore, a *CBS/New York Times* pre-election survey revealed that 71 per cent of those asked did not know of the *Contract*'s existence (Hershey 1997: 208).

***Cousins v. Wigoda* (1975)**   In the *Cousins* ruling the US Supreme Court asserted that the national parties have the right to impose their own rules on state party organisations, even if they are opposed by the state authorities. Although there have been continuing battles between the national parties and the states – and the parties have often backed down – the *Cousins* ruling was confirmed in *Democratic Party of the US v. Wisconsin ex rel. La Follette* (1981). The case established that states could intervene in a party's selection of delegates only if it could demonstrate that there were compelling reasons for doing so.

dealignment   The process by which the loyalties of voters towards a particularly party are progressively eroded.

national party conventions   National or nominating conventions are held during the summer months of presidential election year. Before the primaries became decisive the convention itself selected the presidential candidate, although, in practice, the decision-making process tended to be dominated by small groups of 'barons' and 'bosses' who wielded significant powers of patronage. The last 'brokered' conventions where the selection of the presidential candidate was not simply a foregone conclusion were in 1952 when Governor Adlai Stevenson and General Dwight Eisenhower were chosen as Democratic and Republican candidates respectively.

Today the national convention simply formally confirms the candidate who is victorious in the primary season. It attracts extensive media coverage, and serves as a springboard for the election campaign. A successful convention provides the nominee with a 'bounce' in the public opinion polls. A divided convention, or one that seems unrepresentative of public opinion, can fatally damage a presidential campaign. The Democrats' 1968 national convention, held at the height of the Vietnam War, was bitterly divided, paving the way for a Republican victory. The Republicans' 1992 convention was dominated by Patrick J. Buchanan, a hard-line conservative who had challenged President Bush in the GOP primaries. His prime-time speech – in which he spoke of a 'cultural war' for America's soul – was widely seen as both harsh and abrasive. Bush's campaign was damaged and he was defeated in November.

The convention also confirms the candidate's choice as the vice-presidential candidate and adopts the party's platform for the election.

party 'boss'   The parties – particularly the Democrats in the larger cities – were traditionally dominated by 'bosses' who presided over a 'machine'. There were structured organisations of loyal supporters. The party 'bosses' were powerful figures who controlled nominations and policy. They owed their positions to formidable powers of patronage. They could offer employment or other forms of assistance. Mayor Richard J. Daley of Chicago is widely regarded as the classic 'boss'.

political action committees   Federal law prohibits direct contributions to candidates from companies, unions and interest groups. Their shareholders or members can, however, form PACs and make voluntary contributions to a candidate's funds. They can donate $5,000 to a single candidate and devote unlimited amounts to 'independent' campaigning for or against a particular candidate. PACs play a particularly important role in funding congressional candidates. In 1996, for example, they contributed 31 per cent of the funds raised by those standing for the House of Representatives (Keefe 1998: 145). 'Party decline' theorists claim that PACs have usurped the parties' fund-raising role. (See Chapter 6.)

presidential platform   The platform is a statement of policies adopted by the national convention. It is written by a platform committee following preliminary work by various sub-committees. Public hearings are held, allowing groups to make submissions. The final draft is subject to amendment on the floor of the national convention and is agreed upon by it. Although it tends to reflect the views of the more committed supporters, it is important in defining the party's values.

However, the overall significance of the platform should not be exaggerated. Although it may be written, in part, so as to ensure the loyalty of particular groups, it is also directed towards a very broad coalition of potential supporters. There will therefore be a tendency to 'dilute' policies and beliefs. Furthermore, if elected, a president has only partial freedom of action. The separation of powers places constraints upon an incumbent, and legislative reforms depend upon the willingness of Congress to pass them. Furthermore, modern election campaigns are candidate-centred. The candidate may therefore disregard the platform and the pledges that it may make. In 1996 the Republican challenger, Senator Bob Dole, refused to be bound by the party platform, and publicly stated that he had not read it.

primaries   Primaries are elections that are used by the Democrats, Republicans and some minor parties to select their candidates for public office. The state party's delegation to the national party convention is chosen on the basis of the results. The primary system allows the electorate to play a role in the nominating process. They were introduced to curtail the powers of party 'bosses', who traditionally had a hold over candidate selection.

There are still, however, significant variations in the type of primaries that are conducted in the different states. Some are open in terms of who can vote. Others are closed. Furthermore, there are also differences in the way delegate votes are allocated among the candidates.

realignment   Realignment refers to changes in partisan allegiances. The concept was outlined in its most developed form by V.O. Key. He suggested that there are 'critical elections' in which new, cross-cutting issues emerge and loyalties shift between the parties, although he also acknowledged there are also 'secular' party realignments which are long-term drifts rather than sudden breaks with the past.

soft money   'Soft money' evades the contribution and expenditure limits set by the Federal Election Campaign Act. Although nominally devoted to 'party building' or 'issue ads', there is little to distinguish television advertisements of this type from those promoting a candidate which must – by law – be funded from 'hard money'. Party organisations have played an increasingly important role as contributor of 'soft money' to the election process. Funds are raised and spent by the parties' national committees, congressional committees and senatorial committees.

***Tashjian v. Republican Party of Connecticut* (1986)**   The Supreme Court ruled that state parties could themselves determine the form of delegate selection – such as whether to hold an open or closed primary – that they wished to adopt. It could not be dictated to the party by state laws (Keefe 1998: 83). Many state parties have subsequently chosen to hold open primaries.

ticket splitting   Voters are usually presented with a large number of choices at the same election. They may be voting for the presidency, the House of Representatives, the Senate, state officials, the state legislature and a range of local positions. 'Ticket splitters' back candidates from different parties. It may be a split between the presidency and Congress, between the two houses of Congress, or between state and federal offices.

Resources

References and further reading

Abrahmson, P.R., J.H. Aldrich and D.W. Rohde (1999), *Change and Continuity in the 1996 and 1998 Elections*, Washington DC, Congressional Quarterly Press.

Aldrich, J.H. (1995), *Why Parties? The Origins and Transformation of Parties in America*, Chicago, University of Chicago Press.

Baer, K.S. (2000), *Reinventing Democrats: The Politics of Liberalism from Reagan to Clinton*, Lawrence KS, University Press of Kansas.

Bailey, C.J. (1990), 'Political parties', *Contemporary Record*, 3:3, 12–14.

Collet, C. and M.P. Wattenberg (1999), 'Strategically Unambitious: Minor Party and Independent Candidates in the 1996 Congressional Elections', in J.C. Green and D.M. Shea (eds), *The State of the Parties: The Changing Role of Contemporary American Parties*, Lanham MD, Rowman & Littlefield.

Flanigan, W.H. and N.H. Zingale (1998), *Political Behavior of the American Electorate*, Washington DC, Congressional Quarterly Press.

Frendreis, J. and A.R. Gitelson (1999), 'Local Parties in the 1990s: Spokes in a Candidate-centered Wheel', in J.C. Green and D.M. Shea (eds), *The State of the Parties: The Changing Role of Contemporary American Parties*, Lanham MD: Rowman & Littlefield.

Gillespie, E. and B. Schellhas (eds) (1994), *Contract with America: The Bold Plan by Rep. Newt Gingrich, Rep. Dick Armey, and the House Republicans to Change the Nation*, New York, Times Books.

Green, J.C. and D.M. Shea (1999), *The State of the Parties: The Changing Role of Contemporary American Parties*, Lanham MD: Rowman & Littlefield.

Herrnson, P.S. (1988), *Party Campaigning in the 1980s*, Cambridge MA, Harvard University Press.

Hershey, M.J. (1997), 'The Congressional Elections', in G.M. Pomper *et al.* (eds), *The Election of 1996: Reports and Interpretations*, Chatham NJ, Chatham House.

Keefe, W.J. (1998), *Parties, Politics, and Public Policy in America*, Washington DC, Congressional Quarterly Press.

Keith, B.E. *et al.* (1992), *The Myth of the Independent Voter*, Berkeley CA, University of California Press.

King, A. (1997), 'Running scared', *Atlantic Monthly*, January.

Loomis, B.A. (1998), *The Contemporary Congress*, New York, St Martin's Press.

McSweeney, D. and J. Zvesper (1991), *American Political Parties*, London, Routledge.

The National Election Studies Guide to Public Opinion and Electoral Behavior, www.umich.edu/~nes/nesguide/nesguide.htm.

Ota, A.K. (1999), 'Partisan Voting on the Rise', *Congressional Quarterly Weekly*, 9 January, 79–81.

Pfiffner, J.P. (2000), *The Modern Presidency*, Boston MA, Bedford/St Martin's.

Pomper, G.M. (1999), 'Parliamentary Government in the United States?', in John C. Green and Daniel M. Shea (eds), *The State of the Parties: The Changing Role of Contemporary American Parties*, Lanham MD, Rowman & Littlefield.

Schlesinger, A.M., Jr (1999), *The Cycles of American History*, Boston MA and New York, Houghton Mifflin.

Shafer, B.E. (2000), 'The Partisan Legacy: Are there any New Democrats? (And by the way, was there a Republican Revolution?'), in C. Campbell and B.E. Rockman (eds), *The Clinton Legacy*, New York, Chatham House.

Stanley, H.W. and R.G. Niemi (1998), *Vital Statistics on American Politics,1997–98*, Washington DC, Congressional Quarterly Press.

Wattenberg, M.P. (1991), *The Rise of Candidate-centered Politics*, Cambridge MA, Harvard University Press.

Wattenberg, M.P. (1997), 'The Crisis of Electoral Politics', *Atlantic Monthly*, May.

Wattenberg, M.P. (1998), *The Decline of American Political Parties, 1952–96*, Cambridge MA, Harvard University Press.

Wayne, S.J. (2000), *The Road to the White House, 2000: The Politics of Presidential Elections*, Boston MA and New York, Bedford/St Martin's.

White, J.K. (2000), 'American Party System', *Public Perspective*, March–April, 21–3.

Willis, D. (1999), 'Democrats Feel Blue Dogs' Bite', *Congressional Quarterly Weekly*, 11 December, 2979.

Websites

Democratic National Committee   www.democrats.org

The Democratic National Committee (DNC) includes video clips of the party's television broadcasts, the party platform, and 'GOP Watch', which tracks the Republican Party's campaigns and activities. The DNC also provides e-mails to those who join their mailing list.

Republican National Committee   www.rnc.org

The Republican National Committee (RNC) website offers extensive features, including the Republican Party platform, a guide to the party's elected officials, and GOP-TV webcasts.

Constitution Party   www.constitutionparty.org

The Constitution Party website provides extensive coverage of Howard Phillips's presidential election campaign, a guide to events, the party's platform, audio clips, and links to the different state parties.

Green Parties   www.greenparty.org and www.greenparties.org

Both the Greens/Green Party (USA) and the Association of State Green Parties have websites.

Libertarian Party   www.lp.org

The Libertarian Party's website offers pages covering Harry Browne's 2000 presidential election campaign, press releases, a guide to issues, and party news. There are some video clips from the party's 2000 national convention.

Reform Party   www.reformparty.org

The Reform Party website offers material on the party's history, principles, constitution and platform. It reflects the views of those who backed John Hagelin as the party's 2000 presidential candidate.

Federal Election Commission   www.fec.gov

The Federal Election Commission (FEC) is responsible for monitoring the conduct of presidential and congressional elections. In presidential elections it offers matching funds to primary candidates and total funding to major party candidates. The FEC also enforces the spending limits that are imposed on those who accept federal funding.

8

Elections

This chapter examines the character of both presidential and congressional elections. It considers:

- the nominating process;
- the variables shaping the general election outcome;
- the role of finance;
- the reasons for low levels of electoral turnout;
- the role of the Electoral College;
- congressional elections.

Presidential elections, and almost all other American elections, are a two-stage process:

- In contrast with British politics, the electorate has the opportunity to vote in primaries and caucuses so as to choose the parties' candidates. These usually take place between January and June of election year.
- The primary season is followed – some months later – by the general election campaign. This is a contest between the candidates nominated by the different parties.

The nominating process

The primary system was originally established so as to weaken the hold of the party bosses over the nominating process. **Primaries**, it is said, increase political participation by broadening the franchise, test the qualities of rival candidates, subject them to sustained scrutiny, and build interest for the coming contest between the parties. However, the presidential primaries have also been subject to criticism.

Box 8.1
Stages in US presidential elections

One to three years preceding election year	The 'invisible primary'
January–June	Primaries and caucuses
July–August	National party conventions
Labor Day (the first Monday in September)	The traditional beginning of the campaign
November (the first Tuesday after the first Monday)	Election day
Mid-December	Members of the Electoral College meet in their respective state capitals
6 January	The Electoral College votes are recorded by Congress

---

- The primary season is preceded by the **'invisible primary'**. This has assumed growing importance as candidates have begun to declare their intention to stand for the presidency at an increasingly early stage. During the two or three year period before a presidential election year, individuals seek funds and endorsements from prominent figures and public officials within their party. Straw polls, other tests of public opinion, and television 'talk shows' also play a role. The candidate who is in the lead – in terms of poll ratings – at the beginning of election year has almost always won their party's nomination some months later. This has led some observers to suggest that the **primaries** and **caucuses** are losing their role in the nominating process.
- The first significant caucus and primary are held in Iowa and New Hampshire respectively and they therefore have a pivotal role in the nominating process. Candidates who fail to gain a sizeable share of the poll in the New Hampshire primary generally drop out of the race within weeks. They lose the sense of momentum and the financial backing required to sustain a prolonged campaign. However, both Iowa and New Hampshire are largely rural and overwhelmingly white. They are therefore unrepresentative of metropolitan America
- **Super Tuesday** – when a number of states hold their primaries on the same day – is another major hurdle for candidates. However, many of the states that vote on Super Tuesday are in the south, the most conservative of the regions. Inevitably, therefore, candidates are pulled towards the right.
- The early and decisive contests take place within an increasingly compressed period of time. This represents an advantage for the candidates with extensive financial resources, as they have the ability to campaign in a number of states across the US at the same time.

- The **primaries** and **caucuses** deny opportunities for peer review. In the primaries, candidates are judged by the electorate rather than by those – such as governors, members of Congress, and party officials – who are best qualified to assess the strengths and abilities of a potential president. The skills required in the **primaries** differ from those needed by a president. In a survey of the 1988 primaries, *The Times* reported:

> Candidates for the presidency must travel thousands of miles, wander for months and years through the ballrooms of Holiday Inns, bear the insults of the demonstrators, answer in 20 words or less questions that cannot be answered in 100,000 words, smile steadfastly into the lens of the camera that never sleeps, and display in all circumstances and any weather, not the least sign of fear or disgust. (Quoted in Bennett 1992: 9–10)

On this basis, it can be argued that the primary system has lowered the calibre of US presidents. Indeed, it has been suggested that Jimmy Carter's successes in the 1976 Democratic primaries and the subsequent failings of the Carter White House (1977–81) are testimony to this.

During the summer months of presidential election year, **national party conventions** formally select the presidential candidate. The result is, however, a foregone conclusion. The delegates who – through their state delegations – cast votes at the conventions were chosen on the basis of the primary results. Rival candidates seeking the nominations will – with few exceptions – have withdrawn from the contest long before the convention is held. Nevertheless, although it is in some ways a stage-managed ritual, the national conventions can play an important role.

- They gain media attention and can – if successful – provide the presidential candidate with a 'bounce' in the public opinion polls. In the 2000 presidential election, the Democratic Party's national convention provided Al Gore with a significant 'bounce'. A sixteen percentage point lead for Bush was turned into a one-point Gore lead. Although Bush later regained some support after the televised debates (see below), it remained a finely balanced race until election day.
- The party's platform – outlining its policies – is agreed. Presidential candidates have not, however, always felt bound by its provisions.
- The party chairman is confirmed or selected. He or she will be responsible for organising the party's campaigning and grass-roots activities.
- The keynote speeches by leading figures within the party set the tone and shape the character of the campaign.
- The presidential nominee's choice of vice-presidential nominee is confirmed
- The conventions are held in major cities. They can be used to generate interest and win votes within that state.

Table 8.1a *Primaries and caucuses, 2000: Democratic presidential results*

State	Date	Delegates pledged	Delegates unpledged	Method	Gore vote	Gore %	Bradley vote	Bradley %	Winner
Iowa	24 Jan	47	9	Caucus/convention	1,269	63	698	35	Gore
New Hampshire	1 Feb	22	7	Primary	76,681	52	69,993	48	Gore
Am. Samoa	7 Mar	3	3	Caucus/convention	21	84	4	16	Gore
California	7 Mar	367	68	Primary	1,964,251	81	439,180	18	Gore
Connecticut	7 Mar	54	13	Primary	97,151	55	72,864	42	Gore
Georgia	7 Mar	77	15	Primary	239,015	84	46,215	16	Gore
Hawaii	7 Mar	22	11	Caucus/convention	1,089	80	237	17	Gore
Idaho	7 Mar	18	5	Caucus/convention	240	63	126	33	Gore
Maine	7 Mar	23	9	Primary	34,725	54	26,520	41	Gore
Maryland	7 Mar	68	25	Primary	334,405	67	141,445	29	Gore
Massachusetts	7 Mar	93	25	Primary	337,175	60	210,132	38	Gore
Minnesota	7 Mar	74	17	Caucus/convention	8,051	73	1,543	14	Gore
Missouri	7 Mar	75	17	Primary	171,528	65	89,094	34	Gore
New York	7 Mar	243	51	Primary	598,362	65	311,671	34	Gore
North Dakota	7 Mar	14	8	Caucus/convention	1,780	78	498	22	Gore
Ohio	7 Mar	146	24	Primary	717,389	73	241,298	25	Gore
Rhode Island	7 Mar	22	11	Primary	25,975	57	18,614	41	Gore
Vermont	7 Mar	15	7	Primary	26,719	55	21,561	44	Gore
Washington	7 Mar	75	19	Caucus/convention	148,335	68	68,550	32	Gore
South Carolina	9 Mar	43	9	Party-run primary	9,378	96	172	3	Gore
Colorado	10 Mar	51	10	Primary	63,280	72	20,663	23	Gore
Utah	10 Mar	24	5	Primary	51,302	81	12,106	19	Gore
Wyoming	10 Mar	13	5	Caucus/convention	223	85	13	5	Gore
Arizona	11 Mar	47	8	Party-run primary	55,508	78	14,198	20	Gore
Michigan	11 Mar	129	28	Party-run primary	15,583	83	3,117	16	Gore
Nevada	12 Mar	20	9	Caucus/convention	962	90	24	2	Gore
Florida	14 Mar	161	25	Primary	485,454	82	109,501	18	Gore

Louisiana	14 Mar	61	13	Primary	113,812	73	31,189	20	Gore
Mississippi	14 Mar	37	11	Primary	78,258	90	7,511	8	Gore
Oklahoma	14 Mar	45	8	Primary	92,654	69	34,305	25	Gore
Tennessee	14 Mar	68	13	Primary	196,438	92	11,216	5	Gore
Texas	14 Mar	194	37	Primary/caucus	626,107	80	130,232	17	Gore
Illinois	21 Mar	161	29	Primary	669,771	84	113,697	14	Gore
Alaska[1]	25 Mar	13	6	Caucus/convention	n.a.	n.a.	n.a.	n.a.	Gore
Puerto Rico[2]	26 Mar	51	8	Primary	n.a.	n.a.	n.a.	n.a.	Gore
Delaware	27 Mar	15	7	Caucus/convention	187	100	0	0	Gore
Virgin Islands	1 Apr	3	3	Caucus/convention	748	100	0	0	Gore
Kansas[2]	4 Apr	36	6	Caucus/convention	n.a.	n.a.	n.a.	n.a.	Gore
Pennsylvania	4 Apr	160	31	Primary	517,901	74	145,481	21	Gore
Wisconsin	4 Apr	77	15	Primary	327,436	89	32,324	9	Gore
Virginia[2]	15, 17 Apr	79	18	Caucus/convention	n.a.	n.a.	n.a.	n.a.	Gore
Washington D.C.	2 May	17	15	Primary	17,510	96	0	0	Gore
Indiana	2 May	72	16	Primary	221,040	75	64,262	22	Gore
North Carolina	2 May	86	17	Primary	377,825	79	102,417	21	Gore
Nebraska	9 May	26	6	Primary	72,251	70	27,514	27	Gore
West Virginia	9 May	30	12	Primary	175,337	72	44,894	18	Gore
Oregon	16 May	47	11	Primary	300,922	85	0	0	Gore
Arkansas	23 May	37	11	Primary	193,750	78	0	0	Gore
Kentucky	23 May	49	9	Primary	156,966	71	32,340	15	Gore
Alabama	6 Jun	54	9	Primary	214,541	77	0	0	Gore
Montana	6 Jun	17	7	Primary	68,420	78	0	0	Gore
New Jersey	6 Jun	105	19	Primary	351,701	95	0	0	Gore
New Mexico	6 Jun	26	9	Primary	98,715	75	27,204	21	Gore
South Dakota[3]	6 Jun	15	7	Primary				21	Gore

Notes:
1 Alaska did not compile the votes each candidate received; Gore received all but three unpledged delegates.
2 Virginia, Kansas and Puerto Rico did not compile total votes for each candidate, but all delegates were pledged to Gore.
3 South Dakota didn't have a primary.

Table 8.1b Primaries and caucuses, 2000: Republican presidential results

State	Date	Delegates	Method	Bush vote	Bush %	McCain vote	McCain %	Other vote	Other %	Winner
Iowa	24 Jan	25	Caucus/convention	35,889	41	4,089	5	47,533	54	Bush
New Hampshire	1 Feb	17	Primary	72,262	31	115,490	49	49,050	21	McCain
Delaware	8 Feb	12	Primary	15,102	51	7,547	25	6,995	24	Bush
Hawaii[1]	7–13 Feb	14	Caucus/convention							Bush
South Carolina	19 Feb	37	Primary	301,050	53	237,888	42	26,766	5	Bush
Arizona	22 Feb	30	Primary	106,626	36	179,610	60	11,500	4	McCain
Michigan	22 Feb	58	Primary	535,840	43	626,244	50	76,997	6	McCain
Puerto Rico	27 Feb	14	Primary	86,605	94	5,344	6	45	0	Bush
North Dakota	29 Feb	19	Caucus/convention	6,865	76	1,717	19	484	5	Bush
Virginia	29 Feb	56	Primary	350,185	53	290,779	44	22,424	3	Bush
Washington[2]	29 Feb	12	Primary	214,611	58	141,151	38	12,117	3	Bush
California	7 Mar	162	Primary	1,555,734	60	916,229	35	121,640	5	Bush
Connecticut	7 Mar	25	Primary	82,871	46	87,270	49	5,913	3	McCain
Georgia	7 Mar	54	Primary	431,201	67	179,439	28	33,819	5	Bush
Maine	7 Mar	14	Primary	47,669	53	41,379	43	2,929	3	Bush
Maryland	7 Mar	31	Primary	206,425	56	132,618	36	28,158	8	Bush
Massachusetts	7 Mar	37	Primary	158,208	32	320,617	65	14,014	3	McCain
Minnesota	7 Mar	34	Caucus/convention	11,460	63	3,175	17	3,635	20	Bush
Missouri	7 Mar	35	Primary	275,412	58	167,962	35	30,981	6	Bush
New York	7 Mar	101	Primary	355,958	51	306,443	43	41,676	6	Bush
Ohio	7 Mar	69	Primary	796,848	58	507,943	37	70,310	5	Bush
Rhode Island	7 Mar	14	Primary	12,867	36	21,429	61	1,064	3	McCain
Vermont	7 Mar	12	Primary	28,702	35	48,870	61	3,014	4	McCain
Washington[2]	7 Mar	25	Caucus/convention	2,218	80	407	15	105	5	Bush
Colorado	10 Mar	40	Primary	116,902	65	49,303	27	14,760	8	Bush
Utah	10 Mar	29	Primary	180,529	63	42,945	15	63,004	22	Bush
Wyoming	10 Mar	22	County conventions	732	78	110	12	97	10	Bush
Florida	14 Mar	80	Primary	524,769	74	141,625	20	44,433	6	Bush
Louisiana	14 Mar	28	Primary	85,639	83	9,169	9	7,725	8	Bush

State	Date	Type								
Mississippi	14 Mar	Primary	33	100,085	88	6,260	5	7,579	7	Bush
Oklahoma	14 Mar	Primary	38	98,781	79	12,973	11	13,055	10	Bush
Tennessee	14 Mar	Primary	37	188,094	77	36,097	15	19,270	8	Bush
Texas	14 Mar	Primary	124	1,013,886	88	82,979	7	45,178	4	Bush
Illinois	21 Mar	Primary	74	496,646	68	158,752	22	81,459	10	Bush
Nevada[3]	21 Mar	Caucus/convention	17							
Kansas[4]	4 Apr	Primary	35							Bush
Wisconsin	4 Apr	Primary	37	341,365	71	89,337	19	48,734	10	Bush
Pennsylvania	4 Apr	Primary	80	472,398	73	145,719	22	24,968	4	Bush
Washington DC	2 May	Primary	15	1,771	73	593	24	69	3	Bush
Indiana	2 May	Primary	55	330,095	81	76,569	19	0	0	Bush
North Carolina	2 May	Primary	62	252,031	80	34,813	11	28,506	9	Bush
Nebraska	9 May	Primary	30	142,544	78	27,690	15	11,866	7	Bush
West Virginia	9 May	Primary	18	81,740	79	13,410	13	7,697	8	Bush
Oregon	16 May	Primary	24	292,522	84	0	0	57,309	16	Bush
Alaska[5]	19 May	Caucus/convention	23							
Arkansas	23 May	Primary	24	35,579	80	0	0	8,814	20	Bush
Idaho	23 May	Primary	28	116,385	74	0	0	42,061	27	Bush
Kentucky	23 May	Primary	31	75,783	85	5,780	6	7,931	9	Bush
Alabama	6 Jun	Primary	44	171,077	84	0	0	23,394	16	Bush
Montana	6 Jun	Primary	23	88,194	78	0	0	20,822	22	Bush
New Jersey	6 Jun	Primary	54	358,951	90	0	0	39,601	10	Bush
New Mexico	6 Jun	Primary	21	62,161	83	71,619	10	4,850	6	Bush
South Dakota	6 Jun	Primary	22	35,418	78	6,228	14	3,663	8	Bush

Notes:

1 Hawaii did not hold a caucus, but its delegates were all pledged to Bush at a May convention.

2 Washington has a split system for allocating its convention delegates. Washington's 29 February primary allocated twelve convention delegates on a proportional basis for all candidates who received at least 20 per cent of the total vote. Washington's GOP caucuses on 7 March determined the remaining twenty-five delegates.

3 Nevada did not hold a caucus or pledge its delegates for the convention.

4 Kansas cancelled its primary, but a committee of the state's Republican Party passed a resolution calling for its delegates to nominate Bush.

5 Alaska held a caucus to select delegates, but they were not pledged to candidates.

Source: adapted from the *National Journal*, 12 August 2000.

The variables that shape the election result

The character of the ticket

Conventional wisdom suggested that a **balanced ticket** was required if electoral victory was to be assured. Traditionally, presidential candidates picked vice-presidential nominees – or 'running mates' – who were from other regions and had different backgrounds. Often an 'outsider' would be balanced against a Washington 'insider'. In 1960 the Democratic candidate, John F. Kennedy, selected Lyndon Johnson. Whereas Kennedy came from Massachusetts, Johnson was a native of Texas. Similarly, while Kennedy was a Roman Catholic, Johnson was a Protestant. In 1980 Ronald Reagan – the Republican candidate – picked George Bush. Reagan was a former governor of California while Bush had homes in both Texas and Maine. Reagan had deeply rooted conservative convictions while Bush's politics were characterised by greater pragmatism

There have, however, been some signs of a shift. The concept of the balanced ticket has been modified. Bill Clinton picked Al Gore as his running mate in 1992. Although Gore was an 'insider', while Clinton had little direct experience of Washington politics, both were relatively youthful, from southern states, and belonged to the moderate or centrist wing of the Democratic Party. In 2000 it seemed that the running mates were selected so as to compensate for problems that had arisen in 'selling' the public image of the presidential nominee. Senator Joseph Lieberman had been one of the few Democrats to criticise President Clinton's behaviour in his relationship with Monica Lewinsky. His selection as the vice-presidential candidate thereby distanced Gore from the scandals associated with the Clinton White House. George W. Bush, who was widely seen as inexperienced, particularly in terms of foreign

Table 8.2　*Selected presidential and vice-presidential nominees*

Year	Nominee		Home state	Characteristics
1960	Kennedy	(D)	Massachusetts	Roman Catholic
	Johnson		Texas	Protestant
1980	Reagan	(R)	California	Former film actor and state governor
	Bush		Maine and Texas	UN ambassador and CIA Director
1988	Dukakis	(D)	Massachusetts	State governor – liberal
	Bentsen		Texas	Senator – conservative
1992	Clinton	(D)	Arkansas	State governor
	Gore		Tennesse	Senator
2000	Bush	(R)	Texas	State governor
	Cheney		Wyoming	Congressman and Secretary of Defense
2000	Gore	(D)	Tennessee	Vice-president
	Lieberman		Connecticut	Senator – Jewish

affairs, picked Dick Cheney, a long-serving Washington politician who had been Secretary of Defense in the 1989–93 Bush administration.

The presidential election campaign traditionally began on Labor Day in early September. However, increasingly, the candidates begin their campaigning activities long before this. During the latter stages of the primary season the front runner in the **primaries** will turn his attention to the candidate who is to be nominated by the opposing party. As a consequence, the general election campaign has been elongated and now occupies much of the six-month period preceding election day at the beginning of November.

Attitudes and issues

American public opinion is divided and it would be a mistake to over-generalise. There are, for example, marked differences between the attitudes that can be found in cities such as New York and San Francisco and those held in some other cities and regions. Furthermore, majority opinion is not monolithic. Instead, as Table 8.3 illustrates, it is pulled between liberalism and conservatism.

Table 8.3   *The character of public opinion, 2000 (%)*

Proposal	%
The proportion of the US population favouring policy proposals associated with conservatism	
Mandatory teacher testing in public schools	95
Across-the-board tax cuts	78
National standardised tests for schools	75
Prayer in public schools amendment	69
Privatising part of Social Security	66
Ban on 'partial birth' abortions	63
Reducing government agencies	62
School vouchers	56
The proportion of the US population favouring policy proposals associated with liberalism	
Hate crime legislation	83
Raising the minimum wage	82
Licensing new handguns	72
Assault weapons ban	59
Re-establishing relations with Cuba	56
Opposing the overturn of *Roe v. Wade*	67

Source: adapted from the Gallup Organization, *Poll Releases: Issue referendum reveals mix of liberal and conservative views in America today*, 1 November 2000, www.gallup.com/poll/releases/pr001101.asp.

Table 8.4   *Issues (first and second responses) and the 2000 election (%)*

Issue	%	Issue	%
Medicare	42	Crime	11
Education	41	Defending civil rights	1
Social security	25	Environmental issues	1
Moral values	24	Gun control	1
Taxes	24	Don't know	1
The economy	22		

Source: adapted from the *Washington Post*, Kaiser Family Foundation and Harvard School of Public Health, *Issues 4 Study: Economics*, Media, International Communications Research, 2000, 5.

Nonetheless, despite the ambivalent character of popular attitudes, some broad conclusions can be drawn. At any point in time, certain issues will have a particular importance – or salience in the public mind. During the early 1990s unemployment and crime dominated the agenda. However, as the decade progressed, and both joblessness and rates of criminality fell, other concerns came to the fore. A series of studies, conducted as the 2000 election approached, by the *Washington Post*, the Kaiser Family Foundation and the Harvard School of Public Health examined contemporary opinion. Those interviewed were asked what issues would be the most important in determining their vote in the forthcoming election. The first and second responses of those interviewed in October 2000 are listed – as percentages combined together – in Table 8.4.

These issues draw voters towards one or other of the candidates. Each will have an image in the public mind constructed on the basis of campaign pledges, particular 'sound bites', and personal character.

- Fifty per cent of those who regarded taxation levels as the most important issue – and can be dubbed 'tax voters' – were attracted by the prospect of a large tax cut, a central plank in George W. Bush's election platform (*Washington Post* 2000a).
- A majority of those who saw the future of Medicare (health provision for the aged) as the most important issue were pulled towards Al Gore. Fifty-four per cent of these voters believed that Gore would handle Medicare in a better way than Bush (*Washington Post et al.* 2000).
- Among those who saw moral values as the most critical problem, a large proportion (68 per cent) were intending to vote for George W. Bush. A mere 16 per cent backed Gore. These 'values voters' were guided by the candidates' attitudes to abortion, the break-up of the family, media depictions of sex and violence, and the example a president sets through his own personal conduct (*Washington Post* 2000b).

The televised debates

A significant part of the presidential campaign is directed towards and structured around the televised debates between the principal candidates. The first was held in 1960. After a long gap they resumed in 1976 and have since become an established feature of the election process.

The debates are generally held in October, a few weeks before polling day. The format varies, but there have usually been two or three debates between the presidential candidates and one featuring the vice-presidential 'running mates'. With the single exception of Ross Perot in 1992, minor party candidates have been excluded. By the 1990s there was some flexibility in the structures that were adopted. Some of the debates involve a 'moderator' who asks questions and chairs proceedings. Others have a panel of questioners. There are also debates that involve questions and observations from a studio audience.

Do the televised debates make a difference? Although they attract considerable press comment and speculation, the viewing audience is declining. Table 8.5 shows the average audience ratings for all the debates that were held in a particular election year. The measurement is based upon the proportion of households watching the debates during an average minute.

However, despite the declining audience share evident in the figures, the presidential debates do play an important role.

- Some particularly sharp exchanges are widely remembered and played a part in shaping perceptions of public figures. In 1988 Lloyd Bentsen and Dan Quayle, the Democratic and Republican vice-presidential candidates respectively, took part in a televised debate. Following an attempt by the relatively youthful Quayle to compare himself – in terms of political experience – with President Kennedy, Bentsen, who had known Kennedy personally, sharply retorted, 'Senator, you're no Jack Kennedy.' The comment fuelled the belief that Quayle lacked maturity. In 1992 President George Bush looked at his watch a number of times during a debate before a studio audience with Bill Clinton and Ross Perot. This appeared to confirm claims that Bush was bored and detached from the concerns faced by ordinary citizens.
- A number of the debates appear to have changed opinion and thereby contributed to the election outcome. It has been said that the Nixon–Kennedy

Table 8.5   *Televised presidential and vice-presidential debates: the audience*

Year	Average audience rating (%)	Year	Average audience rating (%)
1960	59.3	1984	44.9
1976	47.3	1988	35.4
1980	58.9	1992	41.4
		1996	25.8

Source: adapted from H.W. Stanley and R.G. Niemi, *Vital Statistics on American Politics 1997–98*, Washington DC, Congressional Quarterly Press, 1998, 187.

Box 8.2
The Electoral College: Maine and Nebraska

In contrast with the forty-eight other states, Maine and Nebraska do not allocate their Electoral votes on a winner-takes-all basis. Instead, they can be split. Under state law, the at-large Electors are required to vote for the winner of the popular vote across the entire state. The other Electors vote for the candidate who has a majority in each of the congressional districts. If such as system was adopted on a nationwide basis, the votes cast in the Electoral College would more closely reflect the distribution of the popular vote. Furthermore, minor party candidates would have a greater opportunity to win Electoral College votes (Bennett 1990).

---

debate changed the result of the 1960 election. In contrast to those who listened on radio, those who watched on television perceived Nixon to be untrustworthy. However, the relationship between the debates and voting behaviour is not straightforward. The significance of the debates depends, in part, upon the expectations that the public has, and the media set, for the candidates. In the 2000 election the three debates were held between 3 and 17 October. George W. Bush was expected to be perform poorly. Conversely, Al Gore was felt to have a sophisticated grasp of policy matters. Both candidates were judged – to Bush's advantage – against this background. Gore's difficulties were compounded by the image that he conveyed to viewers. In the first debate he seemed overbearing. To compensate, he appeared withdrawn in the second of the debates. As Table 8.6 illustrates,

Table 8.6   *The October 2000 televised debates and the opinion polls (% support for each candidate)*

Dates	Gore/Lieberman (D)	Bush/Cheney (R)
1–3	49	41
2–4	51	40
3–5	45	44
4–6	41	48
9–11	45	44
14–16	44	47
16–18	39	49
17–19	40	50
18–20	40	51

Source: adapted from the Gallup Organisation, Poll Releases, 'Bush gains from debates as presidential campaign enters its final phrase', 23 October 2000, www.gallup.com/poll/releases/pr001023.asp.

the 2000 debates appear to have shifted opinion. They thereby contributed to Bush's narrow victory a few weeks afterwards.

Long-term variables

Voting takes place on the first Tuesday after the first Monday in November. Although issues, the character of the campaigns and the televised debates contribute to the outcome, the electorate are also influenced by long-term variables. Alongside other factors, income levels, region, race, ethnicity, and gender play a part in shaping voting decisions.

Income and voting   There is a clear relationship – or *correlation* – between income levels and voting. Although the Democrats have always, in contrast with the European social democratic parties, eschewed socialism or formal identification with class-based politics, the low-paid were an important component of the 'New Deal coalition' that the party constructed as its electoral base during the 1930s. In the 2000 election, for example, those with a family income under $15,000 backed Al Gore by a margin of twenty percentage points over George W. Bush. Correspondingly, as Table 8.7 illustrates, the Republicans draw disproportionate support from those in the higher income brackets. Two points should, however, be added.

- The figures shown in Table 8.7 should be approached with a degree of caution. Family income offers only a limited picture of living standards or the quality of life. The statistics do not reveal either the number of wage earners or of dependent children in the household.
- The impact of income levels upon voting behaviour should be seen within a context of race and gender. From the 1960s onwards, many blue-collar men – including union members in the labour-intensive industries – were drawn away from the Democrats. From their perspective the party had

Table 8.7   *The 2000 presidential election: income levels (% of the vote)*

Income level ($)	Gore	Bush
Under 15,000	57	37
15,000–29,999	54	41
30,000–49,999	49	48
Over 50,000	45	52
Over 75,000	44	53
Over 100,000	43	54

Source: adapted from the *New York Times*, 12 November 2000.

been 'hi-jacked' by the minorities and the advocates of cultural liberalism. Significant numbers voted Republican in presidential and some other elections. They identified, in particular, with the politics of the Reagan administration.

Region and voting   American elections have been marked by increasingly sharp geographical divisions. As Chapter 1 noted, these are derived from the contrasting cultural and economic character of the different regions.

- Many of the metropolitan regions, or 'metros', around the 'rim' of the US have a multi-ethnic character. Cities such as New York, Chicago, Seattle and Los Angeles and the surrounding counties have attracted large numbers of immigrants. Within the white population, a significant proportion are single, highly mobile, and have a college education. A number work in the high-tech sectors of the economy. Identity politics have a hold and there are visible gay communities such as the Castro in San Francisco and Greenwich Village in New York. These cities and the surrounding areas constitute Democratic strongholds. In 2000 states such as Illinois, New York and California, which incorporate multi-ethnic 'metros', voted for Gore by a wide margin. In New York state, for example, there was a 27 percentage point difference between the candidates.
- The hinterland – including the 'metros' that have not attracted a significant proportion of immigrants – has a markedly different character. It is overwhelmingly white or – in the south-eastern states – biracial. Indeed, some metropolitan areas, most notably Phoenix and Las Vegas, are attracting growing numbers of white migrants from other parts of the US. Communities in these regions appear to be more conservative, and lean disproportionately towards the Republicans.

Some observers suggest that population growth in the multi-ethnic 'metros' lays the basis for an 'emerging Democratic majority'. There have been prophecies that, despite the Bush victory in 2000 and the Republican hold over Congress during much of the 1990s, the party will soon be outnumbered by the Democrats' electoral coalition. Some Republicans have responded by calling on their party to broaden the basis of its appeal through 'outreach' efforts towards the minorities.

Race, ethnicity and voting   These regional cleavages are, as noted above, underpinned by racial and ethnic divisions. A majority of whites, particularly white men, are loyal to the Republicans. In contrast, disproportionate numbers from the minorities support the Democrats. In particular, from 1964 onwards, there has been a particularly close relationship between African-Americans and the Democrats. There are three principal reasons for this.

- The Democrats are identified with the civil rights movement and its achievements. A Democratic President, Lyndon Johnson, led calls for legislative reform during the mid-1960s. The 1964 Civil Rights Act brought segregation – a system in the southern states that confined African-Americans to separate and unequal public facilities – to an end. The 1965 Voting Rights Act allowed southern blacks to vote without fear of intimidation. In contrast, the Republicans' 1964 presidential candidate, Senator Barry Goldwater, opposed the Civil Rights Act and appeared to be seeking the votes of white southerners, many of whom opposed desegregation.
- Because the federal government played a pivotal role in compelling state and county officials to abandon segregation, it has, for blacks been an instrument of social justice. Whereas the Democrats are popularly identified associated with an activist federal government, the Republicans have sought to reduce its powers.
- Although they have many wealthy corporate backers, the Democrats are still popularly associated with those on the lower rungs of the socio-economic ladder. Despite some economic success stories, African-Americans still lag far behind whites in terms of *per capita* income (Chapter 1).

The Democrats have also a decisive, although less secure, hold within the Hispanic communities. This can be attributed both to their socio-economic

Table 8.8   *Voting: race and ethnicity in presidential elections (% of the vote)*

Year	Party	White	Black	Hispanic	Asian
1976	Democrat	47	83	76	
	Republican	52	16	24	
1980	Democrat	36	85	56	
	Republican	55	11	35	
	(John Anderson)	7	3	6	
1984	Democrat	35	89	61	
	Republican	64	9	37	
1988	Democrat	40	86	69	
	Republican	59	12	30	
1992	Democrat	39	83	61	31
	Republican	40	10	25	55
	(Ross Perot)	20	7	14	15
1996	Democrat	43	84	72	43
	Republican	46	12	21	48
	(Ross Perot)	9	4	6	8
2000	Democrat	42	90	67	54
	Republican	54	8	31	41
	(Ralph Nader)	3	1	2	4

Source: adapted from the *New York Times*, 12 November 2000.

position and to the Republicans' association with campaigns – particularly around language and immigration – that are popularly regarded as anti-Hispanic. Furthermore, in the 2000 election a majority of Asian-Americans backed the Democratic presidential candidate for the first time. Why has there been a shift in allegiance? Firstly, immigration has led to demographic changes in the character of the Asian communities. Secondly, their opponents had some success in portraying the Republicans as 'anti-Asian', particularly following their opposition to the nomination of Bill Lann Lee as Assistant Attorney General for Civil Rights in 1997.

Gender and voting   Many political observers emphasise the significance of the 'gender gap' in American elections. White men are disproportionately likely to support the Republican Party. In contrast, most women back the Democrats. The gap is evident across almost the racial and socio-economic groupings. It is, however, most clearly evident if the white population alone is considered. In the 2000 election only 36 per cent of white men voted for Al Gore. In contrast, he was supported by 48 per cent of white women.

The gender gap is a relatively recent development. In the 1950s and 1960s women leant towards the Republicans. However, despite some fluctuations, it grew particularly during the Reagan years. Indeed, its scale led some observers to talk of a gender 'canyon'. How should the gap be explained?

Table 8.9   *Voting and gender in presidential elections (% of the vote)*

Year	Party	Men	Women
1976	Democrat	50	50
	Republican	48	48
1980	Democrat	36	45
	Republican	55	47
	(John Anderson)	7	7
1984	Democrat	37	44
	Republican	62	56
1988	Democrat	41	49
	Republican	57	50
1992	Democrat	41	45
	Republican	38	37
	(Ross Perot)	10	7
1996	Democrat	43	54
	Republican	44	38
	(Ross Perot)	10	7
2000	Democrat	42	54
	Republican	53	43
	(Ralph Nader)	3	2

Source: adapted from the *New York Times*, 12 November 2000.

- William Schneider has argued that the principal parties' election campaigns are 'gender-coded'. The Republicans use tough, forceful words about punishment, work and discipline. These correspond to male values and perceptions. In contrast, although Democratic campaign commercials are structured around many of the same issues, they emphasise the importance of prevention and protection. Themes such as these have greater appeal for women (Schneider 1996).
- Feminist organisations such as the National Organization for Women (NOW) have argued that the Republican Party has lost support among women because the party platform and many of its candidates oppose abortion and lesbian rights. However, polling evidence suggests that there are only limited differences in opinion between men and women on these issues.
- Men and women have different attitudes to the role of government. Many women see a role for government in the provision of education and health. In contrast, men are disproportionately more likely to emphasise the need for minimal government. Whereas the Democrats are popularly associated with government programmes, the Republicans are identified with *laissez-faire* notions of government. The Democrats' claims that Republicans would reduce Medicare provision for the elderly appear to have had a particular resonance among women.
- Women are more likely than men to be working in low-paid forms of employment. Gender and socio-economic status are thereby intertwined. As noted above, blue-collar workers are disproportionately drawn to the Democratic Party.
- Some observers suggest that it is a mistake to focus on women's attitudes and voting patterns. They argue that there has been a more significant shift among men. Men, particularly whites, abandoned the Democrats in large numbers from the 1960s onwards. They resented many of the social changes of the 1960s and 1970s and supported conservative policies towards crime, race, and those on welfare.

Nevertheless, despite the attention it has attracted, the scale of the gender gap should be placed in perspective. Firstly, some other divisions and cleavages are larger than the gender gap. The importance of socio-economic, regional and racial differences has already been noted. Secondly, although the gap grew during the Reagan years, and is sometimes attributed to the conservative character of his politics, more women voted for Reagan in both 1980 and 1984 than for his Democratic opponents.

Financing presidential elections

Until the mid-1970s presidential campaigns raised funding for both the nominating process and the general election through donations, large and small, from the candidates' supporters. However, following the Watergate scandal and revelations that the Nixon campaign in 1972 had received large-scale financial contributions from individuals and organisations seeking to influence the administration, Congress passed a radical reform of campaign finance legislation in 1974. Although parts of this law were deemed unconstitutional by the US Supreme Court in the case of *Buckley v. Valeo* in 1976 and amendments were subsequently made, the 1974 legislation has continued to provide the main statutory framework for election funding, although its effectiveness was severely undermined by developments in the 1990s.

Box 8.3
The 1976 presidential election

Jimmy Carter (D) 297 (50 per cent)
Gerald Ford 240 (47.9 per cent)

This was the first post-Watergate election and the first in which the new system of public funding was available to candidates. Gerald Ford had become the first non-elected vice-president under the Twenty-fifth Amendment in 1973 and then took over as president when Nixon resigned over Watergate in August 1974. His pardon of Nixon meant that the former president could not be prosecuted for any offences committed during his tenure in the White House and was criticised by much of the media and the public.

The Republican nomination   Having not been elected to the office, Ford's position as incumbent president was weaker than most. He was defeated in a number of primaries by former California governor Ronald Reagan and had only a small majority of delegates at the Kansas City convention.

The Democratic nomination   This was the first election in which the caucuses in Iowa, held before the New Hampshire primary, came to public attention. An unknown governor from Georgia, Jimmy Carter, had worked hard in the state to gain activist support and went on to gain momentum during the spring primaries, emerging as the victor from a large Democratic field.

The election campaign   Ford's slogan was 'He's making us proud again', arguing that he was returning public trust to the presidency after the scandals of the Nixon era. Carter was the first of several candidates in the post-Watergate climate of greater public cynicism to run as an outsider who was untainted by Washington politics. He promised never to lie to the American people. Ford made a major blunder in a televised debate when he claimed that Eastern Europe was not under the control of the Soviet Union, but the Watergate effect and a sluggish economy were probably the key factors in his defeat. In the popular vote Carter had a plurality of 1.7 million votes out of almost 82 million cast. As a moderate southerner Carter was able to win all the southern states as well as most of the north-east, while Ford won all the west, some Midwestern and a few north-eastern states.

The legislation attempted to restrict the influence of wealthy individuals by limiting donations to $1,000 per election and donations by political action committees to $5,000 per election. These figures have not been raised since 1974 and now are worth only a third of what they were at that time. The law also introduced a substantial element of public financing into presidential elections. This is provided by means of a fund to which taxpayers can voluntarily contribute when they complete their income tax forms. Public funding comes in three ways.

- For the nomination process within the parties, candidates who are successful in raising privately donated funds on a sufficiently broad basis and in small amounts are entitled to claim matching federal money to help finance their campaigns. If they accept the public money in this way candidates are obliged to keep their spending within a 'voluntary' limit as well as accept limits on what they can spend in individual states.
- The political parties receive money to pay for their national nominating conventions.
- The two main parties' candidates receive funding for their general election campaigns, and by accepting this money they agree to abide by official spending limits. Candidates of other parties, such as the Reform Party in 1996 and 2000, receive public funding based on their share of the vote in the last election as long as they received 5 per cent or more.

The *Buckley* decision allows wealthy individuals who are seeking the presidency to spend their own money without limit, based on their rights under the First Amendment. In 1992 Ross Perot financed his independent bid with $65 million of his own resources, and in 1996 and 2000 Steve Forbes used his private fortune to fund his unsuccessful campaigns for the Republican nomination. However, the amounts of public funding available were sufficient for other major candidates from both parties to take the money from 1976 until 2000.

New ground was broken in the 2000 campaign when Texas governor George W. Bush announced that he would not accept federal funding for his nomination campaign. The trend towards 'front loading' in the primary season has meant that candidates have to raise considerable sums of money in the year before the election in order to have any realistic chance of success. Bush had seen that in 1996 Robert Dole, faced by the challenge of Steve Forbes, who was operating without financial constraints, had been adversely affected by the need to spend large amounts of money in the early primaries as well as by the federal spending limits. Although Dole beat Forbes, he was drained financially and his campaign essentially fell silent for several vital months in the spring and summer until he was officially nominated as the Republican candidate at the convention and was entitled to public funding for the general election. This gave President Clinton, who was unopposed in the Democratic primaries, a major advantage in the pre-convention period.

Box 8.4
The 1980 presidential election

Ronald Reagan (R) 489 (51 per cent)
Jimmy Carter (D) 49 (41 per cent)

Jimmy Carter's term of office took place against the backdrop of an inhospitable political environment for the president. Congress was reasserting its powers *vis-à-vis* the executive, unemployment and inflation troubled the economy, queues outside petrol stations attested to an energy crisis, and foreign policy failures, including the fall of Angola and Afghanistan to pro-communist forces, gave the impression of a weak president unable to control events. The seizure of hostages at the US embassy in Tehran by Iranian Islamic militants, an unsuccessful attempt to rescue them and relentless media coverage of their plight were constant reminders to the public in election year of Carter's failings. By July 1980 only 21 per cent approved of Carter's performance in office, the lowest ever recorded by Gallup.

The Democratic nomination   Carter's general unpopularity and the criticisms by liberal Democrats that he had betrayed the New Deal traditions of his party left him vulnerable to challenge. Senator Edward Kennedy duly carried the banner for the liberal wing and won ten primaries to Carter's twenty-four, but the internal battle continued to the convention and was very damaging to the president.

The Republican nomination   Eight candidates entered the early primaries, including well known names such as Howard Baker and Robert Dole, who had been Ford's vice-presidential running mate in 1976. By April only two men were left in the race: Ronald Reagan and George Bush, with Reagan tying up the nomination in May. A liberal Republican, John Anderson, dropped out of the party's race and ran as an independent candidate in the general election, winning 7 per cent of the popular vote. Reagan, having considered former president Ford as his running mate at the Detroit convention, invited his main rival, George Bush, on to the ticket in a successful attempt to unify the party.

The election campaign   Reagan exploited public dissatisfaction with Carter and promised to 'make America great again'. He posed the question in a television debate to the American people: 'Ask yourself whether you are better or worse off than you were four years ago.' The Democrats tried to paint Reagan as a dangerous right-wing extremist but his affable performances in the televised debates reassured many viewers who might have been worried. On election day Reagan's lead was ten points in the popular vote and he won all but a small handful of states which included Carter's and Vice-President Mondale's home states.

Box 8.5
The 1984 presidential election

Ronald Reagan (R) 525 (59 per cent)
Walter Mondale (D) 13 (41 per cent)

President Reagan ran for re-election against the background of a booming economy, renewed public confidence in the nation's future and high presidential approval ratings. The tax cuts and increased defence spending which Reagan had promised in 1980 had been delivered and, following a recovery from the recession of 1982, the president was always likely to win a second term.

The Republican nomination Reagan was, not surprisingly, unchallenged.

The Democratic nomination In contrast the Democratic nomination was hard fought, with nine contenders, although only three (former Vice-President Walter Mondale, Senator Gary Hart and the Reverend Jesse Jackson) made any impact. Mondale, as a traditional New Deal liberal, was challenged from the neo-liberal/moderate wing by Hart and from the left by Jackson, who argued for the building of a 'rainbow coalition' of the poor and minorities in society. Mondale was the favourite of the party establishment but he had only a small lead over Hart in the popular votes cast (38.6 per cent to 36.2 per cent) and Hart actually won more primaries (sixteen to eleven, with Jackson winning in two states). In an attempt to bring some much-needed excitement and interest to his campaign, Mondale named Representative Geraldine Ferraro as his running mate, the first woman to appear on a major party's presidential ticket.

The election campaign Reagan's lead in the opinion polls was never threatened. After a stumbling performance in the first television debate the 'age issue' was briefly raised (he was seventy-three), but the president performed better in the second debate and defused the issue with humour, claiming that he would not exploit for political gain his opponent's relative youth and inexperience. Reagan's landslide victory left Mondale with only the Electoral College votes of his home state of Minnesota and Washington DC.

Bush's record-breaking fund-raising achievements enabled him not only to tie up the Republican nomination very early but also to sustain a full-fledged campaign through until the national party convention in July. Bush raised $93.7 million by May 2000, of which almost $86 million came from individual donors contributing $1,000 or less. He spent more than $83 million in the

Box 8.6
The 1988 presidential election

George Bush (R) 426 (53.4 per cent)
Michael Dukakis (D) 112 (45.7 per cent)

With President Reagan leaving office after two terms, both parties needed to select new candidates. An important development in the nomination process was the introduction of 'Super Tuesday' when sixteen states, mostly in the south, agreed to hold their primaries on the same day in early March. Southern Democrats hoped that by doing so they would strengthen their influence within the party.

The Republican nomination George Bush, as Reagan's loyal deputy for eight years, was always the favourite to win the nomination but as a moderate conservative he faced opposition from five other candidates, including Robert Dole, the former Secretary of State Al Haig, Congressman Jack Kemp and evangelist Pat Robertson. Bush won thirty-seven primaries to Dole's one and gained 68 per cent of the popular votes cast. Bush made a controversial choice of running mate in the largely unknown senator Dan Quayle, who was regarded by many as a lightweight candidate.

The Democratic nomination The early favourite was Gary Hart, who had come so close to upsetting Mondale in 1984. However, revelations of an extra-marital affair wrecked Hart's campaign and he withdrew from the race, only to attempt a come-back later, with minimal effect. Governor Michael Dukakis of Massachusetts emerged victorious, winning twenty-two primaries compared with Jesse Jackson's seven, Al Gore's five, Richard Gephardt's two and Paul Simon's one. However, Dukakis won only 42.4 per cent of the popular vote and Jackson, who gained 29 per cent, continued his fight right up to the convention.

The election campaign Dukakis established a large lead in the polls after the Democratic convention in Atlanta but failed to consolidate this advantage. Bush was seeking to inherit Reagan's popularity and he pointed to his experience as vice-president. His campaign constantly attacked Dukakis for being a liberal and criticised his record as governor, particularly on law and order. A pro-Bush group independently ran a commercial featuring a black murderer named Willie Horton who had been released early from prison in Massachusetts and had gone on to commit further crimes, and this was especially damaging to Dukakis. Following the second television debate Bush opened up a twelve-point lead. Late in the campaign Dukakis accepted the 'liberal' nomenclature and, by energising his party's grassroots support, closed the gap but never seemed likely to overtake Bush. In the event he took only ten states scattered around the Pacific northwest, Midwest and north-east, in addition to Washington DC.

same period, compared with Dole's $46 million in 1996. This level of funding was a major reason why a number of other hopefuls dropped out even before the first primaries. Elizabeth Dole, for example, retired from the race in October 1999, having raised only $5 million and finding herself unable to compete effectively with Bush. This process of narrowing the field of candidates based on fund-raising ability is the most important feature of 'the invisible primary'.

The other significant feature of recent presidential election campaigns has been the increasing importance of 'soft money'. This is money which is contributed by individuals or organisations such as business corporations or trade unions to political party committees and is not affected by the donation limits set for 'hard money' contributions by the 1974 legislation (Table 8.10). In 1979 Congress passed an Act allowing the parties to raise money for 'party-building' activities, such as registration drives and voter mobilisation efforts as well as generic party advertising. Since 1980 the parties have used some of this money to complement their publicly financed presidential campaigns and, in effect, to bypass the official spending limits. The process passed almost unnoticed until the 1990s, when the parties extended their efforts to raise soft money, the scale of spending increased dramatically and the funding was used more directly to support both presidential and congressional campaigns, particularly through television advertising. In the 1995–96 election cycle the Republicans spent $141 million and the Democrats $122 million in soft money, three times what they had spent in 1991–92. In 1999–2000 soft money expenditure by national party committees almost doubled again to $487 million, with the Republicans and Democrats each spending approximately half that sum. As Table 8.10 shows, in 1992 soft money made up

---

Box 8.7
The 1992 presidential election

*Bill Clinton (D) 370 (43.2 per cent)   George Bush (R) 168 (37.7 per cent)
Ross Perot 0 (19 per cent)*

In February 1991, following victory in the Gulf War, President George Bush's approval ratings were at unprecedented levels and he appeared to be sure of re-election in 1992. However, in the autumn, when hopes of recovery from recession began to fade, the president's support dropped noticeably. This new emphasis on the economy and the declining significance of foreign policy as an issue after the collapse of the Soviet Union left Bush vulnerable in 1992.

The Republican nomination   Bush was challenged by the right-winger Patrick Buchanan, who attacked the president for breaking his 1988 promise 'Read my lips: no new taxes' when he reached a budget deal with congressional Democrats in 1990. Buchanan exploited public anger at the impact of the recession, winning 37 per cent of the New Hampshire primary vote. While Bush won 73 per cent of the total primary votes cast and had 98 per cent of the delegates at the convention, Buchanan's challenge proved to be very damaging to the president. In addition, the Houston convention was a public relations disaster, with Buchanan helping to project the image of a strident and narrow party which was obsessed with divisive issues such as abortion.

The Democratic nomination When Bush had the aura of invincibility many leading Democrats were deterred from seeking the presidency in 1992. Therefore the field of candidates in the primaries was really the party's second division. Former Senator Paul Tsongas won the New Hampshire contest and a few other primaries before running out of money and energy, and he withdrew after Super Tuesday. Arkansas Governor Bill Clinton, running as a centrist 'new kind of Democrat', emerged from Super Tuesday ahead of the pack, winning in the Midwest as well as the south, having denied on television allegations that he had had a long-term extra-marital affair. Jerry Brown, the former California governor and now on the radical wing of the party, continued his campaign until the convention, gaining 20 per cent of the primary vote, compared with Clinton's 52 per cent. Clinton chose Al Gore, a well respected and experienced senator from Tennessee, as his running mate.

The election campaign Dissatisfaction among the public with the two major party candidates provide the opportunity for Ross Perot to run as an independent and to emerge as a significant force in the election. Perot financed his campaign with his private fortune and, in securing almost a fifth of the votes, prevented Clinton, the eventual winner, from claiming any popular majority mandate. Perot's constant attacks on the vast federal budget deficit harmed Bush and, unusually for an independent candidate, he was allowed to participate in the television debates because of his relatively high opinion poll ratings.

Clinton enjoyed a 15 per cent poll lead after the Democratic convention and, although this was reduced by almost two-thirds on election day, the Democrat was always ahead. The Democratic campaign was based on the notion that, in the words of one of Clinton's advisers, 'It's the economy, stupid.' Bush, on the other hand, emphasised the issues of trust and character, questioning Clinton's fitness for the presidential office. Clinton's victory included winning California and a number of western and Midwestern states which had voted for Reagan and Bush in the 1980s. Bush managed to win most, but not all, of the south despite the presence of two southerners on the Democratic ticket.

Table 8.10   *Party committees and fund raising, 1991–92 to 1999–2000*
($ million)

Party	1991–92	1993–94	1995–96	1997–98	1999–2000
Democrats					
Hard money	155.5	121.1	210.0	153.4	269.9
Soft money	36.3	49.1	122.3	91.5	243.1
Republicans					
Hard money	266.3	223.7	407.5	273.6	447.4
Soft money	49.8	52.5	141.2	131.0	244.4
Total	507.9	446.4	881.0	649.5	1,204.8

Source: *Congressional Quarterly Weekly*, 10 March 2001, 525.

Box 8.8
The 1996 presidential election

Bill Clinton (D) 379 (49 per cent)   Bob Dole (R) 159 (41 per cent)
Ross Perot (Reform) 0 (8 per cent)

Having won in 1992 as a 'new Democrat', Clinton appeared to move to the left in his first two years in office, working with liberal Democrats in Congress. After the disastrous 1994 mid-term elections, when the Republicans won control of both houses of Congress, Clinton moved back to the centre – his 'triangulation' strategy – positioning himself on issues between the conservative Republican majority and the liberal-dominated Democratic caucus in Congress. Clinton won the public relations battle with the 'extremist' Republican Congress during conflicts over the budget in 1995 when he portrayed himself as the defender of public services against the threat of savage spending cuts. Clinton's poll ratings improved considerably and by the time of the 1996 election campaign he was in a strong position, despite continuing scandals and question marks over his character,

The Democratic nomination   Clinton won renomination without a challenge.

The Republican nomination   There was an initial field of nine candidates, although only five could be said to be serious contenders (Dole, Buchanan, Senator Phil Gramm, former governor Lamar Alexander and the wealthy publisher Steve Forbes). Dole suffered some early setbacks, with defeats by Buchanan and Forbes but, with the party hierarchy rallying to his cause and worrying about the harm which would be done to the party if Buchanan had any further successes, Dole won the vital South Carolina primary on 2 March and swept to victory in the other contests that month to secure the nomination. Overall, Dole won 59 per cent of the primary votes, with 21 per cent going to Buchanan and 10 per cent to Forbes.

The election campaign   A feeling of inevitability about Clinton's re-election grew as every poll carried out showed him well in the lead. Clinton's move to the centre politically left Dole with little scope for attack and Dole himself was hurt by his association, as Senate Majority Leader until May 1996, with the Republican Congress and Newt Gingrich. Dole's age and unexciting television manner did not help his chances either, although frantic campaigning in the final days by the Republican candidate helped mobilise the party's supporters and prevented a Clinton landslide. It also probably secured vital votes that enabled the Republicans to retain control of Congress. Dole won nineteen states, mostly in the south and sparsely populated areas in the Midwest and west. Ross Perot ran in this election as the candidate of the Reform Party that he had created, but his support dropped to 8 per cent and he was a far less significant factor than in 1992.

17 per cent of the parties' total funds; in 2000 it accounted for approximately 40 per cent of their overall financial resources. As the table also demonstrates, while the parties have been able to raise similar amounts in these unlimited donations, the Republicans have a significant advantage in hard money as a result of their greater number of affluent individual contributors.

Critics have argued that competition in presidential election campaigns is now, in financial terms, similar to an arms race without an arms control treaty. The use of soft money for purposes it was not intended for and the failure of the Federal Election Commission, the body set up in 1974 to oversee election spending, to punish and fine the parties in 1996 for the most blatant abuse of the rules have meant that the post-Watergate regulatory structure has been shattered. Senator John McCain of Arizona, a Republican candidate for the presidency in 2000, has been the co-sponsor of a Bill which would ban the parties from raising soft money but the proposal was blocked on several occasions in the Senate during the late 1990s. Although it did pass in the spring of 2001 the House of Representatives failed to act on a similar measure.

Electoral turnout

The level of turnout in American elections has attracted considerable comment. In 1996 less than half the voting-age population (49.08 per cent) cast a vote. Turnout in mid-term elections – half-way through a presidential term when Congress alone faces the electorate – is even lower. As Table 8.11 shows, only about a third of the adult population cast a vote in the 1998 elections.

Box 8.9
The 2000 presidential election

George W. Bush (R) 271 (47.9 per cent)
Al Gore (D) 266 (48.4 per cent)

With President Clinton standing down after two terms, both parties had to find new candidates. The successful economy, with strong growth and budget surpluses, provided a background to the campaign which could be expected to favour the incumbent's party but Clinton's impeachment and the Lewinsky scandal meant that too close association with the president could harm the Democratic candidate.

The Democratic nomination   Clinton's loyal vice-president, Al Gore, was always seen as the favourite to inherit the mantle and head the Democratic ticket. Gore was seen as a hard-working and competent successor but without Clinton's charisma and appeal to the party faithful. He was challenged by former senator Bill Bradley, who came close to upsetting the vice-president in the New Hampshire primary when he won 48 per cent of the vote. However, after the revelation that he was suffering from a heart problem Bradley's campaign faltered and eventually petered out. In order to counter the Bradley threat Gore had espoused more liberal and populist positions, and this approach was exemplified by his acceptance speech at the Los Angeles convention. Gore nominated Senator Joseph Lieberman, an orthodox Jew, as his running mate; Lieberman had been critical of Clinton's behaviour during the Lewinsky affair and the choice was seen as a way of Gore distancing himself from the president.

The Republican nomination   The governor of Texas and son of the former president, George W. Bush became the favourite to win the party's nomination, as he had the benefits of name recognition and huge fund-raising ability. A number of potential candidates dropped out as they realised they could not mount effective challenges to Bush. This left Steve Forbes, who again was prepared to spend his own money in pursuit of the nomination but who again failed to make an impact, and Senator John McCain. McCain had established a reputation as a reformer and he surprised many observers with strong showings in the early primaries, particularly in those states where the rules allowed Democrat and independent voters to participate in the Republican contest. In total he won seven primaries, including New Hampshire, but withdrew after Super Tuesday on 7 March when Bush took all the big states and McCain won only in New England. Bush selected the experienced former Defense Secretary, Dick Cheney, to be the vice-presidential candidate.

The election campaign   Bush had a strong lead after the Republican convention in Philadelphia but Gore closed the gap after his nomination. Thereafter the race was very close up to election day, with the poll lead changing several times. Gore emphasised his experience and the successful economy but confined Clinton to targeted campaigning in black areas where it was hoped he could mobilise African-American voters. Bush stressed that he was a 'compassionate conservative' and a unifier and that he would bring back integrity to the White House. The televised debates helped Bush to counter criticisms that he was unprepared and insufficiently serious to be president.

On election night the closeness of the race was confirmed as both the popular vote and the Electoral College vote resulted in virtual dead heats. The outcome was determined by the result in Florida, as both candidates required its twenty-five electoral votes to obtain the 270 overall majority required to win the presidency. After thirty-six days of legal challenges and confusion over disputed ballots in Florida, a momentous decision by the US Supreme Court stopped recounts in the state and forced Gore to concede defeat. He became the first candidate since 1888 to win the popular vote, albeit by a narrow margin of around 540,000 votes, and lose in the Electoral College.

Table 8.11   *Electoral turnout (% of the voting-age population)*

Year	%	Year	%
1960	62.8	1982	40.09
1962	47.57	1984	53.1
1964	61.9	1986	36.42
1966	48.61	1988	50.2
1968	60.9	1990	36.53
1970	46.78	1992	55.2
1972	55.2	1994	38.79
1974	38.78	1996	49.1
1976	53.6	1998	36.1
1978	37.77	2000	51.2
1980	52.8		

Source: adapted from Committee for the Study of the American Electorate, *Turnout dips to 56 Year Low*, www.gspm.org/csae/cgans4.html.

The level of turnout in the US is amongst the lowest of the Western democracies. Furthermore, from the 1960s onwards observers expected American turnout – as a proportion of the voting age population – to increase rather than fall. There were two principal reasons for this.

- Until the passage of the 1965 Voting Rights Act and the Twenty-fourth Amendment (which prohibited the use of poll taxes to exclude individuals from voting), many African-Americans and some low-income whites living in the southern states were denied the right to vote. Overall turnout – measured as a proportion of the voting-age population – was therefore lower in the south than in other regions. In 1960, for example, just 42.9 per cent of southerners voted. The corresponding figure for the other regions was 69.8 per cent (Teixeira 1992: 6).
- Americans are now educated to a higher level than in earlier years. Whereas, in 1960, only 22 per cent of the population had more than twelve years of education, the figure had risen to 42.3 per cent by 1988. An unprecedented number now have college degrees. At the same time, the proportion of the population to be found in the higher socio-economic groupings has swelled. All else being equal, shifts such as these would be expected to increase electoral turnout.

Why, then, are the turnout figures so low?

- The statistics require close examination. Turnout is not quite as low as it initially appears. It is calculated as a proportion of the total number of eligible adults across the country. However, because the census does not record who is and who is not a citizen, there is no accurate or official count of the number of citizens. Non-citizens are counted as if they were entitled to vote. Furthermore, felons and those who have served sentences of imprisonment are barred from voting in a number of states. Many states also impose residence requirements. An individual must have lived in the state for a specified period of time before being allowed to cast a vote there. Ruy Teixeira suggests that, if the turnout in the 1988 election is recalculated taking these factors into account, the turnout was 54.3 per cent rather than 50.2 per cent. This is still, however, low compared with other nations.
- The electoral system places the burden of responsibility for registration on the individual citizen, making the registration process more difficult in the US than in many other countries. As Teixeira notes:

> This system, based on registration through voluntary, individual initiative, makes it exceptionally difficult by international standards for US citizens to qualify to vote. In most other countries registration is automatic, performed by the state without any individual initiative. (Teixeira 1992: 13–14)

Some initiatives have been launched, although they have not halted the long-term decline in turnout. (1) Application forms – allowing a citizen to register to vote – are now usually available in public libraries, post offices, high schools, and unemployment offices. (2) Some companies, voluntary organisations and pressure groups have encouraged registration. MTV established the Rock the Vote campaign, aimed at young people. As the 1996 elections approached, the Christian Coalition promised 'the most ambitious, aggressive and expensive get-out-the-vote effort in our history'. (3) The 1993 National Voter Registration Act (the 'motor-voter law') allowed citizens to register to vote when applying for a driving licence or other forms of official documentation. Six states, however, allow same-day voter registration: Idaho, Maine, New Hampshire, Minnesota, Wisconsin and Wyoming (Federal Election Commission, 2001). Significantly, they have higher levels of turnout than others. The majority of states require at least twenty to thirty days to elapse between registration and voting. Such a measure, they argue, is required to prevent fraud.

• The numbers sentenced to serve periods of imprisonment increased significantly during the 1990s. Many of these individuals – who were disproportionately African-American – lost the right to vote on either a temporary or a permanent basis. A study by the Sentencing Project estimates that 15 per cent of black men are disenfranchised (Flanigan and Zingale 1998: 31).

• Some suggest that party decline has played a role in reducing turnout. Party activists traditionally mobilised the electorate through meetings and neighbourhood campaigning. Those who assert that the parties have abandoned their campaigning function regard declining turnout as an inevitable consequence.

• There has been a loss of political efficacy (Table 8.12). This is the belief that elected officials will listen to, care about, and respond to the concerns of individuals. A decline suggests that people are feeling increasingly powerless. This may lead them to regard voting as purposeless.

• Many elections have, to use Angus Campbell's description, a low-stimulus character. Mid-term elections – held in the off-year between presidential elections – stimulate less interest than those where the occupancy of the White House is at stake. Primaries and local elections attract even lower levels of interest. The extent of the stimulus offered by a particular election appears

Table 8.12   *Political efficacy: people don't have a say in what the government does, 1960–96 (%)*

Year	Agree	Year	Agree
1960	27	1980	39
1964	29	1984	32
1968	41	1988	41
1972	40	1992	36
1976	41	1996	53

Source: National Election Studies, *The NES Guide to Public Opinion and Electoral Behavior: People Don't Have a Say in What the Government Does 1952–98*, www.umich.edu/~nes/nesguide/toptable/tab5b_2.htm.

to depend on the degree of coverage by the media, the significance of the office in the eyes of voters, the importance of the issues raised in the campaign, and the attractiveness of the candidates. In 1988, for example, both the principal candidates, Michael Dukakis and George Bush, were widely seen as being unattractive. This may, at least in part, explain the very low turnout.

- The competitiveness of the contest may also play a role. Many elections are uncompetitive. The incumbent or the candidate nominated by a particular party is widely regarded – ahead of the election – as a certain winner. Voting therefore appears to serve little purpose. The southern states were for many years – until the 1960s – solidly associated with the Democratic Party. The Republicans offered only token opposition or, sometimes, none at all. More recently it has appeared almost impossible to unseat incumbent congressional candidates. Even in November 1994, when the 'Republican revolution' swept the Democratic Party from power in both houses, 92.3 per cent of the Senate and 90.2 per cent of House members were re-elected.

There is some evidence to suggest that a highly competitive race will increase turnout. There was a 2 per cent rise in turnout between 1996 and 2000. The increase may, in part, be attributable to the closeness of the contest between Al Gore and George W. Bush. However, the 1968, 1976, 1980 and 1988 contests were also relatively close but it did little to raise turnout levels. Furthermore, there was an increase – bucking the long-term trend – in 1984, when Ronald Reagan was assured of re-election.

- The Twenty-sixth Amendment – which was adopted in 1971 – extended the right to vote to all those aged eighteen or over. Those in the youngest age cohorts have relatively little interest in the political process and have particularly low turnout rates. In 1988, for example, just 32.2 per cent cast a vote, compared with 81.6 per cent among those in the sixty-five to seventy-four age bracket (Teixeira 1992: 74). However, this does not explain the extent of the change, as the decline in turnout is evident across all age groups.

- There has been, according to some observers, a decline in 'social connectedness'. In a celebrated, although controversial, study Robert Putnam argues that Americans have become more isolated from each other. There is less participation in both formal and informal groupings. Long-established organisations, such as the trade unions, have lost large numbers of members. Institutions such as neighbourhood bars and restaurants, traditionally the basis of social networks, have been displaced by fast-food outlets. Within the family, individuals are also more alone. For example, the proportion of families eating dinner together fell between the 1970s and the 1990s (Putnam 2000: 101).

From this perspective the decline in electoral turnout is one aspect of a broader picture. It should be placed alongside a fall in other forms of political participation – such as involvement in a party or civic organisation – and the general weakening of social bonds described by Putnam.

Box 8.10
Non-voting: does it matter?

- Ruy Teixeira argues that – if widespread non-voting continues – government will become increasingly delegitimised. Its right to govern will be called into question and it may, as a consequence, shrink from making essential but unpopular decisions.
- If relatively small numbers vote, decision makers will be unrepresentative. The policies that are adopted will not reflect the interests of non-voters. Some suggest that because non-voting is skewed towards those with lower incomes, decision making already discounts their views and needs.
- If elections become less important, the influence of the most influential pressure groups, sometimes called 'special interests', will grow. This reinforces the process by which government becomes less representative of the population as a whole.
- Jack Doppelt and Ellen Shearer argue that low turnout is a source of international embarrassment. The US has sought, particularly since the Second World War, to promote democracy in different parts of the globe. The democratic message has been weakened by low levels of political participation in the US.

How can these processes be explained? The aging and death of the 'long civic generation', whose attitudes and opinions were shaped during the Second World War, appears significant. The war encouraged a sense of solidarity, social obligation and collective purpose. This generation was also the last to grow up without television. Television, Putnam asserts, has done much to break up ties and connections.

- There is also a widely shared distrust of government, particularly the national government. The US has a long-established libertarian tradition whereby government is seen in negative terms. However, from the late 1960s onwards there were markedly higher levels of distrust. Whereas in 1958 73 per cent of the population trusted the government 'to do what is right' either 'most of the time' or 'just about always', the figure had fallen to 40 per cent by 1998 (National Election Studies 2000).
- Some observers adopt a radically different perspective. They point to growing complacency. Low turnout is, they argue, a sign that most Americans are relatively content. David Shribman of the *Boston Globe* describes it as 'hapathy' (Doppelt and Shearer 1999: 10). By this he means that there is a combination of happiness and apathy. However, this explanation should be questioned. The lowest levels of turnout are to be found among those in the lowest socio-economic groupings.

The role of the Electoral College

Until the events that followed the 2000 election the Electoral College was usually regarded as a mere footnote to the electoral process. However, it can play a decisive role.

The US uses an indirect system to elect its presidents. Established under Article II of the Constitution, the Electoral College rests upon the individual states. In almost every state the winner of the vote (or 'popular vote') in each of the states is assigned all that state's Electoral College vote (ECV) or Electors (see Box 8.2). There are, in total, 538 ECV, and to become president a candidate must gain over half of them.

The ECV are cast by the Electors – generally officials and loyalists from the party that has won the presidential vote in a particular state – who meet in their respective state capitals some weeks after the election. The ECV are formally recorded and dispatched to Congress. The president of the Senate (the vice-president) announces the overall results and declares the winner.

The number of ECV allocated to each state is based upon its representation in both houses of Congress. The most populous states therefore have the greatest representation. In contrast, states such as North and South Dakota, that are sparsely populated, are allocated only three ECV. Because there is a process of reapportionment following each decennial census, some states either gain or lose ECV. After the 2000 census, California's ECV rose by one to fifty-five. Correspondingly, New York and Pennsylvania lost two Electors. Box 8.11 outlines the procedures that are followed once the people have voted.

Why did the founding fathers establish the Electoral College? There were three principal reasons.

- It reassured the states, some of which saw dangers of centralisation in the US Constitution, that they could play an institutionalised part in the selection of a president.
- An indirect system allowed the states to maintain their own laws governing the extent of the franchise.
- Although voting rights were limited, the framers feared that the electorate might make an inappropriate choice and sought safeguards against 'popular passion'. The Electoral College was envisaged as a deliberative institution that could, if necessary, disregard such 'passion' and choose the candidate they considered most qualified.

The Electoral College has, however, been subject to considerable criticism. Although it compels candidates to campaign across more of the country than they might otherwise, and gives a role to the smaller states, it has been widely depicted as an anachronism in a modern, democratic age.

Box 8.11
Electoral College procedures

Early November

Voting by the people takes place on the first Tuesday after the first Monday. Following this – except in Maine and Nebraska – the right to cast all the state's Electoral College votes is assigned to the slate put forward by the winning candidate's party. The names of the Electors in each of the states are then certified by the Archivist of the United States, a federal government official.

Mid-December (18 December in 2000)

The Electors meet in their respective state capitals and cast their votes for the presidency by completing certificates. These are then sent to the Archivist of the US and the president of the Senate (the outgoing vice-president, whose term of office finishes on 20 January in the following year).

6 January (or – in some years – another day in early January)

The vice-president presides over a joint session of the new Congress. The tellers read the Electoral votes. If there are objections, and they are backed by at least one Senator and one member of the House, both houses hold separate sessions to decide upon the validity of the disputed Electoral votes. There were challenges in both 1969 and 2001. However, in 2001 House members were unable to find a senator willing to back an objection to the Electoral votes cast in Florida for George W. Bush.

Once these processes have been completed, the vice-president formally announces the winning candidate.

Source: adapted from W. Berns (ed.), *After the People Vote: A Guide to the Electoral College*, Washington DC, AEI Press, 1992, 14–18.

- The system depends – in part – on the personal fidelity of those chosen as Electors. All will be party loyalists, and twenty-five states together with the District of Columbia have laws requiring that Electors respect the result of the popular election in their state. Nevertheless, there have been fourteen instances of 'faithless Electors' who have voted for other individuals. In 1972 a majority of Virginia voters backed Richard Nixon. However, one of the Electors voted for John Hospers, the Libertarian Party candidate. In 1988 a West Virginia Elector supported Senator Lloyd Bentsen, the running mate, rather than Michael Dukakis, the Democratic presidential candidate, who had won the popular vote in the state. In 2000 one Elector from the District of Columbia abstained in protest against the District's lack of representation in Congress. No 'faithless Elector' has changed the outcome of an election, although there was some speculation that this could happen in the aftermath of the 2000 election. Nonetheless, the potential for this in a close race remains. There have been ten presidential elections in which an Elector abstained or voted for an individual other than the candidate to whom they were pledged: 1796, 1820, 1948, 1956, 1960, 1968, 1972, 1976, 1988 and 2000 (Berns, 1992: 13).

- If their votes are dispersed across the US, minor party candidates may attract a significant proportion of the popular vote but will gain no representation in the Electoral College. Ross Perot won 19 per cent of the popular vote in 1992 but no Electoral College votes. It should be noted, however, that minor party candidates whose support is sufficiently concentrated in particular states can overcome this hurdle. In the 1948 and 1968 contests Strom Thurmond and George Wallace attracted votes among white southerners. Although their support was small as a proportion of the national vote, it was concentrated, and they won Electoral College votes.

- The choice between the three leading candidates is assigned to the House of Representatives if no candidate gains over half the ECV (270 votes). However, under the provisions of the Constitution, each state delegation has only one vote, thereby giving the sparsely populated states an equal weighting with those that are most populous. The transfer of the selection process to the legislative branch has also led to claims that this constitutional provision breaches the separation of powers. Two presidential elections – shown in Box 8.12 – have been decided this way.

- Almost all the states use a 'winner-takes-all' system of election (see Box 8.2). Even if a candidate wins the popular vote in a particular state only by a very small margin, she or he will gain all that state's ECV. As a

---

Box 8.12

Presidential elections decided by the House of Representatives

1800   Thomas Jefferson[1]
        Aaron Burr
1824   Andrew Jackson
        John Quincy Adams[1]

Note:
1 Chosen as president. Although Jackson attracted 44.3 per cent of the popular vote, he failed to gain a majority in the Electoral College. Adams was backed by only 30 per cent of the voter (Berns 1992: 38).

Table 8.13   *Elections in which the winner of the popular vote lost the presidency*

Year	Candidate/party	% of the popular vote	ECV
1824	Andrew Jackson	44.3	99
	John Quincy Adams	30.0	84
	William H. Crawford	12.5	41
	Henry Clay	13.2	37
1876	Samuel J. Tilden (D)	51.0	184
	Rutherford B. Hayes (R)	47.9	185
1888	Grover Cleveland (D)	48.6	168
	Benjamin Harrison (R)	47.8	233
2000	Al Gore (D)	48.4	267
	George W. Bush (R)	47.9	271

Note: in 1824 the outcome was decided by the House of Representatives (see Box 8.12). In 1876 Hayes was declared the winner only after Congress had appointed a commission to resolve a dispute arising from contested elections in Florida, Louisiana and South Carolina.
Source: adapted from W. Berns (ed.), *After the People Vote: A Guide to the Electoral College*, Washington DC, AEI Press, 1992, 35–43.

consequence, there are almost always significant discrepancies between the candidates' share of the popular vote and their share of the ECV. Furthermore, in certain circumstances the winner of the popular vote can lose in the Electoral College. This has happened in four elections (Table 8.13).

In 2000 – after a protracted and in some ways unresolved dispute about the allocation of Florida's Electors – Bush won the narrowest of majorities in the Electoral College. However, as Table 8.14 shows, he lost the battle for the popular vote. Some have suggested that the 2000 result will lead to reform of the Electoral College. However, reform proposals face formidable obstacles.

- George W. Bush owes his victory to the Electoral College system. If Republicans support reform, they are denying the legitimacy of his administration.
- It would require a constitutional amendment. This needs the backing of two-thirds of Congress and three-quarters of the states.
- Although the college has its critics, there is little agreement about alternative systems of election. The adoption of a system based upon direct popular election – which was proposed on a number of occasions by Senator Birch Bayh – would undoubtedly be opposed by the smaller rural states. At present, they are over-represented in the process. Furthermore, such a system would – by abandoning representation on the basis of states – undermine the federal principle upon which the US Constitution is constructed.

Table 8.14 *The popular vote and the Electoral College vote: the presidential election, 2000*

	Popular vote[1]					Electoral College votes		
State	Bush/Cheney	% of votes	Gore/Lieberman	% of votes	Total votes	Bush	Gore	Not cast
Alabama	941,173	56.48	692,611	41.57	1,666,272	9	0	
Alaska	167,398	58.84	79,004	27.77	284,492	3	0	
Arizona	781,652	51.02	685,341	44.73	1,532,016	8	0	
Arkansas	472,940	51.31	422,768	45.86	921,781	6	0	
California	4,567,429	41.65	5,861,203	53.45	10,965,856	0	54	
Colorado	883,748	50.75	738,227	42.39	1,741,368	8	0	
Connecticut	561,104	38.43	816,659	55.93	1,460,177	0	8	
Delaware	137,288	41.92	180,068	54.98	327,529	0	3	
District of Columbia	18,073	8.95	171,923	85.16	201,894	0	2	1
Florida	2,912,790	48.85	2,912,253	48.84	5,963,070	25	0	
Georgia	1,419,720	54.96	1,116,230	43.21	2,583,208	13	0	
Hawaii	137,845	37.46	205,286	55.79	367,951	0	4	
Idaho	336,937	67.17	138,637	27.64	501,615	4	0	
Illinois	2,019,421	42.60	2,589,026	54.62	4,739,935	0	22	
Indiana	1,245,836	56.65	901,980	41.01	2,199,302	12	0	
Iowa	634,373	48.26	638,517	48.58	1,314,395	0	7	
Kansas	622,332	58.04	399,276	37.24	1,072,216	6	0	
Kentucky	872,520	56.40	638,923	41.30	1,547,106	8	0	
Louisiana	927,871	52.55	792,344	44.88	1,765,656	9	0	
Maine	286,616	43.97	319,951	49.09	651,790	0	4	
Maryland	813,724	40.24	1,143,888	56.57	2,021,987	0	10	
Massachusetts	878,502	32.55	1,616,487	59.89	2,698,994	0	12	
Michigan	1,953,139	46.15	2,170,418	51.28	4,232,501	0	18	
Minnesota	1,109,659	45.50	1,168,266	47.91	2,438,685	0	10	
Mississippi	572,844	57.62	404,614	40.70	994,184	7	0	
Missouri	1,189,924	50.42	1,111,138	47.08	2,359,892	11	0	
Montana	240,178	58.44	137,126	33.37	410,986	3	0	
Nebraska	433,850	62.23	231,776	33.25	697,132	5	0	
Nevada	301,575	49.79	279,978	46.23	605,655	4	0	

Table 8.14 (cont'd)

State	Popular vote[1]					Electoral College votes		
	Bush/Cheney	% of votes	Gore/Lieberman	% of votes	Total votes	Bush	Gore	Not cast
New Hampshire	273,559	48.18	266,348	46.91	567,795	4	0	
New Jersey	1,284,173	40.29	1,788,850	56.13	3,187,226	0	15	
New Mexico	286,417	47.85	286,783	47.91	598,605	0	5	
New York	2,403,374	35.23	4,107,697	60.21	6,821,999	0	33	
North Carolina	1,631,163	55.96	1,257,692	43.15	2,914,990	14	0	
North Dakota	174,852	60.66	95,284	33.06	288,256	3	0	
Ohio	2,350,363	49.99	2,183,628	46.44	4,701,998	21	0	
Oklahoma	744,337	60.31	474,276	38.43	1,234,229	8	0	
Oregon	713,577	46.62	720,342	47.06	1,530,549	0	7	
Pennsylvania	2,281,127	46.44	2,485,967	50.61	4,912,185	0	23	
Rhode Island	130,555	31.91	249,508	60.99	409,112	0	4	
South Carolina	786,892	56.86	566,037	40.90	1,383,902	8	0	
South Dakota	190,700	60.30	118,804	37.56	316,269	3	0	
Tennessee	1,061,949	51.16	981,720	47.29	2,075,753	11	0	
Texas	3,799,639	59.30	2,433,746	37.98	6,407,637	32	0	
Utah	515,096	67.18	203,053	26.48	766,697	5	0	
Vermont	119,775	40.77	149,022	50.72	293,794	0	3	
Virginia	1,437,490	52.53	1,217,290	44.48	2,736,640	13	0	
Washington	1,108,864	44.58	1,247,652	50.16	2,487,433	0	11	
West Virginia	336,473	51.90	295,497	45.58	648,251	5	0	
Wisconsin	1,237,279	47.61	1,242,987	47.83	2,598,607	0	11	
Wyoming	147,947	69.22	60,481	28.30	213,726	3	0	
Totals[2]	50,456,062	47.89	50,996,582	48.40	105,363,298	271	266	

Notes:

1 Vote totals are as shown on each state's certificate of ascertainment.

2 California submitted an amended certificate of ascertainment 27 December 2000, with amended vote totals, which are reflected here.

Source: adapted from the National Archives and Records Administration, *Electoral College Home Page*, www.nara.gov/fedreg/elctcoll/index.html#top.

Box 8.13
Congressional elections

Although congressional elections are – like presidential contests – shaped by long-term partisan loyalties, the character of the media coverage and issue preferences, both incumbency and financial resources also play a role in determining the outcome.

Incumbency

In congressional elections incumbent members seeking re-election have enormous advantages over potential challengers. These include name recognition, the ability to raise large amounts of campaign funds, and the franking privilege enjoyed by sitting members of Congress which allows regular communication with voters at the taxpayers' expense.

Furthermore, although Congress is not held in high public regard, Roger Davidson and Walter Oleszek point to the contrast between what they call 'the two Congresses'. Individual members of the legislature consistently score much higher approval ratings for their performance in office than Congress as an institution (Davidson and Oleszek 2000: 407–20). Because members successfully cultivate their reputation as a good representative of their district or state and enjoy **seniority** in Congress, they often attract the support of electors who would not normally vote for their party. This has led in recent years to a phenomenally high level of re-election for incumbents, particularly in the House, where 98.3 per cent were returned in 1998 and ninety-three did not face any major party opposition in the November elections. The decline of competitive elections in the House has also been caused by the increasing sophistication, using computerised models, with which state legislatures can draw constituency boundaries to group together homogeneous blocs of votes. This means that party control of the House depends upon:

- elections in the very small number of highly marginal districts;
- the open races where members have decided to retire or have, in a small number of cases, been defeated in primaries.

Table 1 illustrates the way in which, since the beginning of the twentieth century, the majority of members of Congress have become lifetime politicians who repeatedly seek and win re-election. The mean number of terms served by House members that had averaged 2.1 in the nineteenth century had increased to 5.3 by the time of the 106th Congress in 1999–2000.

1   *Length of service in House and Senate, 1789–1999 (%)*

No. of terms	Congress			
	1st–56th (1789–1901)	57th–103rd (1901–95)	104th–105th (1995–99)	106th (1999–2000)
House				
One (up to 2 years)	44.0	23.3	18.2	9.2
Two to six (3–12 years)	53.4	49.7	51.9	61.4
Seven or more (12+ years)	2.6	27.0	30.0	29.4
Mean[1]	2.1	4.8	5.0	5.3
Senate				
One (up to 6 years)	65.6	45.6	33.5	36.0
Two (7–12 years)	23.4	22.4	27.5	31.0
Three or more (12+ years)	11.0	32.0	39.0	33.0
Mean[1]	1.5	2.2	2.4	2.6

Note: 1 Figures are derived from the total number of terms claimed by members whether or not those terms have been served out. For example, members in their initial year of service are counted as having one full term, and so on. Thus the figures cannot be equated precisely with years of service.

Source: Roger H. Davidson and Walter J. Oleszek (2000), *Congress and Its Members*, Washington DC, Congressional Quarterly Press, 36. Adapted from David C. Huckabee, *Length of Service for Representatives and Senators: 1st–103rd Congresses*, Congressional Research Service Report, No. 95-426GOV, 27 March 1995.

The rise of the term limits movement in the early 1990s was a reaction to the decline of competitive elections and the power of incumbency as well as voter dissatisfaction with politicians' failure to deal with the nation's most pressing problems. The movement sought to impose a constitutional restriction on the number of terms members could serve in Congress, just as the Twenty-second Amendment restricts the president to two terms in the White House (Grant 1995). However, the movement faced difficulties.

- A move by states to impose such restrictions on their federal legislators was declared unconstitutional in 1995 by the Supreme Court, and members of the House failed to muster the necessary two-thirds majority to pass a constitutional amendment in 1995 and 1997, despite it being included in proposals that formed the *Contract with America*.

- By rejecting the Democrats in 1994 the voters showed that they could oust large numbers of majority party incumbents when they were in a sufficiently angry mood. Term limits were not necessary.

The term limits movement thereby lost momentum. Polls conducted by the Gallup Organisation indicate that public approval ratings of Congress's performance fell to very low levels at the beginning of the 1990s but rose to around 50 per cent at the end of the decade. This reflected a booming economy and a general sense of satisfaction among the electorate.

Table 2 sets out the number of House and Senate incumbents who sought re-election, were defeated or were re-elected at each election since 1980. It demonstrates the very high success rate of House incumbents who sought re-election, peaking at over 98 per cent in 1988 and 1998. In 1992 and 1994, when economic problems and disenchantment with the Democrats in Congress created an anti-incumbency mood in the country, the success rate fell to relative 'lows' of 88.7 and 90.2 per cent respectively. Another feature of the early 1990s was the marked

2   *The advantage of incumbency in the House and Senate, 1980–98*

	House					Senate				
			Defeated					Defeated		
Year	Seeking re-election	No opponent	Primary	General	% re-elected	Seeking re-election	No opponent	Primary	General	% re-elected
1980	398	53	6	31	90.7	29	1	4	9	55.2
1982	396	53	18	29	90.6	30	0	0	2	93.3
1984	410	60	13	17	95.1	29	1	0	3	89.7
1986	393	71	12	6	98.0	28	0	0	6	75.0
1988	410	79	11	6	98.3	27	0	0	4	85.2
1990	406	74	10	15	96.3	32	5	0	1	96.8
1992	350	17	19	24	87.7	28	0	1	3	85.7
1994	389	38	14	34	90.2	26	0	0	2	92.3
1996	384	14	2	21	94.0	20	0	1	1	90.0
1998	401	93	1	6	98.3	29	0	0	3	89.7

Note: '% re-elected' includes both primary and general election defeats.
Source: adapted from Roger H. Davidson and Walter J. Oleszek, *Congress and its Members*, Washington DC, Congressional Quarterly Press, 2000, 66.

increase in the number of members retiring and not seeking re-election. Many of them said they were disillusioned with life on Capitol Hill, citing factors such as the increased partisanship, the need to raise large sums to finance election campaigns and the stress of rising work loads. However, retirement also reflected the fear among some members that they might be facing defeat, either in their party primary or in the November elections.

The re-election rates of senators show greater variation (from 55.2 per cent in 1980 to 96.8 per cent in 1990). This reflects the fact that states contain more diverse populations and the boundaries cannot be reconstructed, as happens with House seats during reapportionment. As only a third of the Senate is elected every two years the percentage success rate is also a reflection of which members happen to be due for re-election in a particular year. Overall, however, senators also enjoy the advantages of incumbency and have high rates of re-election.

Financing congressional elections

Following the *Buckley* ruling by the US Supreme Court (1976) there are no statutory limits on the amounts which congressional candidates can spend on their campaigns. Congress rejected public funding for elections to the legislature and therefore there are no 'voluntary' limits either; this means that candidates can spend as much as they can raise or as they think is necessary to achieve victory. Table 3 shows that expenditure on congressional campaigns rose from $446.3 million in 1989–90 to $765.3 million in 1995–96 and, having fallen back to $740.4 million in 1997–98, rose dramatically to just over $1 billion in 1999–2000. The rise was explained by the greater number of candidates standing, the competitiveness of the struggle to control both the House and the Senate, and the boom in the economy, which helped

3 *Spending in congressional campaigns, 1989–90 to 1999–2000 ($ million)*

	1989–90	1991–92	1993–94	1995–96	1997–98	1999–2000
Amount spent	446.3	680.2	725.2	765.3	740.4	1,005.6
No. of candidates	1,759	2,950	2,376	2,605	2,100	2,416

Source: Federal Election Commission, *FEC Reports on Congressional Financial Activity for 2000*, 15 May 2001.

fund-raising efforts by candidates and parties. Incumbent members have a major advantage over challengers in fund raising; in 1998 approximately two-thirds of the money raised went to sitting members, while many challengers struggled to find the minimum amount, around $200,000 to $250,000, to finance a competitive campaign.

Candidates for Congress raise money from four main sources:

- donations from individual supporters giving up to the $1,000 limit;
- contributions from political action committees (PACs) which are allowed to donate up to $5,000;
- their own resources in the form of gifts or loans;
- financial support from their political party.

Both parties have sought to recruit wealthy individuals as congressional candidates because they are able to finance their own campaigns. Michael Huffington's 1994 Senate campaign in California, in which he spent $28 million of his own money and failed to win, demonstrates that such individuals are not always successful, but they have a huge advantage in terms of resources that can be decisive. In 2000, the former Wall Street tycoon Jon S. Corzine spent over $50 million of his $400 million fortune in winning a Senate seat in New Jersey, while in Washington state Maria Cantwell, a former computer executive, spent over $5 million of her own money in defeating incumbent Senator Slade Gorton by a few thousand votes after a recount. This Democratic victory had considerable significance in that it deprived the Republicans of their overall majority in the Senate and led to a fifty–fifty split in terms of seats in the 107th Congress.

Glossary

balanced ticket   Presidential candidates would traditionally choose a vice-presidential nominee – or 'running mate' – who had a different character and background to themselves. This gave the 'ticket' a broad appeal to a diverse electorate.

caucuses   Caucuses are meetings of party supporters that are used in some states to decide upon a nominee for the presidency or another post. See Chapter 7.

coat-tails effect   The term 'coat-tails effect' describes the ability of a presidential candidate to attract votes for other candidates standing for other positions on the same party ticket. In 1980, for example, Ronald Reagan had a significant coat-tails effect. Voters drawn to Reagan also supported Republican congressional candidates. Conversely, an unpopular presidential candidate – such as Barry Goldwater in 1964 – may harm the electoral prospects of the party's other candidates.

During the 1990s the coat-tails effect was less evident. Although Bill Clinton won the White House in 1992, sixteen Democratic incumbents (compared with only eight Republicans) were defeated in elections to the House of Representatives. In 1996 the Republicans maintained their majority in both chambers.

invisible primary   The invisible primary precedes the primary season. It is based on fund raising, the winning of endorsements from prominent individuals and interest groups, opinion polling, and the comments of television 'pundits'.

national party conventions   National party conventions formally decide upon the party's nominee for the presidency. See Chapter 7.

platform   The platform is a statement of policies – or manifesto – agreed at a party's **national party convention**. Traditionally, there are battles between different factions and groupings within the party about particular commitments or pledges. The significance of the platform is, however, largely symbolic:

- The campaign is organised by the candidate rather than the party. He is not bound by the platform and will develop his own policies and proposals.
- Once he is in office, many of a president's policies are subject to a process of bartering and negotiation with Congress. Pre-election pledges may, therefore, have to be abandoned.

political action committees   Political action committees (PACs) are established by companies, organisations and individuals so as to fund election candidates. See Chapters 6 and 7.

precinct   A precinct is a small electoral district. It is a subdivision of a city or county. Each precinct contains between 200 and 1,000 voters and a polling place. It is the most basic 'bottom rung' unit of organisation for the political parties.

primaries   Primaries are nominating elections. They are held (in states that do not organise **caucuses**) so as to choose a party's candidate for the presidency or another office. See Chapter 7.

registration   Although the constitution established that citizens aged eighteen or over could vote, the requirements for registration as a voter differ between states:

- Many states do not extend the right to vote to those who have recently moved into the state or to convicted felons.
- Almost all states require a period of time to elapse between registration and voting. It is usually about a month. However, a small number allow same-day registration – voters can register when they come to vote – and appear to enjoy higher turnout levels.

seniority   Traditionally committee chairmanships in Congress were assigned to the longest serving – or most senior – member of the majority party. (See Chapter 3.)

Super Tuesday   This is one of the most important hurdles facing candidates during the primary season. A large number of states, many of which are in the south, hold their primaries on the same day. Candidates' survival in the presidential race depends upon their ability to win – or at least gain a credible share of the vote – on Super Tuesday.

turnout   The proportion of the voting-age population who cast a vote in a particular election.

Resources

References and further reading

Bennett, A.J. (1992), *American Government and Politics*, Godalming, published by the author.

Berns, W. (1992), *After the People Vote: A Guide to the Electoral College*, Washington DC, AEI Press.

Davidson, R.H., and W.J Oleszek (2000), *Congress and its Members*, Washington DC, Congressional Quarterly Press.

Doppelt, J.C., and E. Shearer (1999), *Nonvoters: America's No-shows*, Thousand Oaks CA, Sage.

Federal Election Commission (2001), *FEC Reports on Congressional Financial Activity for 2000*, 15 May.

Flanigan W.H., and N.H. Zingale (1998), *Political Behavior of the American Electorate*, Washington DC, Congressional Quarterly Press.

Grant, A. (1995), 'Financing American elections', *Politics Review*, 5:2, 9–12.

National Election Studies (2000), *The NES Guide to Public Opinion and Electoral Behavior: Trust in Federal Government, 1958–98*, www.umich.edu/~nes/nesguide/toptable/tab5a_1.htm.

Putnam, R.D. (2000), *Bowling Alone: The Collapse and Revival of American Community*, New York, Simon & Schuster.

Schneider W. (1996), 'Coding messages to men, women', CNN Time ALLPOLITICS, 12 June, www.cnn.com/ALLPOLITICS/1996/news/9606/12/gender/index.shtml.

Teixeira, R.A. (1992) *The Disappearing American Voter*, Washington DC, Brookings Institution.

Washington Post (2000a), 26 October, www.washingtonpost.com.

Washington Post (2000b), 'Who are the values voters?', www.washingtonpost.com/wp-srv/politics/polls/vault/stories/harvard093000.htm.

Washington Post, Kaiser Family Foundation and Harvard University (2000), *Issues in the 2000 Election: Health Care*, www.kff.org.

Washington Post, Kaiser Family Foundation and Harvard School of Public Health (2000), *Issues 4 Study: Economics*, International Communications Research, www.kff.org.

Websites

Center for Responsive Politics   www.opensecrets.org
   The Center investigates and publishes details of financial contributions to candidates.
Federal Election Commission   www.fec.gov
   The FEC website offers election statistics, information about state regulations, and candidates' financial returns.
Gallup Organization   www.gallup.com
   Gallup is a long-established and respected source of opinion polls.
National Archives and Records Administration – Electoral College Home Page   www.nara.gov.fedreg/elctcoll/index.html

The NARA website provides information about the popular vote, Electoral College mechanisms, details of those selected as Electors and details of relevant laws.

National Election Studies   www.umich.edu/~nes/

The University of Michigan's National Election Studies website offers data based on polling research. Its coverage includes attitudes to important issues, partisan identification, electoral turnout and split-ticket voting.

9

Federalism and the states

This chapter examines the development of modern federalism and government and politics at state level. It examines:

- recent changes in federal–state relations;
- institutions and political processes at state level;
- the principal characteristics of the individual states (profiled in the appendix).

When the founding fathers drew up the US Constitution in 1787 they created a federal union that James Madison described as 'a happy combination' of a centralised and a decentralised system. A **federation** was a compromise form of unity which avoided the weaknesses of both the **Confederation**, which existed from 1781 until the ratification of the new Constitution, and the dangers of a centralised **unitary system** of government which existed in Europe but which would have been unacceptable to the original thirteen states.

The Constitution's provision for a division of powers between the federal (or national) authority and the states inevitably led to occasional conflicts over the precise boundaries and areas of jurisdiction of the two levels of government. Therefore the debate in American politics today about the size and scope of the federal government's authority relative to the states is not a new one; indeed, the roots of the issue go back to the Philadelphia Convention over 200 years ago.

During the nineteenth and early twentieth centuries something approaching the classical model of 'dual federalism' prevailed (Box 9.1). The powers of the federal government were construed narrowly and it was clearly the junior partner in domestic policy. The 'reserved powers' of the states, as envisaged in the Tenth Amendment to the Constitution, ensured that they were the leading players in providing public services to their citizens, although this was an era when the roles of government at all levels were strictly limited.

From the 1930s onwards, federal intervention in areas that had traditionally been left to the states increased considerably. There were two phases.

Box 9.1
Different models of federalism

Dual federalism

This is the classical model established by the founding fathers, whereby the national (or federal) government and the states each had separate spheres of authority, could act independently within their own areas of jurisdiction and had equal status. Where there was conflict or tension between the two, the US Supreme Court would act as arbiter in the resolution of disputes. Although some writers have argued that the pure form of dual federalism did not exist even in the nineteenth century, until the 1930s the states and their local governments taxed and spent more and provided most public services.

Co-operative federalism

With the onset of the Great Depression, President Franklin Roosevelt's New Deal revolutionised federalism and moved the national government into areas previously left to the states. This was done by a combination of federal funding through grants-in-aid and state involvement in and administration of many new national programmes. A complex system of intergovernmental relations developed, characterised by a sharing of powers and responsibilities between federal, state and local governments. In the 1960s and 1970s further federal intervention, through President Lyndon Johnson's Great Society programmes and civil rights and environmental protection legislation, shifted the balance of power remorselessly towards Washington DC and away from state capitals. Proponents of these changes described the new approach as 'co-operative federalism', a partnership between the different levels of government. Opponents argued that it allowed the federal government to intervene in areas in which it had no constitutional authority.

Coercive federalism

From the 1970s to the 1990s the relationship evolved further into a system that has often been described as 'coercive federalism'. The federal government sought to harness state and local authority resources to achieve its own policy goals but there was less co-operation through grants and state involvement in the design and implementation of new programmes. There was more emphasis on the use of congressional **pre-emption powers** under Article VI of the Constitution, whereby state laws are overridden by federal law in the event of a conflict between them. There was also an increased use of **unfunded mandates** whereby Congress requires states and local governments to act in specific ways but does not compensate them financially for the costs which are incurred in implementing national policy. These changes came about partly because the large federal budget deficit in the 1990s prevented Congress from introducing new grants to the states, while at the same time politicians at national level wanted to respond to public opinion and the demands of their electorates. The heavy-handed nature of much federal intervention in this period provoked a reaction in the states and demands for more **devolution** of power.

- The initial catalyst was the Great Depression and the New Deal programmes introduced by President Franklin Roosevelt to mitigate its effects. Over the next forty years dual federalism effectively gave way to what became known as 'co-operative federalism' (Box 9.1).
- The 1960s saw a second great wave of national government intervention; the Great Society programmes under President Lyndon Johnson included policies aimed at fighting poverty, renewing the inner cities and countering racial discrimination. The federal government was taking the lead role in many areas of domestic policy and using financial grants to the states as incentives to secure their participation in programmes designed in Washington DC. There was a huge growth in spending by the federal government but its staffing levels remained relatively stable because most of the burden of implementation fell upon the other levels of government. Between 1962 and 1995 the net growth of federal civilian employment was 15 per cent, while those employed by state and local governments increased by a full 150 per cent.

Recent changes in federal–state relations

By the 1990s the federal system had evolved further into what some writers have described as 'coercive federalism'. To a degree, it appears that co-operative federalism was a transitional phase between the dual federalism period and the coercive federalism of the modern era. (Zimmerman 1992: 10) (Box 9.1). John Kincaid has argued that, while all levels of government have broadened their involvement with society, the federal government in the 1990s was exercising more power over more aspects of domestic policy than ever before (Kincaid 1994). He contends that the federal system became more coercive and less co-operative as the national government used such methods as **unfunded mandates**, congressional **pre-emption powers** and **cross-over sanctions** whereby states that do not comply with federal laws would lose grant money authorised by earlier legislation.

In the 1970s and 1980s conservative politicians became increasingly critical of this new intergovernmentalism, which, they argued, had led to an undesirable centralisation of power. They attacked federal intervention as lacking a legitimate constitutional basis and also alleged that it was ineffective and hugely expensive. Bureaucratic rules and regulations were stifling state and local initiative and preventing governments at these levels from dealing with problems which they understood much better than remote policy makers in Washington DC. Conservatives alleged that national legislation often failed to recognise the diversity of the US and the differing needs of people in the states. Under President Richard Nixon (1969–74) and Ronald Reagan (1981–89) there were efforts to reverse the tide and shift power and responsibility to the states. Nixon was a managerial conservative who wanted to see the system made more efficient; Reagan was an ideological conservative for whom cutting government at all levels, but particularly in Washington, was central to his political beliefs. As a former Governor of California, Reagan had experienced the frustrations first hand of finding that federal regulations undermined his state's freedom to determine its own policies. He used his inaugural address as president to demand recognition of the distinction between the powers granted to the federal government and those 'reserved to the states or to the people'.

Conservatives argued for the re-establishment of a form of dual federalism and a reversal of the trend by which, since the 1930s, the Tenth Amendment had been in practice ignored by Congress, presidents and the Supreme Court. They criticised the Court for relying in its judgements on phrases in the Constitution which could be interpreted as allowing growing federal interventionism, while at the same time downgrading or disregarding the importance of the Tenth Amendment and its protection of states' rights (see Chapter 2). The Supreme Court in the period up to the 1990s has been described as 'an aggressive nationalizing force' (Nathan 1990: 248); it had to all intents and purposes abdicated its role as the arbiter of the Constitution in settling disputes regarding the federal relationship. This was best demonstrated in the case of *Garcia v. San Antonio Metropolitan Transit Authority* (1985), when the Court declared that the states could not expect the judiciary to protect their powers from federal encroachment by invoking the Tenth Amendment. Instead, they should lobby national politicians like any other pressure group to achieve their aims.

Reagan managed to change the terms of the political debate and place the future of federalism back on the federal agenda. He persuaded Congress to consolidate a number of **categorical grants** – which had many conditions attached to their use – into broad **block grants** which gave the states more discretion. He also reduced the number of federal regulations affecting the states and restrained the growth of federal aid so that by the end of his administration states did not automatically look to Washington for help with their problems. A cultural shift took place in the 1980s that meant that the states were again becoming more self-reliant and looking for their own solutions. Reagan did not succeed in securing the fundamental shift in power he had been seeking, partly because of political opposition in Congress and partly because the public was not ready for such a radical overhaul of the post-New Deal system. What is more, despite its commitment to federalism, the Reagan administration was not always consistent in its defence of the states when such a stance came into conflict with other key priorities. For example, it saw the deregulation of business as one of the central aims of its economic policy and, responding to the arguments of big corporations, it used the federal government's **pre-emption power** to lay down one standard of regulation with which businesses had to comply rather than fifty different sets of state rules, many of which would be more demanding. Reagan also gave into public and congressional pressure and supported federal sanctions for enforcing a national standard age of twenty-one for purchasing alcohol as a way of countering the dangers of drunk driving among teenagers.

Under the presidency of George Bush (1989–93) the emphasis was on consolidating the changes made under Reagan and no major innovations were made in federalism policy. The Democratic-controlled Congress did pass major new Bills on clean air and facilities for disabled people that included costly new obligations for state and local governments that Bush signed into law. Although President Bill Clinton (1993–2001) won election in1992 claiming to be 'a new kind of Democrat', not so committed to '**big government**' programmes as his Democratic predecessors, once in office he moved to left while seeking to work with the liberal members of his own party who controlled the Congress. His most radical and ambitious proposal on health care reform would have substantially increased the federal government's role in this area and proved too complex and expensive even for his own party in the legislature, where it failed to come to a vote. Following this humiliation, Clinton was also widely blamed for the Democrats' significant losses in the 1994 mid-term elections. The Republicans won control of both houses of Congress for the first time in forty years and the results were interpreted as a rejection of '**big government**', reflecting the decline of public confidence in federal institutions which had been detected in opinion polls in the 1990s (see Table 9.1).

President Clinton was obliged to acknowledge voter sentiment on this issue, and in his 1996 State of the Union address he declared that 'the era of big government is over'. Clinton, a former governor himself, who had in the past argued the case for more **devolution** of power to the states, had already recognised the need to streamline the federal bureaucracy with his 'reinventing government' initiative. The Republican Party in both houses of Congress had become more conservative over the years and many members, including the new House Speaker, Newt Gingrich, were committed to a radical restructuring

Table 9.1   *Federalism and public trust (%)*

Which government do you trust to:	State	Federal
Do a better job running things?	70	27
Establish rules about who can receive welfare?	70	25
Set rules for workplace safety?	55	42
Set Medicare and Medicaid regulations?	52	43
Set environmental rules for clean air and clean water?	51	47
Protect civil rights?	35	61

Source: *Washington Post*–ABC poll, reported in Richard Morin, 'Power to the States', *Washington Post National Weekly Edition*, 27 March–2 April 1995, 37.

of the federal relationship in favour of the states. One of the first acts of the new Congress in 1995, and one of considerable symbolic importance, was the passage of a law making it more difficult for the federal government to impose new **unfunded mandates**. Congress also repealed national speed limits and overhauled the Safe Drinking Act to allow states and local authorities more flexibility in implementing the policy.

However, the most radical measure was the welfare reform Bill passed in 1996, which ended the federal government's guarantee to provide welfare assistance to all low-income mothers and children which had been in effect since the New Deal. The legislation transformed the programme into a **block grant** to the states, which would give them more discretion over eligibility levels and benefits. The Republicans claimed that placing a cap on the federal government's commitment on welfare spending was essential if they were to achieve their objective of a balanced budget. However, Congress retained the right to regulate state plans and laid down rules to ensure that states enforced the limits on the time individuals can receive welfare payments and that they made progress towards moving recipients into the work force. President Clinton reluctantly signed the Bill into law despite opposition from most Democrats because he did not wish to be accused of blocking welfare reform in the run-up to the 1996 election. He did succeed, however, in vetoing a proposal to turn Medicaid, the federal–state health insurance programme for the poor, which enjoys more public support than welfare, into a similar **block grant**.

Republican plans to balance the budget, which involved a radical reshaping of the federal relationship, huge cuts in spending and the abolition of many programmes and agencies, also had to be scaled back because of Clinton's veto power. The budget crisis in the winter of 1995–96 was a public relations disaster for the Republicans, enabling Clinton to depict them as extreme and uncaring and himself as the defender of vital public services. Following the re-election of both Clinton and the Republican congressional majorities in 1996 a compromise budget deal was achieved and signed into law in August 1997 which retained the basic principles of the welfare reform legislation. The budget included provision for a children's health insurance programme which gave the states considerable discretion on how they extended coverage to children from poor families not covered by Medicaid but it did not lead to any major new areas of **devolution** to the states. This was primarily because the decline in the federal budget deficit by 1997 had reduced the pressure on Congress to cut spending and because the Republicans, chastened by the failure of their earlier confrontational strategy, were more willing to compromise with the Clinton White House.

As in the Reagan era, conservative Republicans in control of Congress were prepared to increase federal authority when it appeared to be the most effective way of carrying out their political agenda. The commitment to **devolution** to the states often lost out when it came into conflict with other priorities.

For example, Congress laid down requirements for national standards for driving licences and birth certificates as a way of cracking down on illegal immigration; it federalised additional crimes such as inter-state stalking and nullified state laws that restricted competition in the telecommunications industry. Republicans have been inclined to favour national intervention to advance deregulation of the private sector or pursue tougher law-and-order policies, even when these have been areas traditionally left to the states, partly in response to pressure groups and partly because of public opinion in their constituencies. Democrats have tended to support national standards overriding state laws on environmental protection and the health and safety of workers.

Following the retirement of William Brennan and Thurgood Marshall, two of the most liberal justices, the conservative majority on the US Supreme Court began – from 1991 onwards – to provide increased judicial protection to the states. They began to question the constitutional basis of congressional legislation in a way that had not been witnessed since the 1930s (Box 9.2). In particular, the Court laid down the limits of the interstate commerce clause of the Constitution in relation to law-and-order policies. It has emphasised the Tenth Amendment and the reserved powers of the states, as well as the Eleventh Amendment, which prohibits federal courts from adjudicating cases brought against a state by citizens of another state or country.

The federal system is complex and the relationship between the national government and the states is forever changing. The more conservative Supreme Court under Chief Justice William Rehnquist since 1991, coupled with Republican control of Congress since 1995, has allowed a significant if limited reshaping of the terrain of federalism by the beginning of the twenty-first century.

Politics in the states

Each of the fifty states has its own constitution, governmental structures and institutions, as well as its own distinct political history and culture. Although there are many similarities between the states, in that they all have systems based upon the separation of powers principle, there are also many differences and particular features of the political processes in the individual states.

Each state determines its own local government structure, and the pattern of local authorities so established has an important impact on the delivery of services to the public. In 1997 there was a total of 87,453 locally elected councils in the US. This number included 3,043 counties, 19,372 municipal and city administrations, 16,629 towns, all of which have general service responsibilities, as well as district authorities for particular functions such as schools, colleges, parks and fire services which together total 48,409. (*Statistical Abstract of the United States*, 1999: 309).

Box 9.2
The Rehnquist Court and federalism

Since the early 1990s the US Supreme Court has made a number of rulings, often by five votes to four, which have protected the powers of the states. The most significant are set out below.

1992 New York v. United States

The Justices struck down by six votes to three portions of a federal law making states liable for nuclear waste created by commercial reactors. The Court cited the Tenth Amendment and stated that Congress could not 'commandeer' the legislative processes of the states.

1995 United States v. Lopez

The Court struck down by five votes to four parts of an anti-crime law that aimed at banning guns within 1,000 ft of schools. It said that Congress had exceeded its authority under the 'commerce clause', as the statute was concerned with crime and had nothing to do with commercial activities.

1996 Seminole Tribe of Florida v. Florida

Citing the Eleventh Amendment, the justices declared unconstitutional by five votes to four a law that allowed Indian tribes to file federal suits when states failed to negotiate gambling contracts.

1997 City of Boerne v. Flores

The Court ruled by six votes to three that Congress had exceeded its powers under the Fourteenth Amendment's 'equal protection' clause when it passed a law barring states from enacting laws interfering with citizens' First Amendment right of religious expression unless the state had a 'compelling interest'.

1998 Printz v. United States; Mack v. United States

The justices struck down by five votes to four a major part of the Brady handgun control legislation that ordered local sheriffs to check the backgrounds of gun buyers, stating that Congress could not mandate officials of state and local governments to carry out its administrative orders.

1999 Alden v. Maine

The Court cited the Eleventh Amendment in a five–four ruling that Congress exceeded its authority in allowing individuals to sue a state for the payment of overtime wages under fair labour standards legislation which had been extended in 1974 explicitly to cover state employees.

1999 Florida v. College Savings Bank

The Justices ruled by five votes to four that a federal law allowing lawsuits against state agencies alleging violations of federal patent and trade-mark statutes was unconstitutional on the basis of conflict with the Eleventh Amendment.

2000 Kimel v. Florida Board of Regents

The Court found that Congress had exceeded it authority under the Fourteenth Amendment to enforce civil rights laws when it applied to the states a 1967 Act that banned discrimination against older workers.

However, the Court has not always found in favour of the states in this period. Some important exceptions include:

1995 US Term Limits v. Thornton

The justices ruled by five votes to four that states could not impose term limits on members of Congress, thereby invalidating laws passed in twenty-three states. The Court held that such laws would add to the constitutional qualifications for office set out in Article I, Sections 2 and 3, of the US Constitution and this could be done only by an amendment of the Constitution.

2000 Crosby v. National Foreign Trade Council

The Court decided unanimously that a state (Massachusetts) could not introduce its own trade sanctions against Myanmar (formerly Burma) as a reaction to human rights violations in that country. To do so would be impinging on the federal government's exclusive right to make foreign policy.

2001 Bush v. Gore

The justices overruled (by five votes to four), the Florida Supreme Court's decision to order hand recounts of disputed presidential election ballots. They cited equal protection concerns and the insufficient time available for counting to take place which met 'minimal constitutional standards'.

Legislatures

All states except Nebraska have a **bicameral** legislature. As Table 9.2 shows, the lower house (often known as the assembly) usually has two or three times as many members as the upper house, or Senate. State senators generally serve four-year terms while their counterparts in the lower house tend to have only two years in office before having to seek re-election. During the 1990s voters in almost half the states imposed constitutional limits on the number of terms which individual legislators could serve. This movement was a reaction to the growing professionalisation of state legislatures since the 1960s. Until that time members had tended to be part-time, were poorly paid and had little in the way of staff support. Legislatures had short sessions, often met only in alternate years and tended to be dominated by rural interests.

Urban voters secured fairer representation following decisions by the US Supreme Court in the early 1960s which rejected the federal analogy which would allow the state senates to be based on territorial representation and required both lower and upper house to be apportioned on the basis of population. Many states also embarked upon reforms that gave their legislators

Table 9.2 *State legislatures: members, salaries and terms of office*

State	No. of legislators Senate	House	Annual salary ($)[1]	Term (years) Senate	House	Term limit (years) Senate	House
Alabama	35	105	–	4	4	–	–
Alaska	20	40	24,012	4	2	–	–
Arizona	30	60	15,000	2	2	8	8
Arkansas	35	100	12,500	2	2	8	6
California	40	80	75,600	4	2	8	6
Colorado	35	65	17,500	4	2	8	8
Connecticut	36	151	16,760	2	2	–	–
Delaware	21	41	27,500	4	2	–	–
Florida	40	120	24,912	4	2	8	8
Georgia	56	180	11,348	2	2	–	–
Hawaii	25	51	32,000	4	2	–	–
Idaho	35	70	12,360	2	2	8	8
Illinois	59	118	47,039	4/2[3]	2	–	–
Indiana	50	100	11,600	4	2	–	–
Iowa	50	100	20,120	4	2	–	–
Kansas	40	125	–	4	2	–	–
Kentucky	38	100	–	4	2	–	–
Louisiana	39	105	16,800	4	4	12	12
Maine	35	151	10,500	2	2	8	8

Table 9.2   (*cont'd*)

State	No. of legislators		Annual salary ($)[1]	Term (years)		Term limit (years)	
	Senate	House		Senate	House	Senate	House
Maryland	47	141	29,700	4	4	–	–
Massachusetts	40	160	46,410	2	2	–	–
Michigan	38	110	51,895	4	2	8	6
Minnesota	67	134	29,675	4	2	–	–
Mississippi	52	122	10,000	4	4	–	–
Missouri	34	163	26,803	4	2	8	8
Montana	50	100	–	4	2	8	8
Nebraska		49	12,000	unicameral	4		–
Nevada	21	42	–	4	2	12	12
New Hampshire	24	400	200	2	2	–	–
New Jersey	40	80	35,000	4[3]	2	–	–
New Mexico	42	70	–	4	2	–	–
New York	61	150	57,500	2	2	–	–
North Carolina	50	120	13,951	2	2	–	–
North Dakota	49	98	–	4	4	–	–
Ohio	33	99	42,427	4	2	8	8
Oklahoma	48	101	32,000	4	2	12	12
Oregon	30	60	13,104	4	2	8	6
Pennsylvania	50	203	57,367	4	2	–	–
Rhode Island	50	100	10,250	2	2	–	–
South Carolina	46	124	10,400	4	2	–	–
South Dakota	35	70	[2]	2	2	8	8
Tennessee	33	99	16,500	4	2	–	–
Texas	31	150	7,200	4	2	–	–
Utah	29	75	–	4	2	12	12
Vermont	30	150	Week 510	2	2	–	–
Virginia	40	100	S18,000 H17,640	4	2	–	–
Washington	49	98	28,800	4	2	–	–
West Virginia	34	100	15,000	4	2	–	–
Wisconsin	33	99	39,211	4	2	–	–
Wyoming	30	60	–	4	2	12	12

Notes:
1 Salaries as of May 1997. In those states that do not have annual salaries, all but New Mexico have a salary with payments for each day the legislature is in session. Most states also have provision for *per diem* living expenses.
2 South Dakota paid annual salary of $4,267 in odd years; $3,733 for even years.
3 In Illinois senators serve four or two year terms depending upon the district and election cycle. In New Jersey the first senatorial term at the beginning of each decade is two years.
Sources: adapted from *The Book of the States 1998–99, Lexington KY, Council of State Governments, 1999*, 68–9 and 80–1, and US Term Limits.

improved pay and conditions and better administrative and research support. While many observers noted that the legislatures were as a result better equipped to deal with the problems facing state governments, critics argued that the reforms had been exploited by lawmakers who had become 'professional politicians' determined to make life comfortable for themselves. The **term limits** movement managed to persuade voters in many states that there was a need to restrict the number of times incumbent legislators could seek re-election in order to promote more competitive elections and to encourage ordinary people ('citizen legislators' as they called them) to become candidates.

Even today there is great diversity in the way state legislatures operate. Some, like those in New York and California, are almost fully professionalised, have full-time members and regular sessions every year. Others still work with a part-time membership with no proper salaries and meet only for short periods. The principal characteristics of the state legislatures are shown in Table 9.2.

Governors

All fifty states have an elected governor who acts as chief executive of the state. However, the position and powers of these officials vary considerably, particularly in relation to the legislative branch. Overall, there has been a tendency to strengthen the role of the governor, for example, by lengthening the term of office, allowing him or her to serve successive terms and improving the chief executive's control over the budget and administrative organisation. In 1900, of the forty-five states at that, time only twenty had four-year terms for their governors, while Massachusetts, Rhode Island and Tennessee allowed only one-year terms. By 1995 forty-eight out of the fifty state governors had four-year terms, while only New Hampshire and Vermont retained two-year terms. As Table 9.3 shows, thirty-nine states do impose **term limits** on their governors, mostly restricting them to two four-year terms, similar to that imposed on the US president by the Twenty-second Amendment. In all states except North Carolina and North Dakota the governor possesses the power to veto Bills passed by the legislature. Additionally, forty-three state governors also have the power of a line-item veto that allows them to block single parts of a Bill. Normally this applies to appropriations or spending Bills but in some states the line item veto can be used with other Bills as well.

Another factor affecting the power of governors is how far they share executive power with other elected officials and agencies. As Table 9.3 demonstrates, in many states there is a fragmented structure of government and the governor has little opportunity to co-ordinate and control the executive branch. In other states the governor is one of very few executive officials who is elected with a statewide mandate and therefore enjoys greater authority. The governor's deputy is the lieutenant governor but, as the office is elected separately by the people, the successful candidate may possibly be from a different party

Table 9.3 *Governors' term limits, line item veto power and other elected officials*

State	Maximum no. of consecutive terms[1]	Item veto[3]	Other statewide elected officials[2] No. of officials	No. of agencies
Alabama	2	Yes	9	7
Alaska	2[4]	Yes	1	0
Arizona	2	Yes	8	6
Arkansas	2[5]	Yes	6	6
California	2[5]	Yes	7	7
Colorado	2	Yes	4	4
Connecticut	No limit	Yes	5	5
Delaware	2[5]	Yes	1	1
Florida	2	No	7	7
Georgia	2[4]	Yes	12	8
Hawaii	2	Yes	1	1
Idaho	No limit	Yes	6	6
Illinois	No limit	Yes	5	5
Indiana	[6]	No	6	6
Iowa	No limit	Yes	7	6
Kansas	2	Yes	5	5
Kentucky	2	Yes	6	6
Louisiana	2	Yes	7	7
Maine	2	No	0	0
Maryland	2[4]	Yes	3	3
Massachusetts	2[4]	Yes	5	7
Michigan	2	Yes	35	6
Minnesota	No limit	Yes	5	5
Mississippi	2	Yes	7	7
Missouri	2[5]	Yes	5	5
Montana	[8]	Yes	5	5
Nebraska	2[4]	Yes	5	5
Nevada	2	No	5	5
New Hampshire	No limit	No	0	0
New Jersey	2[4]	Yes	0	0
New Mexico	2[4]	Yes	9	7
New York	No limit	Yes	3	3
North Carolina	2	Yes	9	9
North Dakota	No limit	Yes	13	16
Ohio	2[5]	Yes	5	5
Oklahoma	2	Yes	10	8
Oregon	2[6]	Yes	5	5
Pennsylvania	2	Yes	4	4
Rhode Island	2	No	4	4
South Carolina	2	Yes	8	10

Table 9.3   (*cont'd*)

State	Maximum No. of consecutive terms[1]	Item veto[3]	Other statewide elected officials[2]	
			No. of officials	No. of agencies
South Dakota	2	Yes	9	7
Tennessee	2	Yes	0	0
Texas	No limit	Yes	9	7
Utah	3	Yes	4	14
Vermont	No limit	No	5	5
Virginia	1	Yes	2	2
Washington	[7]	Yes	8	8
West Virginia	2	Yes	5	6
Wisconsin	No limit	Yes	5	5
Wyoming	[8]	Yes	4	4

Notes:
1 All governors serve four-year terms, except in New Hampshire and Vermont, which have two-year terms.
2 Number of directly elected executive branch officials on a statewide basis and the number of agencies involving these officials.
3 Provision to override varies, requiring as many as two-thirds of the legislators.
4 After two consecutive terms, must wait for four years before being eligible again.
5 Two terms only, whether or not consecutive.
6 Cannot serve more than eight years in any twelve-year period.
7 Cannot serve more than eight years in any fourteen-year period.
8 Cannot serve more than eight years in any sixteen-year period.
Source: adapted from Harold W. Stanley and Richard G. Niemi, *Vital Statistics on American Politics 1997–98*, Washington DC, Congressional Quarterly Press, 1998, 291–2.

from the governor and a political rival. This contrasts with the position at national level, where the president and vice-president are elected together on a party ticket. Other elected officials usually include the state treasurer, the attorney-general and the secretary of state. The duties of the secretary of state include the administration of elections, as Kathleen Harris's role in the disputed Florida election for president in 2000 highlighted.

Direct democracy

In the early years of the twentieth century the Progressive movement campaigned successfully in many states for ordinary citizens to be given a more direct say in the running of government. The movement succeeded in pushing for the direct election of US senators with the passage of the Seventeenth Amendment in 1913 and the adoption of primaries for the selection and nomination of party candidates for many offices. The movement was particularly influential in the western states and led to many adopting mechanisms such as the initiative, the referendum and recall.

An initiative allows proposed state laws to be placed on the ballot by citizen petition and then enacted or rejected by the electorate. 'Direct' initiatives are measures that can be placed on the ballot following the collection of a specific number of signatures and no action by the legislature is necessary. 'Indirect' initiatives require the measure to be submitted to the legislature for consideration before it can be placed on the ballot.

Referendums allow a state law passed by the legislature to be referred to the voters before it goes into effect. Referendums may be held following a citizen petition or as a result of voluntary submission by the legislature. For certain types of decisions, such as tax increases, referendums may be required by the state constitution. All states except Alabama require changes in the constitution to be submitted by the legislature for voter approval in a referendum. Recall provisions allow voters to remove elected officials from their positions in special elections before the end of their normal term; the number of signatures required ranges from ten to 40 per cent. The recall process is rarely used in practice.

Table 9.4 shows the provision in each state for these methods of direct democracy. Twenty-four states allow either direct or indirect initiatives or both. The direct initiative gives most power to the citizens because they can act without the support of the legislature. Reforms such as legislative term limits and campaign finance limits have been enacted most readily in those states which allow the people to bypass the normal legislative process and the opposition of politicians who would be affected by the changes. The 1980s and 1990s saw a boom in the number of proposals on the ballot, following the 1978 California initiative, Proposition 13, which led to large-scale cuts in property taxes. Since then the initiatives have become more numerous, ambitious and far-reaching. In 1996 a record number of 102 initiatives were placed

Table 9.4   *State provision for initiative, referendum and recall*

State	Initiative	Referendum	Recall
Alabama			
Alaska	Indirect	Legislature and petition	All but judges
Arizona	Indirect	Legislature and petition	All elected officials
Arkansas	Direct	Legislature and petition	
California	Direct	Legislature and petition	All elected officials
Colorado	Direct	Legislature	All elected officials
Connecticut		Legislature	
Delaware		Legislature	
Florida	Direct	Legislature	
Georgia		Legislature	All elected officials

Table 9.4   (*cont'd*)

State	Initiative	Referendum	Recall
Hawaii		Legislature	
Idaho	Direct	Legislature and petition	All but judges
Illinois	Direct	Legislature	
Indiana		Legislature	
Iowa		Legislature	
Kansas		Legislature	All but judges
Kentucky		Legislature and petition	
Louisiana		Legislature	All but certain judges
Maine	Indirect	Legislature and petition	
Maryland		Legislature and petition	
Massachusetts	Indirect	Legislature and petition	
Michigan	Both	Legislature and petition	All but certain judges
Minnesota		Legislature	
Mississippi	Indirect	Legislature	
Missouri	Direct	Legislature and petition	
Montana	Direct	Legislature and petition	All elected or appointed officials
Nebraska	Direct	Legislature and petition	
Nevada	Both	Legislature and petition	All public officers
New Hampshire		Legislature	
New Jersey		Legislature	All elected officials
New Mexico		Legislature and petition	
New York		Legislature	
North Carolina		Legislature	
North Dakota	Direct	Legislature and petition	All elected officials except Congress
Ohio	Both	Legislature and petition	
Oklahoma	Direct	Legislature and petition	
Oregon	Direct	Legislature and petition	All elected officials except Congress
Pennsylvania		Legislature	
Rhode Island		Legislature	Certain elected officials
South Carolina		Legislature	
South Dakota	Direct	Legislature and petition	Certain municipal officials
Tennessee		Legislature	
Texas		Legislature	
Utah	Both	Legislature and petition	
Vermont		Legislature	
Virginia		Legislature	
Washington	Both	Legislature and petition	All but certain judges
West Virginia		Legislature	
Wisconsin		Legislature	All elected officials
Wyoming	Indirect	Legislature and petition	

Sources: *The Book of the States 1998–99*, Lexington KY, Council of State Governments, 1999, 210, and Harold W. Stanley and Richard G. Niemi, *Vital Statistics on American Politics 1997–98*, Washington DC, Congressional Quarterly Press, 1998, 294–5.

on statewide ballots. In 2000 seventy-two initiatives and 133 referendums featured on the voting papers in some forty-two states (*National Journal*, 28 October 2000, 3412). They included such controversial issues as gun control, gay marriages, the legalisation of marijuana for medical use, campaign finance controls, school choice, genetically modified foods and tax cuts. In recent years a higher percentage of the ballot measures have been passed, rising to 61 per cent in 1998. (*National Journal*, 1 July 2000, 2146) While supporters claim that the process allows the public more influence and contributes to a democratic political system, critics express concern that it undermines representative government and cripples state legislatures, while at the same time leading to the exploitation of public opinion by wealthy interest groups and individuals who finance initiative campaigns.

Party politics

The fifty states have their own individual party systems that exhibit a wide variety of partisan competition. The strength of the two main parties depends to a large extent on the particular traditions and political culture of the state as well as its social composition. Patterns of competition vary from close struggles for power in both the legislative and executive branches to those where one party has enjoyed an almost monopoly position in statewide elections. Two trends in recent decades that should be noted are the rise of divided party control of the legislative branch and the governorship within the states and the increasing strength of the Republican Party at state level.

Divided party control of the presidency and Congress at national level has been mirrored by trends in state politics. Whereas in 1960 only 37.5 per cent of states had different parties in control of the legislative and executive branches, the figure had risen to 61 per cent by 1990. In 2001 (excluding Nebraska, which has a non-partisan legislature) only twenty-two states had a single party in control and twenty-seven exhibited divided control, with the governor facing opposition party majorities in one or both legislative chambers.

The Republican Party noticeably increased its influence in state governments during the 1980s and 1990s, particularly in the number of governorships it controlled. For example, in 1985 there were only sixteen Republican governors and thirty-four Democrats. Ten years later, following the party's highly successful 1994 election campaign which enabled it to take control of both houses of the US Congress, the Republicans had thirty governors to the Democrats' nineteen, with one independent. In the same period, Republican control of both houses of state legislatures increased from eleven to nineteen. Following the 2000 elections, the Republicans held twenty-nine governorships and controlled seventeen state legislatures. (See the appendix 'State profiles' for details of party strengths in individual states.) Tables 9.5 and 9.6 provide two indications of party strengths in the states. The former reflects the balance of power between the parties in terms of their control of the

Table 9.5   *Party strengths in state government, 1968–96*

Most Democrat 0–20	21–40	41–60	61–80	Most Republican 81–100
Alabama	California	Alaska	Arizona	Idaho
Arkansas	Connecticut	Delaware	Colorado	New Hampshire
Florida	Maine	Illinois	Indiana	South Dakota
Georgia	Nebraska	Iowa	Kansas	Wyoming
Hawaii	Nevada	Michigan	North Dakota	
Kentucky	New Jersey	Montana	Utah	
Louisiana	Oregon	New York		
Maryland	South Carolina	Ohio		
Massachusetts	Washington	Pennsylvania		
Minnesota	Wisconsin	Vermont		
Mississippi				
Missouri				
New Mexico				
North Carolina				
Oklahoma				
Rhode Island				
Tennessee				
Texas				
Virginia				
West Virginia				

Notes:
Figures are the percentage of Republican wins in elections for governorship and control of
the lower and upper houses of the state legislatures in the period. Nebraska's results include
governorship only as unicameral legislature is non-partisan.
Source: adapted from Harold W. Stanley and Richard G. Niemi, *Vital Statistics on American
Politics, 1997–98*, Washington DC, Congressional Quarterly Press, 1998, 19.

legislature and governorship in individual states in the period from 1968 to
1996. The latter shows the number of times Republican presidential candidates won the states' Electoral College votes in the period from 1968 to 2000.
Taken together, these tables present a picture of which states can be regarded
as 'most Democrat' and which as 'most Republican'. It should be noted that the
Republican Party started to do well in presidential elections in the Deep South,
which had traditionally been solidly Democratic, in the mid to late 1960s.
The generally conservative voters of the region were deterred from supporting
liberal Democratic Party candidates for the White House. It was not until the
Reagan years of the 1980s and during the 1990s that the Republicans increasingly strengthened their position among the congressional delegations
from the southern states and in state government itself. This explains why the
Republicans appear stronger in the south in Table 9.6 than in Table 9.5.

Table 9.6 *Party strength in the states: presidential elections, 1968–2000*

No. of times each state's Electoral College vote went to the Republican candidate				
0	1	2	3	4
District of Columbia	Minnesota	Hawaii Massachusetts Rhode Island	Maryland New York West Virginia	Pennsylvania Washington Wisconsin
5	6	7	8	9
Arkansas Connecticut Delaware Georgia Iowa Louisiana Maine Michigan Oregon	California Illinois Kentucky Missouri New Jersey New Mexico Ohio Tennessee Vermont	Alabama Florida Mississippi Nevada New Hampshire Texas	Arizona Colorado Montana North Carolina South Carolina	Alaska Idaho Indiana Kansas Nebraska North Dakota Oklahoma South Dakota Utah Virginia Wyoming

Source: adapted from Harold W. Stanley and Richard G. Niemi, *Vital Statistics on American Politics 1997–98*, Washington DC, Congressional Quarterly Press, 1998, 17.

State profiles

See the appendix.

Glossary

bicameralism A legislative body that has two separate chambers is known as a bicameral ('two-chamber') legislature. All the American states, with the exception of Nebraska, which has one chamber, have bicameral legislatures. The state senates are smaller in size and often have more senior and experienced legislators among their members than their lower house counterparts. The US Senate has two senators for each state regardless of population and represents the states within a federal system but the US Supreme Court rejected the federal analogy as a justification for having state senators represent grossly unequal constituencies in population terms. Since the mid-1960s state senate and lower house seats must be apportioned on a basis that fairly reflects the state's population.

'**big government**'   The phrase 'big government' has been used as a shorthand way of describing the phenomenon of a large-scale federal government with an increased number of departments, agencies and responsibilities. The term was used mostly in a pejorative sense by conservative critics of the growth of power in Washington DC as a result of the Democratic administration of President Franklin D. Roosevelt following the Great Depression.

block grants   Block grants are a form of federal government financial aid to the states. They have to be spent on broad functional areas, such as education or welfare, but come with relatively few conditions as to their use. States are therefore able to use their discretion as to how they make best use of the money without detailed supervision by federal government departments. Conservatives have generally preferred this type of federal grant to categorical grants (see below) and in 1981, for example, President Reagan managed to persuade Congress to consolidate dozens of such grants into nine block grants.

categorical grants   Categorical grants are funds transferred from the federal government to the states to help pay for specific programmes. They come with conditions attached to them and usually require the state to contribute financially to the programme as well. This form of grant-in-aid has become a significant feature of the federal relationship since the period of the New Deal, and states increasingly became dependent on such funding, with approximately one-fifth of their revenues coming from Washington DC by the 1980s. Proponents of categorical grants saw them as a way of encouraging state participation in federally initiated programmes and a characteristic of *co-operative federalism* (Box 9.1).

confederation   A confederation is an alliance or league of sovereign states that delegates powers on specific issues to a central authority. This central government is deliberately limited and thus may be inherently weak because it has few independent powers. The US was a confederation from 1781 to 1789. The eleven states that sought to secede from the Union and provoked the Civil War of 1861–65 established a short-lived Confederation.

cross-over sanctions   The federal government employed cross-over sanctions to persuade states to adopt uniform laws by threatening a state that failed to comply with a statute that it would lose a federal grant-in-aid authorised by an earlier law. For example, states were obliged to adopt national uniform standards on truck size and a common twenty-one minimum age for the purchase of alcohol by the threat of losing federal highway funds. In 1987 the US Supreme Court in the case of *South Dakota v. Dole* upheld the constitutionality of such sanctions by arguing that a state's participation in a grant-in-aid programme was voluntary. Cross-over sanctions are seen as a feature of *coercive federalism* (Box 9.1).

devolution   In the UK devolution means the transfer of specific powers from a superior to a subordinate parliament or government. The term is not, strictly speaking, appropriate for a federal system with dual sovereignty but in the US it has come to mean the restoration or reviving of state powers or states' rights and a rebalancing of the federal system.

federation   A federation is a system where a national government shares power and constitutional authority with sub-national or state governments. A federal system has certain features: a written constitution that divides power between the central and constituent governments, giving substantial powers and sovereignty to both; the levels of government each exercise power directly over the citizen and have their own authority to raise taxes; the constitutional distribution of power cannot be changed unilaterally by any level of government or by the ordinary process of legislation.

pre-emption power   Article VI of the US Constitution provides that the Constitution and laws of the US shall be the 'supreme law of the land . . . anything in the constitutions or laws of any state to the contrary notwithstanding'. Congressional laws that pre-empt or override state authority have become more common and more directive in nature. The statute may direct the states to initiate specific actions, pass a law or meet national minimum standards in a particular policy area. Pre-emption laws have become a major method by which power is centralised in the national government and a prominent feature of *coercive federalism*.

term limits   Term limits are constitutional restrictions on the number of terms that executive or legislative office holders may serve in the same post. They are seen as a method of preventing individuals from becoming too powerful and as a way of countering the advantages that incumbents enjoy in the electoral process. The US Supreme Court declared in 1995 that states could not constitutionally restrict the number of terms served by their federal legislators but eighteen states have introduced term limits for their state legislators and thirty-nine have placed limits on their governors.

unfunded mandates   Mandates are legal orders requiring state or local government action and have become a common feature of federal legislation. With the growth of the federal government's budget deficit from the 1980s, Congress chose to pass more directive legislation, including mandates, while at the same time failing to provide the necessary reimbursement of the costs involved in implementation. The growth of unfunded mandates became an increasingly costly burden for the states and a source of friction between the federal and state governments. In 1995 members of Congress responded to their states' concerns and passed legislation making it more difficult to introduce new unfunded mandates.

unitary system   A unitary state is a governmental system where one parliament has supreme law-making authority for the whole country and any other sub-national bodies that may be established are subordinate to the national parliament. A unitary state can be contrasted to a federal system where law-making authority is divided between national and sub-national bodies.

Resources

References and further reading

Bailey, C.J. (1998), 'The Changing Federal System', in G. Peele, C.J. Bailey, B. Cain and B. Guy Peters, *Developments in American Politics*, 3, Basingstoke, Macmillan.

Conlan, T.J. (1988), *New Federalism: Intergovernmental Reform from Nixon to Reagan*, Washington DC, Brookings Institution.

Grant, A. (1998), 'Reshaping American Federalism', *Politics Review*, 8:1, 2–6.

Grant A. (2000), 'Devolution and the Reshaping of American Federalism', in A. Grant (ed.), *American Politics: 2000 and Beyond*, Aldershot, Ashgate.

Kincaid, J. (1994), 'Governing the American States', in G. Peele, C.J. Bailey, B. Cain and B.G. Peters (eds), *Developments in American Politics*, 2, Basingstoke, Macmillan.

Nathan, R. (1990), 'Federalism: the Great Composition', in A. King (ed.), *The New American Political System*, Washington DC, AEI Press.

O'Toole, L.J. (1993), *American Intergovernmental Relations*, Washington DC, Congressional Quarterly Press.

Peterson, P.E. (1995), *The Price of Federalism*, Washington DC, Brookings Institution.

Posner, P.L. (1997), 'Unfunded Mandates:1996 and Beyond', *Publius: the Journal of Federalism*, 27:2, 53–71.

Walker, D.B. (1995), *The Rebirth of Federalism*, Chatham NJ, Chatham House.

Zimmerman, J. (1992), *Contemporary American Federalism: The Growth of National Power*, Leicester, Leicester University Press.

Websites

Council of State Governments www.csg.org

Since 1933 the Council has provided a forum by which states can share resources, strategies and ideas. State leaders in both legislative and executive branches cooperate through this association. The website also has links with the home pages of the individual states. These include information about the states and the organisation of their governments.

National Association of Counties www.naco.org

NACO was created in 1935 to speak on behalf of the nation's county level of local government. Today its membership totals almost 2,000 counties, representing three-quarters of the national population. It provides legislative, research and technical assistance to its members and its headquarters are on Capitol Hill.

National Conference of State Legislatures www.ncsl.org

The NCSL was founded in 1975 as a bipartisan organisation committed to serving the lawmakers and staffs of the fifty state legislatures. The conference is a source of research, publications, meetings and seminars, details of which can be found on its website.

National Governors' Association www.nga.org

The NGA is a bipartisan national organisation which was established in 1908 to represent the views of the state governors. Since 1967 it has had an Office of State-Federal Relations in Washington DC. Its website includes analysis of issues affecting the states, details of NGA meetings and press releases on current policy questions.

National League of Cities www.nlc.org

NLC was set up in 1924 and represents more than 18,000 municipal governments, including large and small cities, towns and villages. It encourages membership participation from councillors as well as mayors.

United States Conference of Mayors www.usmayors.org/uscm/

Established in 1933, USCM is the official non-partisan organisation of cities with populations of over 30,000, of which there are about 1,100 today. Each city is represented in the conference by its mayor.

Appendix

State profiles

Alabama

'We dare defend our rights'

State capital Montgomery.

Admittance to the Union 1819 (twenty-third state of the US). Seceded from the Union in January 1861; readmitted in February 1868.

Land area 50,750 square miles (ranked twenty-third in size).

Population 2000 census: 4,447,100. Rank among states by population: 23.

Population change 1990–2000: +10.1 per cent.

Racial composition (1999 estimate): white: 73 per cent; Hispanic: 1 per cent; black: 26 per cent.

Population density: 86.1. Urban population: 60.4 per cent. Rural population: 39.6 per cent. (1990 census figures.)

Voting patterns Voting-age population of 3,293,000, of whom 70 per cent were registered voters (1998). There is no party registration in Alabama.

Presidential elections

Voter turnout (%)

1992	1996	2000
54.6	47.6	50.1 (estimated)

Votes cast

1992	1996	2000
Bush (R) 804,283 (48%)	Dole (R) 768,826 (50%)	Bush (R) 943,799 (56%)
Clinton (D) 690,080 (41%)	Clinton (D) 662,066 (43%)	Gore (D) 696,741 (42%)
Perot (I) 183,109 (11%)	Perot (Reform) 92,628 (6%)	Others 31,904 (2%)

Representation in US Congress (January 2001)

House of Representatives 7: 2 (D), 5 (R).

US senators: J. Sessions (R), elected 1996; R. Shelby (R), elected 1986.

Votes in Electoral College: 9.

State government

Executive branch (maximum two consecutive terms) Governor: Don Siegelman (D), elected 1998. Lieutenant Governor: Steve Windom (R), elected 1998.

Legislature (2001) House of Representatives 105: 68 (D), 37 (R). Senate 35: 24 (D), 11 (R). Both houses serve four-year terms.

Alaska

'North to the future'
State capital Juneau.
Admittance to the Union 1959 (forty-ninth state of the US).
Land area 570,374 square miles (ranked first in size).
Population 2000 census: 626,932. Rank among states by population: 48.
Population change 1990–2000: +14.0 per cent.
Racial composition (1999 estimate): American Indian/Eskimo/Aleut: 6.3 per cent; Asian/Pacific Islander: 4.5 per cent; white: 71.9 per cent; Hispanic: 4 per cent; black: 3.8 per cent.
Population density: 1.1. Urban population: 67.5 per cent. Rural population: 32.5 per cent. (1990 census figures.)
Voting patterns (2001) 480,142 registered voters: 16 per cent D, 25 per cent R, 59 per cent unaffiliated/minor parties.
Presidential elections
Voter turnout (%)

1992	1996	2000
63.8	56.9	52.8 (estimated)

Votes cast

1992	1996	2000
Bush (R) 102,000 (40%)	Dole (R) 122,746 (51%)	Bush (R) 167,398 (59%)
Clinton (D) 78,294 (30%)	Clinton (D) 80,380 (33%)	Gore (D) 79,004 (28%)
Perot (I) 73,481 (28%)	Perot (Reform) 26,333 (11%)	Others 38,090 (13%)

Representation in US Congress (January 2001)
House of Representatives 1: (R).
US senators: Frank Murkowski (R), elected 1980; Ted Stevens (R), appointed 1968.
Votes in Electoral College: 3.
State government
Executive branch (maximum of two consecutive terms) Governor: Tony Knowles (D), elected 1994. Lieutenant Governor: Fran Ulmer (D), elected 1994.
Legislature (2001) House of Representatives 40: 13 (D), 27 (R). Senate 20: 6 (D), 14 (R). Representatives are elected for terms of two years. Members of the Alaska Senate serve four-year terms.

Arizona

'Ditat Deus' (*God enriches*)
State capital Phoenix.
Admittance to the Union 1912 (forty-eighth state of the US).
Land area 113,642 square miles (ranked sixth in size).
Population (2000 census) 5,130,632. Rank among states by population: 20.
Population change 1990–2000: +40.0 per cent.
Racial composition (1999 estimate): white: 67.5 per cent; Hispanic: 22.6 per cent; American Indian: 5.5 per cent; black: 2.2 per cent.
Population density: 42.0. Urban population: 87.5 per cent. Rural population: 12.5 per cent. (1990 census figures.)
Voting patterns Voting-age population of 3,547,000, of whom 64 per cent were registered voters (1998). Of registered voters: 40 per cent D, 45 per cent R, 15 per cent unaffiliated/minor parties.

Presidential elections

Voter turnout (%)

1992	1996	2000
52.9	45.4	59.0 (estimated)

Votes cast

1992	1996	2000
Bush (R) 572,086 (38%)	Clinton (D) 653,288 (47%)	Bush (R) 672,220 (50%)
Clinton (D) 543,050 (37%)	Bush (R) 622,073 (44%)	Gore (D) 608,693 (45%)
Perot (I) 353,741 (24%)	Perot (Reform) 112,074 (8%)	Others 57,504 (5%)

Representation in US Congress   (January 2001)

House of Representatives 6: 5 (R), 1 (D). From 2002 Arizona will have eight Representatives.

US senators: Jon Kyl (R), elected 1994; John McCain (R), elected 1986.

Votes in the Electoral College: 8 (ten votes after 2002).

State government

Executive branch (maximum of two consecutive terms)   Governor: Jane Dee Hull (R), elected November 1998. Secretary of state: Betsey Bayless (R), elected 1998.

Legislature (2001)   House of Representatives 60: 24 (D), 36 (R). Senate 30: 15 (D), 15 (R). Legislators serve two-year terms.

Arkansas

'Regnat populus' (*The people rule*)

State capital   Little Rock.

Admittance to the Union   1836 (twenty-fifth state of the US). Seceded from the Union in May 1861; readmitted in June 1868.

Land area   52,075 square miles (ranked twenty-seventh in size).

Population   2000 census: 2,673,400. Rank among states by population: 33.

Population change 1990–2000: +13.7 per cent.

Racial composition (1999 estimate): white: 80.7 per cent; Hispanic: 2.1 per cent; black: 16.1 per cent.

Population density: 45.1. Urban population: 53.5 per cent. Rural population: 46.5 per cent. (1990 census figures.)

Voting patterns   Voting-age population of 1,882,000, of whom 80.7 per cent were registered voters (1998). There is no party registration in Arkansas.

Presidential elections

Voter turnout (%)

1992	1996	2000
53.6	47.5	48.9 (estimated)

Votes cast

1992	1996	2000
Bush (R) 337,324 (35%)	Dole (R) 325,416 (37%)	Bush (R) 472,940 (51%)
Clinton (D) 505,823 (53%)	Clinton (D) 475,171 (54%)	Gore (D) 422,768 (46%)
Perot (I) 99,132 (10%)	Perot (Reform) 69,884 (8%)	Others 26,073 (3%)
	Others 13,791 (1%)	

Representation in US Congress   (January 2001)

House of Representatives 4: 3 (D), 1 (R).

US senators: Tim Hutchinson (R), elected November 1996; Blanche Lincoln (D), elected November 1998.

Votes in the Electoral College: 6.

State government

Executive branch (maximum of two consecutive terms)   Governor: Mike Huckabee (R), succeeded to office July 1996, elected November 1998. Lieutenant Governor: Win Rockefeller (R), elected November 1996.

Legislature (2001)   House of Representatives 100: 70 (D), 30 (R). Senate 35: 27 (D), 8 (R). Both houses serve two-year terms.

California

'Eureka' (*I have found it*)

State capital   Sacramento.

Admittance to the Union   1850 (thirty-first state of the US).

Land area   155,973 square miles (ranked third in size).

Population   2000 census: 33,871,648. Rank among states by population: 1.

Population change 1990–2000: +13.8 per cent.

Racial composition (1999 estimate): white: 49.8 per cent; Hispanic: 31.5 per cent; black: 7.5 per cent; Asian/Pacific: 12 per cent.

Population density: 190.8. Urban population: 92.6 per cent. Rural population: 7.4 per cent. (1990 census figures.)

Voting patterns   Voting-age population of 23,665,000, of whom 63 per cent were registered voters (1998). Of 14,969,185 registered voters: 47 per cent D, 36 per cent R, 17 per cent unaffiliated and minor parties.

Presidential elections

Voter turnout (%)

1992	1996	2000
49.4	43.3	45.1 (estimated)

Votes cast

1992	1996	2000
Bush (R) 3,630,566 (33%)	Dole (R) 3,828,368 (38%)	Bush (R) 4,437,557 (42%)
Clinton (D) 5,121,249 (46%)	Clinton (D) 5,119,815 (51%)	Gore (D) 5,721,195 (54%)
Perot (I) 2,296,004 (21%)	Perot (Reform) 697,845 (7%)	Others 520,825 (4%)
	Other 372,553 (4%)	

Representation in US Congress   (January 2001)

House of Representatives 52: 32 (D), 20 (R), one vacant. From 2002 California will have 53 Representatives.

US senators: Barbara Boxer (D), elected November 1992; Dianne Feinstein (D), elected November 1992.

Votes in the Electoral College: 54 (55 votes from 2002).

State government

Executive branch (maximum of two consecutive terms)   Governor: Gray Davis (D), elected November 1998. Lieutenant Governor: Cruz Bustamente (D), elected November 1998.

Legislature (2001)   State Assembly 80: 50 (D), 30 (R). Senate 40: 26 (D), 14 (R). Members of the Assembly serve two-year terms. Senators serve terms of four years.

Colorado

'Nil sine Numine' (*Nothing without Providence*)
State capital   Denver.
Admittance to the Union   1876 (thirty-eighth state of the US).
Land area   103,729 square miles (ranked eighth in size).
Population   2000 census: 4,301,261. Rank among states by population: 24.
Population change 1990–2000: +30.6 per cent.
Racial composition (1999 estimate): Asian/Pacific: 2 per cent; white: 78 per cent;
   Hispanic: 14 per cent; black: 4 per cent.
Population density: 31.8. Urban population: 82.4 per cent. Rural population: 17.6 per
   cent. (1990 census figures.)
Voting patterns   Voting-age population of 2,961,000, of whom 86.5 per cent were
   registered voters (1998). Of registered voters, 31 per cent D, 37 per cent R, 34 per
   cent unaffiliated and minor parties.
Presidential elections
Voter turnout (%)

1992	1996	2000
60.8	53.1	59.0 (estimated)

Votes cast

1992	1996	2000
Bush (R) 562,850 (36%)	Dole (R) 691,846 (46%)	Bush (R) 885,147 (51%)
Clinton (D) 629,681 (40%)	Clinton (D) 671,150 (44%)	Gore (D) 738,718 (42%)
Perot (I) 366,010 (23%)	Perot (Reform) 99,628 (7%)	Others 120,223 (7%)
	Other 45,646 (3%)	

Representation in US Congress   (January 2001)
House of Representatives 6: 2 (D), 4 (R). From 2002 Colorado will have seven
   Representatives.
US Senators: Ben Nighthorse Campbell (R), elected November 1992; Wayne A. Allard
   (R), elected November 1996.
Votes in the Electoral College: 8 (nine votes from 2002).
State government
Executive branch (maximum of two consecutive terms)   Governor: Bill Owens (R), elected
   November 1998. Lieutenant Governor: Joe Rogers (R), elected November 1998.
Legislature (2001)   House of Representatives 65: 27 (D), 38 (R). Senate 35: 18 (D),
   17 (R). Representatives serve two-year terms and Senators serve four-year terms.

Connecticut

'Qui transtulit sustinet' (*He who transplants still sustains*)
State capital   Hartford.
Admittance to the Union   1788 (fifth state of the US).
Land area   4,845 square miles (ranked forty-eighth in size).
Population   2000 census: 3,405,565. Rank among states by population: 29.
Population change 1990–2000: +3.6 per cent.
Racial composition (1999 estimate): Asian: 2.5 per cent; white: 80.0 per cent; Hispanic:
   8.5 per cent; black: 9.0 per cent.
Population density: 678.4. Urban population: 79.1 per cent. Rural population: 20.9 per
   cent. (1990 census figures.)

Voting patterns Voting-age population of 2,464,000, of whom 80 per cent were registered voters (1998).
Presidential elections
Voter turnout (%)
| 1992 | 1996 | 2000 |
| 64.4 | 56.4 | 58.7 (estimated) |
Votes cast
1992	1996	2000
Bush (R) 578,313 (36%)	Dole (R) 483,109 (35%)	Bush (R) 558, 069 (39%)
Clinton (D) 682,318 (42%)	Clinton (D) 735,740 (53%)	Gore (D) 808,955 (56%)
Perot (I) 348,771 (22%)	Perot (Reform) 139,523 (10%)	Others 80,449 (5%)

Representation in US Congress (January 2001)
House of Representatives 6: 3 (D), 3 (R). Connecticut will lose one Representative in 2002.
US Senators: Christopher Dodd (D), elected 1980; Joseph Lieberman (D), elected 1988.
Votes in the Electoral College: 8 (seven votes from 2002).
State government
Executive branch Governor: John G. Rowland (R), elected November 1994. Lieutenant Governor: M. Jodi Rell (R), elected November 1994.
Legislature (2001) House of Representatives 151: 100 (D), 51 (R). Senate 36: 21 (D), 15 (R). Both houses serve two-year terms.

Delaware

'Liberty and independence'
State capital Dover.
Admittance to the Union 1787 (first state of the US).
Land area 1,955 square miles (ranked forty-ninth in size).
Population 2000 census: 783,600. Rank among states by population: 45.
Population change 1990–2000: +17.6 per cent.
Racial composition (1999 estimate): white: 74.5 per cent; Hispanic: 3.5 per cent; black: 20 per cent; Asian: 2 per cent.
Population density: 340.8. Urban population: 73 per cent. Rural population: 27 per cent. (1990 census figures.)
Voting patterns Voting-age population of 568,000, of whom 82 per cent were registered voters (1998). Of 467,388 registered voters, 42 per cent D, 36 per cent R and 23 per cent unaffiliated/minor parties.
Presidential elections
Voter turnout (%)
| 1992 | 1996 | 2000 |
| 55.6 | 49.6 | 57.7 (estimated) |
Votes cast *in presidential election*
1992	1996	2000
Bush (R) 102,313 (35%)	Dole (R) 99,062 (37%)	Bush (R) 137,081 (42%)
Clinton (D) 126,054 (44%)	Clinton (D) 140,355 (52%)	Gore (D) 180,638 (55%)
Perot (I) 59,213 (20%)	Perot (Reform) 28,719 (11%)	Others 10,151 (3%)

Representation in US Congress (January 2001)
House of Representatives: 1: (R).

US Senators: Joseph Biden Jr (D), elected November 1972; Thomas Carper (D), elected November 2000.

Votes in the Electoral College: 3.

State government

Executive branch (absolute two-term limits apply; terms need not be consecutive) Governor: Ruth Ann Minner (D), elected November 2000. Lieutenant Governor: John D. Carney (D), elected November 2000.

Legislature (2001)   House of Representatives 41: 15 (D), 26 (R). Senate 21: 13 (D), 8 (R). Representatives serve two-year, senators four-year terms.

Florida

Justitia omnibus (*Justice for all*)

State capital   Tallahassee.

Admittance to the Union   1845 (twenty-seventh state of the US). Seceded from the Union in January 1861; readmitted in July 1868.

Land area   53,937 square miles (ranked twenty-sixth in size).

Population   2000 census: 15,982,378. Rank among states by population: 4.

Population change 1990–2000: +23.5 per cent.

Racial composition (1999 estimate): white: 68 per cent; Hispanic: 15 per cent; black: 15 per cent.

Population density: 239.6. Urban population: 84.8 per cent. Rural population: 15.2 per cent. (1990 census figures.)

Voting patterns   Voting-age population of 11,383,000, of whom 72 per cent were registered voters (1998). Of 8,220,266 registered voters: 45 per cent D, 40 per cent R, 15 per cent unaffiliated and minor parties.

Presidential elections

Voter turnout (%)

1992	1996	2000
51.0	48.0	52.0 (estimated)

Votes cast

1992	1996	2000
Bush (R) 2,171,781 (41%)	Dole (R) 2,242,951 (43%)	Bush (R) 2,912,790 (49%)
Clinton (D) 2,071,651 (39%)	Clinton (D) 2,545,690 (48%)	Gore (D) 2,912,253 (49%)
Perot (I) 1,052,481 (20%)	Perot (Reform) 483,761 (9%)	Others 137,898 (2%)

Representation in US Congress   (January 2001)

House of Representatives 23: 8 (D), 15 (R). From 2002 Florida will have twenty-five Representatives.

US Senators: Bob Graham (D), elected November 1986; Bill Nelson (D), elected November 2000.

Votes in the Electoral College: 25 (27 votes from 2002).

State government

Executive branch (maximum of two consecutive terms)   Governor: Jeb Bush (R), elected November 1998. Lieutenant Governor: Frank T. Brogan (R), elected November 2000.

Legislature (2001)   House of Representatives 120: 43 (D), 77 (R). Senate 40: 15 (D), 25 (R). Representatives serve terms of two years. Senators serve four-year terms.

Georgia

'Wisdom, justice and moderation'
State capital   Atlanta.
Admittance to the Union   1788 (fourth state of the US). Seceded from the Union in January 1861; readmitted in July 1870.
Land area   57,919 square miles (ranked twenty-first in size).
Population   2000 census: 8,186,453. Rank among states by population: 10.
Population change 1990–2000: +26.4 per cent.
Racial composition (1999 estimate): Asian/Pacific: 2 per cent; white: 66 per cent; Hispanic: 3 per cent; black: 28 per cent.
Population density: 111.9. Urban population: 63.2 per cent. Rural population: 36.8 per cent. (1990 census figures.)
Voting patterns   Voting-age population of 5,678,000, of whom 71 per cent were registered voters (1998). There is no party registration in Georgia.
Presidential elections
Voter turnout (%)

1992	1996	2000
46.4	42.6	45.3 (estimated)

Votes cast

1992	1996	2000
Bush (R) 995,252 (43%)	Dole (R) 1,080,840 (47%)	Bush (R) 1,415,277 (55%)
Clinton (D) 1,008,966 (44%)	Clinton (D) 1,053,848 (46%)	Gore (D) 1,110,133 (43%)
Perot (I) 309,657 (13%)	Perot (Reform) 146,337 (6%)	Others 47,367 (2%)

Representation in US Congress   (January 2001)
House of Representatives 11: 3 (D), 8 (R). From 2002 Georgia will have thirteen Representatives.)
US Senators: Max Cleland (D), elected November 1996; Zell Miller (D), appointed 2000.
Votes in the Electoral College: 13 (15 votes from 2002).
State government
Executive branch (maximum of two consecutive terms)   Governor: Roy Barnes (D), elected November 1998. Lieutenant Governor: Mark Taylor (D), elected November 1998.
Legislature (2001)   House of Representatives 180: 104 (D), 76 (R). Senate 56: 31 (D), 24 (R), 1 (I). Both houses serve two-year terms.

Hawaii

'Ua mau ke ea o ka aina ka pono' (*The life of the land is perpetuated in righteousness*)
State capital   Honolulu.
Admittance to the Union   1959 (fiftieth state of the US).
Population   2000 census: 1,211,537. Rank among states by population: 42.
Population change 1990–2000: +9.3 per cent.
Racial composition (1999 estimate): Asian/Pacific: 63 per cent; white: 28 per cent; Hispanic: 8 per cent; black: 2 per cent.
Population density: 172.5. Urban population: 89.0 per cent. Rural population: 11.0 per cent. (1990 census figures.)

Land area 6,423 square miles (ranked forty-seventh in size).
Voting patterns Voting-age population 878,000, of whom 68 per cent were re-
gistered voters (1998). There is no party registration in Hawaii.
Presidential elections
Voter turnout (%)

1992	1996	2000
43.1	40.8	48.3 (estimated)

Votes cast

1992	1996	2000
Bush (R) 136,822 (37%)	Dole (R) 113,943 (32%)	Bush (R) 155,361 (37%)
Clinton (D) 179,310 (48%)	Clinton (D) 205,012 (57%)	Gore (D) 239,621 (56%)
Perot (I) 53,003 (14%)	Perot (Reform) 27,362 (8%)	Others 29,179 (7%)
	Others 13,807 (4%)	

Representation in US Congress (January 2001)
House of Representatives: 2 (D).
US Senators: Daniel Inouye (D), elected November 1962; Daniel Akaka (D), appointed
May 2000.
Votes in the Electoral College: 4.
State government
Executive branch (maximum of two consecutive terms) Governor: Benjamin J. Cayetano
(D), elected November 1994. Lieutenant Governor: Mazie Hirono (D), elected November
1994.
Legislature (2000) House of Representatives: 51: 32 (D), 19 (R). Senate 25: 22 (D),
3 (R). Representatives serve two-year terms. Senators serve four-year terms.

Idaho

'Esto perpetua' (Let it be perpetual)
State capital Boise
Admittance to the Union 1890 (forty-third state of the US).
Land area 82,751 square miles (ranked eleventh in size).
Population 2000 census: 1,293,953. Rank among states by population: 39.
Population change 1990–2000: +28.5 per cent.
Racial composition (1999 estimate): white, 90 per cent; Hispanic, 7.0 per cent; black,
0.6 per cent.
Population density: 12.2. Urban population: 57.4 per cent. Rural population: 42.6
per cent. (1990 census figures.)
Voting patterns Voting-age population of 888,000, of whom 74 per cent were re-
gistered voters (1998). There is no party registration in Idaho.
Presidential elections
Voter turnout (%)

1992	1996	2000
64.3	58.2	55 (estimated)

Votes cast

1992	1996	2000
Bush (R) 202,645 (42%)	Dole (R) 256,595 (52%)	Bush (R) 336,299 (68%)
Clinton (D) 137,013 (28%)	Clinton (D) 165,443 (34%)	Gore (D) 138,354 (28%)
Perot (I) 130,395 (27%)	Perot (Reform) 62,518 (13%)	Others 13,819 (4%)

Representation in US Congress (January 2001)
House of Representatives: 2 (R).
US Senators: Larry E. Craig (R), elected November 1990; Mike Crapo (R), elected November 1998.
Votes in the Electoral College: 4.
State government
Executive branch (maximum of two consecutive terms)   Governor: Dirk Kempthorne (R), elected November 1998. Lieutenant Governor: vacant (January 2001).
Legislature (2001)   House of Representatives 67: 9 (D), 58 (R). Senate 35: 3 (D), 32 (R). Both houses serve two-year terms.

Illinois

'State sovereignty – national union'
State capital   Springfield.
Admittance to the Union   1818 (twenty-first state of the US).
Land area   55,593 square miles (ranked twenty-fourth in size).
Population   2000 census: 12,419,293. Rank among states by population: 5.
Population change 1990–2000: +8.6 per cent.
Racial composition (1999 estimate): Asian/Pacific: 3 per cent; white: 71 per cent; Hispanic: 10 per cent; black: 15 per cent.
Population density: 205.6. Urban population: 84.6 per cent. Rural population: 15.4 per cent. (1990 census figures.)
Voting patterns   Voting-age population of 8,755,000, of whom 77 per cent were registered voters (1998). There is no party registration in Illinois.
Presidential elections
Voter turnout (%)

1992	1996	2000
58.7	49.2	54 (estimated)

Votes cast

1992	1996	2000
Bush (R) 1,734,096 (34%)	Dole (R) 1,587,021 (37%)	Bush (R) 2,025,764 (43%)
Clinton (D) 2,453,350 (49%)	Clinton (D) 2,341,744 (54%)	Gore (D) 2,599,814 (55%)
Perot (I) 840,515 (17%)	Perot (Reform) 346,408 (8%)	Others 133,897 (2%)

Representation in US Congress (January 2001)
House of Representatives 20: 10 (D), 10 (R). Illinois will lose one Representative in 2002.
US Senators: Richard Durbin (D), elected November 1996; Peter Fitzgerald (R), elected November 1998.
Votes in the Electoral College: 22 (21 votes after 2002).
State government
Executive branch   Governor: George H. Ryan (R), elected November 1998. Lieutenant Governor: Corinne Wood (R), elected November 1998.
Legislature (2001)   House of Representatives 118: 62 (D), 56 (R). Senate 59: 27 (D), 32 (R). Representatives serve two-year terms. One-third of senators serve two-year terms, the others serve for four years.

Indiana

'Crossroads of America'
State capital Indianapolis.
Admittance to the Union 1816 (nineteenth state of the US).
Land area 35,870 square miles (ranked thirty-eighth in size).
Population 2000 census: 6,080,485. Rank among states by population: 14.
Population change 1990–2000: +9.7 per cent.
Racial composition (1999 estimate): white: 88 per cent; Hispanic: 2 per cent; black: 8 per cent.
Population density: 154.6. Urban population: 64.9 per cent. Rural population: 35.1 per cent. (1990 census figures.)
Voting patterns Voting-age population of 4,410,000, of whom 83 per cent were registered voters (1998). There is no party registration in Indiana.
Presidential elections
Voter turnout (%)

1992	1996	2000
54.8	48.9	49.0 (estimated)

Votes cast

1992	1996	2000
Bush (R) 989,375 (43%)	Dole (R) 1,006,632 (47%)	Bush (R) 1,242,372 (57%)
Clinton (D) 848,420 (37%)	Clinton (D) 887,454 (42%)	Gore (D) 899,836 (41%)
Perot (I) 455,934 (2%)	Perot (Reform) 224,280 (11%)	Others 34,154 (2%)

Representation in US Congress (January 2001)
House of Representatives 10: 4 (D), 6 (R). Indiana will lose one Representative in 2002.
US Senators: Evan Bayh (D), elected November 1998; Richard Lugar (R), elected November 1976.
Votes in the Electoral College: 12 (eleven votes after 2002).
State government
Executive branch (maximum of two consecutive terms)   Governor: Frank O'Bannon (D), elected November 1996. Lieutenant Governor: Joe Kernan (D), elected November 1996.
Legislature (2001)   House of Representatives 100: 49 (D), 51 (R). Senate 50: 18 (D), 32 (R). Representatives serve two-year terms. Senators serve four-year terms.

Iowa

'Our liberties we prize and our rights we will maintain'
State capital Des Moines.
Admittance to the Union 1846 (twenty-ninth state of the US).
Land area 55,875 square miles (ranked twenty-third in size).
Population 2000 census: 2,926,324. Rank among states by population: 30.
Population change 1990–2000: +5.4 per cent.
Racial composition (1999 estimate): white: 94 per cent; Hispanic: 2 per cent; black: 2 per cent.
Population density: 49.7. Urban population: 60.6 per cent. Rural population: 39.4 per cent. (1990 census figures.)
Voting patterns Voting-age population of 2,157,000, of whom 82 per cent were registered voters (1998). Of 1,769,827 registered voters, 32 per cent D, 33 per cent R and 35 per cent unaffiliated and minor parties.

Presidential elections

Voter turnout (%)

1992	1996	2000
65.3	57.7	61.0 (estimated)

Votes cast

1992	1996	2000
Bush (R) 504,891 (37%)	Dole (R) 492,644 (40%)	Bush (R) 634,225 (48%)
Clinton (D) 586,353 (43%)	Clinton (D) 620,258 (50%)	Gore (D) 638,355 (49%)
Perot (I) 253,468 (19%)	Perot (Reform) 105,159 (9%)	Others 41,615 (3%)

Representation in US Congress   (January 2001)

House of Representatives 5: 1 (D), 4 (R).

US Senators: Chuck Grassley (R), elected November 1980; Tom Harkin (D), elected November 1984.

Votes in the Electoral College: 7.

State government

Executive branch   Governor: Tom Vilsack (D), elected November 1998. Lieutenant Governor: Sally Pederson (D), elected November 1998.

Legislature (2001)   House of Representatives 100: 44 (D), 56 (R). Senate 50: 20 (D), 30 (R). Representatives serve two-year terms. Senators serve four-year terms.

Kansas

'Ad astra per aspera' (*To the stars through difficulties*)

State capital   Topeka.

Admittance to the Union   1861 (thirty-fourth state of the US).

Land area   81,823 square miles (ranked thirteenth in size).

Population   2000 census: 2,688,418. Rank among states by population: 32.

Population change 1990–2000: +8.5 per cent.

Racial composition (1999 estimate): white: 86 per cent; Hispanic: 5.5 per cent; black: 6.0 per cent.

Population density: 30.3. Urban population: 69.1 per cent. Rural population: 30.9 per cent. (1990 census figures.)

Voting patterns   Voting-age population of 1,925,000, of whom 78 per cent were registered voters (1998). Of 1,513,685 registered voters, 29 per cent D, 45 per cent R and 26 per cent unaffiliated and minor parties.

Presidential elections

Voter turnout (%)

1992	1996	2000
62.9	56.6	55.0 (estimated)

Votes cast

1992	1996	2000
Bush (R) 449,469 (39%)	Dole (R) 583,245 (54%)	Bush (R) 616,829 (58%)
Clinton (D) 389,704 (34%)	Clinton (D) 387,659 (36%)	Gore (D) 392,867 (37%)
Perot (I) 311,316 (27%)	Perot (Reform) 92,639 (9%)	Others 50,033 (5%)

Representation in US Congress   (January 2001)

House of Representatives 4: 1 (D), 3 (R).

US Senators: Sam Brownback (R), elected November 1996; Pat Roberts (R), elected November 1996.

Votes in the Electoral College: 6.

State government
Executive branch (maximum of two consecutive terms)   Governor: Bill Graves (R), elected November 1998. Lieutenant Governor: Gary Sherrer (R), elected November 1998.
Legislature (2001)   House of Representatives 125: 46 (D), 79 (R). Senate: 40: 10 (D), 30 (R). Representatives serve two-year terms. Senators serve four-year terms.

Kentucky

'United we stand, divided we fall'
State capital   Frankfort.
Admittance to the Union   1792 (fifteenth state of the US).
Land area   39,732 square miles (ranked thirty-sixth in size).
Population   2000 census: 4,041,769. Rank among states by population: 25.
Population change 1990–2000: +9.7 per cent.
Racial composition (1999 estimate): white: 91 per cent; Hispanic: 1 per cent; black: 7 per cent.
Population density: 92.8. Urban population: 51.8 per cent. Rural population: 48.2 per cent. (1990 census figures.)
Voting patterns   Voting-age population of 2,990,000, of whom 87 per cent were registered voters (1998). Of 2,590,339 registered voters: 61 per cent D, 32 per cent R and 7 per cent unaffiliated and minor parties.
Presidential elections
Voter turnout (%)

1992	1996	2000
53.4	47.5	51.7 (estimated)

Votes cast

1992	1996	2000
Bush (R) 617,196 (41%)	Dole (R) 623,283 (45%)	Bush (R) 872,141 (56%)
Clinton (D) 665,095 (45%)	Clinton (D) 636,614 (46%)	Gore (D) 640,123 (41%)
Perot (I) 203,968 (14%)	Perot (Reform) 120,396 (9%)	Others 35,406 (3%)

Representation in US Congress   (January 2001)
House of Representatives 6: 1 (D), 5 (R).
US Senators: Jim Bunning (R), elected November 1998; Mitch McConnell (R), elected November 1984.
Votes in the Electoral College: 8.
State government
Executive branch (maximum of two consecutive terms)   Governor: Paul E. Patton (D), elected November 1998. Lieutenant Governor: Steve Henry (D), elected November 1998.
Legislature (2001)   House of Representatives 100: 66 (D), 34 (R). Senate 38: 18 (D), 20 (R). Representatives serve two-year terms. Senators serve four-year terms.

Louisiana

'Union, justice, and confidence'
State capital   Baton Rouge.
Admittance to the Union   1812 (eighteenth state of the US). Seceded from the Union in January 1861; readmitted in June 1868.
Land area   43,566 square miles (ranked thirty-third in size).

Population   2000 census: 4,468,976. Rank among states by population: 22.
Population change 1990–2000: +5.9 per cent.
Racial composition (1999 estimate): white: 63.5 per cent; Hispanic: 2.7 per cent; black: 32.3 per cent.
Population density: 96.8. Urban population: 68.1 per cent. Rural population: 31.9 per cent. (1990 census figures.)
Voting patterns   Voting-age population of 3,149,000, of whom 83.6 per cent were registered voters (1998). Of 2,633,626 registered voters: 62 per cent D, 21 per cent R and 16 per cent unaffiliated and minor parties.
Presidential elections
Voter turnout (%)

1992	1996	2000
58.8	56.9	56 (estimated)

Votes cast

1992	1996	2000
Bush (R) 733,386 (42%)	Dole (R) 712,586 (40%)	Bush (R) 927,871 (53%)
Clinton (D) 815,971 (46%)	Clinton (D) 927,836 (53%)	Gore (D) 792,344 (45%)
Perot (I) 211,478 (12%)	Perot (Reform) 123,292 (7%)	Others 45,441 (2%)

Representation in US Congress   (January 2001)
House of Representatives 7: 2 (D), 5 (R).
US Senators: John Breaux (D), elected November 1986; Mary Landrieu (D), elected November 1996.
Votes in the Electoral College: 9.
State government
Executive branch (maximum of two consecutive terms)   Governor: Mike Foster (D), elected November 1995. Lieutenant Governor: Kathleen Blanco (D), elected November 1999.
Legislature (2001)   House of Representatives 105: 71 (D), 32 (R); two seats vacant (January 2001). Senate 39: 26 (D), 13 (R). Both houses serve four-year terms.

Maine

'Dirigo' (*I direct*)
State capital   Augusta.
Admittance to the Union   1820 (twenty-third state of the US).
Land area   30,865 square miles (ranked thirty-ninth in size).
Population   2000 census: 1,274,923. Rank among states by population: 40.
Population change 1990–2000: +3.8 per cent.
Racial composition (1999 estimate): Asian/Pacific: 0.7 per cent; white: 97.6 per cent; Hispanic: 0.7 per cent; black: 0.5 per cent.
Population density: 39.8. Urban population: 44.6 per cent. Rural population: 55.4 per cent. (1990 census figures.)
Voting patterns   Voting-age population of 957,000, of whom 97.5 per cent were registered voters (1998). Of 933,753 registered voters, 32 per cent D, 29 per cent R and 39 per cent unaffiliated and minor parties.
Presidential elections
Voter turnout (%)

1992	1996	2000
72.9	64.5	67.4 (estimated)

Votes cast

1992	1996	2000
Bush (R) 206,504 (31%)	Dole (R) 186,378 (32%)	Bush (R) 283,988 (44%)
Clinton (D) 263,420 (39%)	Clinton (D) 312,788 (53%)	Gore (D) 315,466 (49%)
Perot (I) 206,504 (31%)	Perot (Reform) 85,970 (15%)	Others 45,851 (7%)

Representation in US Congress (January 2001)

House of Representatives: 2 (D).

US Senators: Susan Collins (R), November 1996; Olympia Snowe (R), November 1994.

Votes in the Electoral College: 4.

State government

Executive branch (maximum of two consecutive terms)   Governor: Angus J. King Jr (I), elected November 1994. No Lieutenant Governor. (Governor succeeded by Senate president.)

Legislature (2001) House of Representatives 152: 88 (D), 61 (R), 3 (I). Senate 35: 17 (D), 17 (R), 1 (I). Both houses serve two-year terms.

Maryland

'Fatti maschii, parole femine' (*Manly deeds, womanly words*)

State capital   Annapolis.

Admittance to the Union   1788 (seventh state of the US).

Land area   9,775 square miles (ranked forty-second in size).

Population   2000 census: 5,296,486. Rank among states by population: 19.

Population change 1990–2000: +10.8 per cent.

Racial composition (1999 estimate): Asian/Pacific: 4 per cent; white: 64.2 per cent; Hispanic: 3.8 per cent; black: 28.1 per cent.

Population density: 489.2. Urban population: 81.3 per cent. Rural population: 18.7 per cent. (1990 census figures.)

Voting patterns   Voting-age population of 3,824,000, of whom 67.1 per cent were registered voters (1998). Of 2,569,649 registered voters, 58 per cent D, 20 per cent R, 12 per cent unaffiliated and minor parties.

Presidential elections

Voter turnout (%)

1992	1996	2000
53.6	46.7	50.3 (estimated)

Votes cast

1992	1996	2000
Bush (R) 707,094 (36%)	Dole (R) 681,530 (39%)	Bush (R) 770,911 (40%)
Clinton (D) 988,571 (50%)	Clinton (D) 966,208 (54%)	Gore (D) 1,093,344 (57%)
Perot (I) 281,414 (14%)	Perot (Reform) 115,812 (7%)	Others 61,001 (3%)

Representation in US Congress (January 2001)

House of Representatives 8: 4 (D), 4 (R).

US Senators: Barbara Mikulski (D), elected November 1986; Paul Sarbanes (D), elected November 1976.

Votes in the Electoral College: 10.

State government

Executive branch (maximum of two consecutive terms)   Governor: Parris N. Glendening (D), elected November 1994. Lieutenant Governor: Kathleen Kennedy Townsend (D), elected November 1994.

Legislature (2001)   House of Delegates 141: 106 (D), 35 (R). Senate 47: 33 (D), 14 (R). Both houses serve four-year terms.

Massachusetts

'*Ense petit placidam sub libertate quietem*' (*By the sword we seek peace, but peace only under liberty*)

State capital   Boston.

Admittance to the Union   1788 (sixth state of the US).

Land area   7,838 square miles (ranked forty-fifth in size).

Population   2000 census: 6,349,097. Rank among states by population: 13.

Population change 1990–2000: +5.5 per cent.

Racial composition (1999 estimate): Asian/Pacific: 3.7 per cent; white: 84.4 per cent; Hispanic: 6.3 per cent; black: 6.5 per cent.

Population density: 767.6. Urban population: 84.3 per cent. Rural population: 15.7 per cent. (1990 census figures.)

Voting patterns   Voting-age population of 4,731,000, of whom 78.5 per cent were registered voters (1998). Of 3,718,528 registered voters: 37 per cent D, 13 per cent R, 50 per cent unaffiliated and minor parties.

Presidential elections

Voter turnout (%)

1992	1996	2000
60.1	55.3	56.8 (estimated)

Votes cast

1992	1996	2000
Bush (R) 805,039 (29%)	Dole (R) 718,104 (28%)	Bush (R) 875,658 (33%)
Clinton (D) 1,318,639 (48%)	Clinton (D) 1,571,755 (61%)	Gore (D) 1,609,048 (60%)
Perot (I) 630,731 (22%)	Perot (Reform) 226,787 (9%) Other 39,347 (2%)	Others 203,794 (1%)

Representation in US Congress   (January 2001)

House of Representatives: 10: 10 (D).

US Senators: Edward Kennedy (D), elected November 1962; John Kerry (D), elected November 1984.

Votes in the Electoral College: 12.

State government

Executive branch   Governor: Paul Celucci (R), appointed July 1997, elected November 1998. Lieutenant Governor: Jane Swift (R), elected November 1998.

Legislature (2001)   House of Representatives 160: 135 (D), 24 (R). Senate 40: 34 (D), 6 (R). Both houses serve two-year terms.

Michigan

'*Si quaeris peninsulam amoenam circumspice*' (*If you seek a pleasant peninsula, look about you*)

State capital   Lansing.

Admittance to the Union   1837 (twenty-sixth state of the US).

Land area   56,809 square miles (ranked twenty-second in size).

Population   2000 census: 9,938,444. Rank among states by population: 8.

Population change 1990–2000: +6.9 per cent.

Racial composition (1999 estimate): Asian/Pacific: 1.7 per cent; white: 80.8 per cent; Hispanic: 2.7 per cent; black: 14.3 per cent.

Population density: 163.6. Urban population: 70.5 per cent. Rural population: 29.5 per cent. (1990 census figures.)

Voting patterns   Voting-age population of 7,266,000, of whom 95 per cent were registered voters (1998). There is no party registration in Michigan.

Presidential elections

Voter turnout (%)

1992	1996	2000
61.5	54.5	57.6 (estimate)

Votes cast

1992	1996	2000
Bush (R) 1,554,940 (36%)	Dole (R) 1,481,572 (39%)	Bush (R) 1,947,100 (46%)
Clinton (D) 1,871,182 (44%)	Clinton (D) 1,989,683 (52%)	Gore (D) 2,141,721 (51%)
Perot (I) 824,813 (19%)	Perot (Reform) 336,681 (9%)	Others 103,554 (3%)

Representation in US Congress   (January 2001)

House of Representatives 16: 9 (D), 7 (R). Michigan will lose one Representative in 2002.

US Senators: Carl Levin (D), elected November 1978; Debbie Stabenow (D), elected November 2000.

Votes in the Electoral College: 18 (17 votes from 2002).

State government

Executive branch (maximum of two consecutive terms, but this law was made effective after current incumbent was first elected in 1990)   Governor: John Engler (R), elected November 1990. Lieutenant Governor: Dick Posthumus (R), elected November 1998.

Legislature (2001)   House of Representatives 110: 58 (D), 51 (R); one vacancy. Senate 38: 15 (D), 23 (R). Representatives serve two-year terms. Senators serve terms of four years.

Minnesota

'L'étoile du nord' (*The north star*)

State capital   St Paul.

Admittance to the Union   1858 (thirty-second state of the US).

Land area   79,617 square miles (ranked fourteenth in size).

Population   2000 census: 4,919,479. Rank among states by population: 21.

Population change 1990–2000: +12.4 per cent.

Racial composition (1999 estimate): Asian/Pacific: 2.7 per cent; white: 91.2 per cent; Hispanic: 1.9 per cent; black: 3.1 per cent.

Population density: 55.0. Urban population: 69.1 per cent. Rural population: 30.9 per cent. (1990 census figures.)

Voting patterns   Voting-age population of 3,483,000, of whom 86 per cent were registered voters (1998). There is no party registration in Minnesota.

Presidential elections

Voter turnout (%)

1992	1996	2000
71.8	64.3	70.0 (estimated)

Votes cast

1992	1996	2000
Bush (R) 747,841 (32%)	Dole (R) 766,476 (35%)	Bush (R) 1,110,290 (46%)
Clinton (D) 1,020,997 (44%)	Clinton (D) 1,120,279 (51%)	Gore (D) 1,168,190 (48%)
Perot (I) 562,506 (24%)	Perot (Reform) 257,704 (12%)	Others 160,838 (6%)
	Other 48,425 (2%)	

Representation in US Congress   (January 2001)

House of Representatives 8: 5 (D), 3 (R).

US Senators: Mark Dayton (D), elected November 2000; Paul Wellstone (D), elected November 1990.

Votes in the Electoral College: 10.

State government

Executive branch   Governor: Jesse Ventura (I), elected November 1998. Lieutenant Governor: Mae Schunk (I), elected November 1998.

Legislature (2001)   House of Representatives 134: 65 (Democrat-Farmer-Labor), 69 (R). Senate 67: 39 (DFL), 27 (R), 1 (I). Representatives serve terms of two years. Senators serve four-year terms.

Mississippi

'Virtute et armis' (By valor and arms)

State capital   Jackson.

Admittance to the Union   1817 (twentieth state of the US). Seceded from the Union in January 1861; readmitted in February 1860.

Land area   46,914 square miles (ranked thirty-first in size).

Population   2000 census: 2,844,658. Rank among states by population: 31.

Population change 1990–2000: +10.5 per cent.

Racial composition (1999 estimate): white: 61.7 per cent; black: 36.4 per cent.

Population density: 54.9. Urban population: 47.1 per cent. Rural population: 52.9 per cent. (1990 census figures.)

Voting patterns   Voting-age population of 2,014,000, of whom 88.3 per cent were registered voters (1998). There is no party registration in Mississippi.

Presidential elections

Voter turnout (%)

1992	1996	2000
52.4	45.6	48.0 (estimate)

Votes cast

1992	1996	2000
Bush (R) 487,793 (50%)	Dole (R) 439,833 (49%)	Bush (R) 558,884 (58%)
Clinton (D) 400,258 (41%)	Clinton (D) 394,020 (41%)	Gore (D) 392,587 (41%)
Perot (I) 85,626 (9%)	Perot (Reform) 52,211 (6%)	Others 16,388 (1%)

Representation in US Congress   (November 2000)

House of Representatives 5: 3 (D), 2 (R). Mississippi will lose one Representative in 2002.

US Senators: Thad Cochran (R), elected November 1978; Trent Lott (R), elected November 1988.

Votes in the Electoral College: 7 (six votes from 2002).

State government

Executive branch (maximum of two consecutive terms)   Governor: Ronnie Musgrove (D), elected November 1999. Lieutenant Governor: Amy Tuck (D), elected November 1999.

Legislature (2001)   House of Representatives 122: 85 (D), 33 (R), 3 (I). Senate 52: 34 (D), 18 (R). Both houses serve four-year terms.

Missouri

'Salus populi suprema lex esto' (*The welfare of the people shall be the supreme law*)

State capital   Jefferson City.

Admittance to the Union   1817 (twentieth state of the US).

Land area   68,898 square miles (ranked eighteenth in size).

Population   2000 census: 5,595,211. Rank among states by population: 17.

Population change 1990–2000: +9.3 per cent.

Racial composition (1999 estimate): white: 85.7 per cent; Hispanic: 1.7 per cent; black: 11.3 per cent.

Population density: 74.3. Urban population: 68.7 per cent. Rural population: 31.3 per cent. (1990 census figures.)

Voting patterns   Voting-age population of 4,042,000, of whom 89.9 per cent were registered voters (1998). There is no party registration in Missouri.

Presidential elections

Voter turnout (%)

1992	1996	2000
62.1	54.2	58.3 (estimate)

Votes cast

1992	1996	2000
Bush (R) 811,159 (34%)	Dole (R) 890,014 (41%)	Bush (R) 1,189,52 (50%)
Clinton (D) 1,053,873 (44%)	Clinton (D) 1,025,935 (48%)	Gore (D) 1,110,826 (47%)
Perot (I) 518,741 (22%)	Perot (Reform) 217,219 (10%)	Others 58,795 (3%)

Representation in US Congress   (January 2001)

House of Representatives 9: 4 (D), 5 (R).

US Senators: Christopher Bond (R), elected November 1986; Jean Carnahan (D), appointed November 2000.

Votes in the Electoral College: 11.

State government

Executive branch   Governor: Bob Holden (D), elected November 2000. Lieutenant Governor: Joe Maxwell (D), elected November 2000.

Legislature (2001)   House of Representatives 163: 83 (D), 80 (R). Senate 34: 16 (D), 17 (R), one vacant. Representatives serve two-year terms. Senators serve four-year terms.

Montana

Oro y plata (*Gold and silver*)

State capital   Helena.

Admittance to the Union   1889 (forty-first state of the US).

Land area   145,55 square miles (ranked fourth in size).

Population   2000 census: 902,195. Rank among states by population: 44.

Population change 1990–2000: +12.9 per cent.

Racial composition (1999 estimate): American Indian: 6.5 per cent; white: 91 per cent; Hispanic: 1.8 per cent; black: 0.3 per cent.

Population density: 5.5. Urban population: 52.5 per cent. Rural population: 47.5 per cent (1990 census figures.)

Voting patterns   Voting-age population of 658,000, of whom 97 per cent were registered voters (1998). There is no party registration in Montana.

Presidential elections

Voter turnout (%)

1992	1996	2000
68.4	62.9	62.4 (estimated)

Votes cast

1992	1996	2000
Bush (R) 144,207 (35%)	Dole (R) 179,652 (44%)	Bush (R) 239,775 (58%)
Clinton (D) 154,507 (38%)	Clinton (D) 167,922 (41%)	Gore (D) 137,264 (33%)
Perot (I) 107,225 (26%)	Perot (Reform) 55,229 (14%)	Others 33,779 (7%)

Representation in US Congress   (January 2001)

House of Representatives 1: (R).

US Senators: Max Baucus (D), elected November 1978; Conrad Burns (R), elected November 1988.

Votes in the Electoral College: 3.

State government

Executive branch (absolute limit of eight years of service out of every sixteen years)   Governor: Judy Martz (R), elected November 2000. Lieutenant Governor: Karl Ohs (R), elected November 2000.

Legislature (2001)   House of Representatives 100: 42 (D), 58 (R). Senate 50: 19 (D), 31 (R). Representatives serve two-year terms. Senators serve four-year terms.

Nebraska

'Equality before law'

State capital   Lincoln.

Admittance to the Union   1867 (thirty-seventh state of the US).

Land area   76,878 square miles (ranked fifteenth in size).

Population   2000 census: 1,711,263. Rank among states by population: 38.

Population change 1990–2000: +8.4 per cent.

Racial composition (1999 estimate): white: 89.4 per cent; Hispanic: 4.6 per cent; black: 4.0 per cent.

Population density: 20.5. Urban population: 66.1 per cent. Rural population: 33.9 per cent. (1990 census figures.)

Voting patterns   Voting-age population of 1,231,000, of whom 85.8 per cent were registered voters (1998). Of 1,056,351 registered voters, 37 per cent D, 49 per cent R, 14 per cent unaffiliated/minor parties.

Presidential elections
Voter turnout (%)

1992	1996	2000
63.4	56.1	53.1 (estimated)

Votes cast

1992	1996	2000
Bush (R) 343,678 (47%)	Dole (R) 363,467 (54%)	Bush (R) 408,719 (62.5%)
Clinton (D) 216,864 (29%)	Clinton (D) 236,761 (35%)	Gore (D) 215,616 (32.9%)
Perot (I) 174,104 (24%)	Perot (Reform) 71,278 (11%)	Others 29,397 (4.4%)

Representation in US Congress (January 2001)

House of Representatives: 3 (R).

US Senators: Charles Hagel (R), elected November 1996; Ben Nelson (D), elected November 2000.

Votes in the Electoral College: 5.

State government

Executive branch (after two consecutive terms, candidate must wait four years before becoming eligible to run again) Governor: Mike Johanns (R), elected November 1998. Lieutenant Governor: Dave Maurstad (R), elected November 1998.

Legislature (2001) The legislature has been unicameral since 1937; it is also non-partisan. Senate: 49 (no party affiliations). Senators serve four-year terms.

Nevada

'All for our country'

State capital Carson City.

Admittance to the Union 1864 (thirty-sixth state of the US).

Land area 109,806 square miles (ranked seventh in size).

Population 2000 census: 1,998,257. Rank among states by population: 35.

Population change 1990–2000: +66.3 per cent.

Racial composition (1999 estimate): Asian/Pacific: 4.8 per cent; white: 70.2 per cent; Hispanic: 16.8 per cent; black: 7.7 per cent.

Population density: 10.9. Urban population: 88.3 per cent. Rural population: 11.7 per cent. (1990 census figures.)

Voting patterns Voting-age population of 1,314,000, of whom 68.3 per cent were registered voters (1998). Of 897,865 registered voters, 41 per cent D, 42 per cent R, 17 per cent unaffiliated and minor parties.

Presidential elections
Voter turnout (%)

1992	1996	2000
50.1	39.3	46.3 (estimated)

Votes cast

1992	1996	2000
Bush (R) 175,828 (35%)	Dole (R) 199,244 (43%)	Bush (R) 301,539 (50%)
Clinton (D) 189,148 (37%)	Clinton (D) 203,974 (44%)	Gore (D) 279,749 (46%)
Perot (I) 132,580 (26%)	Perot (Reform) 43,896 (9%)	Others 27,411 (4%)
	Other 17,130 (4%)	

Representation in US Congress (January 2001)

House of Representatives 2: 1 (D), 1 (R). From 2002 Nevada will have three Representatives.)

US Senators: Harry Reid (D), elected November 1986; John Ensign (R), elected November 2000.

Votes in the Electoral College: 4 (five from 2002).

State government

Executive branch (maximum of two consecutive terms)   Governor: Kenny Guinn (R), elected November1998. Lieutenant Governor: Lorraine Hunt (R), elected November 1998.

Legislature (2001)   Assembly 42: 27 (D), 15 (R). Senate 21: 9 (D), 12 (R). Representatives in the Assembly serve two-year terms. Senators serve four-year terms.

New Hampshire

'Live free or die'

State capital   Concord.

Admittance to the Union   1788 (ninth state of the US).

Land area   8,969 square miles (ranked forty-fourth in size).

Population   2000 census: 1,235,786. Rank among states by population: 41.

Population change 1990–2000: +11.4 per cent.

Racial composition (1999 estimate): Asian/Pacific: 1.2 per cent; white: 96.3 per cent; Hispanic: 1.6 per cent; black: 0.7 per cent.

Population density: 123.7. Urban population: 51.0 per cent. Rural population: 49.0 per cent. (1990 census figures.)

Voting patterns   Voting-age population of 890,000, of whom 84 per cent were registered voters (1998). Of 747,608 registered voters, 27 per cent D, 36 per cent R, 36 per cent unaffiliated and minor parties.

Presidential elections

Voter turnout (%)

1992	1996	2000
64.2	58.0	63.6 (estimate)

Votes cast

1992	1996	2000
Bush (R) 202,484 (38%)	Dole (R) 196,486 (39%)	Bush (R) 273,135 (48%)
Clinton (D) 209,040 (39%)	Clinton (D) 246,166 (49%)	Gore (D) 265,853 (47%)
Perot (I) 121,337 (23%)	Perot (Reform) 48,387 (10%)	Others 27,808 (5%)

Representation in US Congress   (January 2001)

House of Representatives: 2 (R).

US Senators: Judd Gregg (R), elected November 1992; Bob Smith (R), elected November 1990.

Votes in the Electoral College: 4.

State government

Executive branch   (Governors serve two year terms with no maximum on number of terms.) Governor: Jeanne Shaheen (D), elected November 1996.

Senate president: Arthur Klemm (R), elected December 2000.

Legislature (2001)   House of Representatives 400: 141 (D), 257 (R), 1 (Libertarian), one vacancy. Senate 24: 11 (D), 13 (R). Both houses serve two-year terms.

New Jersey

'Liberty and prosperity'

State capital   Trenton.

Admittance to the Union   1787 (third state of the US).
Land area   7,419 square miles (ranked forty-sixth in size).
Population   2000 census: 8,414,350. Rank among states by population: 9.
Population change 1990–2000: +8.9 per cent.
Racial composition (1999 estimate): Asian/Pacific: 5.7 per cent; white: 68.3 per cent; Hispanic: 12.6 per cent; black: 14.7 per cent.
Population density: 1042.0. Urban population: 89.4 per cent. Rural population: 10.6 per cent. (1990 census figures.)
Voting patterns   Voting-age population of 6,075,000, of whom 74.7 per cent were registered voters (1998). Of 4,538,944 registered voters, 25 per cent D, 19 per cent R, 56 per cent unaffiliated and minor parties.
Presidential elections
Voter turnout (%)

1992	1996	2000
56.1	51.2	50.8 (estimate)

Votes cast

1992	1996	2000
Bush (R) 1,356,865 (41%)	Dole (R) 1,102,577 (36%)	Bush (R) 1,247,515 (40%)
Clinton (D) 1,436,206 (43%)	Clinton (D) 1,651,019 (54%)	Gore (D) 1,728,956 (56%)
Perot (I) 521,829 (16%)	Perot (Reform) 261,932 (9%)	Others 112,714 (4%)
	Other 59,424 (2%)	

Representation in US Congress   (January 2001)
House of Representatives 13: 7 (D), 6 (R).
US Senators: Robert Torricelli (D), elected November 1996; Jon Corzine (D), elected November 2000.
Votes in the Electoral College: 15.
State government
Executive branch (maximum of two consecutive terms)   Governor: Christine T. Whitman (R), elected November 1993. President of Senate: Donald T. Di Francesco (R), elected 1992.
Legislature   House of Representatives 80: 35 (D), 45 (R). Senate 40: 16 (D), 24 (R). Members of the Assembly serve two-year terms. Senators serve for four years (except for the first term of a new decade, which is of only two years' duration).

New Mexico

'Crescit eundo' (*It grows as it goes*)
State capital   Santa Fe.
Admittance to the Union   1912 (forty-seventh state of the US).
Land area   121,365 square miles (ranked fifth in size).
Population   2000 census: 1,819,046. Rank among states by population: 36.
Population change 1990–2000: +20.1 per cent.
Racial composition (1999 estimate): American/Indian: 9.5 per cent; white: 47.4 per cent; Hispanic: 40.7 per cent; black: 2.6 per cent.
Population density: 12.5. Urban population: 73.0 per cent. Rural population: 27 per cent. (1990 census figures.)
Voting patterns   Voting-age population of 1,250,000, of whom 73.4 per cent were registered voters (1998). There is no party registration in New Mexico.

Presidential elections
Voter turnout

1992	1996	2000
50.8	46.0	47.8 (estimated)

Votes cast

1992	1996	2000
Bush (R) 212,824 (37%)	Dole (R) 232,751 (42%)	Bush (R) 286,079 (48%)
Clinton (D) 261,617 (46%)	Clinton (D) 273,495 (49%)	Gore (D) 286,565 (48%)
Perot (I) 91,895 (16%)	Perot (Reform) 32,271 (6%)	Others 25,430 (4%)
	Other 17,566 (3%)	

Representation in US Congress   (January 2001)
House of Representatives 3: 1 (D), 2 (R).

US Senators: Jeff Bingaman (D), elected November 1982; Pete Domenici (R), elected November 1972.

Votes in the Electoral College: 5.

State government

Executive branch (maximum of two consecutive terms)   Governor: Gary E. Johnson (R), elected November 1994. Lieutenant Governor: Walter Bradley (R), elected November 1994.

Legislature (2001)   House of Representatives 70: 42 (D), 28 (R). Senate 42: 24 (D), 18 (R).

Representatives serve terms of two years. Senators serve four-year terms.

New York

'Excelsior' (*Ever upward*)
State capital   Albany.
Admittance to the Union   1788 (eleventh state of the US).
Land area   47,224 square miles (ranked thirtieth in size).
Population   2000 census: 18,976,457. Rank among states by population: 3.
Population change 1990–2000: +5.5 per cent.
Racial composition (1999 estimate): Asian/Pacific: 5.6 per cent; white: 65.1 per cent; Hispanic: 14.6 per cent; black: 17.7 per cent.
Population density: 381.0. Urban population: 84.3 per cent. Rural population: 15.7 per cent. (1990 census figures.)
Voting patterns   Voting-age population of 13,590,000, of whom 79 per cent were registered voters (1998). Of 10,740,788 registered voters, 47 per cent D, 29 per cent R, 24 per cent unaffiliated and minor parties.
Presidential elections
Voter turnout (%)

1992	1996	2000
50.5	46.5	46.1 (estimated)

Votes cast

1992	1996	2000
Bush (R) 2,342,194 (34%)	Dole (R) 1,932,900 (31%)	Bush (R) 2,222,283 (35.4%)
Clinton (D) 3,435,104 (50%)	Clinton (D) 3,756,565 (61%)	Gore (D) 3,746,839 (59.7%)
Perot (I) 1,089,523 (16%)	Perot (Reform) 503,356 (8%)	Others 300,396 (4.7%)

Representation in US Congress (January 2001)
House of Representatives 31: 19 (D), 12 (R). New York will lose two Representatives in
2002.
US Senators: Charles Schumer (D), elected November 1998; Hillary Clinton (D), elected
November 2000.
Votes in the Electoral College: 33 (31 votes from 2002).
State government
Executive branch   Governor: George E. Pataki (R), elected November 1994. Lieutenant
Governor: Mary Donohue (R), elected November 1998.
Legislature (2001)   House of Representatives 150: 98 (D), 51 (R). Senate: 61: 25 (D),
36 (R). Both houses serve two-year terms.

North Carolina

'Esse quam videri' (*To be rather than to seem*)
State capital   Raleigh.
Admittance to the Union   1789 (twelfth state of the US). Seceded from the Union in
May 1861; readmitted in July 1868.
Land area   48,718 square miles (ranked twenty-ninth in size).
Population   2000 census: 8,049,313. Rank among states by population: 11.
Population change 1990–2000: +21.4 per cent.
Racial composition (1999 estimate): Asian/Pacific: 1.3 per cent; white: 73.2 per cent;
Hispanic: 2.2 per cent; black: 22 per cent.
Population density: 136.1. Urban population: 50.4 per cent. Rural population:
49.6 per cent. (1990 census figures.)
Voting patterns   Voting-age population of 5,685,000, of whom 83 per cent were
registered voters (1998). Of 4,764,036 registered voters, 53 per cent D, 34 per cent
R, 14 per cent unaffiliated and minor parties.
Presidential elections
Voter turnout (%)

1992	1996	2000
50.3	45.8	50.4 (estimate)

Votes cast

1992	1996	2000
Bush (R) 1,131,103 (44%)	Dole (R) 1,213,819 (49%)	Bush (R) 1,608,390 (56%)
Clinton (D) 1,109,953 (43%)	Clinton (D) 1,098,297 (44%)	Gore (D) 1,241,307 (43%)
Perot (I) 357,000 (14%)	Perot (Reform) 167,465 (7%)	Others 21,162 (1%)

Representation in US Congress (January 2001)
House of Representatives 12: 5 (D), 7 (R). From 2002 North Carolina will have thir-
teen Representatives.
US Senators: Jesse Helms (R), elected November 1972; John Edwards (D), elected
November 1998.
Votes in the Electoral College: 14 (15 votes from 2002).
State government
Executive branch (maximum of two consecutive terms)   Governor: Mike Easley (D),
elected November 2000. Lieutenant Governor: Beverly Perdue (D), elected Novem-
ber 2000.
Legislature (2001)   House of Representatives 120: 62 (D), 58 (R). Senate 50: 35 (D),
15 (R). Both houses serve two-year terms.

North Dakota

'Liberty and union, now and for ever, one and inseparable'

State capital   Bismarck.

Admittance to the Union   1889 (thirty-ninth state of the US).

Land area   68,994 square miles (ranked seventeenth in size).

Population   2000 census: 642,200. Rank among states by population: 47.

Population change 1990–2000: +0.5 per cent.

Racial composition (1999 estimate): American Indian: 4.8 per cent; white: 92.7 per
cent; Hispanic: 1.1 per cent; black: 0.6 per cent.

Population density: 9.3. Urban population: 53.3 per cent. Rural population: 46.7 per
cent. (1990 census figures.)

Voting patterns   Voting-age population of 476,000. There is no party registration in
North Dakota.

Presidential elections

Voter turnout (%)

1992	1996	2000
66.7	56.3	60.8 (estimated)

Votes cast

1992	1996	2000
Bush (R) 136,244 (44%)	Dole (R) 125,050 (47%)	Bush (R) 175,558 (61%)
Clinton (D) 99,168 (32%)	Clinton (D) 106,905 (40%)	Gore (D) 95,892 (33%)
Perot (I) 71,084 (23%)	Perot (Reform) 32,515 (12%)	Others 18,185 (6%)

Representation in US Congress   (January 2001)

House of Representatives 1: (D).

US Senators: Byron Dorgan (D), elected November 1992; Kent Conrad (D), elected
November 1986.

Votes in the Electoral College: 3.

State government

Executive branch   Governor: John Hoeven (R), elected November 2000. Lieutenant
Governor: Jack Dalrymple (R), elected November 2000.

Legislature   House of Representatives 98: 29 (D), 69 (R). Senate: 49; 17 (D), 32 (R).
Both houses serve four-year terms.

Ohio

'With God, all things are possible'

State capital   Columbus.

Admittance to the Union   1803 (seventeenth state of the US).

Land area   40,953 square miles (ranked thirty-fifth in size).

Population   2000 census: 11,353,140. Rank among states by population: 7.

Population change 1990–2000: +4.7 per cent.

Racial composition (1999 estimate): white: 85.5 per cent; Hispanic: 1.6 per cent; black:
11.5 per cent.

Population density: 264.9. Urban population: 74.1 per cent. Rural population: 25.9 per
cent. (1990 census figures.)

Voting patterns   Voting-age population of 8,401,000, of whom 84.4 per cent were
registered voters (1998). Of 7,096,423 registered voters, 17 per cent D, 18 per
cent R, 65 per cent unaffiliated and minor parties.

Presidential elections

Voter turnout (%)

1992	1996	2000
60.2	54.3	54.2 (estimated)

Votes cast

1992	1996	2000
Bush (R) 1,894,310 (38%)	Dole (R) 1,860,768 (41%)	Bush (R) 2,284,205 (50%)
Clinton (D) 1,984,942 (40%)	Clinton (D) 2,148,309 (47%)	Gore (D) 2,111,499 (46%)
Perot (I) 1,036,426 (21%)	Perot (Reform) 483,277 (11%)	Others 165,255 (4%)

Representation in US Congress (January 2001)

House of Representatives 19: 8 (D), 11 (R). Ohio will lose one Representative in 2002.

US Senators: Mike DeWine (R), elected November 1994; George Voinovich (R), elected November 1998.

Votes in the Electoral College: 21 (20 votes from 2002).

State government

Executive branch (maximum of two consecutive terms) Governor: Bob Taft (R), elected November1998. Lieutenant Governor: Maureen O'Connor (R), elected November 1998.

Legislature (2001) House of Representatives 99: 40 (D), 59 (R). Senate 33: 12 (D), 20 (R). Representatives serve two-year terms. Senators serve four-year terms.

Oklahoma

'Labor omnia vincit' (*Labor conquers all things*)

State capital Oklahoma City.

Admittance to the Union 1907 (forty-sixth state of the US).

Land area 68,679 square miles (ranked nineteenth in size).

Population 2000 census: 3,450,654. Rank among states by population: 27.

Population change 1990–2000: +9.7 per cent.

Racial composition (1999 estimate): American Indian: 7.8 per cent; white: 79.5 per cent; Hispanic: 4.0 per cent; black: 7.8 per cent.

Population density: 45.8. Urban population: 67.7 per cent. Rural population: 32.3 per cent. (1990 census figures.)

Voting patterns Voting-age population of 2,463,000, of whom 83.6 per cent were registered voters (1998). Of 2,059,817 registered voters, 57 per cent D, 35 per cent R, 8 per cent unaffiliated and minor parties.

Presidential elections

Voter turnout (%)

1992	1996	2000
59.1	49.9	50.2 (estimated)

Votes cast

1992	1996	2000
Bush (R) 592,929 (43%)	Dole (R) 582,315 (48%)	Bush (R) 745,017 (60%)
Clinton (D) 473,066 (34%)	Clinton (D) 488,105 (40%)	Gore (D) 475,596 (38%)
Perot (I) 319,878 (23%)	Perot (Reform) 130,788 (11%)	Others 15,639 (2%)

Representation in US Congress (January 2001)

House of Representatives 6: 1 (D), 5 (R). Oklahoma will lose one Representative in 2002.

US Senators: Don Nickles (R), elected November 1980; James N. Inhofe (R), elected November 1994.

Votes in the Electoral College: 8 (seven votes from 2002).

State government

Executive branch (maximum of two consecutive terms)   Governor: Frank Keating (R), elected November 1994. Lieutenant Governor: Mary Fallin (R), elected November 1994.

Legislature (2001)   House of Representatives 101: 53 (D), 48 (R). Senate 48: 30 (D), 18 (R). Representatives serve two-year terms. Senators serve four-year terms.

Oregon

'The Union'

State capital   Salem.

Admittance to the Union   1859 (thirty-third state of the US).

Land area   96,003 square miles (ranked tenth in size)

Population   2000 census: 3,421,399. Rank among states by population: 28.

Population change 1990–2000: +20.4 per cent.

Racial composition (1999 estimate): Asian/Pacific: 3.3 per cent; white: 87.5 per cent; Hispanic: 6.4 per cent; black: 1.8 per cent.

Population density: 29.6. Urban population: 70.5 per cent. Rural population: 29.5 per cent. (1990 census figures.)

Voting patterns   Voting-age population of 2,484,000, of whom 79.1 per cent were registered voters (1998). Of 1,965,981 registered voters, 40 per cent D, 36 per cent R, 24 per cent unaffiliated and minor parties.

Presidential elections

Voter turnout (%)

1992	1996	2000
65.9	57.5	61.5 (estimated)

Votes cast

1992	1996	2000
Bush (R) 475,757 (33%)	Dole (R) 538,155 (39%)	Bush (R) 712,547 (47%)
Clinton (D) 621,314 (43%)	Clinton (D) 649,631 (47%)	Gore (D) 719,142 (47%)
Perot (I) 354,091 (24%)	Perot (Reform) 121,218 (9%)	Others 96,427 (6%)
	Others 68,746 (5%)	

Representation in US Congress   (January 2001)

House of Representatives 5: 4 (D), 1 (R).

US Senators: Gordon R. Smith (R), elected November 1996; Ron Wyden (D), elected January 1996.

Votes in the Electoral College: 7.

State government

Executive branch   Governor: John A. Kitzhaber (D), elected November 1994. Secretary of state: Bill Bradbury (D), appointed November 1999, elected November 2000.

Legislature (2001)   House of Representatives 60: 27 (D), 33 (R). Senate 30: 14 (D), 16 (R). Representatives serve two-year terms. Senators serve four-year terms.

Pennsylvania

'Virtue, liberty, and independence'

State capital   Harrisburg.

Admittance to the Union   1787 (second state of the US).

Land area   44,820 square miles (ranked thirty-second in size).

Population   2000 census: 12,281,054. Rank among states by population: 6.

Population change 1990–2000: +3.4 per cent.

Racial composition (1999 estimate): Asian/Pacific: 1.6 per cent; white: 86.1 per cent; Hispanic: 2.7 per cent; black: 9.7 per cent.

Population density: 265.1. Urban population: 68.9 per cent. Rural population: 31.1 per cent. (1990 census figures.)

Voting patterns   Voting-age population of 9,118,000, of whom 79.6 per cent were registered voters (1998). Of registered voters, 48 per cent D, 42 per cent R, 9 per cent unaffiliated and minor parties.

Presidential elections

Voter turnout (%)

1992	1996	2000
54.1	49.0	53.4 (estimated)

Votes cast

1992	1996	2000
Bush (R) 1,791,841 (36%)	Dole (R) 1,801,169 (40%)	Bush (R) 2,264,309 (46%)
Clinton (D) 2,239,164 (45%)	Clinton (D) 2,215,819 (49%)	Gore (D) 2,465,412 (51%)
Perot (I) 902,667 (18%)	Perot (Reform) 430,984 (10%)	Others 146,248 (3%)

Representation in US Congress   (January 2001)

House of Representatives 21: 10 (D), 11 (R). Pennsylvania will lose two Representatives in 2002.

US Senators: Arlen Specter (R), elected November 1980; Richard J. Santorum (R), elected November 1994.

Votes in the Electoral College: 23 (21 votes from 2002).

State government

Executive branch (maximum of two consecutive terms)   Governor: Tom Ridge (R), elected November 1994. Lieutenant Governor: Mark Schweiker (R), elected November 1994.

Legislature (2001)   House of Representatives 203: 100 (D), 100 (R) 3 Vacant. Senate: 50: 21 (D), 29 (R). Representatives serve two-year terms. Senators serve four-year terms.

Rhode Island

'Hope'

State capital   Providence.

Admittance to the Union   1790 (thirteenth. state of the US).

Land area   1,045 square miles (ranked fiftieth in size).

Population   2000 census: 1,048,319. Rank among states by population: 43.

Population change 1990–2000: +4.5 per cent.

Racial composition (1999 estimate): white: 86.4 per cent; Hispanic: 6.9 per cent; black: 5.0 per cent.

Population density: 960.3. Urban population: 86.0 per cent. Rural population: 14.0 per cent. (1990 census figures.)

Voting patterns   Voting-age population of 751,000, of whom 84 per cent were registered voters (1998). There is no party registration in Rhode Island.

Presidential elections

Voter turnout (%)

1992	1996	2000
59.0	52.0	54.9 (estimated)

Votes cast

1992	1996	2000
Bush (R) 131,601 (29%)	Dole (R) 104,683 (27%)	Bush (R) 132,212 (32%)
Clinton (D) 213,299 (47%)	Clinton (D) 233,050 (60%)	Gore (D) 252,844 (61%)
Perot (I) 105,045 (23%)	Perot (Reform) 43,723 (11%)	Others 27,848 (7%)
	Others 8,674 (2%)	

Representation in US Congress   (January 2001)

House of Representatives: 2 (D).

US Senators: Lincoln Chafee (R), appointed 1999, elected November 2000; Jack Reed (D), elected November 1996.

Votes in the Electoral College: 4.

State government

Executive branch (maximum of two consecutive terms)   Governor: Lincoln Almond (R), elected November 1994. Lieutenant Governor: Charles J. Fogarty (R), elected November 1998.

Legislature (2001)   House of Representatives 100: 85 (D), 15 (R). Senate 50: 44 (D), 6 (R). Both houses serve two-year terms.

South Carolina

'Animus opibusque parati' (*Prepared in mind and resources*)

State capital   Columbia.

Admittance to the Union   1788 (eighth state of the US). First state to secede from the Union in December 1860; readmitted in June 1868.

Land area   30,111 square miles (ranked fortieth in size).

Population   2000 census: 4,012,012. Rank among states by population: 26.

Population change 1990–2000: +15.1 per cent.

Racial composition (1999 estimate): white: 67.8 per cent; Hispanic: 1.3 per cent; black: 29.7 per cent.

Population density: 115.8. Urban population: 54.6 per cent. Rural population: 45.4 per cent. (1990 census figures.)

Voting patterns   Voting-age population of 2,886,000, of whom 70 per cent were registered voters (1998). There is no party registration in South Carolina.

Presidential elections

Voter turnout (%)

1992	1996	2000
45.1	41.5	49.0 (estimated)

Votes cast

1992	1996	2000
Bush (R) 577,508 (48%)	Dole (R) 573,458 (50%)	Bush (R) 804,826 (57%)
Clinton (D) 479,514 (40%)	Clinton (D) 506,283 (44%)	Gore (D) 578,143 (41%)
Perot (I) 138,782 (12%)	Perot (Reform) 64,386 (6%)	Others 32,461 (2%)

Representation in US Congress   (January 2001)

House of Representatives 6: 2 (D), 4 (R).

US Senators: Ernest Hollings (D), elected November 1966; James Strom Thurmond (R), elected 1954.

Votes in the Electoral College: 8.

State government

Executive branch (maximum of two consecutive terms)   Governor: Jim Hodges (D), elected November 1998. Lieutenant Governor: Robert Lee Peeler (R), elected November 1994.

Legislature (2001)   House of Representatives: 124: 54 (D), 70 (R). Senate 46: 22 (D), 24 (R). Representatives serve two-year terms. Senators serve four-year terms.

South Dakota

'Under God the people rule'

State capital   Pierre.

Admittance to the Union   1889 (fortieth state of the US).

Land area   75,896 square miles (ranked sixteenth in size).

Population   2000 census: 754,844. Rank among states by population: 46.

Population change 1990–2000: +8.5 per cent.

Racial composition (1999 estimate): American Indian: 8.2 per cent; white: 89.4 per cent; Hispanic: 1.2 per cent; black: 0.6 per cent.

Population density: 9.2. Urban population: 50 per cent. Rural population: 50 per cent. (1990 census figures.)

Voting patterns   Voting-age population of 538,000, of whom 84.1 per cent were registered voters (1998). Of 452,901 registered voters, 40 per cent D, 48 per cent (R), 12 per cent unaffiliated and minor parties.

Presidential elections

Voter turnout (%)

1992	1996	2000
66.6	61.1	58.7 (estimated)

Votes cast

1992	1996	2000
Bush (R) 136,718 (41%)	Dole (R) 150,543 (46%)	Bush (R) 190,515 (60%)
Clinton (D) 124,888 (37%)	Clinton (D) 139,333 (43%)	Gore (D) 118,750 (38%)
Perot (I) 73,295 (22%)	Perot (Reform) 31,250 (10%)	Others 6,758 (2%)

Representation in US Congress   (January 2001)

House of Representatives: 1 (R).

US Senators: Thomas Daschle (D), elected November 1986; Tim Johnson (D), elected November 1996.

Votes in the Electoral College: 3.

State government

Executive branch (maximum of two consecutive terms)   Governor: William J. Janklow (R), elected November 1978, November 1982, November 1994. Lieutenant Governor: Carole Hillard (R), elected November 1994.

Legislature (2001)   House of Representatives 70: 20 (D), 50 (R). Senate 35: 11 (D), 24 (R). Both Representatives and Senators serve two-year terms.

Tennessee

'Agriculture and commerce'

State capital   Nashville.

Admittance to the Union   1796 (sixteenth state of the US). Seceded from the Union in June 1861; readmitted in July 1866, the first Confederate state to rejoin.

Land area   41,220 square miles (ranked thirty-fourth in size).

Population   2000 census: 5,689,283. Rank among states by population: 16.

Population change 1990–2000: +16.7 per cent.

Racial composition (1999 estimate): white: 81 per cent; Hispanic: 1.2 per cent; black: 16.6 per cent.

Population density: 118.3. Urban population: 60.9 per cent. Rural population: 39.1 per cent. (1990 census figures.)

Voting patterns   Voting-age population of 4,120,000, of whom 76.5 per cent were registered voters (1998). There is no party registration in Tennessee.

Presidential elections

Voter turnout (%)

1992	1996	2000
52.2	47.1	50.2 (estimated)

Votes cast

1992	1996	2000
Bush (R) 841,300 (42%)	Dole (R) 863,530 (46%)	Bush (R) 1,059,842 (51%)
Clinton (D) 933,521 (47%)	Clinton (D) 909,146 (48%)	Gore (D) 980,353 (47%)
Perot (I) 99,968 (10%)	Perot (Reform) 105,918 (6%)	Others 30,369 (2%)

Representation in US Congress   (January 2001)

House of Representatives 9: 4 (D), 5 (R).

US Senators: Fred Thompson (R), elected November 1994; William Frist (R), elected November 1994.

Votes in the Electoral College: 11.

State government

Executive branch (maximum of two consecutive terms)   Governor: Don Sundquist (R), elected November 1994. Lieutenant Governor and Speaker of Senate: John S. Wilder (D), elected by Senate 1971.

Legislature (2001)   House of Representatives 99: 58 (D), 41 (R). Senate 33: 18 (D), 15 (R). Representatives serve two-year terms, Senators four-year terms.

Texas

'Friendship'

State capital   Austin.

Admittance to the Union   1845 (twenty-eighth state of the US). Seceded from the Union in February 1861; readmitted in March 1870.

Land area   261,914 square miles (ranked second in size).

Population   2000 census: 20,851,820. Rank among states by population: 2.

Population change 1990–2000: +22.8 per cent.

Racial composition (1999 estimate): Asian/Pacific: 1.0 per cent; white: 55.3 per cent; Hispanic: 30.1 per cent; black: 12.3 per cent.

Population density: 64.9. Urban population: 80.3 per cent. Rural population: 19.7 per cent. (1990 census figures.)

Voting patterns   Voting-age population of 14,299,000, of whom 80.6 per cent were registered voters (1998). There is no party registration in Texas.

Presidential elections

Voter turnout (%)

1992	1996	2000
48.5	41.2	44.8 (estimated)

Votes cast

1992	1996	2000
Bush (R) 2,495,608 (41%)	Dole (R) 2,730,085 (49%)	Bush (R) 3,799,639 (59%)
Clinton (D) 2,281,735 (37%)	Clinton (D) 2,455,853 (44%)	Gore (D) 2,433,746 (38%)
Perot (I) 1,354,676 (22%)	Perot (Reform) 378,117 (7%)	Others 174,252 (3%)

Representation in US Congress   (January 2001)

House of Representatives 30: 17 (D), 13 (R). From 2002 Texas will have thirty-two Representatives.

US Senators: Phil Gramm (R), elected November 1984; Kay Bailey Hutchison (R), elected June 1993.

Votes in the Electoral College: 32 (34 votes from 2002).

State government

Executive branch   Governor: Rick Perry (R), inaugurated December 2000 (term expires November 2002). Lieutenant Governor: Bill Ratliff (R), elected by Senate December 2000.

Legislature (2001)   House of Representatives 150: 78 (D), 72 (R). Senate 31: 15 (D), 16 (R). Representatives serve two-year terms. Senators serve terms of four years.

Utah

'Industry'

State capital   Salt Lake City.

Admittance to the Union   1896 (forty-fifth state of the US).

Land area   82,168 square miles (ranked twelfth in size).

Population   2000 census: 2,233,169. Rank among states by population: 34.

Population change 1990–2000: +29.6 per cent.

Racial composition (1999 estimate): Asian/Pacific: 2.6 per cent; white: 88.5 per cent; Hispanic: 7.0 per cent; black: 0.9 per cent.

Population density: 21.0. Urban population: 87.0 per cent. Rural population: 13 per cent. (1990 census figures.)

Voting patterns   Voting-age population of 1,432,000, of whom 77.9 per cent were registered voters (1998). There is no party registration in Utah.

Presidential elections

Voter turnout (%)

1992	1996	2000
63.6	50.3	52.0 (estimated)

Votes cast

1992	1996	2000
Bush (R) 322,632 (43%)	Dole (R) 361,911 (54%)	Bush (R) 512,161 (67%)
Clinton (D) 183,429 (25%)	Clinton (D) 221,633 (33%)	Gore (D) 201,702 (26%)
Perot (I) 203,400 (27%)	Perot (Reform) 66,461 (10%)	Others 32,042 (7%)
	Other 15,623 (2%)	

Representation in US Congress (January 2001)
House of Representatives 3: 1 (D), 2 (R).
US Senators: Robert Bennett (R), elected November 1992; Orrin Hatch (R), elected
November 1976.
Votes in the Electoral College: 5.
State government
Executive branch Governor: Michael O. Leavitt (R), elected November 1992. Lieuten-
ant Governor: Olene S. Walker (R), elected November 1992.
Legislature (2001) House of Representatives 75: 24 (D), 51 (R). Senate 29: 9 (D), 20
(R). Representatives serve two-year terms and Senators four-year terms.

Vermont

'Freedom and unity'
State capital Montpelier.
Admittance to the Union 1791 (fourteenth state of the US).
Land area 9,249 square miles (ranked forty-third in size).
Population 2000 census: 608,827. Rank among states by population: 49.
Population change 1990–2000: +8.2 per cent.
Racial composition (1999 estimate): white: 97.5 per cent; Hispanic: 0.8 per cent; black:
0.5 per cent.
Population density: 60.8. Urban population: 32.2 per cent. Rural population: 67.8 per
cent. (1990 census figures.)
Voting patterns Voting-age population of 448,000, of whom 89 per cent were re-
gistered voters (1998). There is no party registration in Vermont.
Presidential elections
Voter turnout (%)

1992	1996	2000
67.5	58.6	65.1 (estimated)

Votes cast

1992	1996	2000
Bush (R) 88,122 (30%)	Dole (R) 80,352 (31%)	Bush (R) 119,270 (41%)
Clinton (D) 133,592 (46%)	Clinton (D) 137,894 (53%)	Gore (D) 148,166 (51%)
Perot (I) 65,991 (23%)	Perot (Reform) 31,024 (12%)	Others 24,409 (8%)
	Others 9179 (4%)	

Representation in US Congress (January 2001)
House of Representatives 1: (Independent).
US Senators: Patrick Leahy (D), elected 1974; Jim Jeffords (independent), elected 1988.
Votes in the Electoral College: 3.
State government
Executive branch (Governors serve two year terms with no limit on number of terms.)
Governor: Howard Dean (D), succeeded to office in August 1991, elected November
1992. Lieutenant Governor: Douglas Racine (D), elected November 1996.
Legislature (2001) House of Representatives 150: 62 (D), 83 (R), 1 (I), 4 (other).
Senate 30: 16 (D), 14 (R).
Both houses serve two-year terms.

Virginia

'*Sic semper tyrannis*' (*Thus always to tyrants*)

State capital Richmond.

Admittance to the Union 1788 (tenth state of the US). Seceded from Union in April 1861; readmitted in January 1870.

Land area 39,598 square miles (ranked thirty-seventh in size).

Population 2000 census: 7,078,515. Rank among states by population: 12.

Population change 1990–2000: +14.4 per cent.

Racial composition (1999 estimate): Asian/Pacific: 3.7 per cent; white: 72.4 per cent; Hispanic: 3.8 per cent; black: 20.1 per cent.

Population density: 156.3. Urban population: 69.4 per cent. Rural population: 30.6 per cent. (1990 census figures.)

Voting patterns Voting-age population of 5,165,000, of whom 72.1 per cent were registered voters (1998). There is no party registration in Virginia.

Presidential elections

Voter turnout (%)

1992	1996	2000
52.7	47.5	52.8 (estimated)

Votes cast

1992	1996	2000
Bush (R) 1,153,296 (45%)	Dole (R) 1,137,171 (48%)	Bush (R) 1,434,754 (53%)
Clinton (D) 1,040,993 (41%)	Clinton (D) 1,090,219 (46%)	Gore (D) 1,213,714 (44%)
Perot (I) 349,400 (14%)	Perot (Reform) 159,795 (7%)	Others 81,551 (3%)

Representation in US Congress (January 2001)

House of Representatives 11: 4 (D), 5 (R), 1 (I).

US Senators: George Allen (R), elected November 2000; John Warner (R), elected November 1978.

Votes in the Electoral College: 13.

State government

Executive branch (Governor cannot serve two consecutive terms but can seek re-election after four-year respite.) Governor: James S. Gilmore (R), elected November 1997. Lieutenant Governor: John Hager (R), elected November 1997.

Legislature (2001) House of Representatives 100: 47 (D), 52 (R), 1 (I). Senate 40: 18 (D), 22 (R).

Representatives serve two-year terms. Senators serve terms of four years.

Washington

'*Alki*' (*By and by*)

State capital Olympia.

Admittance to the Union 1889 (forty-second state of the US).

Land area 66,581 square miles (ranked twentieth in size).

Population 2000 census: 5,894,121. Rank among states by population: 15.

Population change 1990–2000: +21.1 per cent.

Racial composition (1999 estimate): Asian/Pacific: 5.9 per cent; white: 82.8 per cent; Hispanic: 6.5 per cent; black: 3.5 per cent.

Population density: 73.1. Urban population: 76.4 per cent. Rural population: 23.6 per cent. (1990 census figures.)

Appendix

Voting patterns Voting-age population of 4,257,000, of whom 73.2 per cent were registered voters (1998). There is no party registration in Washington.

Presidential elections

Voter turnout (%)

1992	1996	2000
60.0	54.7	58.4 (estimated)

Votes cast

1992	1996	2000
Bush (R) 731,234 (32%)	Dole (R) 840,712 (37%)	Bush (R) 1,108,864 (45%)
Clinton (D) 993,037 (43%)	Clinton (D) 1,123,323 (50%)	Gore (D) 1,247,652 (50%)
Perot (I) 541,780 (24%)	Perot (Reform) 201,003 (9%)	Others 130,915 (5%)
	Others 90,465 (4%)	

Representation in US Congress (January 2001)

House of Representatives 9: 6 (D), 3 (R).

US Senators: Maria Cantwell (D), elected November 2000; Patty Murray (D), elected November 1992.

Votes in the Electoral College: 11.

State government

Executive branch Governor: Gary Locke (D), elected November 1996. Lieutenant Governor: Brad Owen (D), elected November 1996.

Legislature (2001) House of Representatives 98: 49 (D), 49 (R). Senate 49: 25 (D), 24 (R). Representatives serve two-year terms. Senators serve four-year terms.

West Virginia

'Montani semper liberi' (*Mountaineers are always free*)

State capital Charleston.

Admittance to the Union 1863 (thirty-fifth state of the US).

Land area 24,087 square miles (ranked forty-first in size).

Population 2000 census: 1,808,344. Rank among states by population: 37.

Population change 1990–2000: +0.8 per cent.

Racial composition (1999 estimate): white: 95.7 per cent; Hispanic: 0.5 per cent; black: 3.1 per cent.

Population density: 74.5. Urban population: 36.1 per cent. Rural population: 63.9 per cent. (1990 census figures.)

Voting patterns Voting-age population of 1,406,000, of whom 71.6 per cent were registered voters (1998). Of 1,007,811 registered voters, 63 per cent (D), 29 per cent (R), 8 per cent unaffiliated and minor parties.

Presidential elections

Voter turnout (%)

1992	1996	2000
49.7	45.0	45.4 (estimated)

Votes cast

1992	1996	2000
Bush (R) 241,974 (35%)	Dole (R) 233,946 (37%)	Bush (R) 331,871 (52%)
Clinton (D) 331,001 (48%)	Clinton (D) 327,812 (52%)	Gore (D) 291,204 (46%)
Perot (I) 108,829 (16%)	Perot (Reform) 71,639 (11%)	Others 15,803 (2%)

Representation in US Congress (January 2001)
House of Representatives 3: 2 (D), 1 (R).
US Senators: Robert Byrd (D), elected 1958; John Rockefeller (D), elected 1984.
Votes in the Electoral College: 5.
State government
Executive branch (maximum of two consecutive terms)   Governor: Bob Wise (D), elected 2000. President of Senate: Ray Tomblin (D), elected January 1995.
Legislature (2001)   House of Representatives 100: 75 (D), 25 (R). Senate 34: 28 (D), 6 (R). Representatives serve two-year terms. Senators serve four-year terms.

Wisconsin

'Forward'
State capital   Madison.
Admittance to the Union   1848 (thirtieth state of the US).
Land area   54,314 square miles (ranked twenty-fifth in size).
Population   2000 census: 5,363,675. Rank among states by population: 18.
Population change 1990–2000: +9.6 per cent.
Racial composition (1999 estimate): Asian/Pacific: 1.6 per cent; white: 89.5 per cent; Hispanic: 2.6 per cent; black: 5.6 per cent.
Population density: 90.1. Urban population: 65.6 per cent. Rural population: 34.4 per cent. (1990 census figures.)
Voting patterns   Voting-age population of 3,877,000 (1998). There is no party registration in Wisconsin.
Presidential elections
Voter turnout (%)

1992	1996	2000
68.9	57.4	66.9 (estimated)

Votes cast

1992	1996	2000
Bush (R) 930,855 (37%)	Dole (R) 845,028 (38%)	Bush (R) 1,237,279 (48%)
Clinton (D) 1,041,066 (41%)	Clinton (D) 1,071,970 (49%)	Gore (D) 1,242,987 (48%)
Perot (I) 544,479 (22%)	Perot (Reform) 227,310 (10%)	Others 116,441 (4%)
	Other 51,881 (2%)	

Representation in US Congress (January 2001)
House of Representatives 9: 5 (D), 4 (R). Wisconsin will lose one Representative in 2002.
US Senators: Russell Feingold (D), elected November 1992; Herb Kohl (D), elected November 1988.
Votes in the Electoral College: 11 (10 votes from 2002).
State government
Executive branch   Governor: Tommy G Thompson (R), elected November 1986. Lieutenant Governor: Scott McCallum (R), elected November 1986.
Legislature   House of Representatives 99: 43 (D), 56 (R). Senate 33: 18 (D), 15 (R). Representatives serve two-year terms. Senators serve four-year terms.

Wyoming

'Equal rights'
State capital   Cheyenne.
Admittance to the Union   1890 (forty-fourth state of the US).

Land area   97,105 square miles (ranked ninth in size).

Population   2000 census: 493,782. Rank among states by population: 50.

Population change 1990–2000: +8.9 per cent.

Racial composition (1999 estimate): American Indian: 2.2 per cent; white: 90.3 per cent; Hispanic: 6.0 per cent; black: 0.8 per cent.

Population density: 4.7. Urban population: 65 per cent. Rural population: 35 per cent. (1990 census figures.)

Voting patterns   Voting-age population of 354,000, of whom 67.6 per cent were registered voters (1998). Of 239,304 registered voters, 30 per cent (D), 59 per cent (R), 11 per cent unaffiliated/minor parties.

Presidential elections

Voter turnout

1992	1996	2000
61.0	60.1	60.2 (estimated)

Votes cast

1992	1996	2000
Bush (R) 79,347 (40%)	Dole (R) 105,388 (50%)	Bush (R) 147,674 (69%)
Clinton (D) 68,160 (34%)	Clinton (D) 77,934 (37%)	Gore (D) 60,421 (28%)
Perot (I) 51,263 (26%)	Perot (Reform) 25,928 (12%)	Others 5,331 (3%)

Representation in US Congress   (January 2001)

House of Representatives 1: (R).

US Senators: Thomas Craig (R), elected November 1994; Mike Enzi (R), elected November 1996.

Votes in the Electoral College: 3.

State government

Executive branch (maximum of two consecutive terms)   Governor: Jim Geringer (R), elected November 1994. Lieutenant Governor: Joe Meyer (R), elected November 1998.

Legislature (2001)   House of Representatives 60: 14 (D), 46 (R). Senate 30: 10 (D), 20 (R). Representatives serve two-year terms and Senators four-year terms.

References and further reading

Population

Information on population was taken from tables provided by the US Census Bureau, notably 'Resident population of the fifty states, the District of Columbia, and Puerto Rico: April 1, 2000 (census 2000) and April 1, 1990 (1990 census) and numeric and percent change for 1990 to 2000', http//www.census.gov/population/cen2000/tab05.pdf. Figures for the racial composition of states were provided by the US Census Bureau table (ST-99-29) 'Population estimates for states by race and Hispanic origin, July 1, 1996', http//www.census.gov/population/estimates/state/srh/srh96.txt. Population density and land area are detailed at US Census Bureau table 1, 'Land area, population, and density for states and counties, 1990' (released 12 March 1996, revised 26 June 2000), http//www.census.gov/population/censusdata/90den_stco.txt. Information on the distribution of urban and rural populations is to be found in US Census Bureau table 1, 'Urban and rural population, 1900–90', released October 1995), http//www.census.gov/population/censusdata/urpop0090.txt. Details concerning voting age and voter turnout are to be found in the *Statistical Abstract of the United States* 2000, p.302, table 490, 'Resident population of voting age and percent casting votes, states, 1990–98', http//www.census.gov/prod/99pubs/99statab/sec08.pdf. The number of registered voters and the existence of party registration, or otherwise, are to be found in the *Almanac of American Politics*, as are the figures for the votes cast in the 1992 and 1996 elections. The figures for the votes cast in the 2000 presidential election were supplied by *US Today*.

Congressional representation

Data in this section have been taken from the *Official List of Members of the House of Representatives*, http//clerkweb.house.gov/107/olm107_1.htm, and from the *United States Senate: Senators of the 107th Congress*, http//www.senate.gov/senators/index.cfm.

State government

Information on state governors and term limits was provided by the National Governors' Association, http//www.nga.org/cda/files/GOVLIST2001.PDF, and on lieutenant governors by the National Conference of Lieutenant Governors, http//www.nclg.org/. Details of party representation in state legislatures were provided by the *Guide to the State Legislatures*, US News Online. Information relates to position in the legislative sessions beginning January 2001.

Index